Portable Psychology

Volume 1
USER'S GUIDE

Samuel E. Wood

Ellen Green Wood

Denise Boyd
Houston Community College System

PEARSON

Boston | New York | San Francisco
Mexico City | Montreal | Toronto | London | Madrid | Munich | Paris
Hong Kong | Singapore | Tokyo | Cape Town | Sydney

Editor-in-Chief: Susan Hartman
Development Editors: Deb Hanlon and Julie Swasey
Series Editorial Assistant: Courtney Mullen
Marketing Manager: Jeanette Koskinas
Production Editor: Claudine Bellanton
Editorial Production Service: Nesbitt Graphics, Inc.
Manufacturing Buyer: JoAnne Sweeney
Electronic Composition: Nesbitt Graphics, Inc.
Interior Design: Carol Somberg
Photo Researcher: Sarah Evertson
Cover Administrator/Designer: Joel Gendron

For related titles and support materials, visit our online catalog at
www.pearsonhighered.com.

Between the time website information is gathered and then published, it is not unusual
for some sites to have closed. Also, the transcription of URLs can result in typographical
errors. The publisher would appreciate notification where these errors occur so that
they may be corrected in subsequent editions.

ISBN-13: 978-0-205-56908-3 ISBN-10: 0-205-56908-0

Library of Congress Cataloging-in-Publication Data

Wood, Samuel E.
  Portable psychology / Samuel E. Wood, Ellen Green Wood, Denise Boyd. --
1st ed.
    p. cm.
  Includes bibliographical references and index.
  ISBN 0-205-56908-0
  1. Psychology--Textbooks. I. Wood, Ellen Green. II. Boyd, Denise Roberts.
III. Title.
  BF121.W6566 2009
  150--dc22
                        2008027325

Printed in the United States of America

10 9 8 7 6 5 4 3 2 1 [RRD – IN] 12 11 10 09 08

Credits appear on page C-1, which constitutes an extension of the copyright page.

Sam and Evie dedicate this book with love to their grandchildren: Brittany, Danielle, Ashley, Hayley, Jesse, and Sarah.

Denise dedicates this book to the hundreds of introductory psychology students she has taught over the past 20 years. Their questions, comments, and concerns were the driving force behind her contributions to Portable Psychology.

Brief Contents

Contents

Volume 1

USER'S GUIDE

Volume 2

FOUNDATIONS AND BIOLOGICAL FUNCTIONING

Chapter **Introduction to Psychology** *page 1*

Chapter **3** **Sensation and Perception** *page 96*

Chapter **4** States of Consciousness *page 145*

Volume 3
COGNITIVE FUNCTIONING

Chapter **6** **Memory** *page 230*

Volume 4
HUMAN DEVELOPMENT, MOTIVATION, SEXUALITY, GENDER, AND HEALTH

Chapter **Human Development** *page 320*

Chapter **9** **Motivation and Emotion**   *page 377*

Chapter **11** | **Health and Stress** *page 458*

Volume 5
PERSONALITIES, MENTAL HEALTH, AND SOCIAL PSYCHOLOGY

Chapter **15** Social Psychology   *page 610*

HOW TO USE PORTABLE PSYCHOLOGY

Welcome to *Portable Psychology*!

As today's college students, you and your peers are vastly different from
the students who filled classrooms just a few years ago. Indeed, you are
now more diverse, more mobile, and more technologically savvy than ever
before. *Portable Psychology* is designed for students on the move—those
who, on a daily basis, commute, travel, or work and therefore must study
in nontraditional settings. *Portable Psychology* is separated into five
brief paperback volumes so that you can carry it with you and study
whenever it's most convenient.

1 NAVIGATING *Portable Psychology*

This volume is your User's Guide, or reference volume. It contains a full list of the
learning outcomes, additional practice tests, and all the answers to the study guide
and comprehensive test questions found at the end of each module and at the end
of each chapter. It also contains a full glossary, name and subject
index, and references for the entire book.

Volumes 2–5 contain Chapters 1–15 of the book. The end of
each volume contains an index for that particular
volume. A complete index for all the volumes
can be found in this User's Guide.

Students often benefit from
learning material in smaller units.
Each chapter of *Portable Psychology*
has been broken into chunks we
like to call modules. We have
designed each module as a self-
contained learning unit, complete
with its own summary and study
guide sections. All of the modules
are cross-referenced in the text,
making it easy to navigate back and forth between
relevant discussions. You'll also notice that each
module in a chapter has been color-coded; the
same color appears in the chapter outline, module
title, summary, study guide, and page number.

IMPROVING YOUR GRADE WITH *SQ3R*

The SQ3R method will help you maximize your learning in 5 steps: Survey, Question, Read, Recite, and Review. This chapter, is annotated to show you where each step in the method occurs to help you visualize, practice, and master this learning system.

Our commitment to learning begins with the learning method called SQ3R. Made up of five steps—Survey, Question, Read, Recite, and Review—this method serves as the foundation for your success. Introduced in Chapter 1, Module 1, the SQ3R method is integrated throughout the text to help you make the connection between psychology and life, while promoting a more efficient way to approach reading, studying, and test-taking.

The following pages walk you through a sample chapter, pointing out the features that support our SQ3R learning method.

GETTING STARTED *A Look Inside Each Chapter*

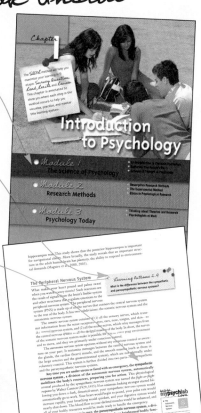

MODULES

The first page of each chapter lists all the modules that will appear in the chapter. An outline of the sections in each module helps you preview the topics.

LEARNING OUTCOMES

Numbered Learning Outcome questions appear in the margins to help focus your reading. They are repeated and answered in the summary section at the end of each module. A complete list of the Learning Outcomes in this text can be found on page xli in Volume 1.

KEY TERMS

Key terms are highlighted throughout the text and their accompanying definitions appear in bold type. Definitions also appear in the complete glossary on pages G-1–G-23 in Volume 1.

MyPsychLab ICONS

Throughout each chapter, you will notice icons in the margins referring you to interactive materials available on this book's MyPsychLab. Go to www.mypsychlab.com to register. (If you did not receive an access code to MyPsychLab with this text and wish to purchase access online, please visit www.mypsychlab.com.)

Once you have registered and logged in, please select your text, *Portable Psychology*. You will have access to an e-book, which exactly matches the layout of your printed book, and contains the multimedia icons in the margins that launch videos (with questions to help guide viewing), activities, and simulations. To get started, test your knowledge by taking a pre-test before reading the chapter. Take a post-test once you have completed a chapter to see how much you have learned.

MULTIMEDIA LIBRARY

You can access a complete list of the interactive materials found in the margins of your book by logging in to your MyPsychLab course and viewing your Multimedia Library. Searchable by chapter, topic, media type, or a combination of the three, this feature in MyPsychLab gives you an easy way to search for interactive materials in each chapter.

Apply It

How to Win the Battle against Procrastination

Have you often thought that you could get better grades if only you had more time? Do you often find yourself studying for an exam or completing a term paper at the last minute? If so, it makes sense for you to learn how to overcome the greatest time waster of all—procrastination. Research indicates that academic procrastination arises partly out of a lack of confidence in one's ability to meet expectations (Wolters, 2003). Once procrastination has become established as a behavior pattern, it often persists for years (Lee, Kelly, & Edwards, 2006). Nevertheless, anyone can overcome procrastination, and gain self-confidence in the process, by using behavior modification techniques. Systematically apply the following suggestions to keep procrastination from interfering with your studying:

- *Identify the environmental cues that habitually interfere with your studying.* Television, computer or video games, and even food can be powerful distractors that consume hours of valuable study time. However, these distractors can be useful positive reinforcers to enjoy after you've finished studying.
- *Schedule your study time and reinforce yourself for adhering to your schedule.* Once you've scheduled it, be just as faithful to your schedule as you would be to a work schedule set by an employer. And be sure to schedule something you enjoy to immediately follow the study time.
- *Get started.* The most difficult part is getting started. Give yourself an extra reward for starting on time and, perhaps, a penalty for starting late.

- *Use visualization.* Much procrastination results from the failure to consider its negative consequences. Visualizing the consequences of not studying, such as trying to get through an exam you haven't adequately prepared for, can be an effective tool for combating procrastination.
- *Beware of jumping to another task when you reach a difficult part of an assignment.* This procrastination tactic gives you the feeling that you are busy and accomplishing something, but it is, nevertheless, an avoidance mechanism.
- *Beware of preparation overkill.* Procrastinators may actually spend hours preparing for a task rather than working on the task itself. For example, they may gather enough library materials to write a book rather than a five-page term paper. This enables them to postpone writing the paper.
- *Keep a record of the reasons you give yourself for postponing studying or completing important assignments.* If a favorite rationalization is "I'll wait until I'm in the mood to do this," count the number of times in a week you are seized with the desire to study. The mood to study typically arrives after you begin, not before.

Don't procrastinate! Begin now! Apply the steps outlined here to gain more control over your behavior and win the battle against procrastination.

www.mypsychlab.com

► Audio: How to Win the Battle against Procrastination   LISTEN

APPLY IT

At the end of each chapter, an application box combines scientific research with practical advice to show how to handle difficult or challenging situations that may occur in your personal, academic, or professional life.

Try It

Mayo Clinic STD Quiz: What You Don't Know Can Hurt You

Answer these questions True or False. (Note: full explanations of the answers to these questions can be found at http://mayoclinic.com/health/stds/QZ00037)

___ 1. The rate of STDs in the United States is on the rise.

___ 2. Condoms—so long as they're still wrapped—will stay effective even if carried around for months at a time in your wallet.

___ 3. Animal skin (lambskin) condoms protect against pregnancy, but don't protect you from STDs, such as HIV/AIDS.

___ 4. You should lubricate condoms with petroleum jelly or baby oil to reduce their risk of tearing.

___ 5. When condoms fail, it's usually because of incorrect use.

___ 6. If you have a history of genital herpes, you can infect your partner even when you don't have symptoms of the disease.

___ 7. Having regular Pap tests will prevent cervical cancer.

___ 8. You can't get an STD from oral sex.

___ 9. Taking birth control pills eliminates your need for a condom.

___ 10. STDs aren't life-threatening.

Answers: 1. T; 2. F; 3. T; 4. F; 5. T; 6. T; 7. F; 8. F; 9. F; 10. F

TRY IT

This interactive feature provides brief applied experiments, self-assessments and hands-on activities, which help personalize psychology, making it simple for you to actively relate psychological principles to your life.

Review and Reflect

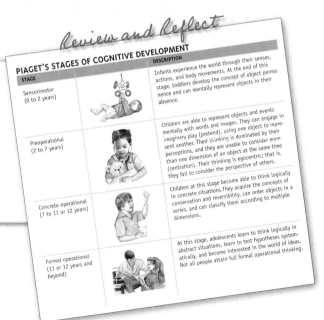

PIAGET'S STAGES OF COGNITIVE DEVELOPMENT

STAGE		DESCRIPTION
Sensorimotor (0 to 2 years)		Infants experience the world through their senses, actions, and body movements. At the end of this stage, toddlers develop the concept of object permanence and can mentally represent objects in their absence.
Preoperational (2 to 7 years)		Children are able to represent objects and events mentally with words and images. They can engage in imaginary play (pretend), using one object to represent another. Their thinking is dominated by their perceptions, and they are unable to consider more than one dimension of an object at the same time (centration). Their thinking is egocentric; that is, they fail to consider the perspective of others.
Concrete operational (7 to 11 or 12 years)		Children at this stage become able to think logically in concrete situations.They acquire the concepts of conservation and reversibility, can order objects in a series, and can classify them according to multiple dimensions.
Formal operational (11 or 12 years and beyond)		At this stage, adolescents learn to think logically in abstract situations, learn to test hypotheses systematically, and become interested in the world of ideas. Not all people attain full formal operational thinking.

WRAPPING UP A MODULE
What Have You Just Learned?

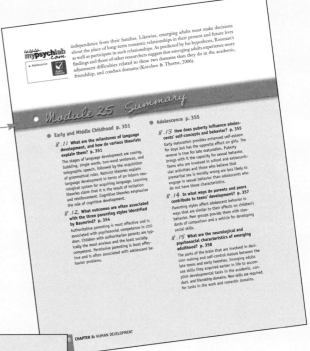

SUMMARY

At the end of each module is a summary section which repeats the Learning Outcome questions, along with brief answers and page references for easy review and study.

KEY TERMS

The key terms are repeated at the end of each module, with their corresponding page references.

STUDY GUIDE

Each module summary leads into a Study Guide—short quizzes to help you assess your knowledge of the subject matter. Answers to all the study guide questions can be found on page SGA-1 in Volume 1.

ONE LAST STEP *Test Prep*

COMPREHENSIVE PRACTICE TEST AND CRITICAL THINKING QUESTIONS

At the end of each chapter is a Comprehensive Test and Critical Thinking questions. These questions are based on material found throughout the chapter. To further test your mastery of the chapter, Volume 1 contains additional Practice Tests beginning on page PTA-1. Answers to the Comprehensive Tests and additional Practice Tests can be found in Volume 1, on pages SGA-1–SGA-3.

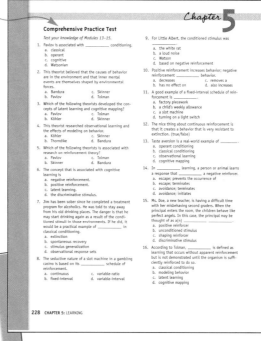

All of these features are designed to help you understand the material presented in this text and better prepare you for test-taking and success in your course. We encourage you to take advantage of the wealth of study materials and interactive applications found throughout this new portable edition and hope you enjoy your study of *Portable Psychology*.

MYPSYCHLAB QUESTIONS

Questions pertaining to select MyPsychLab videos highlighted throughout the text can be found at the very end of each chapter. We encourage you to watch these videos pertaining to relevant topics in your text and try to answer these questions.

Preface

Today's college students are vastly different from students who filled classrooms just a few years ago. Indeed, students today are more diverse, more mobile, and more technologically astute than ever before. It is our belief that an effective and successful psychology textbook must communicate clearly and meaningfully to this diverse audience.

Portable Psychology is written to appeal to students of all educational backgrounds. This text recognizes that different students have different learning preferences, study approaches, and success strategies. It addresses these challenges by offering a wide variety of pedagogical support tools that will help students master the principles of psychology, help them apply these principles to real world situations, and provides micro and macro assessment opportunities along the way. No book on the market does more to help students get better grades while recognizing their daily challenges than *Portable Psychology*.

Portable Psychology is designed specifically for today's student challenged with competing priorities, less time to dedicate to studying, and a results-driven perspective on their educational investment.

Organized into five volumes, *Portable Psychology* adapts to students' lives in a way that no other text has done. Students can read, study, and self-assess anywhere and anytime *they* choose. Each volume is fully self-contained to allow maximum flexibility for students. Within each volume, select chapters are made up of modules or learning units. Each module contains learning outcomes, key terms, section quizzes, integrated online MyPsychLab media icons, and summaries. In addition, each chapter offers a built-in study guide and practice test to allow students to assess their comprehension in a variety of ways. In addition to the ease of use for students, instructors also benefit from using *Portable Psychology* as it allows them more flexibility in assigning materials, integrating media into the classroom, and assessing students.

Our Goals for This Text

We understand that reading about psychology is not enough. We believe that students should be active participants in the learning process. Highly interactive and engaging, *Portable Psychology* encourages students to master the process of critical thinking as they learn about, relate to, and apply the psychological principles that affect their lives. Various tools in the text, including the integrated MyPsychLab icons, help guide students to success. To accomplish our goals, we set the following objectives:

- A Focus on Learning
- A Focus on Application
- A Focus on Assessment

A FOCUS ON LEARNING

MAINTAIN A CLEAR, UNDERSTANDABLE WRITING STYLE First and foremost, a textbook is a teaching instrument. It cannot be a novel, nor should it be an esoteric, academic treatise.

A good psychology textbook must communicate clearly to a diverse audience of various ages and academic abilities. We seek to achieve this objective by explaining concepts in much the same way that we do in our own psychology classes. The text is filled with everyday examples pertinent to students' lives.

PROVIDE AN ACCURATE, CURRENT, AND THOROUGHLY RESEARCHED TEXT FEATURING ORIGINAL SOURCES To introduce the world of psychology accurately and clearly, we have gone back to the original sources and have read and reread the basic works of the major figures in psychology and the classic studies in the field. This reading has enabled us to write with greater clarity and assurance, rather than having to hedge or write tentatively when discussing what experts in the field have actually said. This text is one of the most carefully researched, up-to-date, accurate, and extensively referenced of all the introductory psychology textbooks on the market today.

ENCOURAGE STUDENTS TO BECOME ACTIVE PARTICIPANTS IN THE LEARNING PROCESS Memorizing psychology terms will not guarantee student success. Students should be able to practice what they have learned, both online and in the text, when appropriate. Many of the principles we teach can be demonstrated without elaborate equipment and sometimes, as the student reads. Our *Try It* activities personalize psychology, making it simple for students to actively relate psychology to their lives.

OUR COMMITMENT TO LEARNING *Portable Psychology* reflects our continued commitment to learning. Based on instructor and student feedback, we developed the pedagogical features and organization of each chapter to provide the best possible opportunities for learning. The text's commitment to learning begins with the SQ3R learning method. Made up of five steps—Survey, Question, Read, Recite, and Review—this method serves as the foundation for course success. Introduced in Chapter 1, Module 1, the SQ3R method is integrated throughout the text to help students make the connection between psychology and life, while promoting a more efficient way to approach reading, studying, and test taking.

Among the key learning features that promote use of the SQ3R method are:

CHAPTER OUTLINE

The chapter opener lists all of the modules that will appear in the chapter. An outline of the sections in each module provides a preview of all the topics.

CHAPTER-OPENING VIGNETTES

These stories, based on real world events and people, offer an accessible and interesting introduction to the chapter material.

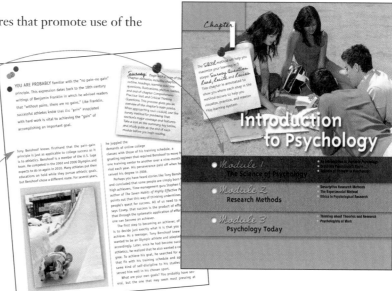

LEARNING OUTCOMES

Numbered Learning Outcome questions appear in the margins to help students focus their reading. These same objectives are repeated and answered in the summary section at the end of each module. A complete list of all the Learning Outcomes for this text can be found on page xli in Volume 1. These Learning Outcomes can also be found in the Instructor's Manual, and are correlated to all the test questions in the Test Bank.

MYPSYCHLAB

Throughout each chapter, icons in the margins refer students to view interactive materials available on this book's MyPsychLab. Students can visit **www.mypsychlab.com** to register, using the access code bundled with this book. On this site, you can view a complete e-book with the interactive activity categories listed to the right. If your students did not recieve an access code to MyPsychLab with their text and they wish to purchase access online, please have them visit **www.mypsychlab.com.**

KEY TERMS

Key terms are highlighted throughout the text and their accompanying definitions appear n bold type. Definitions also appear in the complete glossary on pages G1–G23 in Volume 1.

WATCH These icons direct your students to interesting, relevant video clips that supplement a topic being covered in the textbook. At the end of each chapter of *Portable Psychology*, you will also find a few short answer questions pertaining to some of these videos. We encourage you to assign some of these questions to your students as homework assignments.

SIMULATE At the center of MyPsychLab are highly interactive simulations that allow students to experience psychological phenomena and the research process for themselves.

EXPLORE An Explore icon directs students to an interactive activity that allows them to gain more knowledge of a major topic covered in a chapter, reinforcing key concepts taught in the book.

LISTEN Additional key concepts are explored with audio notes that help clarify important ideas that often cause confusion for students.

TIMELINE The Timeline icons direct you to a visual timeline of factual events tied to material that you are reading about in the text.

QUICK REVIEW These icons link to practice tests that provide reinforcement of key concepts throughout the text. These Quick Review assessments are not graded—so they give your students an opportunity for self-study.

REVIEW AND REFLECT BOXES

These comprehensive summary tables help consolidate major concepts, their components, and their relationships to one another. The tables offer information in a visual form that provides a unique study tool.

MODULE SUMMARIES

At the end of each module is a summary section which repeats the Learning Outcome questions, along with brief answers. This section also lists the key terms in the module, as well as page references to their definitions.

MODULE STUDY GUIDES

Each module summary leads into a study guide— short quizzes made up of multiple choice, true/false, and fill-in-the-blank questions to help students assess their knowledge on the subject matter. Answers to all of the study guide questions can be found beginning on page SGA-1 in Volume 1.

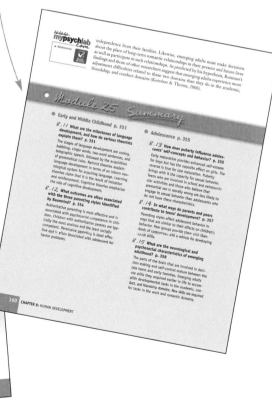

Review and Reflect

PIAGET'S STAGES OF COGNITIVE DEVELOPMENT

STAGE		DESCRIPTION
Sensorimotor (0 to 2 years)		Infants experience the world through their senses, actions, and body movements. At the end of this stage, toddlers develop the concept of object permanence and can mentally represent objects in their absence.
Preoperational (2 to 7 years)		Children are able to represent objects and events mentally with words and images. They can engage in imaginary play (pretend), using one object to represent another. Their thinking is dominated by their perceptions, and they are unable to consider more than one dimension of an object at the same time (centration). Their thinking is egocentric; that is, they fail to consider the perspective of others.
Concrete operational (7 to 11 or 12 years)		Children at this stage become able to think logically in concrete situations. They acquire the concepts of conservation and reversibility, can order objects in a series, and can classify them according to multiple dimensions.
Formal operational (11 or 12 years and beyond)		At this stage, adolescents learn to think logically in abstract situations, learn to test hypotheses systematically, and become interested in the world of ideas. Not all people attain full formal operational thinking.

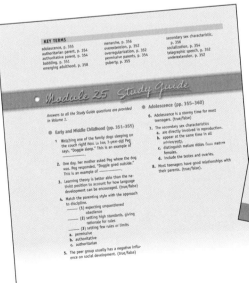

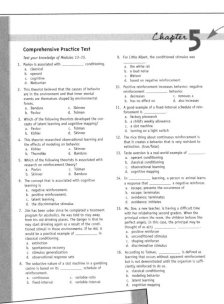

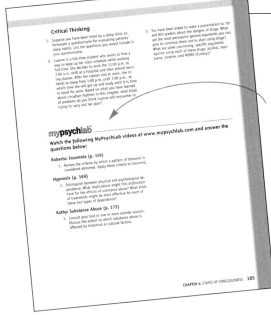

COMPREHENSIVE TEST AND CRITICAL THINKING QUESTIONS

At the end of each chapter is a Comprehensive Test and Critical Thinking questions. These questions are based on material found throughout the chapter. For students seeking more of a challenge, Volume 1 contains additional Practice Tests on page PT1. Answers to the Comprehensive Tests and additional Practice Tests can be found on pages PTA1–PTA9 in Volume 1.

MYPSYCHLAB QUESTIONS

Questions pertaining to select MyPsychLab videos highlighted throughout the text can be found at the very end of each chapter. We encourage you to assign some of these questions as homework for your students.

A FOCUS ON APPLICATION

We recognize that success lies not only in a strong pedagogy, but in the ability to relate key psychological principles to life and career choices. *Portable Psychology* provides a variety of opportunities to make hands-on use of psychological knowledge.

TRY IT

This interactive feature provides brief applied experiments, self-assessments, and hands-on activities, which help personalize psychology, making it simple for students to actively relate psychological principles to everyday life. The following *Try It* boxes appear in the text:

- How Much Do You Know about Psychology? (p. 6)
- A Balancing Act (p. 74)
- Find Your Blind Spot (p. 104)
- A Negative Afterimage (p. 107)
- Lucid Dreaming (p. 162)
- The Relaxation Response (p. 168)
- Using Behavior Modification (p. 215)
- A Penny for Your Thoughts (p. 263)
- Water Lily Problem (p. 282)
- Conservation of Volume (p. 327)
- Stereotypes about Later Adulthood (p. 368)
- Recognizing Basic Emotions (p. 403)
- Mayo Clinic STD Quiz: What You Don't Know Can Hurt You (p. 447)
- Knowledge about AIDS (p. 450)
- Finding a Life Stress Score (p. 462)
- Where Is Your Locus of Control? (p. 516)
- Identifying Anxiety Disorders (p. 544)
- A Possible Hierarchy of Fears (p. 584)
- Choosing a Mate (p. 617)

APPLY IT

At the end of each chapter, an application box combines scientific research with practical advice to show how to handle difficult or challenging situations that may occur in personal, academic, or professional life. These *Apply It* boxes cover the following topics:

- More Tips for Effective Studying (p. 5)
- Should You Consult a Genetic Counselor? (p. 90)
- How Dangerous Is It to Talk on a Cell Phone While Driving? (p. 126)
- How to Get a Good Night's Sleep (p. 160)
- How to Win the Battle Against Procrastination (p. 213)
- Improving Memory with Mnemonic Devices (p. 237)
- How to Build a Powerful Vocabulary (p. 309)
- Where Are You in the Career Development Process? (p. 365)
- The Quest for Happiness (p. 405)
- Rules for Internet Dating (p. 431)
- Interpreting Health Information on the Internet (p. 485)
- Put Your Best Foot Forward (p. 524)
- Overcoming the Fear of Public Speaking (p. 547)
- Is E-Therapy Right for You? (p. 602)
- Unlearning Prejudice (p. 647)

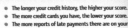

Why Are Credit Scores Useful to Both Lenders and Borrowers?

Correlations are often used to make predictions about future behavior on the basis of past behavior. In fact, correlations underlie one of the most common measures of behavior in our world today, the credit score. A credit score is a numerical summary of an individual's financial history that predicts the likelihood that he or she will have a delinquency in the future. A delinquency is failure to pay back a loan, declaration of bankruptcy, or any instance in which a person makes a payment on a loan or credit card more than 90 days after the original due date.

The higher a person's credit score, the lower the likelihood of a future delinquency (Equifax, 2006). Can you determine the nature (positive or negative) of the correlation between credit scores and delinquency risk? The graph in Figure 1.3 may help you visualize it.

If you compare this graph to the scatterplots in Figure 1.1 on p. 26, you will see that the correlation between credit scores and delinquencies is negative. In other words, the higher your score, the lower your chances of a delinquency. Consequently, using credit scores helps lenders minimize the chances that consumers will fail to pay them back.

The credit score itself is based on several correlations. Some of these correlations are positive, and some are negative. See if you can determine which of the three credit score factors below is based on positive correlations and which is derived from negative correlations (see answers following):

- The longer your credit history, the higher your score.
- The more credit cards you have, the lower your score.
- The more reports of late payments there are on your credit report, the lower your score.

If you guessed that a positive correlation is the basis of the first item on the list, and the others are based on negative correlations, you are correct.

Thanks to the association between length of credit history and credit scores, the scores of young adults tend to go up somewhat automatically during the first few years after they get their first loan or credit card. Of course, young consumers don't benefit from this factor unless they also make payments on time, refrain from running up large credit card balances, and resist the temptation to borrow money excessively as they work to build their credit histories. Financial advisors also suggest that consumers of all ages check their credit reports from time to time for errors that may depress their scores. Thus, for borrowers, credit scores serve as an index of wise financial decision making. And once con-sumers grasp the nature of the correlations that are embodied in credit scores, they can manipulate those correlations in their favor to increase the scores.

www.
mypsychlab
.com

▶ It Video: Why Are Credit Scores Useful to Both Lenders and Borrowers

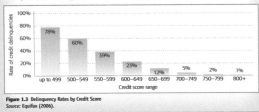

Figure 1.3 Delinquency Rates by Credit Score
Source: Equifax (2006).

EXPLAIN IT

This feature provides psychological explanations to some common everyday occurrences. For instance, have your students ever wondered what a credit score means and how it is used by lenders? Or why some individuals are drawn to dangerous hobbies like skydiving? The following *Explain It* boxes appear in the text:

- Why Are Credit Scores Useful to Both Lenders and Borrowers? (p. 29)
- Why Are Most People Right-Handed? (p. 72)
- Why Can't Everyone Hear the "Mosquito" Ring Tone? (p. 113)
- How Does the Brain Keep Track of Time? (p. 150)
- How Do the Principles of Learning Explain the Behavior of Smoking Cigarettes? (p. 223)
- Why Is Cramming an Ineffective Study Method? (p. 238)
- Why Do People Overestimate the Likelihood of Rare Events? (p. 279)
- Why Are Peer Groups Important in Adolescence? (p. 359)
- Why Are Dangerous Hobbies Appealing to Some People? (p. 383)
- Why Do We Develop Gender Stereotypes? (p. 422)
- Why Do Pop Quizzes Facilitate Learning? (p. 472)
- Why Do Some People Fail to Develop a Conscience? (p. 521)
- How Do Cultural Beliefs about Ideal Emotional States Lead to Depression? (p. 553)
- Why Are Smoking Rates So High among People with Schizophrenia? (p. 593)
- Why Doesn't Groupthink Occur in Every Tightly Knit Group? (p. 627)

A FOCUS ON ASSESSMENT

As instructors we fully understand and support the need for student assessment to meet the needs of instructors and help guide students in their studying. *Portable Psychology* provides a wealth of assessment tools at all levels—by section, chapter, unit—and in many forms—interactive online and traditional quizzing, and hands-on participation—to give students confidence in their progress as well as provide flexibility and choice to the instructor in creating and assigning testing. Among the assessment tools we offer are:

- Learning Outcomes
- Built-in summaries
- Built-in Study Guide (5-15 questions per module)

- Chapter Comprehensive Tests (15-25 questions per chapter)
- Critical Thinking questions (2-3 questions per chapter)
- MyPsychLab activities and questions (2-5 questions per chapter)
- MyPsychLab Pre- and Post-Tests

The Classroom Connection: Denise Boyd, Ed.D.

Denise Boyd of the Houston Community College system resumes her coauthor role along-side veteran authors Samuel Wood and Ellen Green Wood. She brings extensive experience teaching thousands of students of varied ages and economic, educational, and cultural backgrounds to *Portable Psychology*. Dr. Boyd has taught introductory psychology courses both in the traditional classroom and online at Houston Community College for over 20 years. Along with her substantial teaching experience, Dr. Boyd applies her background in learning and development to enhance the quality and craftsmanship of the superior, student-friendly pedagogical system in the text.

Psychology Today: Highlighting Special Coverage

FOCUSING ON HEALTHY AND POSITIVE BEHAVIORS

We have always believed that studying human strengths, virtues, and resilience are an important part of introducing students to the world of psychology. Therefore, examples and discussion of positive psychology can be found throughout the text integrated where appropriate and in context of the discussion at hand. To aid those interested in promoting positive psychology concepts we have provided a sampling of this coverage below. Please see the index in Volume 1 for a full listing of coverage.

- Humanistic Psychology (p. 12)
- How self-awareness is crucial to human interaction (p. 146)
- How circadian rhythms and environmental cues play a role in maintaining a healthy balance in energy and mood (p. 149)
- *How to Get a Good Night's Sleep—Apply It* (p. 160)
- Why meditation or hypnosis can be beneficial for a variety of physical and psychological problems (p. 167)
- How cancer patients can avoid taste aversions and therefore help maintain their body weight during chemotherapy treatments (p. 198)
- *How to Win the Battle Against Procrastination—Apply It* (p. 213)
- Why autobiographical memories may be important for regulating current states of emotional well-being (p. 248)
- *How to Build a Powerful Vocabulary—Apply It* (p. 309)
- Why many people with emotional intelligence experience academic and social success (p. 313)
- Why authoritative parenting leads to more socially competent and responsible children (p. 354)
- *Why Are Peer Groups Important in Adolescence? —Explain It* (p. 359)

- How the careers we choose predict how happy we are (p. 365)
- Positive Psychology and Seligman (p. 378)
- *Six Weight Loss Strategies from the Mayo Clinic* (p. 393)
- Why wellness and health psychology are important (pp. 475–476)
- How to reduce the impact of stress and illness (pp. 480–482)
- Why diet and exercise are important to maintaining a healthy lifestyle (p. 488)
- *How Do Cultural Beliefs About Ideal Emotional States Lead to Depression?—Explain It* (p. 553)

HELPING STUDENTS UNDERSTAND AND APPRECIATE HUMAN DIVERSITY

We are dedicated to the goal of promoting and expanding the understanding of human diversity throughout the text. We all come from diverse backgrounds, cultures, and regions in the United States and internationally. In recognition of this reality, *Portable Psychology* embraces a global perspective in presenting issues of diversity concerning gender, ethnicity, sexuality, and age. In addition to coverage in Chapter 10, Human Sexuality and Gender, some examples of human diversity can be found in the following chapters. Please see the index in Volume 1 for a full listing of coverage.

- Women and minorities in psychology (p. 10)
- Age and gender differences in the brain (p. 81)
- Cultural differences in the perceptions of illusions (p. 138)
- Culture and altered states of consciousness (p. 167)
- Cultural differences in punishment (p. 212)
- Estrogen and memory in older women (p. 255)
- Culture-fair intelligence tests (p. 311)
- Gender-role development (p. 416)
- Social attitudes toward gays and lesbians (p. 441)
- Gender and ethnic differences in health (p. 482)
- Personality and culture (p. 521)
- Race, gender, and age as risk factors for suicide (p. 554)
- Culturally sensitive and gender-sensitive therapy (pp. 604–606)
- Prejudice and discrimination (p. 643)

Supplements

We have designed a collection of instructor resources for *Portable Psychology* that will help you prepare for class, enhance your course presentations, and assess your students' understanding of the material.

MYPSYCHLAB This interactive and instructive multimedia resource can be used to supplement a traditional lecture course or to administer a course entirely online. This all-inclusive tool features an electronic version of the *Portable Psychology* textbook with over 200 embedded video clips (two to four minutes in length, closed-captioned, and with postviewing activities) and over 100 embedded animations and simulations that dynamically illustrate chapter concepts. A new feature, the "It" Video Series, includes audio and video clips dealing with many of the topics in the *Try It*, *Apply It*, and *Explain It* text features. Every video resource will conclude with a quiz question, making this an ideal resource for testing or classroom discussion. Fully customizable and easy to use, MyPsych-Lab meets the individual teaching and learning needs of every instructor and every student. Visit *www.mypsychlab.com* to take a tour and learn more.

INSTRUCTOR'S CLASSROOM KIT VOLUMES 1 & 2 WITH CD-ROM Our unparalleled classroom kit, edited by Nicholas Greco IV, College of Lake County, includes every instructional aid an introductory psychology professor needs to manage the classroom. We have made our resources even easier to use by placing all of our print supplements in two convenient volumes. Organized by chapter, each volume contains instructor's manual resources, test bank questions, and slides from the *Portable Psychology* PowerPoint presentation. Fully revised for this edition, our new classroom kit model organizes all supplementary material by learning outcome, integrating test questions, lecture launchers, MyPsychLab activities, and classroom demonstrations into one comprehensive resource. Electronic versions of the IM, TB, and PPT, which are also searchable by key terms, are available on the Instructor's Classroom Kit CD-ROM.

INSTRUCTOR'S MANUAL Written by Charmaine Jake-Matthews of Prairie State College, this wonderful tool can be used by first-time or experienced teachers. It includes lecture launchers, chapter outlines, suggested reading and video sources, teaching objectives, and more. Each chapter now contains a media resource grid, MyPsychLab Connection activities, and unique in-class and out-of-class activities integrating the boxed features.

TEST BANK Prepared by Paulina Multhaupt of Macomb Community College, the fully reviewed test bank contains over 100 questions per chapter, including traditional multiple-choice, fill-in-the-blank, short-answer, and essay formats. One essay question from each chapter is based on a MyPsychLab asset. Each question has an answer, the page reference, a difficulty rating, skill type, and topic.

POWERPOINT PRESENTATION Carl Granrud of University of Northern Colorado has created an exciting interactive tool for use in the classroom. The PowerPoint presentation for *Portable Psychology* pairs key points covered in the chapters with select figures from the textbook to encourage effective lectures and classroom discussions. A second presentation offers all of the figures from the main text in a convenient PowerPoint format. Both PowerPoint presentations are included on the Instructor's Classroom Kit CD-ROM, and can also be downloaded from our Instructor Resource Center.

ALLYN & BACON TRANSPARENCIES FOR INTRODUCTORY PSYCHOLOGY This set of approximately 200 revised, full-color acetates will enhance classroom lecture and discussion. It includes images from Allyn & Bacon's major introductory psychology texts.

INSIGHTS INTO PSYCHOLOGY, VOLUMES II AND III These video programs include two or three short clips per topic, covering such topics as animal research, parapsychology, health and stress, Alzheimer's disease, bilingual education, genetics and IQ, and much more. A video guide containing critical thinking questions accompanies each video. This is also available on DVD.

***THE BLOCKBUSTER APPROACH*: A GUIDE TO TEACHING INTRODUCTORY PSYCHOLOGY WITH VIDEO** *The Blockbuster Approach* is a unique print resource for instructors who enjoy enhancing their classroom presentations with film. With heavy coverage of general, abnormal, social, and developmental psychology, this guide suggests a wide range of films to use in class, and provides questions for reflection and other pedagogical tools to make the use of film more effective in the classroom.

INTERACTIVE LECTURE QUESTIONS FOR CLICKERS FOR INTRODUCTORY PSYCHOLOGY These lecture questions will jumpstart exciting classroom discussions. We have designed ten multiple-choice questions to accompany each chapter of text.

APA CORRELATION GUIDE Included in the Instructor's Classroom Kits and available in the Instructor's Resource Center, this detailed correlation guide shows how the learning outcomes in *Portable Psychology* correspond to the APA learning goals and assessment guidelines.

Acknowledgments

We are thankful for the support of several people at Allyn and Bacon who helped bring our plans for *Portable Psychology* to fruition. On the editorial side, Susan Hartman monitored the progress of the book and ensured that the final product is an introductory text that achieves the goal of being thorough while also being timely and accessible. We are grateful for the assistance of our developmental editors, Deb Hanlon and Julie Swasey, whose suggestions and encouragement helped immeasurably in the pursuit of this goal. Angela Pickard, Associate Editor, helped us create new and improved ancillaries for both students and instructors. We would also like to acknowledge the fine work of Michael Granger, Managing Editor, and Claudine Bellanton, Production Editor, in overseeing the long and complex process of turning our manuscript into a book. Our copyeditor, Margaret Pinette, provided suggestions that improved our writing and helped us produce a text that is clear, concise, and well organized. Finally, we thank Jeanette Koskinas, Executive Marketing Manager, for her work in promoting the text.

OUR REVIEWERS Numerous reviewers were invaluable to the development of this text as well as *Mastering the World of Psychology*. Their help provided a solid foundation for the creation of *Portable Psychology* and we are grateful for their help.

Sherry Ackerman, College of the Siskiyous
Elaine P. Adams, Houston Community College
David Alfano, Community College of Rhode Island
Jill Barton, Keiser College
Berry J. Daughenbaugh, Wor-Wic Community College
Wendy Domjan, University of Texas
Darlene Earley-Hereford, Southern Union State Community College
Brenda East, Durham Technical Community College
Hallie Feil, Western Nebraska Community College
Julie Feldman, University of Arizona
Chuck Hallock, University of Arizona
Carmon Weaver Hicks, Ivy Tech Community College
Harriet Jardine, Macon State College
Carolyn Kaufman, Columbus State Community College
Bethany Mills, Olivet Nazarene University

Robin Morgan, Indiana University Southeast
Paulina Multhaupt, Macomb Community College
Enrique Otero, North Lake College
Jeffrey Pedroza, Santa Anna College
Ralph Pifer, Sauk Valley College
Cynthia Reed, Tarrant County College Northeast
David Shepard, South Texas College
Jason Spiegelman, Community College of Baltimore County
Robert B. Stennett, Gainesville State College
Linda Weldon, Community College of Baltimore County
Diane Wile, Indiana University Southeast
Edie Woods, Macomb County Community College
Peter Wooldridge, Durham Technical Community College

And, last, to all the instructors and students who have taken time out of their busy lives to send along feedback about their experiences teaching and studying from *Mastering the World of Psychology*, we are grateful to you. Please write drdeniseboyd@sbcglobal.net with your comments about this text.

Samuel E. Wood received his doctorate from the University of Florida. He has taught at West Virginia University and the University of Missouri–St. Louis and was a member of the doctoral faculty at both universities. From 1984 to 1996, he served as the president of the Higher Education Center, a consortium of 14 colleges and universities in the St. Louis area. He is a cofounder of the Higher Education Cable TV channel (HEC-TV) in St. Louis and served as its president and CEP from its founding in 1987 until 1996.

Ellen Green Wood received her doctorate in educational psychology from St. Louis University and was an adjunct professor of psychology at St. Louis Community College at Meramee. She has also taught in the clinical experiences program in education at Washington University and at the University of Missouri–St. Louis. In addition to her teaching, Dr. Wood has developed and taught seminars on critical thinking. She received the Telecourse Pioneer Award from 1982 through 1988 for her contribution to the field of distance learning.

Denise Boyd received her Ed.D. in educational psychology from the University of Houston and has been a psychology instructor in the Houston Community College System since 1988. From 1995 until 1998, she chaired the psychology, sociology, and anthropology department at Houston Community College–Central. She has coauthored seven other Allyn & Bacon texts: with Samuel Wood and Ellen Green Wood, *The World of Psychology* (Sixth Edition), *The World of Psychology: Portable Edition,* and *Mastering the World of Psychology* (Second and Third Editions); with Helen Bee, *Lifespan Development* (Fourth Edition), *The Developing Child* (Eleventh Edition), and the upcoming *The Growing Child*; and with Genevieve Stevens, *Current Readings in Lifespan Development.* A licensed psychologist, she has presented a number of papers at professional meetings, reporting research in child, adolescent, and adult development. She has also presented workshops for teachers whose students range from preschool to college.

Together, Sam, Evie, and Denise have more than 45 years of experience teaching introductory psychology to thousands of students of all ages, backgrounds, and abilities. *Portable Psychology* is the direct result of their teaching experience.

Volume 2

FOUNDATIONS AND BIOLOGICAL FUNCTIONING

Volume 4
HUMAN DEVELOPMENT, MOTIVATION, SEXUALITY, GENDER, AND HEALTH

Volume 5

PERSONALITIES, MENTAL HEALTH, AND SOCIAL PSYCHOLOGY

Chapter 12 **Personality Theory and Assessment** 496

Chapter 13 **Psychological Disorders** 534

Chapter 14 **Therapies**   572

Chapter 15 **Social Psychology**   610

Appendix
Statistical Methods

If you want to know how tall a person is, all you have to do is get hold of a tape measure. But if you want to know whether someone is an extravert or how well he or she solves problems or how large his or her vocabulary is, you have to use a tool that is indispensable to psychological researchers, an operational definition. **An operational definition, is a way of assigning numerical values to a variable that cannot be observed directly.** Tests are one type of operational definition, as are survey results. **The bits of numerical information that researchers get from these operational definitions are known as data. The mathematical techniques that are used to analyze data are collectively called statistics.** Psychologists and other scientists use statistics to organize, describe, and draw conclusions about the quantitative results of their studies. We will explore the two basic types of statistics that psychologists use—descriptive statistics and inferential statistics.

Descriptive Statistics

Descriptive statistics are statistics used to organize, summarize, and describe data. Descriptive statistics include measures of central tendency, variability, and relationship.

Describing Data with Tables and Graphs

Visual representations of data, such as graphs and tables, allow researchers to see data in an organized fashion. For example, a researcher tested 100 students for recall of 20 new vocabulary words 24 hours after they had memorized the list. The researcher organized the scores in a **frequency distribution** —an arrangement showing the numbers of **scores that fall within equal-sized class intervals.** In other words, the frequency distribution shows how many students obtained each score. To organize the 100 test scores, the researcher decided to group the scores into 2-point intervals. Next, the researcher tallied the frequency (number of scores) within each 2-point interval. Table A.1 presents the resulting frequency distribution.

The researcher then made a **histogram, a bar graph that depicts the number of scores within each class interval in the frequency distribution.** The intervals are plotted along the horizontal axis, and the frequency of scores in each interval is plotted along the vertical axis. Figure A.1 shows the histogram for the 100 test scores.

	Frequency Distribution of 100 Vocabulary Test Scores	
CLASS INTERVAL	TALLY OF SCORES IN EACH CLASS INTERVAL	NUMBER OF SCORES IN EACH CLASS INTERVAL (FREQUENCY)
1–2			1
3–4	||	2
5–6	卌		6
7–8	卌 卌 卌 |||	18
9–10	卌 卌 卌 卌 |||	23
11–12	卌 卌 卌 卌 |||	23
13–14	卌 卌 卌 ||	17
15–16	卌 |||	8
17–18			1
19–20			1

Table A.1

   Another common method of representing frequency data is the **frequency polygon a line graph that depicts the frequency, or number, of scores within each class interval in a frequency distribution.** As in a histogram, the class intervals are plotted along the horizontal axis and the frequencies are plotted along the vertical axis. However, in a

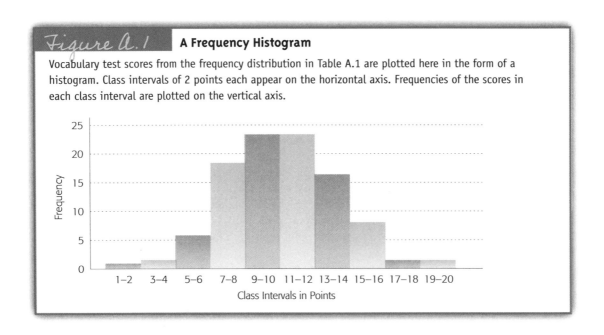

Figure A.1   A Frequency Histogram

Vocabulary test scores from the frequency distribution in Table A.1 are plotted here in the form of a histogram. Class intervals of 2 points each appear on the horizontal axis. Frequencies of the scores in each class interval are plotted on the vertical axis.

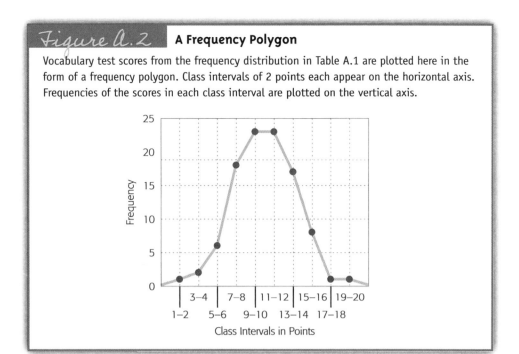

Figure A.2 **A Frequency Polygon**

Vocabulary test scores from the frequency distribution in Table A.1 are plotted here in the form of a frequency polygon. Class intervals of 2 points each appear on the horizontal axis. Frequencies of the scores in each class interval are plotted on the vertical axis.

frequency polygon, each class interval is represented by a graph point that is placed at the middle (midpoint) of the class interval so that its vertical distance above the horizontal axis shows the frequency of that interval. Lines are drawn to connect the points, as shown in Figure A.2. The histogram and the frequency polygon are simply two different ways of presenting data.

Measures of Central Tendency

A measure of central tendency is a measure or score that describes the center, or middle, of a distribution of scores. The most widely used and most familiar measure of central tendency is the **mean, the arithmetic average of a group of scores; computed by adding all the single scores and dividing the sum by the number of scores.**

For instance, consider the case of Carl. Carl sometimes studies and does well in his classes, but he occasionally procrastinates and fails a test. Table A.2 shows how Carl performed on the seven tests in his psychology class last semester. Carl computes his mean score by adding up all his test scores and dividing the sum by the number of tests. Carl's mean, or average, score is 80.

The mean is an important and widely used statistical measure of central tendency, but it can be misleading when a group of scores contains one or several extreme scores. Table A.3 lists the annual incomes of ten people in rank order. When an income of $1 million is averaged with several more modest incomes, the mean does not provide a true picture of the group. Therefore, when one or a few individuals score far above or below

Table A.2	Carl's Psychology Test Scores
Test 1	98
Test 2	74
Test 3	86
Test 4	92
Test 5	56
Test 6	68
Test 7	<u>86</u>
Sum:	560
Mean: 560 ÷ 7 = 80	

the middle range of a group, a different measure of central tendency should be used. **The median is the middle score or value when a group of scores are arranged from highest to lowest.** When there is an odd number of scores, the score in the middle is the median. When there is an even number of scores, the median is the average of the two middle

Table A.3	Annual Income for Ten People
SUBJECT	**ANNUAL INCOME**
1	$1,000,000
2	$50,000
3	$43,000
4	$30,000
5	$28,000
6	$26,000
7	$22,000
8	$22,000
9	$16,000
10	<u>$10,000</u>
Sum:	$1,247,000

$27,000 = Median

Mode

Mean: $1,247,000 ÷ 10 = $124,700
Median: $27,000
Mode: $22,000

scores. For the ten incomes arranged from highest to lowest in Table A.3, the median is $27,000, which is the average of the middle incomes, $28,000 and $26,000. The $27,000 median income is a truer reflection of the comparative income of the group than is the $124,700 mean.

Another measure of central tendency is the **mode**. The mode is easy to find because **it is the score that occurs most frequently in a group of scores.** The mode of the annual income group in Table A.3 is $22,000.

Measures of Variability

In addition to a measure of central tendency, researchers need a measure of the **variability** of a set of scores—**how much the scores spread out, away from the mean.** Both groups in Table A.4 have a mean and a median of 80. However, the scores in Group II cluster tightly around the mean, while the scores in Group I vary widely from the mean.

The simplest measure of variability is the **range —the difference between the highest and lowest scores in a distribution of scores.** Table A.4 reveals that Group I has a range of 47, indicating high variability, while Group II has a range of only 7, showing low variability. Unfortunately, the range reveals only the difference between the lowest score and the highest score; it tells nothing about the scores in between.

The **standard deviation** is a descriptive statistic reflecting the average amount that scores in a distribution deviate, or vary, from their mean. The larger the standard deviation, the greater the variability in a distribution of scores. Refer to Table A.4 and note the standard deviations for the two distributions of test scores. In Group I, the

Table A.4 Comparison of Range and Standard Deviation for Two Small Groups of Scores Having Identical Means and Medians

GROUP I			GROUP II		
TEST	SCORE		TEST	SCORE	
1	99		1	83	
2	99		2	82	
3	98		3	81	
4	80	Median	4	80	Median
5	72		5	79	
6	60		6	79	
7	52		7	76	
Sum:	560		Sum:	560	

Mean: 560 ÷ 7 = 80
Median: 80
Range: 99 − 52 = 47
Standard deviation: 18.1

Mean: 560 ÷ 7 = 80
Median: 80
Range: 83 − 76 = 7
Standard deviation: 2.14

relatively large standard deviation of 18.1 reflects the wide variability in that distribution. By contrast, the small standard deviation of 2.14 in Group II indicates that the variability is low, and you can see that the scores cluster tightly around the mean.

The Normal Curve

Psychologists and other scientists often use descriptive statistics in connection with an important type of frequency distribution known as the normal curve, pictured in Figure A.3. **The normal curve is a symmetrical, bell-shaped frequency distribution that represents how scores are normally distributed in a population.** If a large number of people are measured on any of a wide variety of traits (such as height or IQ score), the great majority of values will cluster in the middle, with fewer and fewer individuals measuring extremely low or high on these variables. Note that slightly more than 68% of the scores in a normal distribution fall within 1 standard deviation of the mean (34.13% within 1 standard deviation above the mean, and 34.13% within 1 standard deviation below the mean). Almost 95.5% of the scores in a normal distribution lie between 2 standard deviations above and below the mean. The vast majority of scores in a normal distribution—99.72%—fall between 3 standard deviations above and below the mean.

Using the properties of the normal curve and knowing the mean and the standard deviation of a normal distribution, we can find where any score stands (how high or low) in relation to all the other scores in the distribution. For example, on the Wechsler

Figure A.3   **The Normal Curve**

The normal curve is a symmetrical, bell-shaped curve that represents how scores are normally distributed in a population. Slightly more than 68% of the scores in a normal distribution fall within 1 standard deviation above and below the mean. Almost 95.5% of the scores lie between 2 standard deviations above and below the mean, and about 99.75% fall between 3 standard deviations above and below the mean.

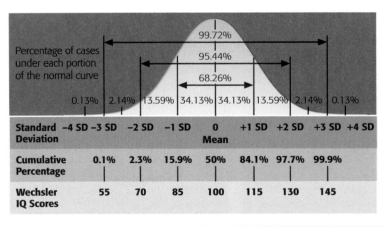

intelligence scales, the mean IQ is 100 and the standard deviation is 15. Thus, 99.72% of the population has an IQ score within 3 standard deviations above and below the mean, ranging from an IQ of 55 to an IQ of 145.

The Correlation Coefficient

As you learned in Chapter 1, Module 2, **a correlation coefficient is a number that indicates the degree and direction of relationship between two variables.** Correlation coefficients can range from +1.00 (a perfect positive correlation) to .00 (no correlation) to −1.00 (a perfect negative correlation), as illustrated in Figure A.4. **A positive correlation indicates that two variables vary in the same direction.** An increase in one variable is associated with an increase in the other variable, or a decrease in one variable is associated with a decrease in the other. There is a positive correlation between the number of hours college students spend studying and their grades. The more hours they study, the higher their grades are likely to be. A **negative correlation means that an increase in one variable is associated with a decrease in the other variable.** There may be a negative correlation between the number of hours students spend watching television and

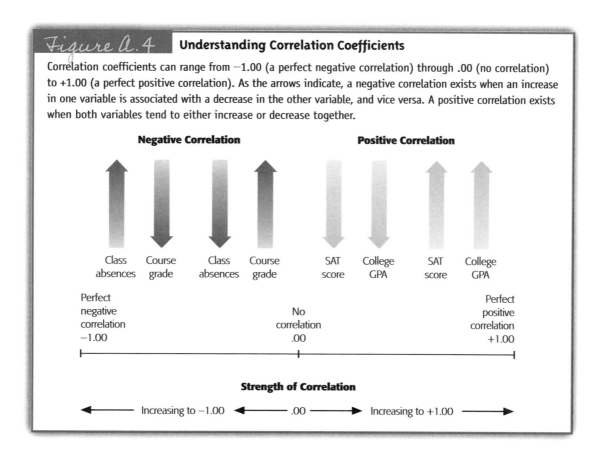

Figure A.4   Understanding Correlation Coefficients

Correlation coefficients can range from −1.00 (a perfect negative correlation) through .00 (no correlation) to +1.00 (a perfect positive correlation). As the arrows indicate, a negative correlation exists when an increase in one variable is associated with a decrease in the other variable, and vice versa. A positive correlation exists when both variables tend to either increase or decrease together.

studying. The more hours they spend watching TV, the fewer hours they may spend studying, and vice versa.

The sign (+ or −) in a correlation coefficient merely tells whether the two variables vary in the same or opposite directions. (If no sign appears, the correlation is assumed to be positive.) The number in a correlation coefficient indicates the relative strength of the relationship between the two variables—the higher the number, the stronger the relationship. For example, a correlation of −.70 is higher than a correlation of +.56; a correlation of −.85 is just as strong as one of +.85. A correlation of .00 indicates that no relationship exists between the variables. IQ and shoe size are examples of two variables that are not correlated.

Table A.5 shows the measurements of two variables—high school GPA and college GPA for 11 college students. Looking at the data, we can see that 6 of the 11 students had a higher GPA in high school, while 5 of the students had a higher GPA in college. A clearer picture of the actual relationship is shown by the *scatterplot* in Figure A.5. High school GPA (variable X) is plotted on the horizontal axis, and college GPA (variable Y) is plotted on the vertical axis.

One dot is plotted for each of the 11 students at the point where high school GPA, variable X, and college GPA, variable Y, intersect. For example, the first student is represented by a dot at the point where her high school GPA of 2.0 on the horizontal (x) axis and college GPA of 1.8 on the vertical (y) axis intersect. The scatterplot in Figure A.5 reveals a relatively high correlation between high school and college GPAs, because the dots cluster near the diagonal line. It also shows that the correlation is positive, because the dots run diagonally upward from left to right. The correlation coefficient for the high

Table A.5	High School and College GPAs for 11 Students	
STUDENT	HIGH SCHOOL GPA (VARIABLE X)	COLLEGE GPA (VARIABLE Y)
1	2.0	1.8
2	2.2	2.5
3	2.3	2.5
4	2.5	3.1
5	2.8	3.2
6	3.0	2.2
7	3.0	2.8
8	3.2	3.3
9	3.3	2.9
10	3.5	3.2
11	3.8	3.5

A Scatterplot

A scatterplot reveals a relatively high positive correlation between the high school and college GPAs of the 11 students listed in Table A.5. One dot is plotted for each of the 11 students at the point where high school GPA (plotted on the horizontal axis) and college GPA (plotted on the vertical axis) intersect.

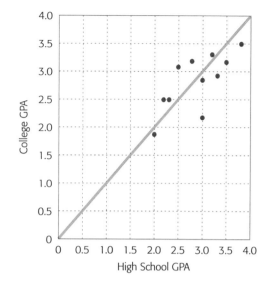

school and college GPAs of these 11 students is .71. If the correlation were perfect (1.00), all the dots would fall exactly on the diagonal line.

A scatterplot shows whether a correlation is low, moderate, or high and whether it is positive or negative. Scatterplots that run diagonally up from left to right reveal positive correlations. Scatterplots that run diagonally down from left to right indicate negative correlations. The closer the dots are to the diagonal line, the higher the correlation. The scatterplots in Figure A.6 depict a variety of correlations. It is important to remember that correlation does not demonstrate cause and effect. Even a perfect correlation (+1.00 or −1.00) does not mean that one variable causes or is caused by the other. Correlation shows only that two variables are related.

Not all relationships between variables are positive or negative. The relationships between some variables are said to be *curvilinear*. A curvilinear relationship exists when two variables correlate positively (or negatively) up to a certain point and then change direction. For example, there is a positive correlation between physical strength and age up to about 40 or 45 years of age. As age increases from childhood to middle age, so does the strength of handgrip pressure. But beyond middle adulthood, the relationship becomes negative, and increasing age is associated with decreasing handgrip strength. Figure A.6(d) shows a scatterplot of this curvilinear relationship.

Figure A.6   A Variety of Scatterplots

A scatterplot moving diagonally up from left to right, as in (a), indicates a positive correlation. A scatter-plot moving diagonally down from left to right, as in (c), indicates a negative correlation. The more closely the dots cluster around a diagonal line, the higher the correlation. Scatterplot (b) indicates no correlation. Scatterplot (d) shows a curvilinear relationship that is positive up to a point and then becomes negative. Age and strength of handgrip have a curvilinear relationship: Handgrip increases in strength up to about age 40 and then decreases with continued aging.

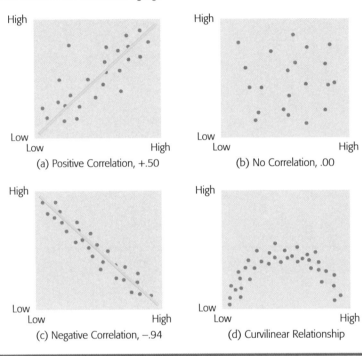

(a) Positive Correlation, +.50

(b) No Correlation, .00

(c) Negative Correlation, −.94

(d) Curvilinear Relationship

● Inferential Statistics

Inferential statistics are statistical procedures that allow researchers (1) to make inferences about the characteristics of the larger population from their observations and measurements of a sample and (2) to derive estimates of how much faith or confidence can be placed in those inferences. In statistical theory, **a population is the entire group that is of interest to researchers—the group to which they wish to apply their findings.** For example, a population could be all the registered voters in the United States. Usually, researchers cannot directly measure and study the entire population of interest. Consequently, they make inferences about a population from a relatively small sample selected from that population. **A sample is defined as the portion of any population that is selected for study and from which generalizations are made about the entire**

population. For researchers to draw conclusions about the larger population, the sample must be representative—that is, its characteristics must mirror those of the larger population. (See Chapter 1 for more information about representative samples.)

Statistical Significance

Suppose 200 students are randomly assigned either to an experimental group that will be taught psychology with innovative materials or to a control group that will receive traditional instruction. At the end of the semester, researchers find that the mean test scores of the experimental group are considerably higher than those of the control group. **To conclude that the instructional methods caused the difference, the researchers must use tests of statistical significance to estimate how often the experimental results could have occurred by chance alone.** The estimates derived from tests of statistical significance are stated as probabilities. A probability of .05 means that the experimental results would be expected to occur by chance no more than 5 times out of 100. The .05 level of significance is usually required as a minimum for researchers to conclude that their findings are statistically significant. Often the level of significance reached is even more impressive, such as the .01 level. The .01 level means that the probability is no more than 1 in 100 that the results occurred by chance.

The inferences researchers make are not absolute. They are based on probability, and there is always a possibility, however small, that experimental results could occur by chance. For this reason, replication of research studies is recommended.

Answers can be found on page PTA-1 in Volume 1.

MULTIPLE CHOICE

1. Psychology is defined as
   a. a survey of the mind's abilities.
   b. an informal study of human behavior and learning processes.
   c. the scientific study of behavior and mental processes.
   d. nothing more than common sense.

2. A counseling psychologist is working with a married couple to promote better communication in their relationship. Which goal of psychology is the psychologist trying to accomplish?
   a. description
   b. explanation
   c. prediction
   d. influence

3. Which of the following is true regarding basic and applied research?
   a. Applied research would seek to find out why memory abilities sometimes change over time.
   b. Basic research would allow us to improve the quality of life for those who suffer from Alzheimer's type dementia.
   c. Neither basic nor applied research allows us to determine cause and effect.
   d. Basic research would allow us to learn about memory changes, and applied research allows us to help those with memory problems cope with everyday life.

4. One of the first psychological laboratories was established by_____where he used_____as the primary method of research.
   a. Ernst Weber; introspection
   b. Gustav Fechner; metromes
   c. Wilhelm Wundt; introspection
   d. Sigmund Freud; behavioral modification

5. The early psychological school of thought devoted to studying the basic elements of conscious mental experiences was_____, developed by_____.
   a. functionalism; Freud
   b. structuralism; Titchener
   c. behaviorism; Skinner
   d. humanism; Watson

6. _____is the school of thought that focuses on unconscious wishes, desires, and impulses.
   a. Humanistic psychology
   b. Behaviorism
   c. Functionalism
   d. Psychoanalytic psychology

7. _____is associated with_____, the school of thought that studies only observable, measurable behavior.
   a. John B. Watson; behaviorism
   b. Sigmund Freud; psychoanalytic psychology
   c. Abraham Maslow; humanistic psychology
   d. Max Wertheimer; structuralism

8. Dr. Smith believes that depression is a consequence of faulty thinking, decision making, and problem solving. With which theoretical perspective would Dr. Smith most agree?
   a. biological
   b. humanistic
   c. psychoanalytic
   d. cognitive

9. A researcher is studying patterns of social play in 8-year-olds by watching children on a playground and documenting their behaviors. Which research method is she using?
   a. survey
   b. laboratory observation
   c. case study
   d. naturalistic observation

10. A survey taker makes sure that the people surveyed closely mirror the population of interest. He is ensuring that he has a
    a. representative sample.
    b. representative population.
    c. biased sample.
    d. random population.

11. A professor asks her class to record how often they study. Her students may tend to report studying more than they really do, thereby giving a
    a. candid response.
    b. social desirability response.
    c. representative response.
    d. random response.

12. The variable that is presumed to vary as a result of the manipulation of another variable is called a(n)
    a. confounding variable.
    b. dependent variable.
    c. independent variable.
    d. mitigating factor.

13. Dr. Needles is testing the effects of a new drug. One group receives the drug, while a comparison group receives an injection of a harmless solution. The group that receives the drug is called the
    a. experimental group.   c. prediction group.
    b. control group.   d. placebo group.

14. In Dr. Needles's experiment, neither he nor the participants know who gets the drug and who gets the harmless solution. This method is called
    a. the single-blind method.
    b. the double-blind technique.
    c. the hidden-purpose method.
    d. deception.

15. Which of the following correlation coefficients indicates the strongest relationship between two variables?
    a. .67   c. −.85
    b. −.43   d. 1.25

16. Research participants must be told the purpose of the study in which they are participating and its potential for harming them. This is the ethical consideration known as
    a. prior approval.
    b. applicable disclosure.
    c. appropriate disclosure.
    d. informed consent.

17. Which of the following is *not* a characteristic exhibited when one engages in critical thinking?
    a. independent thinking
    b. suspension of judgment
    c. open-minded acceptance
    d. willingness to modify prior judgments

18. Dr. Jarrod, a psychologist, is part of an interdisciplinary team that includes biologists, biochemists, and medical researchers, who study the nervous system. To which field does Dr. Jarrod likely belong?
    a. evolutionary psychology
    b. biocultural psychology
    c. chemical psychology
    d. neuroscience

19. Dr. Benson studies the factors that promote productivity in an office environment for a large company. Which type of psychologist is Dr. Benson likely to be?
    a. social psychologist
    b. industrial-organizational psychologist
    c. educational psychologist
    d. counseling psychologist

20. Which type of psychologist is most likely to study how human behavior is affected by the presence of other people?
    a. social psychologist
    b. developmental psychologist
    c. educational psychologist
    d. clinical psychologist

TRUE/FALSE

21. Replication is used to verify a study's findings with a different group of participants.

22. Wilhelm Wundt and John Watson belonged to the same early school of psychology.

23. Humanistic psychology focuses on the uniqueness of human beings and their capacity for growth.

24. Descriptive research methods, such as surveys and observation, accomplish all four goals of psychology equally well.

25. The experimental method allows for the greatest experimenter control as well as permitting cause and effect conclusions to be drawn.

26. A perfect positive correlation is indicated by the coefficient 1.00.

27. If stress and illness are positively correlated, it means that stress causes illness.

28. The APA permits the use of animals in research.

29. Information-processing theory compares the human brain's workings to those of a computer.

30. The view that human behavior is shaped by physiological factors is called the sociocultural approach.

ESSAY

31. Explain what separates the science of psychology from common sense. Include in your response reasons that a theory cannot rely on anecdotal evidence.

32. Name and describe at least four current, major schools of thought in psychology. According to each school selected, what is the primary reason for an individual's behavior?

33. Suppose you wanted to test whether a new drug helped improve scores on a memory test for college students. Design an experiment to do so. Include how you would select your sample and label the independent and dependent variables, as well as the experimental and control groups. Also, describe one confounding variable you would avoid.

MULTIPLE CHOICE

1. The neurons that relay messages from the sense organs to the central nervous system are
   a. afferent (sensory) neurons.
   b. efferent (motor) neurons.
   c. interneurons.
   d. operant neurons.

2. Which part of the neuron receives messages from other cells?
   a. dendrite   c. axon
   b. myelin sheath   d. synapse

3. When a neuron's axon carries a positive electrical potential of about 50 millivolts for a brief moment, it is said to be firing. This is called the
   a. resting potential.   c. action potential.
   b. synaptic charge.   d. ionic storm.

4. Sarah seems to be depressed, isn't sleeping well, and has little appetite. Which neurotransmitter is most likely to be involved in the problem?
   a. serotonin   c. epinephrine
   b. dopamine   d. acetylcholine

5. Jesse is wiring together his home theater system, and he accidentally touches a live wire. He gets a painful shock and quickly jerks his hand away. The reflex of pulling his hand back is dictated by the
   a. hypothalamus.   c. hippocampus.
   b. spinal cord.   d. medulla.

6. A severe injury to the medulla would likely result in
   a. coma.   c. memory loss.
   b. paralysis.   d. death.

7. Which area of the brain regulates several body functions, including hunger, thirst, sexual behavior, and internal body temperature?
   a. thalamus   c. amygdala
   b. hypothalamus   d. substantia nigra

8. Danielle is left-handed. When she is taking notes in class, which part of her brain is directing the movements of her hand?
   a. left frontal lobe   c. left temporal lobe
   b. right frontal lobe   d. right temporal lobe

9. The visual cortex is located in the
   a. frontal lobe.   c. temporal lobe.
   b. parietal lobe.   d. occipital lobe.

10. Coral suffers from epilepsy. Her seizures begin on the left side of her brain and then travel to the right side; this occurs repeatedly. Her doctor wants to perform an operation that he believes will improve the quality of Coral's life. Because medications are not controlling her seizures, which of the following is Coral's doctor likely considering?
    a. He plans to perform a prefrontal lobotomy.
    b. He plans to remove her amygdala.
    c. He plans to sever her corpus callosum.
    d. He plans to scrape the Broca's area.

11. Which part of the nervous system is primarily responsible for regulating the body's involuntary, internal environment?
    a. autonomic nervous system
    b. somatic nervous system
    c. central nervous system
    d. synaptic nervous system

12. During an exam, which brain-wave pattern are you most likely to exhibit?
    a. alpha wave   c. delta wave
    b. beta wave   d. slow wave

13. Kevin is undergoing some tests to look for signs of physical damage to his brain. He also needs to be sure that certain parts of his brain are working properly. Which type of diagnostic technique would reveal both structures and activity?
    a. fMRI   c. CT scan
    b. MRI   d. PET scan

14. Which individual is most likely to recover or at least partially recover a lost brain function following a head injury?
    a. 15-year-old boy   c. 45-year-old woman
    b. 25-year-old man   d. 7-year-old girl

15. Which of the following statements about gender differences in the adult brain is true?
    a. Men have less white matter in the brain than do women.
    b. Women have more white matter in the left brain than do men.
    c. Women have more gray matter in the area of the brain that controls emotions than do men.
    d. There is no evidence of gender differences in the adult brain.

16. Marisa is riding a roller coaster. As it surges over the high point to plunge downward, her heart races, her breathing quickens, and blood flow to her skeletal muscles increases. Which division of the peripheral nervous system is most active?
    a. somatic
    b. central
    c. sympathetic
    d. parasympathetic

17. _____ are to the central nervous system as _____ are to the endocrine system.
    a. Neurons; electrons
    b. Electrons; neurons
    c. Hormones; neurotransmitters
    d. Neurotransmitters; hormones

18. Which organ is responsible for regulating blood sugar by releasing insulin and glucagon into the bloodstream?
    a. pancreas
    b. pituitary
    c. spleen
    d. thyroid

19. In a dominant-recessive pattern set of inheritance rules, which pair of genes would result in the expression of a recessive trait?
    a. two dominant genes
    b. one dominant gene and one recessive gene
    c. two recessive genes
    d. none of the above

20. Which of the following is *true* regarding the field of behavioral genetics?
    a. The researchers are trying to understand how heredity affects behavior.
    b. Twin studies are used in the field of behavioral genetics.
    c. Adoption studies are used in the field of behavioral genetics.
    d. All of the above are true.

TRUE/FALSE

21. The myelin sheath allows neural impulses to travel faster.

22. Any neurotransmitter can fit into any receptor.

23. The limbic system is a series of brain structures involved in emotion.

24. Wernicke's aphasia involves difficulty with comprehension of speech.

25. The right hemisphere of the brain is responsible for most language functions.

26. Pain perception occurs in the somatosensory area of the cerebrum.

27. The somatic nervous system can be divided into the sympathetic and parasympathetic nervous systems.

28. An MRI is a more powerful way to view the brain's structures than an EEG.

29. The gonads are primarily responsible for the production of sex hormones.

30. There are 22 pairs of chromosomes in the human body.

ESSAY

31. Describe the process of neural transmission across the synapse.

32. Name and describe the effects of five neurotransmitters.

33. Name and describe the components that make up the peripheral nervous system.

CHAPTER 3: Sensation and Perception

MULTIPLE CHOICE

1. Jenna accidentally steps on a pin. The stimulation of her skin and transmission of the information regarding this touch to the central nervous system is the process of
   a. penetration.
   b. sensation.
   c. perception.
   d. registration.

2. To sense a change in weights being carried, the additional weight added must be 2% higher than what you carried before. This difference threshold is calculated using
   a. Weber's law.
   b. an absolute threshold.
   c. Planck's law.
   d. Gestalt laws.

3. The process of converting sensory information into neural impulses is called
   a. sensory conduction.
   b. transformation.
   c. sensory adaptation.
   d. transduction.

4. The outer part of the eye that serves to protect the eye, and on which you would place your contact lenses, is called the
   a. lens.
   b. cornea.
   c. pupil.
   d. iris.

5. Jake and Abby walked into their local Starbucks to get some coffee. Jake immediately noticed the smell of freshly ground coffee beans. Abby couldn't smell them until she walked closer to the counter where the beans were being ground. Jake and Abby likely have different
   a. sensory adaptation abilities.
   b. olfactory accommodations.
   c. absolute thresholds.
   d. saturation levels.

6. The_____is the structure responsible for transduction for vision.
   a. retina   c. fovea
   b. optic nerve   d. iris

7. Which theory best explains visual phenomena such as afterimages?
   a. trichromatic theory
   b. opponent-process theory
   c. Weber's law
   d. signal detection theory

8. The loudness of a sound corresponds to which physical characteristic of a sound wave?
   a. amplitude   c. wavelength
   b. frequency   d. timbre

9. Which of the following best describes where transduction for hearing takes place?
   a. eardrum   c. ossicles
   b. pinna   d. hair cells in the cochlea

10. Which theory of hearing best explains how sensory receptors in our ear encode sound-wave frequencies over 1,000 Hz?
    a. frequency theory
    b. place theory
    c. both frequency theory and place theory
    d. neither frequency theory nor place theory

11. Glenda purchases some new perfume to attract her boyfriend's attention. The perfume is meant to stimulate which sensory system?
    a. olfactory   c. tactile
    b. gustatory   d. auditory

12. Linda's friends all drink coffee, but Linda finds the taste of coffee very bitter, more so than do her friends. Which is one explanation for Linda's dislike of coffee?
    a. She is has an aversion to caffeine.
    b. She is a "nontaster."
    c. She is a "supertaster."
    d. She has damaged taste buds.

13. Monique experiences a leg cramp in her calf. She massages the muscle while gritting her teeth and finds she feels less pain. Which theory explains this decrease in pain?
    a. place theory
    b. frequency theory
    c. opponent-process theory
    d. gate-control theory

14. A toddler plays with blocks by sorting them into piles by color, so that the red blocks make up one pile, the blue blocks make up a second pile, and the green blocks make up a third pile. He is using which Gestalt principle of perceptual organization?
    a. proximity   c. continuity
    b. similarity   d. closure

15. Gary sees a friend standing near a fence. The fence partially blocks his view of his friend, so Gary realizes the fence is closer to him than is his friend. Which monocular depth cue is Gary using?
    a. linear perspective c. interposition
    b. relative size   d. texture gradient

16. The "old woman/young woman" image is an example of
    a. the phi phenomenon.   c. an ambiguous figure.
    b. an impossible figure. d. an autokinetic illusion.

17. Which of the following involves an illusion using two equal lines with diagonals extending outward from one line, making it appear longer than the line with diagonals extending inward?
    a. Müller-Lyer illusion c. Ponzo illusion
    b. moon illusion   d. linear perspective illusion

18. Brandi is learning to read by sounding out a word one letter at a time. Which type of processing is she using?
    a. bottom-up processing
    b. top-down processing
    c. perceptual set
    d. Gestalt principle of closure

19. Leroy is studying and trying to ignore his roommate's phone conversation in the other room. He is engrossed in his psychology textbook until he hears his name mentioned, when he suddenly becomes aware of what his roommate is saying on the phone. Which perceptual concept does this example demonstrate?
    a. phi phenomenon
    b. cross-modal perception
    c. just noticeable difference
    d. cocktail party phenomenon

20. Which type of extrasensory perception might be claimed by individuals who try to predict the outcome of a football game?
    a. clairvoyance
    b. synesthesia
    c. precognition
    d. telepathy

TRUE/FALSE

21. The lens in the eye is a muscle that dilates or constricts depending on the amount of light in the environment.

22. A blind spot exists in our vision due to an area on the retina that lacks rods and cones.

23. Someone with color blindness cannot perceive any colors at all.

24. The same note played on different musical instruments sounds different because of a change in timbre.

25. The sensory receptors for the olfactory system are located in the olfactory bulbs.

26. Specific areas of the tongue specialize in processing different taste sensations.

27. The body has the ability to produce natural painkillers called endorphins in times of need.

28. Receptors in our muscles, joints, and ligaments allow us to obtain information as to where our body is in space.

29. Illusions fool our perceptual system only when our attention decreases.

30. Subliminal perception can influence behavior to some degree.

ESSAY

31. Explain the progression of a sound wave from its arrival at the pinna to its arrival in the brain.

32. Describe how the gate-control theory explains our perception of pain. How do psychological factors affect this perception?

33. Name and describe five Gestalt principles of perceptual organization.

CHAPTER 4: States of Consciousness

MULTIPLE CHOICE

1. A mental state other than wakefulness, such as sleep or meditation, is called
    a. consciousness.
    b. meta-consciousness.
    c. an altered state of consciousness.
    d. conscientiousness.

2. Circadian rhythms exist for
    a. appetite.
    b. learning efficiency.
    c. energy level.
    d. all of the above.

3. Which hormone is most related to the sleep/wake cycle?
    a. adrenaline
    b. serotonin
    c. melatonin
    d. glucagons

4. _____occurs in four stages.
    a. Biorhythm
    b. Consciousness
    c. REM sleep
    d. NREM sleep

5. Which EEG pattern is typical of someone who is relaxed and drowsy but not yet asleep?
    a. alpha waves
    b. beta waves
    c. delta waves
    d. sleep spindles

6. Jonas stayed up all night at a party. The next night, he had nightmares when he slept. This was probably because of
    a. somnambulism.
    b. REM rebound effect.
    c. NREM sleep disturbance.
    d. more time spent in stage 3 sleep.

7. Which theory explains the function of sleep in humans?
    a. restorative theory of sleep
    b. circadian theory of sleep
    c. a combination of both the restorative and circadian theories of sleep
    d. neither the restorative nor the circadian theory of sleep

8. Laura describes a dream she had to her friend, Jessica. Jessica explains her view of what the dream means. According to Freud, Jessica is offering her opinion of which aspect of Laura's dream?
    a. manifest content
    b. latent content
    c. lucid content
    d. symbiotic content

9. Which of the following best describes the activation-synthesis hypothesis of dreaming?
   a. Dreams are symbolic of unconscious conflicts.
   b. Dreams offer a symbolic opportunity to rehearse solutions to real-world problems.
   c. Dreams are the brain's way of consolidating memories.
   d. Dreams are the brain's attempt to make sense of the random firing of brain cells during REM sleep.

10. The technical term for talking in one's sleep is
    a. somniloquy.
    b. somnambulism.
    c. parasomnia.
    d. hypersomnia.

11. Which of the following major sleep disorders may be treated through surgery?
    a. insomnia
    b. sleep apnea
    c. narcolepsy
    d. somniloquy

12. Nightmares and sleep terrors
    a. occur during different stages of sleep.
    b. are both seen during REM sleep.
    c. are the same thing.
    d. predict mental illness.

13. Terrell spends time every morning sitting alone, quietly concentrating on the sound of his own breathing. He says that the 20 minutes of quiet time clear his mind and cause him to feel rested and alert. Terrell is experiencing the benefits of
    a. hypnosis.
    b. somniloquy.
    c. dyssomnia.
    d. meditation.

14. Which of the following statements about hypnosis is true?
    a. Memory is more accurate under hypnosis.
    b. People can perform superhuman acts while under hypnosis.
    c. People are more suggestible while hypnotized.
    d. Hypnosis can be used to regress adults back to their childhood.

15. Which theory of hypnosis states that the behavior of a hypnotized person is a function of his or her own expectations about how people behave while hypnotized?
    a. sociocognitive theory of hypnosis
    b. theory of dissociated control
    c. cognitive dissonance theory
    d. neodissociated theory of hypnosis

16. Which of the following is not a psychoactive drug?
    a. marijuana
    b. nicotine
    c. caffeine
    d. All of the above are psychoactive drugs.

17. Alcohol is classified as a
    a. stimulant.
    b. depressant.
    c. hallucinogen.
    d. narcotic.

18. Blake uses cocaine. He finds he needs more cocaine now to receive the same effect he once received from smaller amounts of the drug. This symptom of cocaine dependence is called
    a. withdrawal.
    b. drug escalation.
    c. drug tolerance.
    d. psychological drug dependence.

19. According to psychologists, at what point does casual use of a psychoactive drug become abuse?
    a. when the use of the substance occurs regularly
    b. when the individual feels a craving for the drug
    c. when use of the drug has begun to negatively affect important aspects of the person's life and functioning
    d. when the individual realizes that he or she wants to stop using the substance

20. The neurotransmitter associated with the feelings of reward or pleasure produced by many psychoactive substances is
    a. serotonin.
    b. dopamine.
    c. acetylcholine.
    d. diazepam.

TRUE/FALSE

21. Chronic jet lag can result in permanent memory deficits.

22. Exposure to bright sunlight during early morning hours and avoidance of bright light in the evening may help restore circadian rhythms for those experiencing jet lag.

23. Sleep deprivation may negatively affect mood but has little effect on cognitive performance.

24. Dreams occur only during REM sleep.

25. Chronic insomnia can last for years and affects about 10% of all adults.

26. Meditation can help some people with depression.

27. Hypnosis has been effective in helping patients control pain.

28. Substance abuse is a more severe problem than substance dependence.

29. An individual who is addicted to cocaine and tries to quit using will often feel nervous and "hyper."

30. Marijuana has been associated with apathy and a decline in school performance.

ESSAY

31. Describe the NREM and REM progression of the sleep cycle. Include the EEG pattern typical of each stage.

32. Distinguish between the dream theories espoused by Freud and Hobson.

33. Distinguish between the general effects of stimulants, depressants, and hallucinogens, including the typical pattern of withdrawal symptoms for each.

CHAPTER 5: Learning

MULTIPLE CHOICE

1. The individual most directly responsible for the process of classical conditioning is
  a. B. F. Skinner.
  c. John B. Watson.
  b. Ivan Pavlov.
  d. Edward Thorndike.

2. Vinny's professor always says, "Here we go!!" before administering an exam. For some reason now, Vinny becomes nervous every time he hears someone say, "Here we go!!" In this example of classical conditioning, which is the conditioned stimulus?
  a. the exam
  b. becoming nervous
  c. hearing the phrase, "Here we go!!"
  d. Vinny's professor

3. Twenty-two year old Sofia drank too much vodka and cranberry juice one evening and became very ill. Now, anytime Sofia tastes cranberry juice, she feels very ill. Based on classical conditioning,_____is the unconditioned stimulus whereas_____is the conditioned stimulus.
  a. too much vodka; cranberry juice
  b. feeling very ill; too much vodka
  c. cranberry juice; feeling very ill
  d. cranberry juice; vodka

4. The weakening and eventual disappearance of a conditioned response that is caused by repeated presentation of the conditioned stimulus without the presence of the unconditioned stimulus is called
  a. discrimination.
  c. spontaneous recovery.
  b. generalization.
  d. extinction.

5. Jerry bought a dog specifically to serve as a watch dog. He teaches his dog to bark whenever the doorbell rings. However, the dog also barks at the telephone or a doorbell rung on television. Which process explains these additional responses?

  a. spontaneous recovery
  c. generalization
  b. higher-order conditioning
  d. discrimination

6. John B. Watson's work with Little Albert was significant because it demonstrated
  a. a conditioned fear response.
  b. the limitations of classical conditioning.
  c. discrimination procedures.
  d. conditioning the behavior of a rat.

7. Janie once ate fish at a restaurant and later felt ill. Now the very smell of cooked fish makes her nauseous. What has Janie experienced?
  a. a conditioned fear response
  b. a taste aversion
  c. a taste generalization
  d. an unconditioned aversion response

8. Bill completes his drug rehabilitation program. His counselor strongly urges him to avoid going to places where he used to use drugs. His counselor, knowledge-able about classical conditioning, says this so that
  a. Bill doesn't experience peer pressure to use drugs.
  b. Bill can start fresh in more areas of his life.
  c. Bill doesn't get rewarded for drug use.
  d. Bill doesn't come into contact with stimuli previously associated with drug use.

9. Thorndike's experiments using the cat that had to learn to escape the puzzle box for food illustrated which behavioral law?
  a. law of rewards
  c. law of effect
  b. law of consequence
  d. law of gravity

10. _____are the major concepts of operant conditioning, a type of learning devised by_____.
  a. Positive and negative reinforcement; Pavlov
  b. Stimulus and reinforcement; Skinner
  c. The law of effect and classical conditioning; Thorndike
  d. Reinforcement and punishment; Skinner

11. The process of shaping a response involves reinforcing each of a series of steps that become increasingly more similar to the desired response. This is called
    a. successive approximations.
    b. gradual discovery.
    c. the "eureka" phenomenon.
    d. planning with foresight.

12. What causes extinction in operant conditioning?
    a. withholding punishment
    b. withholding reinforcement
    c. shaping
    d. reinforcing successive approximations

13. Cindy cries for candy when in the store with her mother. Her mother, wanting Cindy to be quiet, gives in and gets her some candy, at which point Cindy becomes silent. The next time they go to the store, the process repeats itself. Which of the following best describes what has happened?
    a. Cindy's behavior is positively reinforced, and her mother's behavior is positively reinforced.
    b. Cindy's behavior is positively reinforced, and her mother's behavior is negatively reinforced.
    c. Cindy's behavior is negatively reinforced, and her mother's behavior is positively reinforced.
    d. Cindy's behavior is negatively reinforced, and her mother's behavior is negatively reinforced.

14. Positive reinforcement_____the likelihood of a behavior happening again; negative reinforcement_____the likelihood of a behavior happening again.
    a. decreases; increases   c. decreases; decreases
    b. increases; decreases   d. increases; increases

15. Which of the following is the best example of a primary reinforcer?
    a. money   c. water
    b. a diploma   d. a greeting card

16. A professor gives his class a quiz each Monday. Consequently, students do not study much during the week, but "cram" throughout the weekend to earn a good grade. Their behavior best corresponds to which schedule of reinforcement?
    a. fixed ratio   c. fixed interval
    b. variable ratio   d. variable interval

17. When Billy misbehaves, his parents make sure to apply punishment immediately and consistently and to use the harshest possible punishment so that Billy will "get the message." According to the research in your text, which of the following is a recommendation you might make to help their use of punishment be more effective?
    a. make punishment less severe
    b. make punishment more severe
    c. punish him less consistently
    d. wait a bit after his misbehavior before punishing him

18. Seligman's experiments with dogs that did not escape the shock administered, even when they could have, demonstrates which principle?
    a. avoidance learning
    b. learned helplessness
    c. escape learning
    d. positive reinforcement

19. Carrie is trying to complete a jigsaw puzzle. She struggles with it for some time until she suddenly sees how the pieces fit together. Which type of learning is Carrie exhibiting?
    a. insight learning   c. shaping
    b. latent learning   d. observational learning

20. Carl learned how to change a flat tire by watching his mother do so. She would change a tire and then have him show her each step as well. Which type of learning does this demonstrate?
    a. insight learning   c. classical conditioning
    b. latent learning   d. observational learning

TRUE/FALSE

21. Memorizing a phone number long enough to dial it, and then forgetting it, fits the text definition of learning.

22. Classical conditioning takes place most readily when the unconditioned stimulus occurs just before the conditioned stimulus.

23. John B. Watson was one of the researchers who demonstrated that fear could be conditioned in humans.

24. Rescorla's cognitive view of classical conditioning suggests that the repeated pairing of the conditioned stimulus and the unconditioned stimulus is the critical element for conditioning to occur.

25. The "operant" in operant conditioning refers to a voluntary behavior.

26. Negative reinforcement is designed to have the same outcome as punishment.

27. According to Skinner, punishment can suppress behavior but not extinguish it.

28. Biofeedback can be used to train individuals to control internal responses such as heart rate and anxiety-tension states.

29. Behavior modification programs require a therapist to administer them.

30. The process of latent learning depends on reinforcement taking place.

ESSAY

31. Distinguish between the process of extinction in classical conditioning and the process of extinction in operant conditioning.

32. Design a reinforcement plan to teach your dog to roll over. Include the type of reinforcement used, the schedule of reinforcement, and the reason why you made those particular choices.

33. Describe Bandura's "Bobo doll" study and its implications for television violence.

CHAPTER 6: Memory

MULTIPLE CHOICE

1. Any steps you take to try to commit something to memory are part of the_____process.
   a. consolidation
   b. encoding
   c. retrieval
   d. placement

2. When you call information for a phone number, but you don't have a pen to write down the number, which part of your memory must attempt to maintain the number while you run around looking for a pen?
   a. implicit memory
   b. long-term memory
   c. short-term memory
   d. nondeclarative memory

3. The strategy of grouping bits of information into larger units that are easier to remember is called
   a. displacement.
   b. rehearsal.
   c. assimilation.
   d. chunking.

4. For information stored in long-term memory to be used, it must first be
   a. grouped.
   b. moved into sensory memory.
   c. retrieved.
   d. chunked.

5. Memories of a vacation spent with your family would be considered
   a. implicit memories.
   b. episodic memories.
   c. procedural memories.
   d. nondeclarative memories.

6. Which of the following is not one of the three types of nondeclarative memories?
   a. information learned in class
   b. motor skills
   c. simple classically conditioned responses
   d. habits

7. A memory researcher asks subjects to memorize a list of words and finds it takes them 30 minutes to do so. Two weeks later, he asks the same subjects to memorize the list of words again, and they do so in 15 minutes. The percentage of time saved, 50%, is known as the
   a. savings score.
   b. relearning score.
   c. rote score.
   d. recognition score.

8. An integrated framework about people, objects, and events that is stored in long-term memory is called a
   a. memory.
   b. schema.
   c. reconstruction.
   d. retrieval cue.

9. Henry, a college student, has difficulty remembering events from the first few years of his life. This is likely due to
   a. repression of early traumas.
   b. a negative bias.
   c. infantile amnesia.
   d. the fact that he has yet to experience recovered memories.

10. There is a good chance that you remember exactly where you were and what you were doing when you first heard about the attacks on September 11, 2001. Such a vivid memory is called a(n) _____ memory.
    a. flashbulb
    b. snapshot
    c. autobiographical
    d. first-order

11. According to the serial position effect, which items on a list are least likely to be recalled?
    a. the first few
    b. the middle few
    c. the last few
    d. All items are equally likely to be remembered or forgotten.

12. Vern had a bit too much to drink at a party one night. The next day he got a phone call from a woman he met at the party, but he cannot remember her name. According to the state-dependent memory effect, under which condition will Vern most likely remember her name?
    a. when he is sober
    b. when he hears her voice
    c. when he sees her face
    d. when he has a bit too much to drink

13. Which of the following techniques is used to measure memory?
    a. the relearning method   c. tests of recognition
    b. tests of recall   d. all of the above

14. Which of the following hormones has *not* been related to memory processes, according to your text?
    a. cortisol   c. testosterone
    b. estrogen   d. noradrenalin (norepinephrine)

15. Jacquez believes that as you get older, memories that haven't been used will just fade away and disappear. His position is most consistent with which cause of forgetting?
    a. decay theory   c. consolidation failure
    b. encoding failure   d. proactive interference

16. David studied French in high school but switched to learning Italian in college. Whenever he tries to speak French, he catches himself instead translating his English phrases into Italian. Why is David forgetting his French?
    a. encoding failure
    b. proactive interference
    c. retroactive interference
    d. decay theory

17. Which of the following is not a form of motivated forgetting according to your text?
    a. repression   c. suppression
    b. progressive forgetting   d. retrograde amnesia

18. Cassie is playing Trivial Pursuit with friends. She is asked a question and knows she knows the answer. However, she becomes frustrated because although she knows the answer, she cannot seem to retrieve it. What is Cassie likely experiencing?
    a. state-dependent memory
    b. the tip-of-the-tongue phenomenon
    c. retrograde amnesia
    d. repression

19. Another name for "cramming"—generally considered less effective than other methods of studying—is
    a. distributed practice.   c. massed practice.
    b. elaborative rehearsal.   d. motivated learning.

20. ROY G. BIV, an acronym representing the colors of the visual spectrum, is a type of
    a. chunking exercise.   c. pegging.
    b. elaborative rehearsal.   d. mnemonic device.

TRUE/FALSE

21. Elaborative rehearsal is the best method for remembering complex information like material for this class.

22. Recall tasks are typically considered to be easier than recognition tasks.

23. A reconstruction of an event may sometimes be based on inaccurate information.

24. Research suggests that eyewitness testimony is too unreliable to be considered as evidence in criminal court cases.

25. Repressed memories are controversial in that the event never really occurred.

26. Your strongest, most long-lasting memories are usually those fueled by your emotions.

27. Hermann Ebbinghaus conducted the first experimental studies on learning and memory.

28. The tip-of-the-tongue phenomenon is an example of retrieval failure.

29. Overlearning involves studying so hard you can't remember what you studied.

30. Engaging in spaced practice will help you remember more in less study time.

ESSAY

31. Describe the "reconstructive" nature of memory, including the impact of schemas and cognitive bias.

32. What is long-term potentiation, and how is it related to learning?

33. Describe a plan for studying that incorporates at least two recommendations from your text to improve your memory.

MULTIPLE CHOICE

1. Acquiring, storing, retrieving, and using information, based on sensation, perception, problem solving, and conceptualizing, is called
   - **a.** a formal concept.
   - **b.** memorizing.
   - **c.** cognition.
   - **d.** recognition.

2. Which of the following would not be considered a concept?
   - **a.** animals
   - **b.** your cat Spike
   - **c.** mammals
   - **d.** dogs

3. Individual instances of a concept that are stored in memory based on personal experience are called
   - **a.** prototypes.
   - **b.** specifics.
   - **c.** phonemes.
   - **d.** exemplars.

4. Which of the following is the most likely prototype of a bird?
   - **a.** sparrow
   - **b.** penguin
   - **c.** ostrich
   - **d.** turkey

5. You are trying to decide what kind of breakfast cereal to buy. You notice a new cereal that you recall seeing advertised on television and choose to buy it. This kind of decision making fits best with the concept of the
   - **a.** elimination by aspects strategy.
   - **b.** recognition heuristic.
   - **c.** algorithm.
   - **d.** representativeness heuristic.

6. The_____is a sort of mental short cut that helps us make decisions based on what is easiest to call to mind.
   - **a.** probability heuristic
   - **b.** representative heuristic
   - **c.** recognition heuristic
   - **d.** availability heuristic

7. Kayla is playing blackjack and has a hand totaling 17. She knows that she will likely lose if she gets another card but she does so anyway because she has a "gut feeling" she will get a lucky card. On what is Kayla's decision making based?
   - **a.** probability heuristic
   - **b.** elimination by aspects
   - **c.** intuition
   - **d.** analogy heuristic

8. When you use a specific procedure for solving a math problem that will always lead you to the correct answer, providing you correctly follow the steps, you are using a(n)
   - **a.** analogy.
   - **b.** availability heuristic.
   - **c.** algorithm.
   - **d.** means-end analysis.

9. Juanita visits her advisor at college and afterward figures out when she will graduate by counting how many classes she has left and determining how many terms it will take to complete them. She is using
   - **a.** the recognition heuristic.
   - **b.** means-end analysis.
   - **c.** pragmatics.
   - **d.** an algorithm.

10. _____refers to word arrangement, whereas_____refers to the meaning of words.
    - **a.** Syntax; semantics
    - **b.** Semantics; phonemes
    - **c.** Morphemes; pragmatics
    - **d.** Semantics; syntax

11. How many phonemes are in the word *psychology?*
    - **a.** 4
    - **b.** 6
    - **c.** 8
    - **d.** 10

12. Intonation and social rules are part of which component of language?
    - **a.** phonics
    - **b.** pragmatics
    - **c.** syntax
    - **d.** semantics

13. The language in which you think largely determines the nature of your thoughts. This is called the
    - **a.** bilingual theory.
    - **b.** relative cognition model.
    - **c.** meta-cognitive strategy.
    - **d.** linguistic relativity hypothesis.

14. Thurston believed that seven distinct capabilities are involved in all intellectual activities, which he referred to as
    - **a.** primary mental abilities.
    - **b.** the *g* factor.
    - **c.** IQ.
    - **d.** the triarchic theory.

15. Wes is a con artist who flunked out of school, though he always got along with teachers and students. He is currently unemployed but runs "scams" to earn his living. He has played a bum, a cop, a priest, and a businessman as part of his efforts to cheat people, and he has never been caught. Wes would likely have a high degree of Gardner's_____intelligence.
    - **a.** interpersonal
    - **b.** musical
    - **c.** componential intelligence
    - **d.** existential

16. Phillip is an 8-year-old with a mental age of 6. According to Stern's formula, what is his IQ?
    - **a.** 60
    - **b.** 75
    - **c.** 100
    - **d.** 133

17. When you take a psychology test and afterward believe it did not accurately measure your knowledge of the psychology, you are questioning the test's
    a. validity.
    b. cultural fairness.
    c. reliability.
    d. standardization.

18. When administered properly, the results of a standardized intelligence test
    a. can be used to determine which individuals will enjoy a successful life.
    b. should not be considered at all because IQ tests are culturally unfair.
    c. can help explain why a child may be struggling in school.
    d. are completely useless.

19. Early interventions designed to enrich the environment of poor children
    a. rarely have an effect.
    b. have demonstrated that such efforts can have lasting effects.
    c. support the heritability of intelligence.
    d. demonstrate that nature cannot be altered by nurturing.

20. When you figure out a solution to your problem and you put it into action, you are engaging in the process of
    a. preparation.
    b. incubation.
    c. illumination.
    d. translation.

TRUE/FALSE

21. A rose would be a likely prototype for the concept of flowers.

22. Framing, or presenting information a certain way to emphasize an outcome or gain, has a limited effect on decision making.

23. Anything the human brain can do, an artificial intelligence program can do just as well or better.

24. Morphemes, the smallest units of meaning in the English language, are always words.

25. Bilingualism during childhood is associated with an improved ability to think about language.

26. The SAT is an aptitude test designed to predict college performance.

27. Mental retardation is based solely on one's IQ score.

28. Lewis Terman's study found that mentally gifted individuals had more mental health/psychological problems than the general population.

29. Research shows that racial differences in IQ are largely due to genetic factors.

ESSAY

30. Discuss the advantages and disadvantages of relying on heuristics in making decisions.

31. What have attempts to teach language to nonhuman primates demonstrated?

32. Distinguish between Spearman's *g* factor approach to intelligence and Gardner's theory of multiple intelligences.

CHAPTER 8: Human Development

MULTIPLE CHOICE

1. The idea that development occurs in distinctive phases that are easily distinguishable from each other is the central premise of
    a. continuous development.
    b. stage theories.
    c. environmental theory.
    d. nature versus nurture

2. Genevieve is studying language development among elementary-school aged children by comparing the vocabulary test scores of first-graders to those of fourth-graders. Genevieve is using the
    a. cross-sectional method.
    b. longitudinal method.
    c. sequential method.
    d. discontinuous method.

3. Wendy is 18 months old and just learning to speak. She meows whenever she sees a cat. One day, while she is watching television, a rabbit appears, and Wendy points and meows. What process has Wendy attempted regarding her existing scheme of cats?
    a. assimilation
    b. conservation
    c. accommodation
    d. hypothetico-deductive thinking

4. Sanford enjoys playing hide-and-seek with his mother. Sanford can play this game only because he has achieved what Piaget would call
   a. conservation.
   b. reversibility.
   c. hypothetico-deductive thinking.
   d. object permanence.

5. Piaget's cognitive stages in chronological order are
   a. sensorimotor, concrete operations, preoperations, formal operations.
   b. preoperations, concrete operations, formal operations, sensorimotor.
   c. preoperations, formal operations, concrete operations, sensorimotor.
   d. sensorimotor, preoperations, concrete operations, formal operations.

6. During which of Piaget's stages are children able to understand abstract concepts such as "freedom"?
   a. formal operations
   b. preoperations
   c. concrete operations
   d. sensorimotor

7. Luis behaves well at school because he wants to please his teacher. Which of Kohlberg's levels of moral development best fits Luis?
   a. sensorimotor
   b. preconventional
   c. conventional
   d. postconventional

8. According the Erikson, adolescence is known as the period of
   a. industry versus inferiority.
   b. autonomy versus shame and doubt.
   c. identity versus role confusion.
   d. trust versus mistrust.

9. Ginny is 82 years old. She often looks back on her life with satisfaction, believing that she accomplished a lot, had a loving family, and contributed to the world. Which of Erikson's stages best fits Ginny?
   a. industry versus inferiority
   b. ego integrity versus despair
   c. generativity versus stagnation
   d. autonomy versus shame and doubt

10. The developing human organism as it develops from the ninth week until birth is called a(n)
   a. embryo.
   b. zygote.
   c. gamete.
   d. fetus.

11. Because of the risk of fetal alcohol syndrome, pregnant women are advised to
   a. drink no more than one glass of wine per day.
   b. limit their drinking during the first trimester of pregnancy.
   c. completely abstain from alcohol during pregnancy.
   d. abstain from all hard liquor and limit consumption of other alcoholic beverages.

12. Harmful agents in the environment that can have a negative effect on prenatal development are called
   a. critical periods.
   b. teratogens.
   c. prenatal poisons.
   d. antagonists.

13. Brandi is 2 months old. She is generally happy most of the time, enjoys meeting new people, and has a regular routine to her day. Which temperament best describes her?
   a. slow-to-warm-up
   b. inconsistent
   c. easy
   d. difficult

14. Shawn is 18 months old. Lately, whenever his mother leaves him with his grandmother, he cries as if he is afraid. Their pediatrician said not to worry because_____is common among children his age.
   a. stranger anxiety
   b. separation anxiety
   c. attachment disorder
   d. avoidance anxiety

15. "Want cookie!" could be an example of
   a. babbling.
   b. underextension.
   c. overextension.
   d. telegraphic speech.

16. Barry tells his father that he and his mother "goed to the store." This error is an example of
   a. overextension.
   b. overregularization.
   c. underextension.
   d. underregularization.

17. Which parenting style generally appears to be the most effective in the United States?
   a. authoritative
   b. authoritarian
   c. permissive
   d. indulgent

18. Cassandra is a teenager who hates school. She has developed a plan to have a perfect life that involves quitting school with her boyfriend and getting rich and famous by being on *American Idol*. Cassandra's plan would best be described by which term?
   a. a personal fable
   b. naive idealism
   c. imaginary audience
   d. hypothetico-deductive thinking

19. The most common symptom of menopause is
   a. menarche.
   b. hot flashes.
   c. dizziness.
   d. high blood pressure.

20. The only intellectual ability to show a continuous decline from about the mid-20s to 80 is
    a. spatial ability.
    b. perceptual speed.
    c. creativity.
    d. general mathematic ability.

21. Which of the following is *false* regarding Americans over 65 years of age?
    a. More than 90% live alone or with a spouse.
    b. At least one out of four (about 25%) have an income level at or below poverty.
    c. About 50% are sexually active.
    d. Most need no help with daily living activities.

TRUE/FALSE

22. Developmental psychology as it is studied today focuses on childhood and adolescence as times of change and adulthood as a time of stagnation.

23. According to Piaget, a 3-year-old child would assume that you can see what she sees.

24. Vygotsky's sociocultural approach to cognitive development puts more emphasis on the impact of language development than does Piaget's theory.

25. Newborns can recognize some stimuli to which they were exposed prior to birth.

26. One conclusion drawn from the visual cliff experiment was that babies have no perception of depth until they learn to walk.

27. Securely attached infants tend to develop more advanced social skills when they are preschoolers than their peers who were not securely attached.

28. The nativist position suggests that language development occurs primarily through operant conditioning.

29. Fluid intelligence peaks in one's 20s, but crystallized intelligence increases throughout the life span.

30. Kübler-Ross' stages of death and dying appear to be universal.

ESSAY

31. Name and describe the stages of prenatal development.

32. Distinguish between how learning theorists, nativists, and interactionists explain language development.

CHAPTER 9: Motivation and Emotion

MULTIPLE CHOICE

1. Keisha wants to make good grades because her parents promised her a new car if she makes the honor roll. Keisha's motivation is
   a. intrinsic.
   b. extrinsic.
   c. social.
   d. homeostatic.

2. Human behavior is motivated by certain innate tendencies shared by all individuals, according to
   a. instinct.
   b. drive-reduction theory.
   c. Maslow's theory.
   d. set-point theory.

3. Which of the following statements is true according to the Yerkes-Dodson law?
   a. Performance on simple tasks is best when the arousal level is low.
   b. Performance on both simple and difficult tasks is best when the arousal level is high.
   c. Performance on moderately difficult tasks is best when the arousal level is low.
   d. Performance on difficult tasks is better when arousal is low.

4. Which needs did Maslow believe must be satisfied first?
   a. need to feel competent and respected
   b. need for security and shelter
   c. need for basic necessities
   d. need for connectedness and affiliation

5. Which of the following factors *inhibits* eating?
   a. low blood levels of glucose
   b. stomach contractions
   c. increased levels of cholecystokinin (CCK)
   d. increased levels of insulin

6. All of the following are true *except*
   a. a taste aversion may inhibit eating.
   b. foods high in fat and sugar may stimulate eating.
   c. raised blood glucose levels stimulate eating.
   d. a full (or distended) stomach may inhibit eating.

7. You conduct a hunger experiment with rats. In one rat, you damage the ventromedial hypothalamus. In the second rat, you stimulate the lateral hypothalamus. Then you offer food to each of the rats. What will happen?
   a. The first rat will eat; the second rat will not eat.
   b. The first rat will not eat; the second rat will eat.
   c. Both rats will eat.
   d. Neither rat will eat.

8. Cherelle has weighed approximately 120 pounds for most of her adult life. She doesn't work hard to lose weight, nor does she try to gain weight. You conclude that 120 pounds represents Cherelle's
   a. set point.
   b. metabolic rate.
   c. body mass index.
   d. homeostatic score.

9. The hormone, produced in the body's fat tissues, that affects the hypothalamus and plays a primary role in weight regulation is
   a. adrenalin.
   b. leptin.
   c. serotonin.
   d. insulin.

10. Based on the research with males, which factor seems most highly correlated with bulimia?
    a. age
    b. education
    c. sexual orientation
    d. intelligence

11. Inez devotes all of her energy to school. She sets high standards of performance for herself in an effort to accomplish all she can. According to research on motivation, Inez could be said to have a high need for
    a. success.
    b. recognition.
    c. achievement.
    d. glory.

12. Yvonne insists she must get the highest grade on every test so that she can exceed her peers and enhance her own self-worth. According to goal orientation theory, which goal orientation best fits Yvonne?
    a. mastery approach orientation
    b. mastery avoidance orientation
    c. performance approach orientation
    d. performance avoidance orientation

13. On realizing that the shadow behind you is a man with a gun, your heart begins to race *just as* you feel afraid. With which of the following theories of emotion is this scenario most consistent?
    a. Cannon-Bard theory
    b. Lazarus theory
    c. James-Lange theory
    d. Schachter-Singer theory

14. Which two-factor theory of emotion says that physiological arousal is followed by a cognitive interpretation of the situation?
    a. James-Lange theory
    b. Cannon-Bard theory
    c. Schachter-Singer theory
    d. Lazarus theory

15. Which of the following would not be considered a basic emotion?
    a. embarrassment
    b. fear
    c. anger
    d. joy/happiness

16. Many members of traditional British culture consider Americans to be vulgar because of Americans' tendency to spontaneously demonstrate whatever emotion they feel. The conflict between cultures is caused by differing
    a. impressions.
    b. display rules.
    c. emotional ranges.
    d. basic emotions.

17. The facial feedback hypothesis states that
    a. we recognize the emotions of others in their facial expression and change our own emotions to match.
    b. our emotions directly affect our facial muscles so that we produce an expression to match the emotion.
    c. muscular movements involved in certain facial expressions produce the corresponding emotion.
    d. seeing an individual's emotional response innately triggers a corresponding emotion.

18. Mary Ann is at a restaurant when she sees someone she thinks she knows. He turns around, and she realizes it is her ex-boyfriend. She decides that this is not a good situation. She becomes nervous, and sweaty palms and an increased heart rate follow. Which theory of motivation best describes this scenario?
    a. Lazarus theory
    b. Cannon-Bard theory
    c. James-Lange theory
    d. Schachter-Singer theory

TRUE/FALSE

19. According to psychologists, motivation is thought to have three basic components: activation, persistence, and intensity.

20. Extrinsic motivation is consistent with Skinner's concept of reinforcement.

21. Drive-reduction theory is largely based on the concepts of tension and homeostasis.

22. With regard to bulimia, bingeing is characterized by eating an extraordinary amount of food coupled with the feeling of loss of control over one's eating.

23. The amygdala is activated by fear before any direct involvement of the cerebral cortex occurs.

24. Facial expressions for the basic emotions are very similar across cultures.

ESSAY

25. Describe environmental cues for hunger.

26. Define anorexia nervosa and bulimia nervosa and describe the negative effects of each disorder.

27. Discuss the role of cognition in each of the four theories of emotion discussed in this chapter.

CHAPTER 10: Human Sexuality and Gender

MULTIPLE CHOICE

1. The area of the hypothalamus that governs sexual behavior is twice as large in heterosexual men than it is in homosexual men, according to research done by LeVay. What is the *main* criticism of LeVay's research?
   a. He did not use universal precautions.
   b. He did not account for AIDS as a variable.
   c. LeVay used only CT scans of the subjects' brains.
   d. His research was never replicated.

2. In the early 1950s, this researcher published ground-breaking surveys of sexual behavior among men and women in the United States.
   a. Virginia Johnson
   b. William Masters
   c. Alfred Kinsey
   d. Margaret Mead

3. Which of the following hormones is manufactured in the testes?
   a. estrogen
   b. progesterone
   c. androgen
   d. oxcytocin

4. What is the shortest of the four phases in the sexual response cycle?
   a. plateau
   b. resolution
   c. excitement
   d. orgasm

5. Michael, a gay man in his early 20s, recalls having been more interested in cross-gender activities than other boys when he was a child. According to research, Michael's experience
   a. is highly unusual.
   b. is more common among homosexual than heterosexual men.
   c. is more common among lesbians than among gay men.
   d. was probably the result of his having grown up with two older sisters.

6. The direction of a person's sexual preference toward members of the opposite sex or members of their own sex is referred to as
   a. sexual orientation.
   b. sexual identity.
   c. sexual role.
   d. sexual bias.

7. This researcher proposed the concept of androgyny.
   a. Virginia Johnson
   b. Alfred Kinsey
   c. Sandra Bem
   d. Lawrence Kohlberg

8. _____ % of men and _____% of women think about sex at least once a day.
   a. 50, 50
   b. 87, 13
   c. 70, 33
   d. 95, 25

9. Historically, homosexuality has been reported
   a. only in the last 20 years or so.
   b. in all societies and throughout history.
   c. until recently only in non-religious societies.
   d. generally in Western cultures, but not Eastern societies.

10. Initially, when she was very young, Billy would sometimes insist to her parents that she was a boy just like her brothers. However, prior to Billy's third birthday, she stopped insisting that she was a boy and started actively engaging in "little girl" games. This is indicative of which of Kohlberg's stages?
    a. gender constancy
    b. gender development
    c. gender stability
    d. gender identity

11. Research indicates the most consistent and prominent difference between males and females is a significant variation in levels of
    a. verbal ability.
    b. aggression.
    c. mathematical ability.
    d. spatial ability.

12. _____ is the only sexually transmitted disease in the following group for which there is a cure.
    a. Genital warts
    b. Syphilis
    c. Genital herpes
    d. AIDS

13. On tests of which of these cognitive abilities do males tend to score much higher than females?

   a. spelling   **c.** calculation skills

   b. reading comprehension   **d.** mental rotation

14. This STD is linked with as many as 85% of the cervical cancer cases in the United States.

   a. gonorrhea   **c.** syphilis

   b. herpes   **d.** human papillomavirus

15. Gender roles are

   a. cultural expectations about appropriate behaviors for males and females.

   b. the psychological sense of being male and female.

   c. social manifestations of the X and Y chromosomes.

   d. influenced more by learning than by hormones.

16. Four-year-old Tommy tells his friend, "Don't play with sister's baby dolls cause I got in trouble for playing with dolls. My momma told me boys don't play with dolls!" Tommy's admonition to his friend illustrates:

   a. cognitive theory of gender role development.

   b. social learning theory of gender role development.

   c. psychoanalytic theory of gender role development.

   d. gender-schema theory of gender role development.

17. HPV, or the human papillomavirus, is the virus that causes

   a. genital warts.   **c.** syphilis.

   b. genital herpes.   **d.** AIDS.

18. In order for embryos with an XY chromosome combination to develop primary male sex characteristics _____ must be present in the testes.

   a. androgens   **c.** metabolites

   b. estrogens   **d.** endocrines

19. The most common sexual dysfunction in women is

   a. sexually transmitted disease.

   b. female orgasmic disorder.

   c. vaginismus.

   d. dyspareunia.

TRUE/FALSE

20. In general, men are more likely to interrupt others than women are.

21. Cross-cultural studies suggest that Kohlberg's stages do not occur in the same order in diverse populations.

22. On average, men are more likely than women to be interested in purely physical sex and think about it more often.

23. Homophobia is a purely male reaction to being around gay people.

24. The words sex and gender should be used interchangeably.

25. According to the gender-schema theory of gender-role development, children are motivated to attend to and behave in ways consistent with the gender stereotypes of the culture.

26. Research suggests an association between higher incidence of sexual fantasies and a more satisfactory sex life.

27. Some studies show that women are more attuned to verbal and nonverbal expressions of emotions than men are.

28. In childhood, lesbians were more often labeled as "tomboys" than were heterosexual women.

29. A truly exclusive homosexual orientation is found to be common.

ESSAY

30. Many homophobic individuals believe that AIDS is the "gay disease." Which facts about AIDS and HIV speak against this myth? Why do you think this myth persists?

31. Explain the differences between the social learning and cognitive theories of gender-role development. What role do parents and the media play within each theory?

32. Describe the various biological factors that have been implicated as possible influences in the development of sexual orientation.

MULTIPLE CHOICE

1. Based on the Social Readjustment Rating Scale (SRRS), which of the following have the largest life-changing unit value?
   a. change in school
   b. jail term
   c. getting fired at work
   d. death of a spouse

2. According to Lazarus, which types of stressors seem to cause more stress?
   a. hassles
   b. uplifts
   c. annoyances
   d. catastrophes

3. Hank has a stressful job, but he always looks forward to coming home to his wife, who never fails to bring a smile to his face and relieve some of his stress. According to Richard Lazarus, Hank's time with his wife would be described as
   a. a hassle.
   b. an approach-approach situation.
   c. a counter-stressor.
   d. an uplift.

4. Would you rather have a terrible toothache or the undesirable experience of having the tooth drilled and the cavity filled? This choice represents which type of conflict?
   a. approach-avoidance
   b. approach-approach
   c. avoidance-avoidance
   d. avoidance-approach

5. According to Albrecht (1979), which of the following factors is *not* related to job satisfaction and effective functioning at work?
   a. the clarity of the job description and evaluation criteria
   b. having a variety of tasks to accomplish
   c. being one's own boss
   d. having some amount of accountability on the job

6. A prolonged stress reaction following a catastrophic experience is called
   a. acute stress disorder.
   b. posttraumatic stress disorder.
   c. general adaptation syndrome.
   d. reactive attachment disorder.

7. According to Utsey (2002),_____has been found to moderate the levels of racial stress in African Americans.
   a. a strong sense of ethnic identity
   b. a high degree of hostility
   c. historical racism
   d. being one of only a few African Americans in a given setting, such as a classroom or workplace

8. According to Seyle's General Adaptation Syndrome theory, what happens when an organism fails in its efforts to resist or adapt to a stressor?
   a. resistance failure
   b. exhaustion
   c. fight-or-flight syndrome
   d. alarm

9. According to Richard Lazarus, an event appraised as stressful could involve
   a. harm or loss.
   b. threat.
   c. challenge.
   d. all of the above

10. Which of the following statements reflects a secondary appraisal?
   a. "I refuse to accept that I have cancer."
   b. "It's good to know my sister can watch my kids while I have chemotherapy. At least I don't have to worry about that."
   c. "It is not fair that I have been diagnosed with cancer at such a young age!"
   d. "Why is this happening to *me?*"

11. Mrs. Genova has been told that she has terminal cancer and only a few months left to live. After a brief time, she set out to tie up the loose ends of her life, updating her will, giving away special possessions, and saying her goodbyes. Mrs. Genova is employing which approach to coping with her illness?
   a. variate-focused
   b. problem-focused
   c. emotion-focused
   d. solution-focused

12. Blake has been at his friend's party for about two hours now. He has consumed a large amount of alcohol (about five drinks) in those few hours. He gets a call from his girlfriend who tells him to sober up and come to the party she is attending. Based on the research in your text, which of the following is the best advice Blake gets from his friends?
   a. "Blake, wait another hour, and you should be sober enough to drive."
   b. "Blake, just go crash on my bed for one or two hours . . . you can sleep it off and then leave."
   c. "Blake, buddy, there is no way to sober up in time for you to get to that party. Looks like you are staying here tonight."
   d. "Blake, drink two cans of Red Bull and then take a walk outside. The fresh air and caffeine will help you sober up before you leave."

13. Which element of the Type A behavior pattern is most strongly related to coronary heart disease?
    a. time urgency
    b. hostility
    c. competitiveness
    d. impatience

14. Which of the following is a risk factor for cancer, according to health psychologists?
    a. smoking
    b. promiscuous sexual behavior
    c. excessive alcohol consumption
    d. all of the above

15. The key components of the immune system are the white blood cells known as
    a. antigens.
    b. antibodies.
    c. lymphocytes.
    d. leukocytes.

16. Which of the following infectious diseases has *not* been correlated with periods of high stress?
    a. rubella
    b. mononucleosis
    c. flu
    d. genital herpes

17. All of the following are qualities of the hardiness trait *except*
    a. control.
    b. commitment.
    c. caring.
    d. challenge.

18. What percentage of the adult population in the United States still smokes, according to your text?
    a. 65%
    b. less than 25%
    c. 35%
    d. 50%

19. Though research shows exercise is the simplest and most effective way to enhance one's health, what percentage of Americans still don't exercise at all?
    a. about 40%
    b. about 30%
    c. about 20%
    d. about 10%

TRUE/FALSE

20. The parasympathetic nervous system initiates the fight-or-flight response.

21. The hassle most commonly cited by college students is not getting enough sleep.

22. Survivor guilt may be a symptom experienced by individuals who live through a catastrophic event.

23. According to Selye, prolonged stress can lead to permanent increases in blood pressure, suppression of the immune system, and weakening of muscles.

24. Engaging in problem-focused coping helps manage stress by reducing, modifying, or eliminating the stressor.

25. A sedentary lifestyle is the primary modifiable risk factor contributing to death from coronary heart disease.

26. The Type D behavior pattern appears to buffer the negative effects of stress.

27. Women are more likely than men to seek medical care.

28. Being exposed to secondhand smoke doubles one's risk of having a heart attack when compared to those who are not exposed to it.

ESSAY

29. Describe the biopsychosocial model of health and illness.

30. Describe the Type A, Type B, and Type D behavior patterns.

31. Describe four factors that reduce the impact of stress and illness.

CHAPTER 12: Personality Theory and Assessment

MULTIPLE CHOICE

1. You don't usually think about your phone number, but if someone asked you for it, you could easily recall it and make yourself aware of it. According to Freud's levels of consciousness, your phone number is likely stored in your
    a. unconscious.
    b. conscious.
    c. preconscious.
    d. subconscious.

2. George wants a new stereo badly. He decides he will buy a new one by putting it on his credit card, without worrying too much about the debt he is accruing. George is acting based on the wishes of his
    a. id.
    b. ego.
    c. superego.
    d. unconscious mind.

3. Alice feels good about how neat and organized she keeps her room. This pride represents her
    a. ego.
    b. conscience.
    c. id.
    d. ego ideal.

4. Lysette cannot believe it when her friends tell her that her boyfriend is cheating on her. She insists they must be mistaken. Which Freudian defense mechanism might Lysette be exhibiting?
    a. repression
    b. projection
    c. displacement
    d. denial

5. Tabitha has always been a flirtatious and promiscuous woman. She is very vain, and she tends to seek attention from anyone around her. Freud might suggest that she had problems at which psychosexual stage of development?
   a. anal
   b. phallic
   c. oral
   d. latency

6. Which theorist suggested that we share the universal experiences of humankind throughout evolution?
   a. Carl Jung
   b. Sigmund Freud
   c. Karen Horney
   d. Alfred Adler

7. Which theorist suggested that behavior, cognitive factors, and the environment have a mutually influential relationship?
   a. Abraham Maslow
   b. Julian Rotter
   c. Albert Bandura
   d. Karen Horney

8. Which of the following statements about the differences between people with high self-efficacy and low self-efficacy is *false*?
   a. People with high self-efficacy show greater persistence than those with low self-efficacy.
   b. People with high self-efficacy set lower goals that are more realistic than those with low self-efficacy.
   c. People with high self-efficacy have more confidence than those with low self-efficacy.
   d. People with low self-efficacy appear to have higher rate of depression than those with high self-efficacy.

9. Someone with an internal locus of control is most likely to explain a high test grade as due to
   a. luck.
   b. an easy exam.
   c. hard work.
   d. prayer.

10. Which group of theories is most likely to suggest that individuals can reach their full potential for growth?
    a. psychoanalytic
    b. trait
    c. learning
    d. humanistic

11. Ben goes along with what his friends want to do even though he would prefer to do something else. He does so because he wants to be accepted. Carl Rogers would explain Ben's behavior by saying that he has been exposed to conditions of
    a. worth.
    b. self-actualization.
    c. unconditional positive regard.
    d. friendship.

12. You are trying to set up two of your friends for a date. One asks you to describe the other's personality, which you do using the four characteristics the person is known for. According to Allport, what kind of traits have you listed?
    a. cardinal traits
    b. surface traits
    c. central traits
    d. source traits

13. Zach is an emotional, nervous, and moody person, but he is always good-natured, warm, and cooperative. On which two Big Five traits would Zach likely be rated highly?
    a. extroversion and neuroticism
    b. openness to experience and agreeableness
    c. conscientiousness and extroversion
    d. agreeableness and neuroticism

14. According to the Minnesota twin study, which of the following statements concerning twins and personality is true?
    a. Identical twins are similar on several personality factors, whether reared together or apart.
    b. Identical twins are similar on several personality factors, but only if they were reared together.
    c. Identical twins are similar on several personality factors, but only if they were reared apart.
    d. Identical twins are not similar on any personality factors.

15. Genes exert more influence on which Big Five traits?
    a. extraversion and neuroticism
    b. openness to experience and agreeableness
    c. conscientiousness and extroversion
    d. agreeableness and neuroticism

16. Nicole responds to some questionnaires that ask her questions about her behaviors and personality characteristics. What kind of personality assessment has she undergone?
    a. behavioral assessment
    b. personality inventory
    c. projective test
    d. structured interview

17. Which of the following provides a standardized format for the data from observations or interviews?
    a. personality inventory
    b. rating scale
    c. projective test
    d. the TAT

18. Which of the following is often used by career counselors?
    a. Minnesota Multiphasic Personality Inventory (MMPI)
    b. Myers-Briggs Type Indicator (MBTI)
    c. Thematic Apperception Test (TAT)
    d. California Personality Inventory (CPI)

19. Which of the following is a projective test?
    a. Minnesota Multiphasic Personality Inventory (MMPI)
    b. Myers-Briggs Type Indicator (MBTI)
    c. Thematic Apperception Test (TAT)
    d. California Personality Inventory (CPI)

20. Which of the following is considered by the examiner in evaluating responses to the Rorschach Inkblot method?
    a. the content of the response
    b. whether shape or color influenced the response
    c. whether the whole blot or only part of it is used in the response
    d. all of the above

TRUE/FALSE

21. The ego operates according to a principle that demands immediate gratification.

22. Freud's theories, when tested, show no scientific evidence supporting them.

23. Low self-efficacy is correlated with an increased risk for depression.

24. People with an internal locus of control are more likely to procrastinate than people with an external locus of control.

25. According to Maslow, self-actualized individuals are autonomous and thus do not pursue personal relationships.

26. According to Raymond Cattell, observable qualities of personality are referred to as source traits.

27. The Big Five traits have been found in cross-cultural studies in Canada, Poland, Germany, Hong Kong, and Russia.

28. The trait of aggressiveness is solely influenced by parental upbringing.

29. The MMPI contains validity scales to detect faking or lying.

30. The Rorschach Inkblot method continues to have poor interrater agreement due to the lack of a scoring system.

ESSAY

31. What are the primary distinctions between the theories of the neo-Freudians and Freud's theory?

32. Describe the situation versus trait debate.

33. How does personality differ based on the individualism/collectivism dimension of a culture?

CHAPTER 13: Psychological Disorders

MULTIPLE CHOICE

1. Gretchen likes to keep everything. She has things stacked in corners, and every closet is filled to the top. Lots of people save things, but Gretchen's "saving" has reached the point that every surface in her home is covered. She is embarrassed to have company, to the point that she refuses to allow anyone in her house. However, she continues to save things. What is it about Gretchen's behavior that makes it considered abnormal?
    a. It is illegal.
    b. It is maladaptive.
    c. It is dangerous.
    d. It is culturally influenced.

2. Which perspective contends that early childhood experiences are behind the manifestation of psychological disorders?
    a. psychosocial
    b. psychodynamic
    c. cognitive
    d. biopsychosocial

3. Which of the following is considered an anxiety disorder?
    a. schizophrenia
    b. bipolar disorder
    c. substance abuse/dependence
    d. panic disorder

4. Eric does not like to be in public places—especially where there are a lot of people, and escape would be difficult. He fears he will have a panic attack and will not be able to get away or obtain help. Eric could probably be diagnosed with
    a. agoraphobia.
    b. obsessive-compulsive disorder.
    c. bipolar disorder.
    d. generalized anxiety disorder.

5. Which of the following would be considered a social phobia?
    a. fear of enclosed places
    b. fear of injections
    c. fear of public speaking
    d. fear of flying

6. Mark spends hours upon hours mopping, dusting, and in general sanitizing his house. This cleaning behavior is Mark's way to mute the frightening visual images that frequently pop into his mind. Mark's cleaning behaviors might be described as a(n)
   a. phobia.
   b. obsession.
   c. delusion.
   d. compulsion.

7. Which individual is *most* at risk for a recurrent episode of depression?
   a. John, who first became depressed at age 24
   b. Mary, who first became depressed at age 50
   c. Carol, who first became depressed at age 14
   d. Henry, who first became depressed at age 40

8. The rate of depression among women is generally _____ that of men.
   a. about half
   b. twice
   c. about four times
   d. one-fourth

9. How does the prevalence of bipolar disorder compare to the prevalence of major depressive disorder?
   a. Bipolar disorder is much less common.
   b. Major depressive disorder is much less common.
   c. Bipolar disorder is three times more common.
   d. Their prevalence rates are strikingly similar.

10. In the field of psychology, the word *psychosis* refers to
    a. dangerousness.
    b. nervousness.
    c. a loss of contact with reality.
    d. social isolation.

11. Marianne truly believes that she is a world-famous movie star. Her neighbors see her occasionally in her front yard, waving to them as if they were her adoring crowd. Marianne likely suffers from
    a. delusions of grandeur.
    b. delusions of persecution.
    c. an anxiety disorder.
    d. dissociative identity disorder.

12. Which of the following neurotransmitters has been associated with schizophrenia?
    a. serotonin
    b. norepinephrine
    c. acetylcholine
    d. dopamine

13. Individuals with which type of schizophrenia have periods where they display little or no body movement, often remaining in bizarre positions for hours?
    a. undifferentiated
    b. disorganized
    c. paranoid
    d. catatonic

14. Which of the following disorders is diagnosed more often in men than in women?
    a. major depression
    b. generalized anxiety disorder
    c. schizophrenia
    d. phobia

15. On waking one morning, Michael could not see. However, doctors could find no medical cause for his blindness. They should consider a diagnosis of
    a. conversion disorder.
    b. dissociative disorder.
    c. reaction formation.
    d. hypochondriasis.

16. The disorder that involves an individual having more than one personality, generally one host and at least one alter, is called
    a. dissociative identity disorder.
    b. dissociative fugue.
    c. dissociative amnesia.
    d. conversion disorder.

17. Which cluster of personality disorders includes disorders that are most likely to be confused with schizophrenia, especially paranoid schizophrenia?
    a. cluster A
    b. cluster B
    c. cluster C
    d. cluster D

18. Tina is one of those people you can never predict. One minute she's your best friend; the next, she hates you and considers you to be her worst enemy. She has fits of inappropriate anger, recklessness, and occasional suicidal gestures. Tina may be an example of a(n)
    a. histrionic personality.
    b. dependent personality.
    c. borderline personality.
    d. antisocial personality.

TRUE/FALSE

19. *Insanity* is a term used by mental health professionals to describe those suffering from psychological disorders.

20. Mental illness is diagnosed in about 44 million adult Americans every year.

21. Antidepressant drugs are effective in the treatment of obsessive-compulsive disorder (OCD) for some individuals.

22. Research indicates that one year after their initial diagnosis of major depressive disorder, more than 90% of individuals still show symptoms.

23. About 90% of individuals who commit suicide leave clues.

24. Schizophrenia involves the possession of multiple personalities within the same body.

25. Smelling something that is not there is an example of a hallucination.

26. An individual with hypochondriasis is someone who fakes an illness to get attention.

27. Dissociative amnesia is typically caused by a traumatic head injury that impairs the functioning of the hippocampus.

ESSAY

28. Review the questions that may be asked to determine whether someone's behavior is abnormal.

29. Describe the risk factors for suicide, including gender, age, and ethnic differences in suicide rates.

30. Distinguish between the positive and the negative symptoms of schizophrenia.

CHAPTER 14: Therapies

MULTIPLE CHOICE

1. Which group of psychotherapy approaches is based on the notion is that psychological well-being depends on self-understanding?
   a. behavior therapies
   b. relationship therapies
   c. insight therapies
   d. All forms of psychotherapy are based on that notion.

2. Which approach attempts to uncover repressed childhood experiences in an effort to explain a person's current difficulties?
   a. psychodynamic therapy
   b. interpersonal therapy
   c. person-centered therapy
   d. cognitive therapy

3. Valora became angry with her therapist and shouted at him, "You are just like my father!" Freud would consider her outburst to be an example of
   a. dissociation.   c. transference.
   b. empathy.   d. genuineness.

4. What is the goal of person-centered therapy?
   a. to uncover unconscious conflicts and resolve them
   b. to assist clients' growth toward self-actualization
   c. to replace maladaptive behaviors with more adaptive responses
   d. to challenge clients' irrational beliefs about themselves and others

5. The individual most closely associated with Gestalt therapy is
   a. Fritz Perls.   c. Carl Rogers.
   b. Sigmund Freud.   d. Aaron Beck.

6. Interpersonal therapy (IPT) is especially helpful in treating
   a. alcoholism.   c. specific phobias.
   b. narcissism.   d. depression.

7. Which type of problem is interpersonal therapy (IPT) not specifically designed to address?
   a. severe problems in coping with the death of a loved one
   b. deficits in interpersonal skills
   c. the highs and lows of bipolar disorder
   d. difficulties in adjusting to life after a divorce

8. Which of the following is true regarding behavior therapy?
   a. It is based on the idea that inappropriate thoughts are the basis for abnormal behavior.
   b. It is based on the notion that abnormal behavior is learned.
   c. It is a type of therapy that uses medication to control behaviors.
   d. It assumes that abnormal behavior is primarily caused by aggressive forces within the unconscious.

9. Juan's school uses a reward system to encourage students to do their homework and have good behavior. Children earn gold stars for completing assignments and paying attention to the teacher and later can exchange stars for snacks or even a day without homework. Which behavior modification technique is Juan's school using?
   a. time out
   b. systematic desensitization
   c. flooding
   d. token economy

10. Which technique is designed to treat phobias by exposing the client to extended periods of contact with the feared object or event until the anxiety decreases?
    a. aversion therapy
    b. flooding
    c. systematic desensitization
    d. free association

11. Exposure and response prevention is an approach that has proved successful in treating
    a. personality disorders.
    b. narcissism.
    c. depression.
    d. obsessive-compulsive disorder.

12. In Ellis's ABC model, the *A* represents the
    a. action taken.
    b. actual problem.
    c. activity of the client.
    d. activating event.

13. Joan's therapist encourages her to look for unrealistic thoughts that may be "automatic." Joan's therapist is likely providing therapy based on the theory proposed by
    a. Sigmund Freud
    b. Fritz Perls
    c. Carl Rogers
    d. Aaron Beck

14. *Neuroleptics* is another term for
    a. antipsychotics.
    b. benzodiazepines.
    c. mood stabilizers.
    d. antidepressants.

15. Which of the following drugs is most likely to be prescribed for bipolar disorder?
    a. Xanax
    b. Clozapine
    c. Lithium
    d. Prozac (fluoxetine)

16. Cynthia wants to be a psychiatrist. What degree will she need after college?
    a. Ph.D.
    b. M.D.
    c. Psy.D.
    d. Ed.D.

17. The bond between therapist and client that is thought to be a factor in the effectiveness of psychotherapy is called
    a. attachment.
    b. counselor–client bonding.
    c. the psychosocial relationship.
    d. the therapeutic alliance.

18. What does research suggest about the success of psychotherapy?
    a. It is most successful with single adults.
    b. The longer someone is in therapy, the more improvement he or she seems to make.
    c. Psychotherapy is not nearly as effective as treatment involving medication.
    d. Patients in therapy do better with psychologists than with psychiatrists.

19. All of the following behaviors would be considered ethical for a therapist *except*
    a. informing clients about the cost and expected duration of a therapy.
    b. alerting the authorities if a client confesses to a crime.
    c. treating an ex-girlfriend in therapy.
    d. explaining the purpose of tests given to clients as part of therapy.

20. Culturally sensitive therapy is important because
    a. it ensures that proper medication will be prescribed.
    b. cultural factors need to be considered when choosing a therapeutic intervention.
    c. the development of a therapeutic alliance is not possible if the client and therapist have different backgrounds.
    d. cultural insensitivity is the underlying cause of most mood disorders.

TRUE/FALSE

21. A psychodynamic therapist would interpret a client's being late to a session as a form of resistance.

22. Person-centered therapy is an example of a directive therapy.

23. A Gestalt therapist might help a client with unfinished business using the empty chair technique.

24. Family therapy, in addition to medication, tends to be effective as a treatment option for schizophrenia.

25. Alcoholics Anonymous (AA) is a form of self-help group.

26. Aversion therapy is no longer used due to ethical concerns about it.

27. Tardive dyskinesia is a movement disorder brought on by long-term use of antidepressants.

28. Tricyclics, SSRIs, and MAO inhibitors are forms of antipsychotic medications.

29. Rapid transcranial magnetic stimulation (rTMS) appears to have the same benefits as electroconvulsive therapy (ECT) with significantly fewer risks.

30. Acknowledging that there are, in fact, differences between males and females is an important facet of gender-sensitive therapy.

ESSAY

31. Compare and contrast Ellis's rational emotive therapy and Beck's cognitive therapy.

32. What are the three types of antidepressant drugs, and how do they work?

33. Explain the similarities and differences between psychologists and psychiatrists.

PRACTICE TESTS

MULTIPLE CHOICE

1. In Stanley Milgram's obedience study, the "learner" was a(n)
   a. confederate.
   c. unwilling participant.
   b. naive subject.
   d. victim.

2. Your grandmother always told you that first impressions create lasting impressions. She is essentially describing
   a. the actor-observer effect.
   b. the recency effect.
   c. the primacy effect.
   d. a situational attribution.

3. Creighton's boss is particularly grumpy today. He knows that she's been under a lot of stress at home and figures that is the reason for her grumpiness. Creighton is making a
   a. self-serving bias.
   b. random attribution.
   c. dispositional attribution.
   d. situational attribution.

4. Shea failed her law school entrance exams. She said it was because there was too much noise in the room and the questions were ridiculous. When she passed on taking it a second time, she concluded she was intellectually gifted. Shea demonstrated
   a. a false attribution.
   b. the primacy effect.
   c. the actor-observer effect.
   d. the self-serving bias.

5. Heather never gave Bobby much thought until she found out that he likes her. Lately she's been thinking that she likes him, too. Her attraction is largely based on
   a. the mere-exposure effect.
   b. proximity.
   c. reciprocity.
   d. a situational attribution.

6. All of the following factors influence attraction *except*
   a. physical attractiveness.
   b. the mere-exposure effect.
   c. proximity.
   d. deindividuation.

7. The matching hypothesis is similar to the idea that
   a. birds of a feather flock together.
   b. opposites attract.
   c. a bird in the hand is worth two in the bush.
   d. familiarity breeds contempt.

8. Changing or adopting an attitude or behavior to be consistent with the social norms of a group or their expectation is called
   a. obedience.
   c. familiarity.
   b. conformity.
   d. triangulation.

9. All of the following are true regarding Asch's study of conformity *except*
   a. 70% of the true subjects conformed at least some of the time.
   b. 5% of the true subjects conformed all of the time.
   c. 25% of the true subjects did not conform.
   d. the majority of participants refused to conform.

10. Phillip was offered a job that provided the majority of the weekends off. Once he said yes and gave notice at his old job, the new employer told him he would have to work every Saturday until noon. Phillip's new boss used the
    a. mere-exposure effect.
    b. door-in-the-face technique.
    c. foot-in-the-door technique.
    d. low-ball technique.

11. Two teams were playing a game of tug-of-war. Gerald was tired, so he just pretended to be pulling, knowing that no one could tell the difference. Gerald's approach to the game is an example of
    a. socialization.
    b. social facilitation.
    c. social loafing.
    d. the triangular effect.

12. If you work better in front of other people, the effect of those other people is called a(n)
    a. audience effect in social facilitation.
    b. coaction effect in social facilitation.
    c. audience effect in social loafing.
    d. coaction effect in social loafing.

13. Investigations following the latest NASA shuttle disaster suggested that many of the engineers and other workers saw problems but failed to speak up because no one else did. They all work well together and were accustomed to everything going right. In their zeal to launch the shuttle and continue to work effectively and cohesively, they failed to investigate problems that were quite evident. Some suggested that the NASA scientists were victims of
    a. groupthink.   c. obedience.
    b. social facilitation. d. compliance.

14. Zimbardo's prison study showed that
    a. social roles influence behavior.
    b. behavior is beyond the influence of social bias.
    c. prisons are inherently corrupt.
    d. social loafing is culturally bound.

15. Which of the following is a deliberate attempt to change the attitude or behavior of another person?
    a. stereotyping   c. extortion
    b. persuasion   d. cognitive dissonance

16. Frank is overweight and seems unable to stick to any diet. Although his diet efforts suggest that he wants to lose weight, he denies it and says that he is happy with his body the way it is. Frank is trying to reduce his feelings of
    a. cognitive dissonance.
    b. negative persuasion.
    c. self-esteem.
    d. attributional asymmetry.

17. According to your text, which of the following is *not* one of the identified elements of persuasion?
    a. the source of the communication
    b. the message
    c. the decision-making process
    d. the audience

18. When Kitty Genovese was stabbed to death near her apartment, later investigations found that nearly 40 people witnessed the attack—yet no one called for help. Some would say that this case is an example of
    a. altruism.   c. the bystander effect.
    b. prejudice.   d. antisocial behavior.

19. Which of the following has been shown to help people unlearn prejudice?
    a. an open discussion on prejudice and discrimination
    b. the jigsaw technique
    c. intergroup contact
    d. all of the above

20. Kathy's sorority has a rule against dating boys from certain fraternities. Kathy may date only boys who belong to two specific fraternities. Her sorority considers any other boys to be "undesirables." According to the definitions in your chapter, Kathy's sorority is an example of_____whereas the "undesirables" are an example of_____.
    a. an in-group; an in-group
    b. an out-group; an in-group
    c. an out-group; an out-group
    d. an in-group; an out-group

TRUE/FALSE

21. Research has indicated that culture contributes to attributional biases.

22. There are significant cultural differences in attractiveness ratings of the opposite sex.

23. In Asch's conformity experiments, 75% of the participants conformed to the incorrect response of the majority at least once.

24. Some research indicates that in the presence of others, an individual has lower performance on easier tasks but excels at more difficult tasks.

25. Social loafing is more common in collectivistic cultures such as China than in the United States.

26. Zimbardo's Stanford prison experiment had to be ended in six days because the behavior of the participants began to get out of hand.

27. Generally speaking, people with low IQs are easier to persuade than people with high IQs.

28. Altruistic acts are usually performed for some gain.

29. Individuals who were abused as children are more likely to be aggressive than adults who were not abused in childhood.

30. According to some research, people perceive more diversity among members of their own ethnic group and more similarity among members of other groups.

ESSAY

31. What do men and women rate as the most important qualities in a mate? Review both the similarities and the differences in what men and women seek.

32. Describe Stanley Milgram's obedience study. What conclusions could be drawn from it? Could the same study be conducted today?

33. Describe the social learning theory of aggression. What does the research say about a relationship between TV violence and viewer aggression?

Answers to Practice Tests

Multiple Choice: 1. c; 2. d; 3. d; 4. c; 5. b; 6. d; 7. a ; 8. d; 9. d; 10. a; 11. b; 12. b; 13. a; 14. b; 15. c; 16. d; 17. c; 18. d; 19. b; 20. a

True/False: 21. true; 22. false; 23. true; 24. false; 25. true; 26. true; 27. false; 28. true; 29. true; 30. false

Essay

31. Common sense propositions are made based on experience or folklore. Common sense sayings may also contradict. For example, do "opposites attract" or do "birds of a feather flock together"? Psychology, as a science, employs the scientific method to investigate propositions through the use of research. The scientific method consists of the orderly, systematic process that researchers follow as they identify a research problem, design a study to investigate the problem, collect and analyze data, draw conclusions, and then communicate their findings.

32. Psychologists seek to explain behavior and may do so in a number of different ways. Those who believe behavior is a product of our environment and focus on learning and environment as determinants of behavior take on the behavioral school of thought (also called **behaviorism**). Psychologists who take a **biological perspective** look to the functioning of the nervous system and the structure of the brain to explain human behavior. Psychologists who take a **cognitive school of thought** focus on thinking as a means of explaining behavior, that how one thinks influences how one acts. **Humanistic psychologists** look at our desire to be the best that we can be as the guiding force behind our behavior, while the Freudian approach, **psychoanalytic psychology**, sees most of our behavior as the product of the unconscious.

33. Volunteers from one or more college campuses should be randomly assigned to the experimental group, the group that will receive the drug, and a control group, who will not receive the drug. This random assignment ensures that the two groups are roughly equivalent in all respects other than the receipt of the drug or a placebo. The use of a single-blind or double-blind design may prevent biases on the part of the participants or the researcher from impacting the results. All participants will then take a test of memory. The drug is the independent variable, and scores on the memory test are the dependent variable.

If the drug is effective, the experimental group will outperform the control group on the test of memory.

Multiple Choice: 1. a; 2. a; 3. c; 4. a; 5. b; 6. d; 7. b; 8. b; 9. d; 10. c; 11. a; 12. b; 13. a; 14. d; 15. c; 16. c; 17. d; 18. a; 19. c; 20. d

True/False: 21. true; 22. false; 23. true; 24. true; 25. false; 26. true; 27. false; 28. true; 29. true; 30. false

Essay

31. The action potential is transmitted down the length of the axon, and reaches the axon terminal. Inside the axon terminal are small containers called synaptic vesicles, which hold chemicals called neurotransmitters. These neurotransmitters are released into the synaptic cleft. They have a distinctive molecular shape, which fit into specific receptor sites on the surfaces of cell bodies and dendrites. Once the neurotransmitter binds to a receptor site, it may have an excitatory (influencing the neuron to fire) or inhibitory (influencing the neuron not to fire) effect on the receiving neuron.

32. **Acetylcholine** exerts excitatory effects on skeletal muscle fibers, influencing them to contract so the body can move. It also has an inhibitory effect on muscle fibers in the heart, so that the heart does not beat too rapidly. Acetylcholine also has an excitatory effect in stimulating neurons involved in learning new information and storing information in memory. **Dopamine** is related to functions such as learning, attention, movement, and reinforcement. Neurons in the brains of people with Parkinson's disease and schizophrenia appear to be less sensitive to the effects of dopamine. **Norepinephrine** affects eating, alertness, and sleep. **Epinephrine** affects the metabolism of glucose and nutrient energy stored in muscles to be released during strenuous exercise. **Serotonin** plays an important role in regulating mood, sleep, impulsivity, aggression, and appetite. **Glutamate** is the primary excitatory neurotransmitter in the brain, and is active in areas of the brain involved in learning, thought, and emotions. **GABA** is the main inhibitory neurotransmitter in the brain, and facilitates the control of anxiety in humans. Finally, **endorphins** are a class of neurotransmitters that reduce pain and the stress of vigorous exercise, and positively affect mood.

33. The **peripheral nervous system** connects the central nervous system (CNS) to the rest of the body. The peripheral nervous system is made up of the *somatic nervous system* (which controls voluntary movement) and the *autonomic nervous system* (which control involuntary muscles such as the heart and digestive system). The autonomic nervous system further breaks down into the *sympathetic nervous system* (engages body in the fight-or-flight response) and the *parasympathetic nervous system* (calms body after fight-or-flight response and helps to bring body back to homeostasis).

CHAPTER 3

Multiple Choice: 1. b; 2. a; 3. d; 4. b; 5. c; 6. a; 7. b; 8. a; 9. d; 10. b; 11. a; 12. c; 13. d; 14. b; 15. c; 16. c; 17. a; 18. a; 19. d; 20. c

True/False: 21. false; 22. true; 23. false; 24. true; 25. false; 26. false; 27. true; 28. true; 29. false; 30. true

Essay

31. Sound waves are created by movement of the air. These waves enter the pinna and travel through the auditory canal to the eardrum (tympanic membrane). The waves strike the eardrum and the eardrum vibrates. The movement of the eardrum sets in motion the bones of the middle ear. The bones of the middle ear amplify the sound wave which then strikes the oval window. On the other side of the oval window is the inner ear, a structure called the cochlea. When the oval window receives the sound wave, it sets the fluid contained in the cochlea into motion. In the cochlea are hair cells that bend as the fluid moves. When the hair cells bend, an electrical impulse is generated. The impulse travels down the optic nerve, to the thalamus, to the occipital lobe for processing.

32. The gate-control theory of Melzack and Wall suggests that there is an area in the spinal cord that can act like a gate and either block pain messages or transmit them to the brain. Pain is experienced when pain messages carried by small, slow-conducting nerve fibers reach the gate and cause it to open. Other sensory messages from other parts of the body are carried by large, fast-conducting nerve fibers and block the pain messages at the gate. This theory also suggests that messages from the brain to the spinal cord can block the pain messages at the gate, explaining how psychological factors can influence pain perception.

33. The Gestalt psychologists argued that what we perceive is more than what we have sensed. They identified several basic principles that explain how we make sense out of the world by organizing our sensory experiences. We tend to perceive, for example, those things that have similar characteristics as belonging together, as being of one group. This is the Gestalt principle of **similarity**. The Gestalt principle of **proximity** states that things that are close together are perceived as belonging together. **Closure** implies that when there is a gap in an image, we tend to fill in the gap automatically. **Continuity** is our tendency to perceive objects as belonging together if they appear to form a continuous pattern. Finally, **figure-ground** states that as we view the world, an object (the figure) seems to stand out from the background (the ground).

CHAPTER 4

Multiple Choice: 1. c; 2. d; 3. c; 4. d; 5. a; 6. b; 7. c; 8. b; 9. d; 10. a; 11. b; 12. a; 13. d; 14. c; 15. a; 16. d; 17. b; 18. c; 19. c; 20. b

True/False: 21. true; 22. true; 23. false; 24. false; 25. true; 26. true; 27. true; 28. false; 29. false; 30. true

Essay

31. There are four NREM stages of sleep: Stages 1, 2, 3, and 4. Stage 1 is the lightest stage of sleep and Stage 4 is the deepest. REM sleep is characterized by rapid eye movements, an active brain, and inhibition of the large muscles of the body. Throughout the night, sleep cycles progress from Stage 1 through Stage 4 and then back down to Stage 2. From Stage 2 you progress into REM sleep, instead of back to Stage 1. After the first two full sleep cycles, the pattern changes and most sleep time is spent alternating between Stage 2 and REM sleep. As the night goes on, more time is spent in REM sleep. Each stage of sleep has a characteristic pattern of brain wave activity as indicated by EEG. Stage 1 sleep is characterized by small, irregular brain patterns and some alpha waves. In Stage 2 the typical pattern is that of sleep spindles. By Stage 3, delta waves appear, and Stage 4 is characterized by mostly delta waves.

32. Freud believed that dreaming was a means of expressing unacceptable wishes or impulses. He thought that these unacceptable desires were expressed symbolically so as not to upset the dreamer. The dream as it was recalled is the manifest content and the true meaning behind the dream is the latent content. A very different explanation of dreaming is Hobson's activation-synthesis hypothesis. This proposes that dreams occur because the brain is trying to make sense of the random

firing of brain cells that occurs during REM sleep. From the random activity (activation), a story is synthesized.

33. **Stimulants** speed up activity in the central nervous system, suppress appetite, and can make a person feel more awake, alert, and energetic. Stimulants increase pulse rate, blood pressure, and respiration rate, and reduce cerebral blood flow. Withdrawal symptoms for different stimulants may include fatigue, long periods of sleep, depression, anxiety, and increased irritability. **Depressants** decrease activity in the central nervous system, slow down bodily functions, and reduce sensitivity to outside stimulation. Withdrawal symptoms for different depressants may include anxiety, nausea, irritability, muscle tension, tremors, or cramps, sleeping problems, and in some cases severe and life-threatening physiological difficulties. **Hallucinogens** alter or distort the perception of time and space, alter mood, and produce feelings of unreality. Hallucinogens tend to magnify the mood of the user at the time the drug is taken, and tend to hamper creative thinking. Withdrawal symptoms for different hallucinogens may include anxiety, depression, fatigue, decreased appetite, and hyperactivity.

CHAPTER 5

Multiple Choice: 1. b; 2. c; 3. a; 4. d; 5. c; 6. a; 7. b; 8. d; 9. c; 10. d; 11. a; 12. b; 13. b; 14. d; 15. c; 16. c; 17. a; 18. b; 19. a; 20. d

True/False: 21. false; 22. false; 23. true; 24. false; 25. true; 26. false; 27. true; 28. true; 29. false; 30. false

Essay

31. In classical conditioning, extinction represents the weakening and eventual disappearance of the conditioned response as a result of repeated presentation of the conditioned stimulus without the unconditioned stimulus. In operant conditioning, extinction represents the weakening and eventual disappearance of a response as a result of the withholding of reinforcement. So in both forms of learning, a response is weakened and disappears, but extinction occurs due to different processes in each form of learning.

32. A dog is unlikely to spontaneously roll over, much less to do so on command the first time. In order to teach a dog this complex behavior, you can reinforce approximations of the desired behavior, an application called shaping. You might, for example, reward the dog for sitting. Then you would reward it for lying down. You might need to encourage the dog by pressing on his backside to

get him to sit, or to get him to roll over by holding the treat as he lies down so that he must reach for it and tumble. To first train him to roll over, every response of rolling over should be rewarded. Later, an intermittent reinforcement schedule, such as a variable ratio schedule, will maintain the behavior at a high rate yet keep it resistant to extinction.

33. Albert Bandura conducted a study on the process of observational learning, or sociocognitive learning, as a means of children learning aggressive behaviors. One classic study involved preschoolers. One group of children observed an adult model punching, kicking, and hitting a 5-foot, inflated plastic "Bobo Doll," a second group observed a nonaggressive model who ignored the Bobo Doll and played quietly with other toys, while a third group was a control group did not observe a model. Later, each child was observed playing, and children exposed to the aggressive model imitated much of the aggression they witnessed, and engaged in more nonimitative aggression than did children in the other groups. The implications of this study are that children may engage in increased levels of aggressive behavior when viewing such actions on television.

CHAPTER 6

Multiple Choice: 1. b; 2. c; 3. d; 4. c; 5. b; 6. a; 7. a; 8. b; 9. c; 10. a; 11. b; 12. d; 13. d; 14. c; 15. a; 16. c; 17. b; 18. b; 19. c; 20. d

True/False: 21. true; 22. false; 23. true; 24. false; 25. false; 26. true; 27. true; 28. true; 29. false; 30. true

Essay

31. Memory is not a "snapshot" of an event, but an account of an event that has been pieced together from a few highlights, using information that may or may not be accurate. Memories are recreations, with remembered material supplemented with details that fit expectations or beliefs. As such, schemas, which are frameworks of knowledge and assumptions we have about people, objects, and events, influence our memories. We are more likely to recall, or even create, details that are consistent with our schemas. Positive bias is a distortion of autobiographical memories, in that we are more likely to remember pleasant events than unpleasant ones, and to distort unpleasant memories so that they become more pleasant over time.

32. Long-term potentiation (LTP) is a strengthening of neuronal transmission at a synapse that lasts for at least

several hours and is thought to be the physiological process that is behind the formation of memories. This assertion is supported by research that demonstrates that blocking LTP disrupts or prevents some forms of learning.

33. *Organizing* information when encoding can facilitate retrieval. Organization is a strategy one can use by writing out headings and subheadings of text material or class notes. One can even integrate the two into one organized set of notes so that studying from each source isn't seen as a separate project. *Overlearning* is a strategy that involves practicing or studying material beyond the point where it can be repeated once without error. So when trying to memorize a definition or list of terms, instead of stopping with one error-free repetition from memory, continuing to study and recite the material will lead to superior and more long-term retrieval. If one typically engages in cramming, or massed practice, which involves trying to learn in a long session without rest, it might be better to try spaced practice. *Spaced practice* involves using shorter study periods broken up with breaks between each period. Finally, using *recitation* involves closing one's eyes and seeing how much of the information can be repeated aloud from memory.

CHAPTER 7

Multiple Choice: 1. c; 2. b; 3. d; 4. a; 5. b; 6. d; 7. c; 8. c; 9. b; 10. a; 11. c; 12. b; 13. d; 14. a; 15. a; 16. b; 17. a; 18. c; 19. b; 20. d

True/False: 21. true; 22. false; 23. false; 24. false; 25. true; 26. true; 27. false; 28. false; 29. false

Essay

30. Heuristics are rules of thumb or mental short cuts that are derived from experience and used in decision-making and problem solving. There is no guarantee that a heuristic will be accurate or useful. In general, heuristics enable us to make quick decisions with little mental effort. However, on some of these occasions, more effort would result in more accurate decision-making. Moreover, knowledge about heuristics by advertisers, politicians, and salespeople can lead us to make decisions we might not otherwise have made.

31. While virtually all animal species have some form of communication, language appears to be a uniquely human ability. Other primates can be taught to use some components of human language, but they do not appear capable of learning and using the language laws that humans readily internalize. Nonhuman primates are not capable of human speech, so studies have focused on the use of sign language and other symbols for communication. The most impressive results have been obtained with Kanzi, the offspring of a pygmy chimpanzee that had been taught to use symbols for communication. Kanzi has demonstrated an ability to respond to novel commands and has been more prolific than most primates trained to communicate. But despite his success, Kanzi's language abilities are far from what is achieved by human children with little effort.

32. Spearman's g-factor of intelligence suggests that intelligence consists of a single factor, which represents a general intellectual ability that underlies all mental operations. Spearman believed that intelligence tests tap this general factor, as well as several specific factors representing more specific intellectual abilities. In stark contrast, Gardner denies the existence of a general factor; instead, he suggests that there are eight independent forms of intelligence, which he labeled frames of mind. The eight frames of mind are: linguistic, logical-mathematical, spatial, bodily-kinesthetic, musical, interpersonal, intrapersonal, and naturalistic. The controversial aspect of Gardner's theory is his assertion that all forms of intelligence are of equal importance.

CHAPTER 8

Multiple Choice: 1. b; 2. a; 3. a; 4. d; 5. d; 6. a; 7. c; 8. c; 9. b; 10. d; 11. c; 12. b; 13. c; 14. b; 15. d; 16. b; 17. a; 18. b; 19. b; 20. b; 21. b

True/False: 22. false; 23. true; 24. true; 25. true; 26. false; 27. true; 28. false; 29. true; 30. false

Essay

31. The three stages are (1) period of the zygote, (2) period of the embryo, and (3) period of the fetus. The period of the zygote (also called germinal period) begins at conception and ends around week 2 of gestation. The major event going on in that stage is cell division. The period of the embryo (week 3 until week 8) is most negatively affected by teratogens, as this is the timeframe in which all major organs and structures form. The fetal period begins at week 9 and continues until birth. It is during this time that the organism is growing rapidly and major organs and structures are gaining function.

32. **Nativists** argue that humans are born prepared to acquire language. A famous linguist, Noam Chomsky, has even argued that humans are born with a language acquisition device (LAD), which enables children to

extract the rules of their native language from what they hear. While the LAD has not been located, an examination of the universal commonalities in language learning supports the notion of an inborn ability to decipher the rules of language. Further evidence of a role for nature in language learning is found in the manner in which language is acquired, because all children pass through the same identifiable stages in learning language. **Learning theorists** argue that language is learned through reinforcement and imitation. Thus, they support the nurture side of the nature vs. nurture issue as it relates to language. While certainly children appear to acquire aspects of language through these processes, this theory is inconsistent with the errors observed because they are errors that a child is unlikely to have ever heard or been rewarded for. Finally, the **interactionist theory** suggests that both nature and nurture are essential for the proper development of language. As such, a child's inborn capacity for language acquisition needs the environmental influences to support its development.

CHAPTER 9

Multiple Choice: 1. b; 2. a; 3. d; 4. c; 5. c; 6. c; 7. c; 8. a; 9. b; 10. c; 11. c; 12. c; 13. a; 14. c; 15. a; 16. b; 17. c; 18. a

True/False: 19. true; 20. true; 21. true; 22. true; 23. true; 24. true

Essay

25. Hunger is influenced by both physiological processes and environmental factors. Environmental cues that stimulate eating include an appetizing smell, taste, or appearance of food, acquired food preferences, being around others who are eating, foods high in fat and sugar, learned eating habits, and eating as a reaction to boredom, stress, or an unpleasant emotional state. Environmental cues that inhibit eating include an unappetizing smell, taste, or appearance of food, acquired taste aversions, learned eating habits, a desire to be thin, and not eating as a reaction to boredom, stress, or an unpleasant emotional state.

26. Anorexia nervosa and bulimia nervosa are both eating disorders. Anorexia nervosa is characterized by an overwhelming, irrational fear of gaining weight or becoming fat, compulsive dieting to the point of self-starvation, and excessive weight loss. Individuals with anorexia have a grossly distorted perception of their body size. These individuals may also attempt to lose weight through relentless exercise. Negative effects of anorexia nervosa include amenorrhea, low blood pressure, impaired heart function, dehydration, electrolyte disturbances, sterility, and potentially death.

Bulimia nervosa is characterized by repeated and uncontrolled episodes of binge eating, which involves the consumption of large amounts of food and a feeling of being unable to control eating behavior during a binge. Individuals with bulimia may follow binges with purges, attempts to maintain their weight with self-induced vomiting or the use of laxatives. Negative effects of bulimia nervosa include tooth decay due to the presence of stomach acids during vomiting, chronic sore throat, dehydration, swelling of the salivary glands, kidney damage, hair loss, and potentially death. Depression, guilt, and shame are common feelings among those with bulimia as well.

27. The role of cognition, the influence of thinking, in emotion has long been a subject of debate. Do we respond automatically to a snake with fear, or do we consider first whether or not it is poisonous? Interestingly, the two earliest theories of emotion virtually ignored the role of cognition in emotion. Neither the James-Lange nor the Cannon-Bard theory addressed the role of cognition in emotion. Each of these theories envisioned an emotional response as an automatic response to a stimulus. A very different approach was introduced by Schachter and Singer. These researchers cited cognition as a key element in determining what emotion would be experienced. According to the Schachter-Singer theory, an emotion is felt after two things have occurred: physiological arousal and a labeling of that arousal. In other words, arousal is felt and then this arousal is interpreted according to the situation. A very different view is offered by Lazarus. While James-Lange and Cannon-Bard ignored cognition and Schachter-Singer saw it as following arousal, Lazarus proposed that the first step in an emotional response is cognitive. According to Lazarus, an emotion is not felt until the situation has been subjected to a cognitive appraisal. No theory is without its flaws, but all invite a more careful consideration of the processes involved in the experience of an emotion.

CHAPTER 10

Multiple Choice: 1. b; 2. c; 3. c; 4. d; 5. b; 6. a; 7. c; 8. c; 9. b; 10. d; 11. b; 12. b; 13. d; 14. d; 15. a; 16. b; 17. a; 18. a; 19. b

True/False: 20. false; 21. false; 22. true; 23. false; 24. false; 25. true; 26. true; 27. true; 28. true; 29. false

Essay

30. HIV is transmitted through exchange of blood, semen, or vaginal secretions, and is therefore not limited to homosexual activity. It is also spread through IV drug use. Twenty-five percent of those in America infected are IV drug users. It is common for gay men to be infected, especially if they have multiple partners. It appears that HIV might be more easily spread through anal intercourse. However, heterosexual women are one of the fastest growing groups of new AIDS cases; about 30% of AIDS sufferers are women.

31. Answers for this question should emphasize that social learning theory involves observation, imitation, and reinforcement, while cognitive theory proposes that children must first understand gender and its relative permanence when developing their identities. Media and parents provide models within both theories, provide reinforcement according to social learning theory, and they help children understand the permanence of gender and develop gender appropriate behaviors as per cognitive theory.

32. Biological factors include abnormal levels of androgen during prenatal development, which can either influence the brain of the developing fetus, or cause structural differences in the hypothalamus between gay and heterosexual males. Genetic factors include possible feminizing genes that may shift male brain development in a female direction and DNA carried on the X chromosome of the mother.

CHAPTER 11

Multiple Choice: 1. d; 2. a; 3. d; 4. c; 5. c; 6. b; 7. a; 8. b; 9. d; 10. b; 11. c; 12. c; 13. b; 14. d; 15. c; 16. a; 17. c; 18. b; 19. b

True/False: 20. false; 21. false; 22. true; 23. true; 24. true; 25. true; 26. false; 27. true; 28. true

Essay

29. The biopsychosocial model considers health and illness to be determined by a combination of biological, psychological, and social factors. Biological factors favoring health and wellness include genetics, homeostasis, relaxation, and a healthy lifestyle (diet and exercise). Those biological factors working against health and wellness include lack of exercise, poor diet, disease and injury, toxic chemicals, and pollution. Psychological factors favoring health and wellness include self-regulation, stress management, giving and receiving love, positive imagery, positive thoughts, and a healthy personality. Psychological factors working against health and wellness include depression, negative thoughts, worry, anxiety, poor coping skills, an unhealthy personality, and stress. Social factors favoring health and wellness include social responsibility, social policy, and social groups. Social factors working against health and wellness include loneliness, poverty, exploitation, and violence.

30. The Type A behavior pattern is associated with a high rate of coronary heart disease. People with the Type A behavior pattern have a strong sense of time urgency, are impatient, excessively competitive, hostile, and easily angered. People with the Type B behavior pattern are relaxed and easygoing and are not driven by a sense of time urgency. They are not impatient or hostile and are able to relax without guilt.
(Note: The relaxed and easygoing nature of the Type B folks does not come at the expense of success. Type B folks are as bright and ambitious as the others and may even be more successful than the Type A or D counterparts.)
The Type D behavior pattern is characterized by chronic emotional distress coupled with the tendency to suppress negative emotions.

31. Four personal factors that reduce the impact of stress and illness are optimism, hardiness, religious faith, and social support. Optimists generally expect good outcomes, and these positive expectations make them more stress-resistant than pessimists, who generally expect bad outcomes. Hardiness is a combination of three psychological qualities—commitment, control, and change—shared by people who can handle high levels of stress and remain healthy. People with this characteristic tend to act to solve their problems, and to welcome life's challenges, seeing them as opportunities for growth and improvement. Research also indicates that religious involvement is positively associated with measures of physical health and lower rates of cancer, heart disease, and stroke. Finally, social support refers to tangible and/or emotional support provided in times of need by family members, friends, and others; such support provides a feeling of being loved, valued, and cared for by those toward whom we feel a similar obligation.

CHAPTER 12

Multiple Choice: 1. c; 2. a; 3. d; 4. d; 5. b; 6. a; 7. c; 8. b; 9. c; 10. d; 11. a; 12. a; 13. d; 14. a; 15. a; 16. b; 17. b; 18. b; 19. c; 20. d

True/False: 21. false; 22. false; 23. true; 24. false; 25. false; 26. false; 27. true; 28. false; 29. true; 30. false

Essay

31. Compared to Freud's psychoanalytic theory, the Neo-Freudians, including Jung, Adler, and Horney, tended to look more at the life span of an individual in shaping personality, rather than suggesting that personality was completely formed in childhood. They focused more on the unity of the individual self than on intrapsychic conflicts, and they tended to place less emphasis on sexual impulses, and the id in general, than did Freud. Greater emphasis was placed on the development of one's identity. Horney in particular argued against Freud's views of women, including his notion that a woman's desire to have a child and a man is a conversion of her unfulfilled wish for a penis.

32. The situation-trait debate is an ongoing discussion among psychologists about the relative importance of factors within the situation and factors within the person in accounting for behavior. Mischel and others argue that individuals behave differently in different situations. Advocates of the trait side of the debate argue that support for trait theories has come from many longitudinal studies. Current evidence supports the view that there are internal traits that strongly influence behavior across situations, but that situational variables do affect personality traits.

33. In individualist cultures, more emphasis is placed on individual achievement than on group achievement. High achieving individuals are accorded honor and prestige. The United States is an individualistic culture. People in collectivist cultures, on the other hand, tend to be more interdependent and define themselves and their personal interests in terms of their group membership. Several Latin American cultures, such as Guatemala and Ecuador, are collectivist cultures. The culture's emphasis is thought to predict which types of behaviors and traits would thus be more valued within that culture. For example, autonomy is thought to be more valued in individualist cultures, whereas respect for harmonious social relationships may be more valued in collectivist cultures. Some psychologists warn against overemphasizing cultural differences in personality, arguing that the goal of all individuals, regardless of cultural context, is to enhance self-esteem.

CHAPTER 13

Multiple Choice: 1. b; 2. b; 3. d; 4. a; 5. c; 6. d; 7. c; 8. b; 9. a; 10. c; 11. a; 12. d; 13. d; 14. c; 15. a; 16. a; 17. a; 18. c

True/False: 19. false; 20. true; 21. true; 22. false; 23. true; 24. false; 25. true; 26. false; 27. false

Essay

28. Human behavior lies along a continuum, ranging from well-adjusted to maladaptive. Several questions may be asked to determine where along this continuum behavior becomes abnormal. First, is the behavior considered strange within the person's own culture? One reason for this question is to rule out judging someone as abnormal because of a specific cultural custom or behavior. Does the behavior cause personal distress? If a behavior causes an individual considerable emotional distress, the behavior may warrant being considered abnormal. Is the behavior maladaptive? A normal behavior should not lead to impaired functioning. Is the person a danger to self or others? To be committed to a mental hospital a person must be considered mentally ill and endangering themselves or someone else. Is the person legally responsible for their acts? The legal term insanity is used to describe someone whose psychiatric state makes them not legally responsible for their actions.

29. Depression is one significant risk factor for suicide, but not all depressed people are suicidal. Other risk factors include other mood disorders, schizophrenia, and substance abuse. Life stressors can also increase suicide risk. In the U.S., White Americans and Native Americans have similar suicide rates, and both groups are more likely to commit suicide than African Americans and Hispanic Americans. Asian Americans have the lowest suicide rate of all ethnic groups in the United States. Women are generally four times more likely than men to attempt suicide, but men are more likely to succeed, as they tend to choose more lethal methods. Finally, older Americans are at a higher risk of suicide than teens and young adults. Risk factors for older adults to commit suicide include poor general health, serious illness, loneliness, and decline in economic status.

30. Schizophrenia is a serious and complicated mental illness and each of its symptoms can be classified as either positive or negative. Positive, in this instance, refers to something being present whereas negative, to something being absent. Positive symptoms (indicating the presence of abnormal behavior) seen in those with schizophrenia might include hallucinations of any kind, delusions of any kind, disorganized behavior, inappropriate affect, and derailment (derailment is an example of incoherent, disorganized speech). Negative symptoms (the absence of expected or anticipated behavior) would include social withdrawal, a lack of emotion, and limited movement (immobility), flat affect, and apathy.

CHAPTER 14

Multiple Choice: 1. c; 2. a; 3. c; 4. b; 5. a; 6. d; 7. c; 8. b; 9. d; 10. b; 11. d; 12. d; 13. d; 14. a; 15. c; 16. b; 17. d; 18. b; 19. c; 20. b

True/False: 21. true; 22. false; 23. true; 24. true; 25. true; 26. false; 27. false; 28. false; 29. true; 30. true

Essay

31. Both Ellis's rational emotive therapy and Beck's cognitive therapy are forms of cognitive therapies, which assume that maladaptive behavior can result from irrational thoughts, beliefs, and ideas, which the therapist tries to change. Ellis's rational emotive therapy approach relies on his ABC theory, in which the activating event (A) does not cause emotions, but the person's belief (B) about the event that causes emotional consequences (C). Ellis's approach does not involve a warm, supportive therapist, but one who challenges the client's irrational thinking that leads to emotional distress. Beck's cognitive therapy traces emotional distress to an individual's automatic thoughts, unreasonable but unquestioned ideas that rule the person's life. Beck's approach is designed to help clients stop their negative thoughts and replace them with more objective thoughts. Beck's warm approach accomplishes this goal through guidance of the client so that personal experiences can provide evidence in the real world to refute the false beliefs. Both approaches have similar goals, but accomplish them through differing strategies.

32. The antidepressants are the tricyclics, the selective serotonin reuptake inhibitors (SSRIs), and the monoamine oxidase (MAO) inhibitors. The **tricyclic antidepressants** act to block the reuptake of norepinephrine and serotonin. This treats the symptoms of depression by increasing the amount of time of these neurotransmitters have in the synapse. Drugs like Prozac, Paxil, and Zoloft are **SSRIs** and also work by blocking neurotransmitter reuptake, but block reuptake selectively of serotonin. **MAO inhibitors** work by blocking the activity of the enzyme that breaks down norepinephrine and serotonin. Thus, all the drugs used to treat depression are drugs that increase the availability of serotonin only (the SSRIs) or of serotonin and norepinephrine. The effectiveness of these drugs suggests that a decrease in the activity of these neurotransmitters is what underlies depression.

33. Psychiatrists attend medical school and earn a medical degree (MD or DO) and undergo a residency in psychiatry. They can provide psychotherapy and prescribe drug therapy (psychiatric medications).

They can also conduct research. Clinical psychologists attend graduate school and earn a Ph.D. or Psy.D. and complete an internship in clinical psychology. In some states, with additional training, they can also provide drug therapy. Psychologists can conduct research, and provide psychotherapy as well as administer psychological tests.

CHAPTER 15

Multiple Choice: 1. a; 2. c; 3. d; 4. d; 5. c; 6. d; 7. a; 8. b; 9. d; 10. d; 11. c; 12. a; 13. a; 14. a; 15. b; 16. a; 17. c; 18. c; 19. d; 20. d

True/False: 21. true; 22. false; 23. true; 24. false; 25. false; 26. true; 27. true; 28. false; 29. false; 30. true

Essay

31. Men and women both consider the physical attractiveness of a partner as a primary consideration in mate selection. Another factor that is important according to research is someone who is similar in personality, physical traits, intellectual ability, education, religion, ethnicity, socioeconomic status, and attitudes. Generally, men and women across a variety of cultures rate four qualities as most important in mate selection: mutual attraction/love, dependable character, emotional stability and maturity, and a pleasing disposition. According to evolutionary psychologists, men prefer young and beautiful women, because they suggest health and fertility, whereas women prefer someone offering resources and social status. Both sets of qualities are considered adaptive for the next generation.

32. Stanley Milgram conducted a study of obedience utilizing male volunteers, in which the student was assigned to be a "teacher" and deliver electric shocks to a "learner" when the learner made errors on a memory task. The teacher was instructed to administer escalating levels of shock with each error by the learner, who was in actuality a confederate of the experimenter. Whenever the teacher hesitated, the experimenter instructed him to continue. At the 20th switch, 300 volts, the learner cried out in pain and pleaded to be let out of the experiment. After the next shock, the learner ceased to respond, and the teacher was instructed to continue. Out of the 40 participants, 26 (or 65%) continued administering shocks to the maximum level, and none stopped before the 20th switch, when the learned cried out and protested. The results of this study suggested that people will follow the orders of an authority figure even if harm may potentially come to another. This study is not as likely to be

conducted in that form today because of concerns about the harm to the teacher participants, even if they are told afterward that the learner is a confederate and was never being shocked at all.

33. The social learning theory of aggression suggests that people learn to behave aggressively by observing aggressive models and by having their aggressive responses reinforced. Aggression is known to be higher in groups and subcultures that condone violent behavior. Albert Bandura's classic "Bobo doll" studies, in which children observed a model playing aggressively with an inflated clown doll (AKA a bobo doll) were more likely to copy those aggressive behaviors than other children who did not see the aggressive model, demonstrated the potential for aggressive behavior being acquired through observational learning. Research evidence strongly supports a relationship between TV violence and viewer aggression. This relationship is even stronger among individuals who are already highly aggressive. TV violence may stimulate physiological arousal, lower inhibitions, cause unpleasant feelings, and decrease sensitivity to violence, making it more acceptable.

Answers to Module Study Guides and Chapter Comprehensive Practice Tests

CHAPTER 1

MODULE 1: 1. scientific method; 2. describe, explain, predict, influence; 3. true; 4. (1) c (2) c (3) c (4) b,a (5) b (6) a (7) a,b,c; 5. structuralism; 6. functionalism; 7. (1) c (2) a (3) d (4) e (5) b; 8. (1) d (2) c (3) b (4) a (5) c (6) b; 9. (1) d (2) a (3) f (4) e (5) b (6) c; 10. psychoanalysis; 11. (1) b (2) c (3) a (4) b (5) a (6) c; 12. (1) b (2) c (3) d (4) a (5) e (6) g (7) f; 13. (1) Yes (2) No (3) No (4) No

MODULE 2: 1. (1) d (2) a (3) b (4) c; 2. naturalistic observation; 3. representative sample; 4. case studies; 5. false; 6. false; 7. correlation coefficient; 8. b; 9. positive; 10. negative; 11. false; 12. true; 13. independent variable, dependent variable; 14. (1) d (2) c (3) a (4) b; 15. c; 16. d; 17. b; 18. true

MODULE 3: 1. d; 2. independent thinking, suspension of judgment, willingness to modify prior judgments; 3. b; 4. c; 5. many; 6. clinical, counseling psychologists

Comprehensive Practice Test: 1. b; 2. b; 3. d; 4. c; 5. c; 6. b; 7. a; 8. d; 9. c; 10. a; 11. c; 12. false; 13. false; 14. true; 15. false; 16. true; 17. false; 18. false; 19. false; 20. false

CHAPTER 2

MODULE 4: 1. a; 2. glial cells; 3. c; 4.d; 5. action; 6. b; 7. b; 8. norepinephrine; 9. endorphins; 10. serotonin, GABA; 11. central, peripheral; 12. (1) b (2) a (3) f (4) c (5) e (6) d (7) g; 13. b; 14. hippocampus; 15. amygdala, hippocampus; 16. b; 17. c

MODULE 5: 1. (1) b (2) c (3) a; 2. b; 3. a; 4. c; 5. c; 6. b; 7. a; 8. (1) d (2) c (3) a (4) b; 9. (1) d (2) a (3) e (4) b (5) c; 10. (1) a (2) b (3) a (4) a (5) b; 11. c; 12. c; 13. synaptogenesis, myelination; 14. white matter; 15. navigation, location of sound; 16. decreases; 17. stroke

MODULE 6: 1. (1) d (2) a (3) e (4) c (5) b (6) f; 2. recessive; 3. d; 4. twin studies, adoption studies

Comprehensive Practice Test: 1. b; 2. d; 3. d; 4. a; 5. c; 6. b; 7. c; 8. b; 9. d; 10. b; 11. a; 12. c; 13. c;

14. d; 15. true; 16. true; 17. spatial perception; 18. parietal; 19. X chromosome; 20. (1) frontal lobe, (2) motor cortex, (3) parietal lobe, (4) occipital lobe; (5) cerebellum; (6) pons, (7) medulla, (8) corpus callosum, (9) pituitary gland

CHAPTER 3

MODULE 7: 1. sensation; 2. raw material, finished product; 3. absolute; 4. false; 5. c; 6. transduction; 7. b; 8. (1) d (2) c (3) b (4) e (5) a; 9. d; 10. rods, cones; 11. c; 12. opponent-process

MODULE 8: 1. d; 2. hertz, decibels; 3. (1) b (2) a (3) c; 4. d; 5. c; 6. olfaction; 7. c; 8. sweet, sour, salty, bitter, umami; 9. taste bud; 10. false; 11. kinesthetic; 12. vestibular, inner ear

MODULE 9: 1. inattentional blindness; 2. bottom-up processing; 3. cross-modal perception; 4. (1) c (2) a (3) b; 5. binocular; 6. (1) c (2) b (3) a (4) d; 7. false; 8. c; 9. b; 10. top-down; 11. c; 12. false; 13. Ganzfeld procedure

Comprehensive Practice Test: 1. c; 2. a; 3. d; 4. c; 5. b; 6. d; 7. a; 8. c; 9. a; 10. c; 11. c; 12. b; 13. d; 14. a; 15. d; 16. b; 17. false; 18. d; 19. true; 20. c; 21. false; 22. a; 23. c; 24. d; 25. c; 26. b; 27. a; 28. a; 29. d

CHAPTER 4

MODULE 10: 1. a; 2. suprachiasmatic nucleus; 3. d; 4. false; 5. circadian, restorative; 6. (1) a (2) b (3) a (4) a (5) a; 7. c; 8. false; 9. d; 10. b; 11. (1) c (2) b (3) a; 12. c; 13. false; 14. (1) d (2) a (3) c (4) b; 15. c; 16. false; 17. b; 18. false

MODULE 11: 1. Meditation; 2. b; 3. true; 4. true; 5. c; 6. a; 7. sociocognitive, neodissociation, dissociated control

MODULE 12: 1. nucleus accumbens; 2. d; 3. true; 4. true; 5. (1) b (2) a (3) d (4) c; 6. b; 7. b; 8. a; 9. c; 10. d; 11. c; 12. (1) b (2) d (3) f (4) c (5) e (6) a (7) g

Comprehensive Practice Test: 1. melatonin; 2. b; 3. c; 4. c; 5. b; 6. b; 7. false; 8. d; 9. c; 10. d; 11. true; 12. b; 13. b; 14. false; 15. false; 16. c; 17. c; 18. false

CHAPTER 5

MODULE 13: 1. Pavlov; 2. sound of truck; 3. food; 4. conditioned; 5. salivation; 6. extinction; 7. existing conditioned stimulus; 8. b; 9. conditioned, unconditioned; 10. a; 11. biological predispositions; 12. true; 13. true

MODULE 14: 1. b; 2. c; 3. d; 4. negative; 5. continuous; 6. d; 7. a; 8. false; 9. false; 10. true; 11. learned helplessness; 12. biofeedback; 13. behavior modification

MODULE 15: 1. insight; 2. d; 3. b; 4. b; 5. (1) c (2) a (3) d (4) b; 6. (1) c (2) a (3) b

Comprehensive Practice Test: 1. a; 2. c; 3. c; 4. d; 5. b; 6. c; 7. b; 8. c; 9. a; 10. d; 11. b; 12. false; 13. b; 14. b; 15. d; 16. c

CHAPTER 6

MODULE 16: 1. encoding; 2. d; 3. rehearsal; 4. working; 5. long; 6. (1) b (2) c (3) a; 7. semantic; 8. (1) b (2) c (3) a; 9. c

MODULE 17: 1. c; 2. (1) a (2) c (3) b (4) a,b (5) c; 3. c; 4. true; 5. true; 6. b; 7. true; 8. a; 9. c; 10. d; 11. a; 12. false; 13. true; 14. episodic, semantic; 15. a; 16. true

MODULE 18: 1. d; 2. a; 3. (1) c (2) e (3) a (4) b (5) d; 4. a; 5. false; 6. true; 7. c; 8. d

Comprehensive Practice Test: 1. c; 2. a; 3. c; 4. b; 5. nondeclarative; 6. a; 7. d; 8. b; 9. true; 10. false; 11. false; 12. d; 13. a; 14. c; 15. false; 16. true; 17. false; 18. a; 19. b; 20. true; 21. (1) large (2) visual, fraction of a second, auditory, 2 seconds; (3) 7 +/- 2; (4) <30 seconds without rehearsal; (5) unlimited; (6) minutes to a lifetime; (7) declarative; (8) semantic; (9) motor; (10) classically

CHAPTER 7

MODULE 19: 1. d; 2. b; 3. d; 4. framing; 5. a; 6. b; 7. c; 8. elimination by aspects; 9. false; 10. false

MODULE 20: 1. (1) c (2) d (3) b (4) e (5) a; 2. false; 3. true; 4. false; 5. psycholinguistics; 6. pragmatics; 7. linguistic relativity

MODULE 21: 1. (1) b (2) c (3) a; 2. validity; 3. contextual; 4. reliability; 5. a; 6. b; 7. a

MODULE 22: 1. false; 2. true; 3. c; 4. false; 5. c

Comprehensive Practice Test: 1. b; 2. b; 3. prototype; 4. false; 5. a; 6. a; 7. d; 8. a; 9. false; 10. true; 11. false; 12. c; 13. a; 14. b; 15. false; 16. true; 17. true

CHAPTER 8

MODULE 23: 1. d; 2. b; 3. (1) a (2) b (3) a (4) b (5) b (6) a,b; 4. b; 5. scheme; 6. d; 7. personal fable; 8. (1) b (2) c (3) a; 9. conventional; 10. true; 11. identity versus role confusion

MODULE 24: 1. (1) c (2) a (3) b; 2. zygote; 3. teratogens; 4. maturation; 5. a; 6. b; 7. c; 8. true;

MODULE 25: 1. telegraphic speech; 2. overregularization; 3. false; 4. (1) c (2) b (3) a; 5. false; 6. (1) c (2) b (3) a (4) e (5) d 7. false; 8. c; 9. true

MODULE 26: 1. c; 2. presbyopia; 3. crystallized, fluid; 4. b; 5. a; 6. d; 7. bargaining

Comprehensive Practice Test: 1. d; 2. c; 3. b; 4. b; 5. b; 6. d; 7. b; 8. a; 9. b; 10. a; 11. true; 12. b; 13. d; 14. b; 15. c; 16. c; 17. true; 18. b; 19. c; 20. b; 21. true; 22. b

CHAPTER 9

MODULE 27: 1. extrinsic; 2. a; 3. d; 4. c; 5. true; 6. true; 7. false; 8. mastery; 9. d; 10. feeding, satiety; 11. c; 12. c; 13. d; 14. maintain; 15. d; 16. biological; 17. c; 18. anorexia nervosa, bulimia nervosa

MODULE 28: 1. c; 2. a; 3. b; 4. c; 5. d; 6. c; 7. a; 8. c

Comprehensive Practice Test: 1. a; 2. a; 3. c; 4. a; 5. c; 6. d; 7. true; 8. d; 9. b; 10. c; 11. c; 12. false; 13. c; 14. true; 15. false

CHAPTER 10

MODULE 29: 1. a; 2. c; 3. a; 4. androgens; 5. intersex; 6. biological sex, psychological gender; 7. (1) e (2) f (3) a (4) d (5) b (6) c; 8. masculinity; 9. (1) b (2) a (3) a (4) b (5) b; 10. b; 11. mating; 12. hurt sad, disappointed; anger

MODULE 30: 1. a; 2. c; 3. true; 4. true; 5. (1) Sexual response cycle, (2) Correlation between brain structure and sexual orientation, (3) Absence of correlation between sexual orientation and family variables, (4) Gay and lesbian adults' recollections of cross-gender childhood behavior, (5) Sexual behavior among American adults, (6) Influence of heredity in sexual orientation; 6. Males, females; 7. female circumcision; 8. four; 9. testosterone; 10. b; 11. (1) b; (2) b; (3) a; (4) b; (5) a; 12. orientation; 13. males; females

MODULE 31: 1. (1) d (2) e (3) b (4) a (5) f (6) c; 2. sexual dysfunction; 3. sexual aversion disorder; 4. false; 5. a; 6. true; 7. (1) a; (2) a; (3) b; (4) a; (5) b; (6) b; (7) b; 8. syphilis; 9. herpes; 10. gonorrhea, Chlamydia; 11. immune; 12. homosexual men; 13. pelvic inflammatory disease

Comprehensive Practice Test: 1. c; 2. d; 3. c; 4. d; 5. c; 6. a; 7. a; 8. d; 9. d; 10. a; 11. c; 12. a; 13. false; 14. false; 15. false; 16. true; 17. false; 18. true; 19. true; 20. false

CHAPTER 11

MODULE 32: 1. false; 2. false; 3. true; 4. true; 5. c; 6. d; 7. d; 8. false; 9. false; 10. d; 11. resistance; 12. exhaustion; 13. physiological, psychological; 14. a; 15. problem-focused, emotion-focused; 16. true

MODULE 33: 1. c; 2. b; 3. a; 4. c; 5. true; 6. d; 7. false; 8. a; 9. b; 10. alcohol; 11. d; 12. false

Comprehensive Practice Test: 1. false; 2. b; 3. a; 4. c; 5. a; 6. true; 7. true; 8. c; 9. racism; 10. true; 11. a; 12. false; 13. a

CHAPTER 12

MODULE 34: 1. true; 2. unconscious; 3. a; 4. c; 5. b; 6. false; 7. true; 8. birth; 9. d; 10. b; 11. Oedipal complex; 12. c; 13. collective; 14. c; 15. c

MODULE 35: 1. d; 2. c; 3. a; 4. d; 5. true; 6. a; 7. b; 8. b; 9. c; 10. a; 11. d

MODULE 36: 1. negligible; 2. false; 3. (1) a (2) c (3) d (4) b (5) e; 4. d; 5. c; 6. Jung's; 7. projective; 8. MMPI; 9. collectivism, individualism/collectivism

Comprehensive Practice Test: 1. c; 2. c; 3. b; 4. false; 5. b; 6. c; 7. a; 8. a; 9. b; 10. d; 11. b; 12. c; 13. true; 14. false; 15. c; 16. d

CHAPTER 13

MODULE 37: 1. false; 2. a; 3. (1) c (2) a (3) b (4) d; 4. biological

MODULE 38: 1. false; 2. true; 3. false; 4. (1) e (2) d (3) b (4) c (5) a (6) f; 5. c; 6. (1) b (2) c (3) a; 7. false; 8. b

MODULE 39: 1. (1) a (2) d (3) b (4) c; 2. d; 3. (1) c (2) a (3) b (4) d; 4. false; 5. true; 6. (1) d (2) b (3) e (4) c (5) a; 7. paraphilias; 8. c; 9. c

Comprehensive Practice Test: 1. c; 2. b; 3. d; 4. b; 5. true; 6. b; 7. a; 8. false; 9. d; 10. b; 11. true; 12. d; 13. c; 14. true; 15. d; 16. c; 17. false; 18. b

CHAPTER 14

MODULE 40: 1. d; 2. Gestalt; 3. Person-centered; 4. psychodynamic; 5. c; 6. c; 7. false

MODULE 41: 1. operant; 2. b; 3. d; 4. (1) c (2) b (3) a (4) d; 5. c; 6. false; 7. b; 8. d; 9. true; 10. (1) c (2) b (3) a (4) c (5) c; 11. b; 12. d; 13. a; 14. false; 15. false

MODULE 42: 1. b; 2. (1) a (2) c (3) b (4) c; 3. c; 4. are; 5. gender-based prejudices

Comprehensive Practice Test: 1. c; 2. c; 3. c; 4. false; 5. d; 6. a; 7. b; 8. a; 9. a; 10. b; 11. b; 12. a; 13. c; 14. c; 15. b; 16. d; 17. c; 18. true; 19. false; 20. false; 21. (1) e (2) a (3) d (4) f (5) b (6) g (7) c

CHAPTER 15

MODULE 43: 1. d; 2. b; 3. true; 4. (1) c (2) b (3) a; 5. true; 6. false

MODULE 44: 1. (1) c (2) a (3) b; 2. c; 3. b; 4. c; 5. d; 6. a; 7. c; 8. d; 9. true; 10. b; 11. true; 12. true

MODULE 45: 1. b; 2. true; 3. true; 4. false; 5. false; 6. true; 7. b; 8. c; 9. c; 10. false; 11. true; 12. (1) b (2) a (3) c; 13. c; 14. false; 15. true

Comprehensive Practice Test: 1. d; 2. false; 3. c; 4. b; 5. false; 6. d; 7. c; 8. true; 9. b; 10. false; 11. b; 12. c; 13. c; 14. c; 15. true; 16. b; 17. true; 18. a

absolute threshold The minimum amount of sensory stimulation that can be detected 50% of the time.

accommodation In vision, the flattening and bulging action of the lens as it focuses images of objects on the retina. In learning, the process by which existing schemes are modified and new schemes are created to incorporate new objects, events, experiences, or information.

acetylcholine (ah-SEET-ul-KOH-leen) A neurotransmitter that plays a role in learning new information, causes the skeletal muscle fibers to contract, and keeps the heart from beating too rapidly.

acquired immune deficiency syndrome (AIDS) A devastating and incurable illness that is caused by infection with the human immunodeficiency virus (HIV) and progressively weakens the body's immune system, leaving the person vulnerable to opportunistic infections that usually cause death.

action potential The sudden reversal of the resting potential, which initiates the firing of a neuron.

activation-synthesis hypothesis of dreaming The hypothesis that dreams are the brain's attempt to make sense of the random firing of brain cells during REM sleep.

actor-observer effect The tendency to attribute one's own behavior primarily to situational factors and the behavior of others primarily to dispositional factors.

adolescence The developmental stage that begins at puberty and encompasses the period from the end of childhood to the beginning of adulthood.

adrenal glands (ah-DREE-nal) A pair of endocrine glands that release hormones that prepare the body for emergencies and stressful situations and also release corticoids and small amounts of the sex hormones.

aerobic exercise Exercise that uses the large muscle groups in continuous, repetitive action and increases oxygen intake and breathing and heart rates.

afterimage A visual sensation that remains after a stimulus is withdrawn.

aggression The intentional infliction of physical or psychological harm on others.

agoraphobia (AG-or-uh-FO-bee-ah) An intense fear of being in a situation from which escape is not possible or in which help would not be available if one experienced overwhelming anxiety or a panic attack.

alarm stage The first stage of the general adaptation syndrome, in which the person experiences a burst of energy that aids in dealing with the stressful situation.

algorithm A systematic, step-by-step procedure, such as a mathematical formula, that guarantees a solution to a problem of a certain type if applied appropriately and executed properly.

alpha wave The brain-wave pattern associated with deep relaxation.

altered state of consciousness Changes in awareness produced by sleep, meditation, hypnosis, and drugs.

alternative medicine Any treatment or therapy that has not been scientifically demonstrated to be effective.

altruism Behavior that is aimed at helping another, requires some self-sacrifice, and is not performed for personal gain.

Alzheimer disease (ALZ-hye-mer) An incurable form of dementia characterized by progressive deterioration of intellect and personality, resulting from widespread degeneration of brain cells.

amnesia A partial or complete loss of memory due to loss of consciousness, brain damage, or some psychological cause.

amplitude The measure of the loudness of a sound; expressed in the unit called the decibel.

amygdala (ah-MIG-da-la) A structure in the limbic system that plays an important role in emotion, particularly in response to unpleasant or punishing stimuli.

analogy heuristic A rule of thumb that applies a solution that solved a problem in the past to a current problem that shares many features with the past problem.

androgens Male sex hormones.

androgyny (an-DROJ-uh-nee) A combination of desirable masculine and feminine characteristics in one person.

anorexia nervosa An eating disorder characterized by an overwhelming, irrational fear of gaining weight or becoming fat, compulsive dieting to the point of self-starvation, and excessive weight loss.

anterograde amnesia The inability to form long-term memories of events occurring after a brain injury or brain surgery, although memories formed before the trauma are usually intact and short-term memory is unaffected.

antidepressant drugs Drugs that act as mood elevators for severely depressed people and are also prescribed to treat some anxiety disorders.

antipsychotic drugs Drugs used to control severe psychotic symptoms, such as delusions, hallucinations, disorganized speech, and disorganized behavior, by inhibiting dopamine activity; also known as neuroleptics.

anxiety disorders Psychological disorders characterized by frequent fearful thoughts about what might happen in the future.

aphasia (uh-FAY-zyah) A loss or impairment of the ability to use or understand language, resulting from damage to the brain.

applied research Research conducted specifically to solve practical problems and improve the quality of life.

approach-approach conflict A conflict arising from having to choose between equally desirable alternatives.

approach-avoidance conflict A conflict arising when the same choice has both desirable and undesirable features.

aptitude test A test designed to predict a person's achievement or performance at some future time.

archetype (AR-ka-type) Existing in the collective unconscious, an inherited tendency to respond to universal human situations in particular ways.

arousal A state of alertness and mental and physical activation.

arousal theory A theory of motivation suggesting that people are motivated to maintain an optimal level of alertness and physical and mental activation.

artificial intelligence The programming of computer systems to simulate human thinking in solving problems and in making judgments and decisions.

artificial neural networks (ANNs) Computer systems that are intended to mimic the human brain.

assimilation The process by which new objects, events, experiences, or information is incorporated into existing schemes.

association areas Areas of the cerebral cortex that house memories and are involved in thought, perception, and language.

attachment The strong affectionate bond a child forms with the mother or primary caregiver.

attention The process of sorting through sensations and selecting some of them for further processing.

attitude A relatively stable evaluation of a person, object, situation, or issue, along a continuum ranging from positive to negative.

attribution An assignment of a cause to explain one's own or another's behavior.

audience effects The impact of passive spectators on performance.

audition The sensation and process of hearing.

authoritarian parents Parents who make arbitrary rules, expect unquestioned obedience from their children, punish transgressions, and value obedience to authority.

authoritative parents Parents who set high but realistic standards, reason with the child, enforce limits, and encourage open communication and independence.

availability heuristic A cognitive rule of thumb that says that the probability of an event or the importance assigned to it is based on its availability in memory.

aversion therapy A behavior therapy in which an aversive stimulus is paired with a harmful or socially undesirable behavior until the behavior becomes associated with pain or discomfort.

avoidance learning Learning to avoid events or conditions associated with aversive consequences or phobias.

avoidance-avoidance conflict A conflict arising from having to choose between undesirable alternatives.

axon (AK-sahn) The slender, tail-like extension of the neuron that transmits signals to the dendrites or cell body of other neurons and to muscles, glands, and other parts of the body.

babbling Vocalization of the basic speech sounds (phonemes), which begins between 4 and 6 months.

bacterial STDs Sexually transmitted diseases that are caused by bacteria and can be treated with antibiotics.

basic emotions Emotions that are unlearned and universal, that are reflected in the same facial expressions across cultures, and that emerge in children according to their biological timetable of development; fear, anger, disgust, surprise, happiness, and sadness are usually considered basic emotions.

basic research Research conducted to seek new knowledge and to explore and advance general scientific understanding.

behavior modification A method of changing behavior through a systematic program based on the learning principles of classical conditioning, operant conditioning, or observational learning. An approach to therapy that uses learning principles to eliminate inappropriate or maladaptive behaviors and replace them with more adaptive responses.

behavior therapy A treatment approach that is based on the idea that abnormal behavior is learned and that applies the principles of operant conditioning, classical conditioning, and/or observational learning to eliminate inappropriate or maladaptive behaviors and replace them with more adaptive responses.

behavioral genetics A field of research that uses twin studies and adoption studies to investigate the relative effects of heredity and environment on behavior.

behaviorism The school of psychology that views observable, measurable behavior as the appropriate subject matter for psychology and emphasizes the key role of environment as a determinant of behavior.

beta wave (BAY-tuh) The brain-wave pattern associated with mental or physical activity.

binocular depth cues Depth cues that depend on both eyes working together.

biofeedback The use of sensitive equipment to give people precise feedback about internal physiological processes so that they can learn, with practice, to exercise control over them.

biological psychology The school of psychology that looks for links between specific behaviors and equally specific biological processes that often help explain individual differences.

biological sex Physiological status as male or female.

biological therapy A therapy (drug therapy, electroconvulsive therapy, or psychosurgery) that is based on the assumption that psychological disorders are symptoms of underlying physical problems.

biomedical model A perspective that explains illness solely in terms of biological factors.

biopsychosocial model A perspective that focuses on health as well as illness and holds that both are determined by a combination of biological, psychological, and social factors.

bipolar disorder A mood disorder in which manic episodes alternate with periods of depression, usually with relatively normal periods in between.

blind spot The point in each retina where there are no rods or cones because the cable of ganglion cells is extending through the retinal wall.

body mass index (BMI) A measure of weight relative to height.

bottom-up processing Information processing in which individual components or bits of data are combined until a complete perception is formed.

brainstem The structure that begins at the point where the spinal cord enlarges as it enters the brain and handles functions critical to physical survival. It includes the medulla, the pons, and the reticular formation.

brightness The dimension of visual sensation that is dependent on the intensity of light reflected from a surface and that corresponds to the amplitude (height) of the light wave.

Broca's aphasia (BRO-kuz uh-FAY-zyah) An impairment in the physical ability to produce speech sounds or, in extreme cases, an inability to speak at all; caused by damage to Broca's area.

Broca's area (BRO-kuz) The area in the frontal lobe, usually in the left hemisphere, that controls the production of speech sounds.

bulimia nervosa An eating disorder characterized by repeated and uncontrolled (and often secretive) episodes of binge eating.

bystander effect A social factor that affects prosocial behavior: As the number of bystanders at an emergency increases, the probability that the victim will receive help decreases, and the help, if given, is likely to be delayed.

California Personality Inventory (CPI) A highly regarded personality test developed especially for normal individuals aged 13 and older.

Cannon-Bard theory The theory that an emotion-provoking stimulus is transmitted simultaneously to the cerebral cortex, providing the conscious mental experience of the emotion, and to the sympathetic nervous system, causing the physiological arousal.

case study A descriptive research method in which a single individual or a small number of persons are studied in great depth.

catatonic schizophrenia (KAT-uh-TAHN-ik) A type of schizophrenia characterized by complete stillness or stupor or great excitement and agitation; patients may assume an unusual posture and remain in it for long periods of time.

cell body The part of a neuron that contains the nucleus and carries out the metabolic functions of the neuron.

central nervous system (CNS) The part of the nervous system comprising the brain and the spinal cord.

cerebellum (sehr-uh-BELL-um) The brain structure that helps the body execute smooth, skilled movements and regulates muscle tone and posture.

cerebral cortex (seh-REE-brul KOR-tex) The gray, convoluted covering of the cerebral hemispheres that is responsible for the higher mental processes of language, memory, and thinking.

cerebral hemispheres (seh-REE-brul) The right and left halves of the cerebrum, covered by the cerebral cortex and connected by the corpus callosum; they control movement and feeling on the opposing sides of the body.

cerebrum (seh-REE-brum) The largest structure of the human brain, consisting of the two cerebral hemispheres connected by the corpus callosum and covered by the cerebral cortex.

chlamydia (klah-MIH-dee-uh) A highly infectious bacterial STD that is found in both sexes and can cause infertility in females.

chromosomes Rod-shaped structures in the nuclei of body cells, which contain all the genes and carry all the genetic information necessary to make a human being.

chunking A memory strategy that involves grouping or organizing bits of information into larger units, which are easier to remember.

circadian rhythm (sur-KAY-dee-un) Within each 24-hour period, the regular fluctuation from high to low points of certain bodily functions and behaviors.

circadian theory of sleep The theory that sleep evolved to keep humans out of harm's way during the night; also known as the evolutionary theory.

classical conditioning A type of learning through which an organism learns to associate one stimulus with another.

co-action effects The impact on performance of the presence of other people engaged in the same task.

cochlea (KOK-lee-uh) The fluid-filled, snail-shaped, bony chamber in the inner ear that contains the basilar membrane and its hair cells (the sound receptors).

cognition The mental processes that are involved in acquiring, storing, retrieving, and using information and that include sensation, perception, imagery, concept formation, reasoning, decision making, problem solving, and language.

cognitive dissonance The unpleasant state that can occur when people become aware of inconsistencies between their attitudes or between their attitudes and their behavior.

cognitive map A mental representation of a spatial arrangement such as a maze.

cognitive processes (COG-nih-tiv) Mental processes such as thinking, knowing, problem solving, remembering, and forming mental representations.

cognitive psychology The school of psychology that sees humans as active participants in their environment; studies mental processes such as memory, problem solving, reasoning, decision making, perception, language, and other forms of cognition.

cognitive therapies Therapies that assume maladaptive behavior can result from irrational thoughts, beliefs, and ideas.

cognitive therapy A therapy designed by Aaron Beck to help patients stop their negative thoughts as they occur and replace them with more objective thoughts.

coitus (KOY-tus) Penile-vaginal intercourse.

collective unconscious In Jung's theory, the most inaccessible layer of the unconscious, which contains the universal experiences of humankind throughout evolution.

coitus (KOY-tus) Penile-vaginal intercourse.

color blindness The inability to distinguish certain colors from one another.

compliance Acting in accordance with the wishes, suggestions, or direct requests of other people.

compulsion A persistent, irresistible, and irrational urge to perform an act or ritual repeatedly.

concept A mental category used to represent a class or group of objects, people, organizations, events, situations, or relations that share common characteristics or attributes.

conditioned response (CR) The learned response that comes to be elicited by a conditioned stimulus as a result of its repeated pairing with an unconditioned stimulus.

conditioned stimulus (CS) A neutral stimulus that, after repeated pairing with an unconditioned stimulus, becomes associated with it and elicits a conditioned response.

conditions of worth Conditions on which the positive regard of others rests.

cones The light-sensitive receptor cells in the retina that enable humans to see color and fine detail in adequate light but do not function in very dim light.

confederate A person who poses as a participant in an experiment but is actually assisting the experimenter.

conformity Changing or adopting a behavior or an attitude in an effort to be consistent with the social norms of a group or the expectations of other people.

confounding variables Factors or conditions other than the independent variable(s) that are not equivalent across groups and could cause differences among the groups with respect to the dependent variable.

conscious (KON-shus) The thoughts, feelings, sensations, or memories of which a person is aware at any given moment.

consciousness Everything of which we are aware at any given time—our thoughts, feelings, sensations, and external environment.

conservation The concept that a given quantity of matter remains the same despite being rearranged or changed in appearance, as long as nothing is added or taken away.

consolidation A physiological change in the brain that allows encoded information to be stored in memory.

consolidation failure Any disruption in the consolidation process that prevents a long-term memory from forming.

control group In an experiment, a group similar to the experimental group that is exposed to the same experimental environment but is not given the treatment; used for purposes of comparison.

conventional level Kohlberg's second level of moral development, in which right and wrong are based on the internalized standards of others; "right" is whatever helps or is approved of by others, or whatever is consistent with the laws of society.

conversion disorder A somatoform disorder in which a person suffers a loss of motor or sensory functioning in some part of the body; the loss has no physical cause but solves some psychological problem.

coping Efforts through action and thought to deal with demands that are perceived as taxing or overwhelming.

cornea (KOR-nee-uh) The tough, transparent, protective layer that covers the front of the eye and bends light rays inward through the pupil.

corpus callosum (KOR-pus kah-LO-sum) The thick band of nerve fibers that connects the two cerebral hemispheres and makes possible the transfer of information and the synchronization of activity between the hemispheres.

correlation coefficient A numerical value that indicates the strength and direction of the relationship between two variables; ranges from +1.00 (a perfect positive correlation) to −1.00 (a perfect negative correlation).

correlational method A research method used to establish the degree of relationship (correlation) between two characteristics, events, or behaviors.

creativity The ability to produce original, appropriate, and valuable ideas and/or solutions to problems.

critical period A period so important to development that a harmful environmental influence at that time can keep a bodily structure from developing normally or can impair later intellectual or social development.

critical thinking The process of objectively evaluating claims, propositions, and conclusions to determine whether they follow logically from the evidence presented.

cross-modal perception A process whereby the brain integrates information from more than one sense.

cross-sectional study A type of developmental study in which researchers compare groups of participants of differentages on various characteristics to determine age-related differences.

crowding The subjective judgment that there are too many people in a confined space.

crystallized intelligence Aspects of intelligence, including verbal ability and accumulated knowledge, that tend to increase over the lifespan.

CT scan (computerized axial tomography) A brain-scanning technique that uses a rotating, computerized X-ray tube to produce cross-sectional images of the structures of the brain.

culturally sensitive therapy An approach to therapy in which knowledge of clients' cultural backgrounds guides the choice of therapeutic interventions.

culture-fair intelligence test An intelligence test that uses questions that will not penalize those whose culture differs from the mainstream or dominant culture.

decay theory The oldest theory of forgetting, which holds that memories, if not used, fade with time and ultimately disappear altogether.

decibel (dB) (DES-ih-bel) A unit of measurement for the loudness of sounds.

decision making The process of considering alternatives and choosing among them.

declarative memory The subsystem within long-term memory that stores facts, information, and personal life events that can be brought to mind verbally or in the form of images and then declared or stated; also called explicit memory.

defense mechanism A means used by the ego to defend against anxiety and to maintain self-esteem.

delta wave The brain-wave pattern associated with slow-wave (deep) sleep. The slowest brain-wave pattern; associated with Stage 3 and Stage 4 NREM sleep.

delusion A false belief, not generally shared by others in the culture.

delusion of grandeur A false belief that one is a famous person or a powerful or important person who has some great knowledge, ability, or authority.

delusion of persecution A false belief that some person or agency is trying in some way to harm one.

dementia A state of mental deterioration characterized by impaired memory and intellect and by altered personality and behavior.

dendrites (DEN-drytes) In a neuron, the branchlike extensions of the cell body that receive signals from other neurons.

dependent variable The factor or condition that is measured at the end of an experiment and is presumed to vary as a result of the manipulations of the independent variable(s).

depressants A category of drugs that decrease activity in the central nervous system, slow down bodily functions, and reduce sensitivity to outside stimulation; also called "downers."

depth perception The ability to perceive the visual world in three dimensions and to judge distances accurately.

descriptive research methods Research methods that yield descriptions of behavior.

developmental psychology The study of how humans grow, develop, and change throughout the lifespan.

difference threshold A measure of the smallest increase or decrease in a physical stimulus that is required to produce a difference in sensation that is noticeable 50% of the time.

diffusion of responsibility The feeling among bystanders at an emergency that the responsibility for helping is shared by the group, making each person feel less compelled to act than if he or she alone bore the total responsibility.

directive therapy Any type of psychotherapy in which the therapist takes an active role in determining the course of therapy sessions and provides answers and suggestions to the patient; an example is Gestalt therapy.

discrimination Behavior (usually negative) directed toward others based on their gender, religion, race, or membership in a particular group. The learned ability to distinguish between similar stimuli so that the conditioned response occurs only to the original conditioned stimulus but not to similar stimuli.

discriminative stimulus A stimulus that signals whether a certain response or behavior is likely to be rewarded, ignored, or punished.

disinhibitory effect Displaying a previously suppressed behavior because a model does so without receiving punishment.

disorganized schizophrenia The most serious type of schizophrenia, marked by extreme social withdrawal, hallucinations, delusions, silliness, inappropriate laughter, grotesque mannerisms, and other bizarre behavior.

displacement The event that occurs when short-term memory is filled to capacity and each new, incoming item pushes out an existing item, which is then forgotten.

display rules Cultural rules that dictate how emotions should generally be expressed and when and where their expression is appropriate.

dispositional attribution Attributing a behavior to some internal cause, such as a personal trait, motive, or attitude; an internal attribution.

dissociative amnesia A dissociative disorder in which there is a complete or partial loss of the ability to recall personal information or identify past experiences.

dissociative disorders Disorders in which, under unbearable stress, consciousness becomes dissociated from a person's identity or her or his memories of important personal events, or both.

dissociative fugue (FEWG) A dissociative disorder in which one has a complete loss of memory of one's entire identity, travels away from home, and may assume a new identity.

dissociative identity disorder (DID) A dissociative disorder in which two or more distinct, unique personalities occur in the same person, and there is severe memory disruption concerning personal information about the other personalities.

divergent thinking The ability to produce multiple ideas, answers, or solutions to a problem for which there is no agreed-on solution.

dominant-recessive pattern A set of inheritance rules in which the presence of a single dominant gene causes a trait to be expressed but two genes must be present for the expression of a recessive trait.

door-in-the-face technique A strategy in which someone makes a large, unreasonable request with the expectation that the person will refuse but will then be more likely to respond favorably to a smaller request later.

dopamine (DOE-pah-meen) A neurotransmitter that plays a role in learning, attention, movement, and reinforcement.

double-blind technique A procedure in which neither the participants nor the experimenter knows who is in the experimental and control groups until after the data have been gathered; a control for experimenter bias.

drive An internal state of tension or arousal that is brought about by an underlying need and that an organism is motivated to reduce.

drive-reduction theory A theory of motivation suggesting that biological needs create internal states of tension or arousal—called drives—which organisms are motivated to reduce.

drug tolerance A condition in which the user becomes progressively less affected by the drug and must take increasingly larger doses to maintain the same effect or high.

DSM-IV-TR *Diagnostic and Statistical Manual of Mental Disorders*, 4th edition, text revision a manual published by the American Psychiatric Association, which describes the criteria used to classify and diagnose mental disorders.

dyspareunia (dis-PAH-roo-nee-yah) A sexual pain disorder marked by genital pain associated with sexual intercourse; more common in females than in males.

ego (EE-go) In Freud's theory, the logical, rational, largely conscious system of personality, which operates according to the reality principle.

elaborative rehearsal A memory strategy that involves relating new information to something that is already known.

electroconvulsive therapy (ECT) A biological therapy in which an electric current is passed through the right hemisphere of the brain; usually reserved for severely depressed patients who are suicidal.

electroencephalogram (EEG) (ee-lek-tro-en-SEFF-uh-lo-gram) A record of brain-wave activity made by a machine called the electroencephalograph.

elicitation effect Exhibiting a behavior similar to that shown by a model in an unfamiliar situation.

elimination by aspects A decision-making approach in which alternatives are evaluated against criteria that have been ranked according to importance.

embryo The developing human organism during the period (week 3 through week 8) when the major systems, organs, and structures of the body develop.

emotion An identifiable feeling state involving physiological arousal, a cognitive appraisal of the situation or stimulus causing that internal body state, and an outward behavior expressing the state.

emotional intelligence The ability to apply knowledge about emotions to everyday life.

emotion-focused coping A response involving reappraisal of a stressor to reduce its emotional impact.

encoding The process of transforming information into a form that can be stored in memory.

encoding failure A cause of forgetting that occurs when information was never put into long-term memory.

endocrine system (EN-duh-krin) A system of ductless glands in various parts of the body that manufacture hormones and secrete them into the bloodstream, thus affecting cells in other parts of the body.

endorphins (en-DOR-fins) The body's own natural painkillers, which block pain and produce a feeling of well-being. Chemicals produced naturally by the brain that reduce pain and the stress of vigorous exercise and positively affect mood.

epinephrine (EP-ih-NEF-rin) A neurotransmitter that affects the metabolism of glucose and nutrient energy stored in muscles to be released during strenuous exercise.

episodic memory (ep-ih-SOD-ik) The type of declarative memory that records events as they have been subjectively experienced.

erectile dysfunction A sexual dysfunction in which a man experiences the repeated inability to hear or sustain an erection firm enough for coitus; also known as impotence.

estrogen (ES-truh-jen) A female sex hormone that promotes the secondary sex characteristics in females and controls the menstrual cycle.

ethnocentrism The tendency to look at situations from one's own racial or cultural perspective.

evolutionary psychology The school of psychology that studies how humans have adapted the behaviors required for survival in the face of environmental pressures over the long course of evolution.

exemplars The individual instances, or examples, of a concept that are stored in memory from personal experience.

excitement phase The first stage of the sexual response cycle, characterized by an erection in males and a swelling of the clitoris and vaginal lubrication in females.

exhaustion stage The third stage of the general adaptation syndrome, which occurs if the organism fails in its efforts to resist the stressor.

experimental group In an experiment, the group that is exposed to an independent variable.

experimental method The only research method that can be used to identify cause-effect relationships between two or more conditions or variables.

experimenter bias A phenomenon that occurs when a researcher's preconceived notions or expectations in some way influence participants' behavior and/or the researcher's interpretation of experimental results.

expert systems Computer programs designed to carry out highly specific functions within a limited domain.

exposure and response prevention A behavior therapy that exposes patients with obsessive-compulsive disorder to stimuli that trigger obsessions and compulsive rituals, while patients resist performing the compulsive rituals for progressively longer periods of time.

extinction In classical conditioning, the weakening and eventual disappearance of the conditioned response as a result of repeated presentation of the conditioned stimulus without the unconditioned stimulus. In operant conditioning, the weakening and eventual disappearance of the conditioned response as a result of the withholding of reinforcement.

extrasensory perception (ESP) Gaining information about objects, events, or another person's thoughts through some means other than the known sensory channels.

extrinsic motivation The desire to behave in a certain way to gain some external reward or to avoid some undesirable consequence.

facial-feedback hypothesis The idea that the muscular movements involved in certain facial expressions produce the corresponding emotions (for example, smiling makes one feel happy).

family therapy Therapy involving an entire family, with the goal of helping family members reach agreement on changes that will help heal the family unit, improve communication problems, and create more understanding and harmony within the group.

feature detectors Neurons in the brain that respond only to specific visual patterns (for example, to lines or angles).

fetal alcohol syndrome A condition, caused by maternal alcohol intake during pregnancy, in which the baby is born mentally retarded, with a small head and facial, organ, and behavioral abnormalities.

fetus The developing human organism during the period (week 9 until birth) when rapid growth and further development of the structures, organs, and systems of the body occur.

female orgasmic disorder A sexual dysfunction in which a woman is persistently unable to reach orgasm or delays in reaching orgasm, despite adequate sexual stimulation.

female sexual arousal disorder A sexual dysfunction in which a woman may not feel sexually aroused in response to sexual stimulation or may be unable to achieve or sustain an adequate lubrication-swelling response to sexual excitement.

fight-or-flight response A response to stress in which the sympathetic nervous system and the endocrine glands prepare the body to fight or flee.

five-factor theory A trait theory that attempts to explain personality using five broad dimensions, each of which is composed of a constellation of personality traits.

fixation Arrested development at a psychosexual stage occurring because of excessive gratification or frustration at that stage.

fixed-interval schedule A schedule in which a reinforcer is given following the first correct response after a specific period of time has elapsed.

fixed-ratio schedule A schedule in which a reinforcer is given after a fixed number of correct, nonreinforced responses.

flashbulb memory An extremely vivid memory of the conditions surrounding one's first hearing the news of a surprising, shocking, or highly emotional event.

flooding A behavior therapy based on classical conditioning and used to treat phobias by exposing clients to the feared object or event (or asking them to imagine it vividly) for an extended period, until their anxiety decreases.

fluid intelligence Aspects of intelligence involving abstract reasoning and mental flexibility, which peak in the early 20s and decline slowly as people age.

foot-in-the-door technique A strategy designed to gain a favorable response to a small request at first, with the intent of making the person more likely to agree later to a larger request.

formal concept A concept that is clearly defined by a set of rules, a formal definition, or a classification system; also known as an artificial concept.

fovea (FO-vee-uh) A small area at the center of the retina that provides the clearest and sharpest vision because it has the largest concentration of cones.

framing The way information is presented so as to emphasize either a potential gain or a potential loss as the outcome.

free association A psychoanalytic technique used to explore the unconscious by having patients reveal whatever thoughts, feelings, or images come to mind.

frequency The number of cycles completed by a sound wave in one second, determining the pitch of the sound; expressed in the unit called the hertz.

frequency theory The theory of hearing that holds that hair cell receptors vibrate the same number of times per second as the sounds that reach them.

frontal lobes The largest of the brain's lobes, which contain the motor cortex, Broca's area, and the frontal association areas.

frustration-aggression hypothesis The hypothesis that frustration produces aggression.

functional fixedness The failure to use familiar objects in novel ways to solve problems because of a tendency to view objects only in terms of their customary functions.

functional MRI (fMRI) A brain-imaging technique that reveals both brain structure and brain activity more precisely and rapidly than PET.

functionalism An early school of psychology that was concerned with how humans and animals use mental processes in adapting to their environment.

***g* factor** Spearman's term for a general intellectual ability that underlies all mental operations to some degree.

GABA Primary inhibitory neurotransmitter in the brain.

gender (JEN-der) The psychological and sociocultural definition of masculinity or femininity, based on the expected behaviors for males and females.

gender constancy The understanding that activities and clothes do not affect gender stability; acquired between ages 6 and 8.

gender identity The sense of being male or female; acquired between ages 2 and 3.

gender identity disorder Sexual disorder characterized by a problem accepting one's identity as male or female.

gender roles Cultural expectations about the behavior appropriate for each gender.

gender schema theory A theory suggesting that young children are motivated to attend to and behave in ways consistent with gender-based standards and stereotypes of their culture.

gender-sensitive therapy An approach to therapy that takes into account the effects of gender on both the therapist's and the client's behavior.

gender stability The awareness that gender is a permanent characteristic; acquired between ages 4 and 5.

general adaptation syndrome (GAS) The predictable sequence of reactions (alarm, resistance, and exhaustion stages) that organisms show in response to stressors.

generalization In classical conditioning, the tendency to make a conditioned response to a stimulus that is similar to the original conditioned stimulus. In operant conditioning, the tendency to make the learned response to a stimulus similar to that for which the response was originally reinforced.

generalized anxiety disorder An anxiety disorder in which people experience chronic, excessive worry for 6 months or more.

genes The segments of DNA that are located on the chromosomes and are the basic units for the transmission of all hereditary traits.

genital herpes An STD that is caused by the herpes simplex virus and results in painful blisters on the genitals; presently incurable, the infection usually recurs and is highly contagious during outbreaks.

genital warts Growths on the genitals that are caused by the human papillomavirus (HPV).

genitals (JEN-uh-tulz) The internal and external reproductive organs of males or females.

Gestalt (geh-SHTALT) A German word that roughly refers to the whole form, pattern, or configuration that a person perceives.

Gestalt psychology The school of psychology that emphasizes that individuals perceive objects and patterns as whole units and that the perceived whole is more than the sum of its parts.

Gestalt therapy A therapy that was originated by Fritz Perls and that emphasizes the importance of clients' fully experiencing, in the present moment, their feelings, thoughts, and actions and then taking responsibility for them.

glial cells (GLEE-ul) Specialized cells in the brain and spinal cord that support neurons, remove waste products such as dead neurons, and perform other manufacturing, nourishing, and cleanup tasks.

glutamate (GLOO-tah-mate) Primary excitatory neurotransmitter in the brain.

goal orientation theory The view that achievement motivation depends on which of four goal orientations (mastery-approach, mastery-avoidance, performance-approach, performance-avoidance) an individual adopts.

gonads The ovaries in females and the testes in males; endocrine glands that produce sex hormones.

gonorrhea (gahn-ah-REE-ah) A bacterial STD that, in males, causes a pus-like discharge from the penis and painful urination; if untreated, females can develop pelvic inflammatory disease and possibly infertility.

group therapy A form of therapy in which several clients (usually 7 to 10) meet regularly with one or more therapists to resolve personal problems.

groupthink The tendency for members of a tightly knit group to be more concerned with preserving group solidarity and uniformity than with objectively evaluating all alternatives in decision making.

gustation The sense of taste.

hair cells Sensory receptors for hearing that are attached to the basilar membrane in the cochlea.

hallucination An imaginary sensation.

hallucinogens (hal-LU-sin-o-jenz) A category of drugs that can alter and distort perceptions of time and space, alter mood, produce feelings of unreality, and cause hallucinations; also called *psychedelics*.

halo effect The tendency to assume that a person has generally positive or negative traits as a result of observing one major positive or negative trait.

hardiness A combination of three psychological qualities—commitment, control, and challenge—shared by people who can handle high levels of stress and remain healthy.

hassles Little stressors, including the irritating demands that can occur daily, that may cause more stress than major life changes do.

health psychology The subfield within psychology that is concerned with the psychological factors that contribute to health, illness, and recovery.

heritability An index of the degree to which a characteristic is estimated to be influenced by heredity.

heuristic (yur-RIS-tik) A rule of thumb that is derived from experience and used in decision making and problem solving, even though there is no guarantee of its accuracy or usefulness.

higher-order conditioning Conditioning that occurs when conditioned stimuli are linked together to form a series of signals.

hippocampal region A part of the limbic system, which includes the hippocampus itself and the underlying cortical areas, involved in the formation of semantic memories.

hippocampus (hip-po-CAM-pus) A structure in the limbic system that plays a central role in the storing of new memories, the response to new or unexpected stimuli, and navigational ability.

homeostasis The natural tendency of the body to maintain a balanced internal state in an effort to ensure physical survival.

homophobia An intense, irrational hostility toward or fear of homosexuals.

hormone A chemical substance that is manufactured and released in one part of the body and affects other parts of the body.

hue The dimension of light that refers to the specific color perceived.

human immunodeficiency virus (HIV) The virus that causes AIDS.

human papillomavirus (HPV) A virus that causes genital warts; also believed to contribute to cervical cancer.

humanistic psychology The school of psychology that focuses on the uniqueness of human beings and their capacity for choice, growth, and psychological health.

humanistic therapies Psychotherapies that assume that people have the ability and freedom to lead rational lives and make rational choices.

hypnosis A procedure through which one person, the hypnotist, uses the power of suggestion to induce changes in thoughts, feelings, sensations, perceptions, or behavior in another person, the subject.

hypoactive sexual desire disorder A sexual dysfunction marked by low or nonexistent sexual desire or interest in sexual activity.

hypochondriasis (HI-poh-kahn-DRY-uh-sis) A somatoform disorder in which persons are preoccupied with their health and fear that their physical symptoms are a sign of some serious disease, despite reassurance from doctors to the contrary.

hypothalamus (HY-po-THAL-uh-mus) A small but influential brain structure that regulates hunger, thirst, sexual behavior, internal body temperature, other body functions, and a wide variety of emotional behaviors.

hypothesis A testable prediction about the conditions under which a particular behavior or mental process may occur.

hypothetico-deductive thinking The ability to base logical reasoning on a hypothetical premise.

id The unconscious system of the personality, which contains the life and death instincts and operates on the pleasure principle; source of the libido.

illusion A false perception or a misperception of an actual stimulus in the environment.

imagery The representation in the mind of a sensory experience—visual, auditory, gustatory, motor, olfactory, or tactile.

imaginary audience A belief of adolescents that they are or will be the focus of attention in social situations and that others will be as critical or approving as they are of themselves.

inattentional blindness The phenomenon in which we shift our focus from one object to another and, in the process, fail to notice changes in objects to which we are not directly paying attention.

incentive An external stimulus that motivates behavior (for example, money or fame).

inclusion Educating students with mental retardation in regular rather than special schools by placing them in regular classes for part of the day or having special classrooms in regular schools; also called *mainstreaming*.

independent variable In an experiment, a factor or condition that is deliberately manipulated to determine whether it causes any change in another behavior or condition.

individualism/collectivism dimension A measure of a culture's emphasis on either individual achievement or social relationships.

infantile amnesia The relative inability of older children and adults to recall events from the first few years of life.

information-processing theory An approach to the study of mental structures and processes that uses the computer as a model for human thinking.

in-group A social group with a strong sense of togetherness, from which others are excluded.

inhibitory effect Suppressing a behavior because a model is punished for displaying the behavior.

inner ear The innermost portion of the ear, containing the cochlea, the vestibular sacs, and the semicircular canals.

insight The sudden realization of the relationship between elements in a problem situation, which makes the solution apparent.

insight therapies Approaches to psychotherapy based on the notion that psychological well-being depends on self-understanding.

insomnia A sleep disorder characterized by difficulty falling or staying asleep, by waking too early, or by sleep that is light, restless, or of poor quality.

intelligence An individual's ability to understand complex ideas, to adapt effectively to the environment, to learn from experience, to engage in various forms of reasoning, and to overcome obstacles through mental effort.

intelligence quotient (IQ) An index of intelligence, originally derived by dividing mental age by chronological age and then multiplying by 100, but now derived by comparing an individual's score with the scores of others of the same age.

interference A cause of forgetting that occurs because information or associations stored either before or after a given memory hinder the ability to remember it.

interpersonal therapy (IPT) A brief psychotherapy designed to help depressed people better understand and cope with problems relating to their interpersonal relationships.

intersex The condition in which a person's internal organs differ from his or her external genitalia.

intrinsic motivation The desire to behave in a certain way because it is enjoyable or satisfying in and of itself.

intuition Rapidly formed judgments based on "gut feelings" or "instincts."

inventory A paper-and-pencil test with questions about a person's thoughts, feelings, and behaviors, which measures several dimensions of personality and can be scored according to a standard procedure.

James-Lange theory The theory that emotional feelings result when an individual becomes aware of a physiological response to an emotion-provoking stimulus (for example, feeling fear because of trembling).

just noticeable difference (JND) The smallest change in sensation that a person is able to detect 50% of the time.

kinesthetic sense The sense providing information about the position of body parts in relation to each other and the movement of the entire body or its parts.

laboratory observation A descriptive research method in which behavior is studied in a laboratory setting.

language A means of communicating thoughts and feelings, using a system of socially shared but arbitrary symbols (sounds, signs, or written symbols) arranged according to rules of grammar.

latent content Freud's term for the underlying meaning of a dream.

latent learning Learning that occurs without apparent reinforcement and is not demonstrated until the organism is motivated to do so.

lateral hypothalamus (LH) The part of the hypothalamus that acts as a feeding center to incite eating.

lateralization The specialization of one of the cerebral hemispheres to handle a particular function.

law of effect One of Thorndike's laws of learning, which states that the consequence, or effect, of a response will determine whether the tendency to respond in the same way in the future will be strengthened or weakened.

Lazarus theory The theory that a cognitive appraisal is the first step in an emotional response and all other aspects of an emotion, including physiological arousal, depend on it.

learned helplessness A passive resignation to aversive conditions that is learned through repeated exposure to inescapable or unavoidable aversive events.

learning A relatively permanent change in behavior, knowledge, capability, or attitude that is acquired through experience and cannot be attributed to illness, injury, or maturation.

left hemisphere The hemisphere that controls the right side of the body, coordinates complex movements, and, in most people, handles most of the language functions.

lens The transparent disk-shaped structure behind the iris and the pupil that changes shape as it focuses on objects at varying distances.

limbic system A group of structures in the brain, including the amygdala and hippocampus, that are collectively involved in emotional expression, memory, and motivation.

linguistic relativity hypothesis The notion that the language a person speaks largely determines the nature of that person's thoughts.

lithium A drug used to treat bipolar disorder, which at proper maintenance dosage reduces both manic and depressive episodes.

locus of control Rotter's concept of a cognitive factor that explains how people account for what happens in their lives—either seeing themselves as primarily in control of their behavior and its consequences (internal locus of control) or perceiving what happens to them to be in the hands of fate, luck, or chance (external locus of control).

longitudinal study A type of developmental study in which the same group of participants is followed and measured at different ages.

long-term memory (LTM) The memory system with a virtually unlimited capacity that contains vast stores of a person's permanent or relatively permanent memories.

long-term potentiation (LTP) An increase in the efficiency of neural transmission at the synapses that lasts for hours or longer.

low-ball technique A strategy in which someone makes a very attractive initial offer to get a person to commit to an action and then makes the terms less favorable.

low-birth-weight baby A baby weighing less than 5.5 pounds.

lucid dream A dream that an individual is aware of dreaming and whose content the individual is often able to influence while the dream is in progress.

lymphocytes The white blood cells—including B cells and T cells—that are the key components of the immune system.

maintenance rehearsal Repeating information over and over again until it is no longer needed; may eventually lead to storage of information in long-term memory.

major depressive disorder A mood disorder marked by feelings of great sadness, despair, and hopelessness as well as the loss of the ability to experience pleasure.

male orgasmic disorder A sexual dysfunction in which a man experiences the absence of ejaculation, or ejaculation occurs only after strenuous effort over a prolonged period.

manic episode (MAN-ik) A period of excessive euphoria, inflated self-esteem, wild optimism, and hyperactivity, often accompanied by delusions of grandeur and by hostility if activity is blocked.

manifest content Freud's term for the content of a dream as recalled by the dreamer.

massed practice Learning in one long practice session without rest periods.

matching hypothesis The notion that people tend to have lovers or spouses who are similar to themselves in physical attractiveness and other assets.

maturation Changes that occur according to one's genetically determined biological timetable of development.

means–end analysis A heuristic strategy in which the current position is compared with the desired goal and a series of steps are formulated and taken to close the gap between them.

meditation (concentrative) A group of techniques that involve focusing attention on an object, a word, one's breathing, or one's body movements in an effort to block out all distractions, to enhance well-being, and to achieve an altered state of consciousness.

medulla (muh-DUL-uh) The part of the brainstem that controls heartbeat, blood pressure, breathing, coughing, and swallowing.

memory The process of encoding, storage, consolidation, and retrieval of information.

menarche (men-AR-kee) The onset of menstruation.

menopause The cessation of menstruation, occurring between ages 45 and 55 and signifying the end of reproductive capacity.

mental set The tendency to apply a familiar strategy to the solution of a problem without carefully considering the special requirements of that problem.

mentally retarded Subnormal intelligence reflected by an IQ below 70 and by adaptive functioning severely deficient for one's age.

mere-exposure effect The tendency to feel more positively toward a stimulus as a result of repeated exposure to it.

metabolic rate (meh-tuh-BALL-ik) The rate at which the body burns calories to produce energy.

microelectrode A small wire used to monitor the electrical activity of or stimulate activity within a single neuron.

middle ear The portion of the ear containing the ossicles, which connect the eardrum to the oval window and amplify sound waves.

Minnesota Multiphasic Personality Inventory (MMPI) The most extensively researched and widely used personality test, which is used to screen for and diagnose psychiatric problems and disorders; revised as MMPI-2.

model The individual who demonstrates a behavior or whose behavior is imitated.

modeling Another name for observational learning.

modeling effect Learning a new behavior from a model through the acquisition of new responses.

monocular depth cues (mah-NOK-yu-ler) Depth cues that can be perceived by one eye alone.

mood disorders Disorders characterized by extreme and unwarranted disturbances in emotion or mood.

morphemes The smallest units of meaning in a language.

motivated forgetting Forgetting through suppression or repression in an effort to protect oneself from material that is painful, frightening, or otherwise unpleasant.

motivation All the processes that initiate, direct, and sustain behavior.

motives Needs or desires that energize and direct behavior toward a goal.

motor cortex The strip of tissue at the rear of the frontal lobes that controls voluntary body movement and participates in learning and cognitive events.

MRI (magnetic resonance imagery) A diagnostic scanning technique that produces high-resolution images of the structures of the brain.

multifactorial inheritance A pattern of inheritance in which a trait is influenced by both genes and environmental factors.

myelin sheath (MY-uh-lin) The white, fatty coating wrapped around some axons that acts as insulation and enables impulses to travel much faster.

Myers-Briggs Type Indicator (MBTI) A personality inventory useful for measuring normal individual differences; based on Jung's theory of personality.

naive idealism A type of thought in which adolescents construct ideal solutions for problems.

naive subject A person who has agreed to participate in an experiment but is not aware that deception is being used to conceal its real purpose.

narcolepsy An incurable sleep disorder characterized by excessive daytime sleepiness and uncontrollable attacks of REM sleep.

narcotics A class of depressant drugs derived from the opium poppy that produce both pain-relieving and calming effects.

natural concept A concept acquired not from a definition but through everyday perceptions and experiences; also known as a fuzzy concept.

naturalistic observation A descriptive research method in which researchers observe and record behavior in its natural setting, without attempting to influence or control it.

nature–nurture controversy The debate over whether intelligence and other traits are primarily the result of heredity or environment.

need for achievement (*n* Ach) The need to accomplish something difficult and to perform at a high standard of excellence.

negative reinforcement The termination of an unpleasant condition after a response, which increases the probability that the response will be repeated.

neodissociation theory of hypnosis A theory proposing that hypnosis induces a split, or dissociation, between two aspects of the control of consciousness: the planning function and the monitoring function.

neonate A newborn infant up to 1 month old.

neuron (NEW-ron) A specialized cell that conducts impulses through the nervous system and contains three major parts—a cell body, dendrites, and an axon.

neuroscience An interdisciplinary field that combines the work of psychologists, biologists, biochemists, medical researchers, and others in the study of the structure and function of the nervous system.

neurotransmitter (NEW-ro-TRANS-mit-er) A chemical substance that is released into the synaptic cleft from the axon terminal of a sending neuron, crosses a synapse, and binds to appropriate receptor sites on the dendrites or cell body of a receiving neuron, influencing the cell either to fire or not to fire.

nondeclarative memory The subsystem within long-term memory that stores motor skills, habits, and simple classically conditioned responses; also called implicit memory.

nondirective therapy Any type of psychotherapy in which the therapist allows the direction of the therapy sessions to be controlled by the client; an example is person-centered therapy.

norepinephrine (nor-EP-ih-NEF-rin) A neurotransmitter affecting eating, alertness, and sleep.

norms Standards based on the range of test scores of a large group of people who are selected to provide the bases of comparison for those who take the test later.

NREM dream A type of dream occurring during NREM sleep that is typically less frequent and memorable than REM dreams are.

NREM sleep Non–rapid eye movement sleep, which consists of four sleep stages and is characterized by slow, regular respiration and heart rate, little body movement, an absence of rapid eye movements, and blood pressure and brain activity that are at their 24-hour low points.

obesity BMI over 30.

object permanence The realization that objects continue to exist, even when they can no longer be perceived.

observational learning Learning by observing the behavior of others and the consequences of that behavior; learning by imitation.

obsession A persistent, involuntary thought, image, or impulse that invades consciousness and causes great distress.

obsessive-compulsive disorder (OCD) An anxiety disorder in which a person suffers from recurrent obsessions and/or compulsions.

occipital lobes (ahk-SIP-uh-tul) The lobes that are involved in the reception and interpretation of visual information; they contain the primary visual cortex.

Oedipus complex (ED-uh-pus) Occurring in the phallic stage, a conflict in which the child is sexually attracted to the opposite-sex parent and feels hostility toward the same-sex parent.

olfaction (ol-FAK-shun) The sense of smell.

olfactory bulbs Two matchstick-sized structures above the nasal cavities, where smell sensations first register in the brain.

olfactory epithelium Two 1-square-inch patches of tissue, one at the top of each nasal cavity, which together contain about 10 million olfactory neurons, the receptors for smell.

operant A voluntary behavior that accidentally brings about a consequence.

operant conditioning A type of learning in which the consequences of behavior are manipulated so as to increase or decrease the frequency of an existing response or to shape an entirely new response.

opponent-process theory The theory of color vision suggesting that three kinds of cells respond by increasing or decreasing their rate of firing when different colors are present.

optic nerve The nerve that carries visual information from each retina to both sides of the brain.

orgasm The third stage of the sexual response cycle, marked by a sudden discharge of accumulated sexual tension and involuntary muscle contractions.

outer ear The visible part of the ear, consisting of the pinna and the auditory canal.

out-group A social group made up of individuals specifically identified by the in-group as not belonging.

overextension The act of using a word, on the basis of some shared feature, to apply to a broader range of objects than is appropriate.

overlearning Practicing or studying material beyond the point where it can be repeated once without error.

overregularization The act of inappropriately applying the grammatical rules for forming plurals and past tenses to irregular nouns and verbs.

pancreas The endocrine gland responsible for regulating the amount of sugar in the bloodstream.

panic attack An episode of overwhelming anxiety, fear, or terror.

panic disorder An anxiety disorder in which a person experiences recurring, unpredictable episodes of overwhelming anxiety, fear, or terror.

paranoid schizophrenia (PAIR-uh-noid) A type of schizophrenia characterized by delusions of grandeur or persecution.

paraphilias Sexual disorders in which recurrent sexual urges, fantasies, or behavior involve nonhuman objects, children, other nonconsenting persons, or the suffering or humiliation of the individual or his or her partner.

parasomnias Sleep disturbances in which behaviors and physiological states that normally take place only in the waking state occur while a person is sleeping.

parasympathetic nervous system The division of the autonomic nervous system that brings the heightened bodily responses back to normal following an emergency.

parathyroid glands The endocrine glands that produce PTH, a hormone that helps the body absorb minerals from the diet.

parental investment A term used by evolutionary psychologists to denote the amount of time and effort men or women must devote to parenthood.

parietal lobes (puh-RY-uh-tul) The lobes that contain the somatosensory cortex (where touch, pressure, temperature, and pain register) and other areas that are responsible for body awareness and spatial orientation.

participant modeling A behavior therapy in which an appropriate response to a feared stimulus is modeled in graduated steps and the client attempts to imitate the model step by step, encouraged and supported by the therapist.

pelvic inflammatory disease (PID) An infection in the female pelvic organs, which can result from untreated chlamydia or gonorrhea and can cause pain, scarring of tissue, and even infertility or an ectopic pregnancy.

perception The process by which the brain actively organizes and interprets sensory information.

perceptual constancy The phenomenon that allows us to perceive objects as maintaining stable properties, such as size, shape, and brightness, despite differences in distance, viewing angle, and lighting.

perceptual set An expectation of what will be perceived, which can affect what actually is perceived.

peripheral nervous system (PNS) (peh-RIF-er-ul) The nerves connecting the central nervous system to the rest of the body.

permeability (perm-ee-uh-BIL-uh-tee) The capability of being penetrated or passed through.

permissive parents Parents who make few rules or demands and allow children to make their own decisions and control their own behavior.

personal fable An exaggerated sense of personal uniqueness and indestructibility, which may be the basis for adolescent risk taking.

personal space An area surrounding each person, much like an invisible bubble, that the person considers part of himself or herself and uses to regulate the level of intimacy with others.

personal unconscious In Jung's theory, the layer of the unconscious that contains all of the thoughts, perceptions, and experiences accessible to the conscious, as well as repressed memories, wishes, and impulses.

personality A person's characteristic patterns of behaving, thinking, and feeling.

personality disorder A long-standing, inflexible, maladaptive pattern of behaving and relating to others, which usually begins in early childhood or adolescence.

person-centered therapy A nondirective, humanistic therapy developed by Carl Rogers, in which the therapist creates an accepting climate and shows empathy, freeing clients to be themselves and releasing their natural tendency toward self-actualization.

persuasion A deliberate attempt to influence the attitudes and/or behavior of another person.

PET scan (positron-emission tomography) A brain-imaging technique that reveals activity in various parts of the brain, based on patterns of blood flow, oxygen use, and glucose consumption.

phobia (FO-bee-ah) A persistent, irrational fear of some specific object, situation, or activity that poses little or no real danger.

phonemes The smallest units of sound in a spoken language.

physical drug dependence A compulsive pattern of drug use in which the user develops a drug tolerance coupled with unpleasant withdrawal symptoms when the drug use is discontinued.

pineal gland The endocrine gland that secretes the hormone that controls the sleep/wakefulness cycle.

pituitary gland The endocrine gland located in the brain that releases hormones that activate other endocrine glands as well as growth hormone; often called the "master gland."

place theory The theory of hearing that holds that each individual pitch a person hears is determined by the particular location along the basilar membrane of the cochlea that vibrates the most.

placebo (pluh-SEE-bo) An inert or harmless substance given to the control group in an experiment as a control for the placebo effect.

placebo effect The phenomenon that occurs in an experiment when a participant's response to a treatment is due to his or her expectations about the treatment rather than to the treatment itself.

plasticity The capacity of the brain to adapt to changes such as brain damage.

plateau phase The second stage of the sexual response cycle, during which muscle tension and blood flow to the genitals increase in preparation for orgasm.

population The entire group of interest to researchers, to which they wish to generalize their findings; the group from which a sample is selected.

positive reinforcement Any pleasant or desirable consequence that follows a response and increases the probability that the response will be repeated.

postconventional level Kohlberg's highest level of moral development, in which moral reasoning involves weighing moral alternatives; "right" is whatever furthers basic human rights.

posttraumatic stress disorder (PTSD) A prolonged and severe stress reaction to a catastrophic event or to severe, chronic stress.

pragmatics The patterns of intonation and social roles associated with a language.

preconscious The thoughts, feelings, and memories that a person is not consciously aware of at the moment but that may be easily brought to consciousness.

preconventional level Kohlberg's lowest level of moral development, in which moral reasoning is based on the physical consequences of an act; "right" is whatever avoids punishment or gains a reward.

prejudice Attitudes (usually negative) toward others based on their gender, religion, race, or membership in a particular group.

premature ejaculation A chronic or recurring orgasmic disorder in which orgasm and ejaculation occur with little stimulation, before, during, or shortly after penetration and before the man wishes; the most common sexual dysfunction in males.

prenatal development Development from conception to birth.

presbyopia (prez-bee-O-pee-uh) A condition, occurring in the mid- to late 40s, in which the lenses of the eyes no longer accommodate adequately for near vision, and reading glasses or bifocals are required for reading.

preterm infant An infant born before the 37th week and weighing less than 5.5 pounds; a premature infant.

primacy effect The tendency for an overall impression of another to be influenced more by the first information that is received about that person than by information that comes later. The tendency to recall the first items in a sequence more readily than the middle items.

primary appraisal A cognitive evaluation of a potentially stressful event to determine whether its effect is positive, irrelevant, or negative.

primary auditory cortex The part of each temporal lobe where hearing registers in the cerebral cortex.

primary drives A state of tension or arousal that arises from a biological need and is unlearned.

primary mental abilities According to Thurstone, seven relatively distinct capabilities that singly or in combination are involved in all intellectual activities.

primary reinforcer A reinforcer that fulfills a basic physical need for survival and does not depend on learning.

primary sex characteristics The internal and external reproductive organs; the genitals.

primary visual cortex The area at the rear of the occipital lobes where vision registers in the cerebral cortex. The part of the brain in which visual information is processed.

problem solving Thoughts and actions required to achieve a desired goal that is not readily attainable.

problem-focused coping A direct response aimed at reducing, modifying, or eliminating a source of stress.

progesterone (pro-JES-tah-rone) A female sex hormone that plays a role in the regulation of the menstrual cycle and prepares the lining of the uterus for pregnancy.

projective test A personality test in which people respond to inkblots, drawings of ambiguous human situations, or incomplete sentences by projecting their inner thoughts, feelings, fears, or conflicts onto the test materials.

prosocial behavior Behavior that benefits others, such as helping, cooperation, and sympathy.

prospective forgetting Not remembering to carry out some intended action.

prototype An example that embodies the most common and typical features of a concept.

proximity Physical or geographic closeness; a major influence on attraction.

pruning The process through which the developing brain eliminates unnecessary or redundant synapses.

psychiatrist A mental health professional who is a medical doctor.

psychoactive drug Any substance that alters mood, perception, or thought; called a controlled substance if approved for medical use.

psychoanalysis (SY-ko-ah-NAL-ih-sis) The term Freud used for both his theory of personality and his therapy for the treatment of psychological disorders; the unconscious is the primary focus of psychoanalytic theory. The first psychodynamic therapy, which was developed by Freud and uses free association, dream analysis, and transference.

psychodynamic therapies Psychotherapies that attempt to uncover repressed childhood experiences that are thought to explain a patient's current difficulties.

psycholinguistics The study of how language is acquired, produced, and used and how the sounds and symbols of language are translated into meaning.

psychological disorders Mental processes and/or behavior patterns that cause emotional distress and/or substantial impairment in functioning.

psychological drug dependence A craving or irresistible urge for a drug's pleasurable effects.

psychological perspectives General points of view used for explaining people's behavior and thinking, whether normal or abnormal.

psychologist A mental health professional who possesses a doctoral degree in psychology.

psychology The scientific study of behavior and mental processes.

psychoneuroimmunology (sye-ko-NEW-ro-IM-you-NOLL-oh-gee) A field in which psychologists, biologists, and medical researchers combine their expertise to study the effects of psychological factors on the immune system.

psychosexual stages A series of stages through which the sexual instinct develops; each stage is defined by an erogenous zone around which conflict arises.

psychosis (sy-CO-sis) A condition characterized by loss of contact with reality.

psychosocial stages Erikson's eight developmental stages for the entire lifespan; each is defined by a conflict that must be resolved satisfactorily for healthy personality development to occur.

psychosurgery Brain surgery performed to alleviate serious psychological disorders or unbearable chronic pain.

psychotherapy Any type of approach that uses psychological rather than biological means to treat psychological disorders.

puberty A period of rapid physical growth and change that culminates in sexual maturity.

punishment The removal of a pleasant stimulus or the application of an unpleasant stimulus, thereby lowering the probability of a response.

random assignment The process of selecting participants for experimental and control groups by using a chance procedure to guarantee that each participant has an equal probability of being assigned to any of the groups; a control for selection bias.

rational emotive therapy A directive form of psychotherapy, developed by Albert Ellis and designed to challenge clients' irrational beliefs about themselves and others.

realistic conflict theory The view that as competition increases among social groups for scarce resources, so do prejudice, discrimination, and hatred.

recall A memory task in which a person must produce required information by searching memory.

recency effect The tendency to recall the last items in a sequence more readily than those in the middle.

receptors Protein molecules on the surfaces of dendrites and cell bodies that have distinctive shapes and will interact only with specific neurotransmitters.

reciprocal determinism Bandura's concept of a mutual influential relationship among behavior, cognitive factors, and environment.

recognition A memory task in which a person must simply identify material as familiar or as having been encountered before.

recognition heuristic A strategy in which decision making stops as soon as a factor that moves one toward a decision has been recognized.

reconstruction An account of an event that has been pieced together from a few highlights, using information that may or may not be accurate.

reflexes Built-in responses to certain stimuli that neonates need to ensure survival in their new world.

rehearsal The act of purposely repeating information to maintain it in short-term memory.

reinforcement Any event that follows a response and strengthens or increases the probability that the response will be repeated.

reinforcer Anything that follows a response and strengthens it or increases the probability that it will occur.

relationship therapies Therapies that attempt to improve patients' interpersonal relationships or create new relationships to support patients' efforts to address psychological problems.

relearning method A measure of memory in which retention is expressed as the percentage of time saved when material is relearned compared with the time required to learn the material originally.

reliability The ability of a test to yield nearly the same score when the same people are tested and then retested on the same test or an alternative form of the test.

REM dream A type of dream occurring almost continuously during each REM period and having a storylike quality; typically more vivid, visual, and emotional than NREM dreams.

REM rebound The increased amount of REM sleep that occurs after REM deprivation; often associated with unpleasant dreams or nightmares.

REM sleep A type of sleep characterized by rapid eye movements, paralysis of large muscles, fast and irregular heart and respiration rates, increased brain-wave activity, and vivid dreams.

replication The process of repeating a study to verify research findings.

representative sample A sample that mirrors the population of interest; it includes important subgroups in the same proportions as they are found in that population.

representative heuristic A thinking strategy based on how closely a new object or situation is judged to resemble or match an existing prototype of that object or situation.

repression Completely removing unpleasant memories from one's consciousness, so that one is no longer aware that a painful event occurred.

resistance stage The second stage of the general adaptation syndrome, when there are intense physiological efforts to either resist or adapt to the stressor.

resolution phase The final stage of the sexual response cycle, during which the body returns to an unaroused state.

resting potential The slight negative electrical potential of the axon membrane of a neuron at rest, about −70 millivolts.

restorative theory of sleep The theory that the function of sleep is to restore body and mind.

reticular formation A structure in the brainstem that plays a crucial role in arousal and attention and that screens sensory messages entering the brain.

retina The layer of tissue that is located on the inner surface of the eyeball and contains the sensory receptors for vision.

retrieval The process of bringing to mind information that has been stored in memory.

retrieval cue Any stimulus or bit of information that aids in retrieving particular information from long-term memory.

retrieval failure Not remembering something one is certain of knowing.

retrograde amnesia (RET-ro-grade) A loss of memory for experiences that occurred shortly before a loss of consciousness.

reuptake The process by which neurotransmitters are taken from the synaptic cleft back into the axon terminal for later use, thus terminating their excitatory or inhibitory effect on the receiving neuron.

reversibility The realization that any change in the shape, position, or order of matter can be reversed mentally.

right hemisphere The hemisphere that controls the left side of the body and, in most people, is specialized for visual-spatial perception.

rods The light-sensitive receptor cells in the retina that look like slender cylinders and allow the eye to respond to as few as five photons of light.

Rorschach Inkblot Method (ROR-shok) A projective test composed of 10 inkblots that the test taker is asked to describe; used to assess personality, make differential diagnoses, plan and evaluate treatment, and predict behavior.

sample A part of a population that is studied to reach conclusions about the entire population.

saturation The purity of a color, or the degree to which the light waves producing it are of the same wavelength.

scaffolding A type of instruction in which an adult adjusts the amount of guidance provided to match a child's present level of ability.

scapegoating Displacing aggression onto members of minority groups or other innocent targets not responsible for the frustrating situation.

Schachter-Singer theory A two-factor theory stating that for an emotion to occur, there must be (1) physiological arousal and (2) a cognitive interpretation or explanation of the arousal, allowing it to be labeled as a specific emotion.

schedule of reinforcement A systematic process for administering reinforcement.

schemas The integrated frameworks of knowledge and assumptions a person has about people, objects, and events, which affect how the person encodes and recalls information.

scheme Piaget's term for a cognitive structure or concept used to identify and interpret information.

schizophrenia (SKIT-soh-FREE-nee-ah) A severe psychological disorder characterized by loss of contact with reality, hallucinations, delusions, inappropriate or flat affect, some disturbance in thinking, social withdrawal, and/or other bizarre behavior.

scientific method The orderly, systematic procedures that researchers follow as they identify a research problem, design a study to investigate the problem, collect and analyze data, draw conclusions, and communicate their findings.

secondary appraisal A cognitive evaluation of available resources and options prior to deciding how to deal with a stressor.

secondary reinforcer A reinforcer that is acquired or learned through association with other reinforcers.

secondary sex characteristics Those physical characteristics that are not directly involved in reproduction but distinguish the mature male from the mature female.

selection bias The assignment of participants to experimental or control groups in such a way that systematic differences among the groups are present at the beginning of the experiment.

self-actualization Developing to one's fullest potential.

self-efficacy The perception a person has of his or her ability to perform competently whatever is attempted.

self-serving bias The tendency to attribute one's successes to dispositional causes and one's failures to situational causes.

semantic memory The type of declarative memory that stores general knowledge, or objective facts and information.

semantics The meaning or the study of meaning derived from morphemes, words, and sentences.

semicircular canals Three fluid-filled tubular canals in the inner ear that sense the rotation of the head.

sensation The process through which the senses pick up visual, auditory, and other sensory stimuli and transmit them to the brain.

sensory adaptation The process in which sensory receptors grow accustomed to constant, unchanging levels of stimuli over time.

sensory memory The memory system that holds information from the senses for a period of time ranging from only a fraction of a second to about 2 seconds.

sensory receptors Highly specialized cells in the sense organs that detect and respond to one type of sensory stimulus light, sound, or odor, for example—and transduce (convert) the stimuli into neural impulses.

separation anxiety The fear and distress shown by a toddler when the parent leaves, occurring from 8 to 24 months and reaching a peak between 12 and 18 months.

serial position effect The finding that, for information learned in a sequence, recall is better for the beginning and ending items than for the middle items in the sequence.

serotonin (ser-oh-TOE-nin) A neurotransmitter that plays an important role in regulating mood, sleep, impulsivity, aggression, and appetite.

set point The weight the body normally maintains when one is trying neither to gain nor to lose weight.

sex assignment The decision to bring up a child with ambiguous genitalia as either male or female.

sex chromosomes The pair of chromosomes that determines the biological sex of a person (XX in females and XY in males).

sexual aversion disorder A sexual dysfunction characterized by an aversion to and active avoidance of genital contact with a sexual partner.

sexual disorders Disorders with a sexual basis that are destructive, guilt- or anxiety-producing, compulsive, or a cause of discomfort or harm to one or both parties involved.

sexual dysfunction A persistent or recurrent problem that causes marked distress and interpersonal difficulty and that may involve some combination of the following: sexual desire, sexual arousal or the pleasure associated with sex, or orgasm.

sexual orientation The direction of one's sexual preference—toward members of the opposite sex (heterosexuality), toward one's own sex (homosexuality), or toward both sexes (bisexuality).

sexual response cycle The four phases—excitement, plateau, orgasm, and resolution—that make up the human sexual response in both males and females, according to Masters and Johnson.

sexually transmitted diseases Infections that are spread primarily through intimate sexual contact.

shaping An operant conditioning technique that consists of gradually molding a desired behavior (response) by reinforcing any movement in the direction of the desired response, thereby gradually guiding the responses toward the ultimate goal.

short-term memory (STM) The memory system that codes information according to sound and holds about seven (from five to nine) items for less than 30 seconds without rehearsal; also called working memory.

situational attribution Attributing a behavior to some external cause or factor operating within the situation; an external attribution.

Skinner box A soundproof chamber with a device for delivering food to an animal subject; used in operant conditioning experiments.

sleep apnea A sleep disorder characterized by periods during sleep when breathing stops and the individual must awaken briefly to breathe.

sleep cycle A period of sleep lasting about 90 minutes and including one or more stages of NREM sleep, followed by REM sleep.

sleep spindles Sleep Stage 2 brain waves that feature short periods of calm interrupted by brief flashes of intense activity.

slow-wave sleep Deep sleep; associated with Stage 3 and Stage 4 sleep.

social cognition The mental processes that people use to notice, interpret, and remember information about the social world.

social facilitation Any positive or negative effect on performance that can be attributed to the presence of others, either as an audience or as co-actors.

social loafing The tendency to put forth less effort when working with others on a common task than when working alone.

social norms The attitudes and standards of behavior expected of members of a particular group.

social phobia An irrational fear and avoidance of any social or performance situation in which one might embarrass or humiliate oneself in front of others by appearing clumsy, foolish, or incompetent.

social psychology The subfield that attempts to explain how the actual, imagined, or implied presence of others influences the thoughts, feelings, and behavior of individuals.

Social Readjustment Rating Scale (SRRS) Holmes and Rahe's measure of stress, which ranks 43 life events from most to least stressful and assigns a point value to each.

social roles Socially defined behaviors considered appropriate for individuals occupying certain positions within a given group.

social support Tangible and/or emotional support provided in time of need by family members, friends, and others; the feeling of being loved, valued, and cared for by those toward whom we feel a similar obligation.

socialization The process of learning socially acceptable behaviors, attitudes, and values.

sociocognitive theory of hypnosis A theory suggesting that the behavior of a hypnotized person is a function of that person's expectations about how subjects behave under hypnosis.

sociocultural approach The view that social and cultural factors may be just as powerful as evolutionary and physiological factors in affecting behavior and mental processing and that these factors must be understood when interpreting the behavior of others.

somatoform disorders (so-MAT-uh-form) Disorders in which physical symptoms are present that are due to psychological causes rather than any known medical condition.

somatosensory cortex (so-MAT-oh-SENS-or-ee) The strip of tissue at the front of the parietal lobes where touch, pressure, temperature, and pain register in the cerebral cortex.

spaced practice Learning in short practice sessions with rest periods in between.

specific phobia A marked fear of a specific object or situation; a general label for any phobia other than agoraphobia and social phobia.

spinal cord An extension of the brain, from the base of the brain through the neck and spinal column, that transmits messages between the brain and the peripheral nervous system.

split-brain operation A surgical procedure, performed to treat severe cases of epilepsy, in which the corpus callosum is cut, separating the cerebral hemispheres.

spontaneous recovery The reappearance of an extinguished response (in a weaker form) when an organism is exposed to the original conditioned stimulus following a rest period.

SQ3R method A study method involving the following five steps: (1) survey, (2) question, (3) read, (4) recite, and (5) review.

Stage 4 sleep The deepest stage of NREM sleep, characterized by an EEG pattern of more than 50% delta waves.

standardization Establishing norms for comparing the scores of people who will take a test in the future; administering tests using a prescribed procedure.

state-dependent memory effect The tendency to recall information better if one is in the same pharmacological or psychological state as when the information was encoded.

stereotypes Widely shared beliefs about the characteristic traits, attitudes, and behaviors of members of various social groups (racial, ethnic, or religious), including the assumption that the members of such groups are usually all alike.

stimulants A category of drugs that speed up activity in the central nervous system, suppress appetite, and can cause a person to feel more awake, alert, and energetic; also called "uppers."

stimulus (STIM-yu-lus) Any event or object in the environment to which an organism responds; plural is *stimuli.*

stimulus motives Motives that cause humans and other animals to increase stimulation when the level of arousal is too low (examples are curiosity and the motive to explore).

storage The process of keeping or maintaining information in memory.

stranger anxiety A fear of strangers common in infants at about 6 months and increasing in intensity until about 12 months, and then declining in the second year.

stress The physiological and psychological response to a condition that threatens or challenges a person and requires some form of adaptation or adjustment.

stressor Any stimulus or event capable of producing physical or emotional stress.

stroke The most common cause of damage to adult brains, arising when blockage of an artery cuts off the blood supply to a particular area of the brain or when a blood vessel bursts.

structuralism The first formal school of thought in psychology, aimed at analyzing the basic elements, or structure, of conscious mental experience.

subjective night The time during a 24-hour period when the biological clock is telling a person to go to sleep.

subliminal perception The capacity to perceive and respond to stimuli that are presented below the threshold of awareness.

substance abuse Continued use of a substance after several episodes in which use of the substance has negatively affected an individual's work, education, and social relationships.

substantia nigra (sub-STAN-sha NI-gra) The structure in the midbrain that controls unconscious motor movements.

successful aging Maintaining one's physical health, mental abilities, social competence, and overall satisfaction with life as one gets older.

successive approximations A series of gradual steps, each of which is more similar to the final desired response.

superego (sue-per-EE-go) The moral system of the personality, which consists of the conscience and the ego ideal.

suprachiasmatic nucleus (SCN) A pair of tiny structures in the brain's hypothalamus that control the timing of circadian rhythms; the biological clock.

survey A descriptive research method in which researchers use interviews and/or questionnaires to gather information about the attitudes, beliefs, experiences, or behaviors of a group of people.

symbolic function The understanding that one thing—an object, a word, a drawing—can stand for another.

sympathetic nervous system The division of the autonomic nervous system that mobilizes the body's resources during stress and emergencies, preparing the body for action.

synapse (SIN-aps) The junction where the axon terminal of a sending neuron communicates with a receiving neuron across the synaptic cleft.

synesthesia The capacity for responding to stimuli simultaneously with normal and unusual perceptions.

syntax The aspect of grammar that specifies the rules for arranging and combining words to form phrases and sentences.

syphilis A bacterial STD that progresses through three predictable stages; if untreated, it can eventually be fatal.

systematic desensitization A behavior therapy that is based on classical conditioning and used to treat fears by training clients in deep muscle relaxation and then having them confront a graduated series of anxiety-producing situations (real or imagined) until they can remain relaxed while confronting even the most feared situation.

tactile Pertaining to the sense of touch.

taste aversion The intense dislike and/or avoidance of a particular food that has been associated with nausea or discomfort.

taste buds Structures in many of the tongue's papillae that are composed of 60 to 100 receptor cells for taste.

telegraphic speech Short sentences that follow a strict word order and contain only essential content words.

temperament A person's behavioral style or characteristic way of responding to the environment.

temporal lobes The lobes that are involved in the reception and interpretation of auditory information; they contain the primary auditory cortex, Wernicke's area, and the temporal association areas.

teratogens Harmful agents in the prenatal environment, which can have a negative impact on prenatal development or even cause birth defects.

testosterone (tes-TOS-tah-rone) The most important androgen, which influences the development and maintenance of male sex characteristics and sexual motivation and, in small amounts, maintains sexual interest and responsiveness in females.

thalamus (THAL-uh-mus) The structure, located above the brainstem, that acts as a relay station for information flowing into or out of the forebrain.

Thematic Apperception Test (TAT) A projective test consisting of drawings of ambiguous human situations, which the test taker describes; thought to reveal inner feelings, conflicts, and motives, which are projected onto the test materials.

theory A general principle or set of principles proposed to explain how a number of separate facts are related.

theory of dissociated control The theory that hypnosis is an authentic altered state of consciousness in which the control the executive function exerts over other subsystems of consciousness is weakened.

thymus gland The endocrine gland that produces hormones that are essential to immune system functioning.

timbre (TAM-burr) The distinctive quality of a sound that distinguishes it from other sounds of the same pitch and loudness.

time out A behavior modification technique used to eliminate undesirable behavior, especially in children and adolescents, by withdrawing all reinforcers for a period of time.

token economy A behavior modification technique that motivates and rewards appropriate behavior with tokens that can be exchanged later for desired goods or privileges.

top-down processing Information processing in which previous experience and conceptual knowledge are applied to recognize the whole of a perception and thus easily identify the simpler elements of that whole.

trait A personal characteristic that is stable across situations and is used to describe or explain personality.

transduction The process through which sensory receptors convert the sensory stimulation into neural impulses.

transference An emotional reaction that occurs during psychoanalysis, in which the patient displays feelings and attitudes toward the analyst that were present in another significant relationship.

transgendered The condition in which an individual's biological sex and psychological gender do not match.

transsexual An individual who lives as the opposite gender on a fulltime basis.

triarchic theory of intelligence Sternberg's theory that there are three types of intelligence: componential (analytical), experiential (creative), and contextual (practical).

trichromatic theory The theory of color vision suggesting that three types of cones in the retina each make a maximal chemical response to one of three colors—blue, green, or red.

true hermaphrodite An individual who has both ovarian and testicular tissue.

Type A behavior pattern A behavior pattern marked by a sense of time urgency, impatience, excessive competitiveness, hostility, and anger; considered a risk factor in coronary heart disease.

Type B behavior pattern A behavior pattern marked by a relaxed, easygoing approach to life, without the time urgency, impatience, and hostility of the Type A pattern.

unconditional positive regard Unqualified caring and nonjudgmental acceptance of another.

unconditioned response (UR) A response that is elicited by an unconditioned stimulus without prior learning.

unconditioned stimulus (US) A stimulus that elicits a specific unconditioned response without prior learning.

unconscious (un-KON-shus) For Freud, the primary motivating force of human behavior, containing repressed memories as well as instincts, wishes, and desires that have never been conscious.

underextension Restricting the use of a word to only a few, rather than to all, members of a class of objects.

undifferentiated schizophrenia A catchall term used when schizophrenic symptoms either do not conform to the criteria of any one type of schizophrenia or conform to more than one type.

uplifts The positive experiences in life, which may neutralize the effects of many hassles.

vaginismus (VAJ-ah-NIZ-mus) A sexual pain disorder in which involuntary muscle contractions tighten and even close the vagina, making intercourse painful or impossible.

validity The ability of a test to measure what it is intended to measure.

variable Any condition or factor that can be manipulated, controlled, or measured.

variable-interval schedule A schedule in which a reinforcer is given after the first correct response that follows a varying time of nonreinforcement, based on an average time.

variable-ratio schedule A schedule in which a reinforcer is given after a varying number of nonreinforced responses, based on an average ratio.

ventromedial hypothalamus (VMH) The part of the hypothalamus that acts as a satiety (fullness) center to inhibit eating.

vestibular sense (ves-TIB-yu-ler) The sense that detects movement and provides information about the body's orientation in space.

viral STDs Sexually transmitted diseases that are caused by viruses and are considered to be incurable.

visible spectrum The narrow band of electromagnetic waves that are visible to the human eye.

visual cliff An apparatus used to test depth perception in infants and young animals.

wavelength A measure of the distance from the peak of a light wave to the peak of the next.

Weber's law The law stating that the just noticeable difference (JND) for all the senses depends on a proportion or percentage of change in a stimulus rather than on a fixed amount of change.

Wernicke's aphasia (VUR-nih-keys) Aphasia that results from damage to Wernicke's area and in which the person's speech is fluent and clearly articulated but does not make sense to listeners.

Wernicke's area The language area in the left temporal lobe involved in comprehending the spoken word and in formulating coherent speech and written language.

withdrawal symptoms The physical and psychological symptoms (usually the exact opposite of the effects produced by the drug) that occur when a regularly used drug is discontinued and that terminate when the drug is taken again.

working backward A heuristic strategy in which a person discovers the steps needed to solve a problem by defining the desired goal and working backward to the current condition; also called *backward search*.

Yerkes-Dodson law The principle that performance on tasks is best when the arousal level is appropriate to the difficulty of the task: higher arousal for simple tasks, moderate arousal for tasks of moderate difficulty, and lower arousal for complex tasks.

zone of proximal development A range of cognitive tasks that a child cannot yet do but can learn to do through the guidance of an older child or adult.

zygote Cell that results from the union of a sperm and an ovum.

REFERENCES

Aaltola, E. (2005). The politics and ethics of animal experimentation. *International Journal of Biotechnology, 7,* 234–249.

Abraham, H., & Duffy, F. (2001). EEG coherence in post-LSD visual hallucinations. *Psychiatry Research: Neuroimaging, 107,* 151–163.

Abramowitz, J. S. (1997). Effectiveness of psychological and pharmacological treatments for obsessive-compulsive disorder: A quantitative review. *Journal of Consulting and Clinical Psychology, 65,* 44–52.

Abrams, D., Wetherell, M., Cochrane, S., Hogg, M. A., & Turner, J. C. (1990). Knowing what to think by knowing who you are: Self-categorization and the nature of norm formation, conformity and group polarization. *British Journal of Social Psychology, 29*(Pt. 2), 97–119.

Adam, M., & Reyna, V. (2005). Coherence and correspondence criteria for rationality: Experts' estimation of risks of sexually transmitted infections. *Journal of Behavioral Decision Making, 18,* 169–186.

Adams, J. H., Graham, D. I., & Jennett, B. (2000). The neuropathology of the vegetative state after an acute brain insult. *Brain, 123,* 1327–1338.

Adams, R., and Boscarino, J. (2006). Predictors of PTSD and delayed PTSD after disaster: The impact of exposure and psychosocial resources. *Journal of Nervous and Mental Disease, 194,* 485–493.

Addis, M., Hatgis, C., Krasnow, A., Jacob, K., Bourne, L., & Mansfield, A. (2004). Effectiveness of cognitive-behavioral treatment for panic disorder versus treatment as usual in a managed care setting. *Journal of Consulting & Clinical Psychology, 72,* 625–635.

Addis, M., & Mahalik, J. (2003). Men, masculinity, and the contexts of help seeking. *American Psychologist, 58,* 5–14.

Ader, R. (2000). On the development of psychoneuroimmunology. *European Journal of Pharmacology, 405,* 167–176.

Adesman, A. (1996). Fragile X syndrome. In A. Capute & P. Accardo (Eds.). *Developmental disabilities in infancy and childhood* (2nd ed., Vol. 2, pp. 255–269). Baltimore: Brookes.

Adler, A. (1927). *Understanding human nature.* New York: Greenberg.

Adler, A. (1956). In H. L. Ansbacher & R. R. Ansbacher (Eds.), *The individual psychology of Alfred Adler: A systematic presentation in selections from his writings.* New York: Harper & Row.

Adler, J. (1997, Spring/Summer). It's a wise father who knows. . . . *Newsweek* [Special Edition], 73.

Agras, W. S., Walsh, T., Fairburn, C. G., Wilson, T., & Kraemer, H. C. (2000). A multicenter comparison of cognitive-behavioral therapy and interpersonal psychotherapy for bulimia nervosa. *Archives of General Psychiatry, 57,* 459–466.

Ainsworth, M. (2000). ABCs of "internet therapy." *Metanoia* [Electronic version]. Retrieved 2000 from www.metanoia.org

Ainsworth, M. D. S. (1973). The development of infant-mother attachment. In B. Caldwell & H. Ricciuti (Eds.), *Review of child development research* (Vol. 3). Chicago: University of Chicago Press.

Ainsworth, M. D. S. (1979). Infant-mother attachment. *American Psychologist, 34,* 932–937.

Ainsworth, M. D. S., Blehar, M. C., Walters, E., & Wall, S. (1978). *Patterns of attachment.* Hillsdale, NJ: Erlbaum.

Åkerstedt, T. (1990). Psychological and psychophysiological effects of shift work. *Scandinavian Journal of Work and Environmental Health, 16,* 67–73.

Aksan, N., & Kochanska, G. (2005). Conscience in childhood: Old questions, new answers. *Developmental Psychology, 41,* 506–516.

Al'absi, M., Hugdahl, K., & Lovallo, W. (2002). Adrenocortical stress responses and altered working memory performance. *Psychophysiology, 39,* 95–99.

Albrecht, K. (1979). *Stress and the manager: Making it work for you.* Englewood Cliffs, NJ: Prentice-Hall.

Alexander, G. E., Furey, M. L., Grady, C. L., Pietrini, P., Brady, D. R., Mentis, M. J., et al. (1997). Association of premorbid intellectual function with cerebral metabolism in Alzheimer's disease: Implications for the cognitive reserve hypotheses. *American Journal of Psychiatry, 154,* 165–172.

Alleman, J. (2002). Online counseling: The Internet and mental health treatment. *Psychotherapy: Theory, Research, Practice, Training, 39,* 199–209.

Allen, B. P. (1997). *Personality theories: Development, growth, and diversity* (2nd ed.). Boston: Allyn & Bacon.

Allen, G., Buxton, R. B., Wong, E. C., & Courchesne, E. (1997). Attentional activation of the cerebellum independent of motor involvement. *Science, 275,* 1940–1943.

Allen, K. W. (1996). Chronic nailbiting: A controlled comparison of competing response and mild aversion treatments. *Behaviour Research and Therapy, 34,* 269–272.

Allison, T., Puce, A., & McCarthy, G. (2000). Social perception from visual cues: Role of the STS region. *Trends in Cognitive Sciences, 4,* 267–278.

Allport, G. W. (1954). *The nature of prejudice.* Reading, MA: Addison-Wesley.

Allport, G. W. (1961). *Pattern and growth in personality.* New York: Holt, Rinehart & Winston.

Allport, G. W., & Odbert, J. S. (1936). Trait names: A psycholexical study. *Psychological Monographs, 47*(1, Whole No. 211), 1–171.

Alsaker, F. D. (1995). Timing of puberty and reactions to pubertal changes. In M. Rutter (Ed.), *Psychosocial disturbances in young people* (pp. 37–82). New York: Cambridge University Press.

Altermatt, E., & Pomerantz, E. (2003). The development of competence-related and motivational beliefs: An investigation of similarity and influence among friends. *Journal of Educational Psychology, 95,* 111–123.

Aluja, A., & Blanch, A. (2004). Replicability of first-order 16PF-5 factors: An analysis of three parcelling methods. *Personality & Individual Differences, 37,* 667–677.

Amado, S., & Ulupinar, P. (2005). The effects of conversation on attention and peripheral detection: Is talking with a passenger and talking on the cell phone different? *Transportation Research, 8,* 383–395.

Amato, S. (1998). Human genetics and dysmorphy. In R. Behrman & R. Kliegman (Eds.), *Nelson essentials of pediatrics* (3rd ed., pp. 167–225). Philadelphia: W. B. Saunders.

American Association of Retired Persons. (2002). *Evaluating health information on the Internet: How good are your sources?* Retrieved November 1, 2002, from http://www.aarp.org/confacts/health/wwwhealth.html

American Cancer Society. (2002). *Cancer facts & figures/2002.* Retrieved November 10, 2002, from http://www.cancer.org/downloads/STT/CancerFacts&Figures2002TM

American Medical Association. (1994). *Report of the Council on Scientific Affairs: Memories of childhood abuse.* CSA Report 5-A-94.

American Psychiatric Association. (1993a). *Statement approved by the Board of Trustees, December 12, 1993.* Washington, DC: Author.

American Psychiatric Association. (1994). *Diagnostic and statistical manual of mental disorders* (4th ed.). Washington DC: Author.

American Psychiatric Association. (1997). Practice guideline for the treatment of patients with Alzheimer's disease and other dementias of late life. *American Journal of Psychiatry, 154,* 1–39.

American Psychiatric Association. (2000a). *The Diagnostic and Statistical Manual of Mental Disorders* (4th ed., Text Revision). Washington, DC: Author.

American Psychiatric Association. (2000b). *Practice guidelines for eating disorders.* Retrieved January 31, 2005, from http://www.psych.org.

American Psychological Association (APA). (1994). *Interim report of the APA Working Group on Investigation of Memories of Childhood Abuse.* Washington, DC: Author.

American Psychological Association (APA). (1995). *Psychology: Scientific problem-solvers—Careers for the 21st century.* Retrieved March 7, 2002, from http://www.apa.org/students/brochure/outlook.html#bachelors

American Psychological Association (APA). (2000). *Psychologists in the red* [Online factsheet]. Retrieved March 7, 2002, from http://www.apa.org/ppo/issues/ebsinthered.html

American Psychological Association (APA). (2002). *Ethical principles of psychologists and code of conduct. American Psychologist, 57,* 1060–1073.

American Psychological Association (APA). (2003a). *Graduate study in psychology.* Washington, DC: APA.

American Psychological Association (APA). (2003b). Guidelines on multicultural education, training, research, practice, and organizational change for psychologists. *American Psychologist, 58,* 377–402.

American Psychological Association (APA). (2006a). *Practice guidelines for treatment of patients with eating disorders* (3rd edition). Retrieved October 12, 2006, from http://psych.org/psych_pract/treatg/pg/EatingDisorders3ePG_04-28-06.pdf

American Society of Bariatric Surgeons. (2005). *Rationale for the surgical treatment of morbid obesity.* Retrieved January 25, 2007, from http://www.asbs.org/html/patients/rationale.html

Amsterdam, B. (1972). Mirror self-image reactions before age two. *Developmental Psychobiology, 5,* 297–305.

Anand, B. K., & Brobeck, J. R. (1951). Hypothalamic control of food intake in rats and cats. *Yale Journal of Biological Medicine, 24,* 123–140.

Andersen, B. L., & Cyranowski, J. M. (1995). Women's sexuality: Behaviors, responses, and individual differences. *Journal of Consulting and Clinical Psychology, 63,* 891–906.

Anderson, C., & Bushman, B. (2001). Effects of violent video games on aggressive behavior, aggressive cognition, aggressive affect, physiological arousal, and prosocial behavior: A meta-analytic review of the scientific literature. *Psychological Science, 12,* 353–359.

Anderson, C. A., & Anderson, K. B. (1996). Violent crime rate studies in philosophical context: A destructive testing approach to heat and southern culture of violence effects. *Journal of Personality and Social Psychology, 70,* 740–756.

Anderson, C. A., & Dill, K. E. (2000). Video games and aggressive thoughts, feelings, and behavior in the laboratory and in life. *Journal of Personality & Social Psychology, 78,* 772–790.

Anderson, R. (2002). Deaths: Leading causes for 2000. *National Vital Statistics Reports, 50*(16), 1–86.

Anderson, S. M., Klatzky, R. L., & Murray, J. (1990). Traits and social stereotypes: Efficiency differences in social information processing. *Journal of Personality and Social Psychology, 59,* 192–201.

Andreasen, N. C., Arndt, S., Alliger, R., Miller, D., & Flaum, M. (1995). Symptoms of schizophrenia: Methods, meanings, and mechanisms. *Archives of General Psychiatry, 52,* 341–351.

Andreasen, N. C., & Black, D. W. (1991). *Introductory textbook of psychiatry.* Washington, DC: American Psychiatric Press.

Andreasen, N. C., Flaum, M., Swayze, V., O'Leary, D. S., Alliger, R., Cohen, G., Ehrhardt, J., & Yuh, W. T. C. (1993). Intelligence and brain structure in normal individuals. *American Journal of Psychiatry, 150,* 130–134.

Andrews, G., & Erskine, A. (2003). Reducing the burden of anxiety and depressive disorders: The role of computerized clinician assistance. *Current Opinion in Psychiatry, 16,* 41–44.

Angeleri, F., Angeleri, V. A., Foschi, N., Giaquinto, S., Nolfe, G., Saginario, A., & Signorino, M. (1997). Depression after stroke: An investigation through catamnesis. *Journal of Clinical Psychiatry, 58,* 261–265.

Anglin, J. (1995, March). *Word learning and the growth of potentially knowable vocabulary.* Paper presented at the biennial meetings of the Society for Research in Child Development, Indianapolis, IN.

Anokhin, A., Vedeniapin, A., Sitevaag, E., Bauer, L., O'Connor, S., Kuperman, S., et al. (2000). The P300 brain potential is reduced in smokers. *Psychopharmacology, 149,* 409–413.

Apgar, V., & Beck, J. (1982). A perfect baby. In H. E. Fitzgerald & T. H. Carr (Eds.), *Human Development 82/83* (pp. 66–70). Guilford, CT: Dushkin.

Aram, D., & Levitt, I. (2002). Mother-child joint writing and storybook reading: Relations with literacy among low SES kindergarteners. *Merrill-Palmer Quarterly, 48,* 202–224.

Archer, J. (1991). The influence of testosterone on human aggression. *British Journal of Social Psychology, 82*(Pt. 1), 1–28.

Archer, J. (1996). Sex differences in social behavior: Are the social role and evolutionary explanations compatible? *American Psychologist, 51,* 909–917.

Arehart-Treichel, J. (2002). Researchers explore link between animal cruelty, personality disorders. *Psychiatric News, 37,* 22.

Armstrong, M., & Shikani, A. (1996). Nasal septal necrosis mimicking Wegener's granulomatosis in a cocaine abuser. *Ear Nose Throat Journal, 75,* 623–626.

Arnett, J. (2000). Emerging adulthood: A theory of development from the late teens through the twenties. *American Psychologist, 57,* 774–783.

Aronson, E. (1976). Dissonance theory: Progress and problems. In E. P. Hollander & R. C. Hunt (Eds.), *Current perspectives in social psychology* (4th ed., pp. 316–328). New York: Oxford University Press.

Aronson, E. (1988). *The social animal* (3rd ed.). San Francisco: W. H. Freeman.

Aronson, E., Stephan, W., Sikes, J., Blaney, N., & Snapp, M. (1978). *Cooperation in the classroom.* Beverly Hills, CA: Sage.

Arriaga, P., Esteyes, F., Carneiro, P., & Monteiro, M. (2006). Violent computer games and their effects on state hostility and physiological arousal. *Aggressive Behavior, 32,* 146–158.

Arushanyan, E., & Shikina, I. (2004). Effect of caffeine on light and color sensitivity of the retina in healthy subjects depending on psychophysiological features and time of day. *Human Physiology, 30,* 56–61.

Asch, S. E. (1955). Opinions and social pressure. *Scientific American, 193,* 31–35.

Assadi, S., Noroozian, M., Pakravannejad, M., Yahyazadeh, O., Aghayan, S., Shariat, S., et al. (2006). Psychiatric morbidity among sentenced prisoners: Prevalence study in Iran. *British Journal of Psychiatry, 188,* 159–164.

Assefi, S., & Garry, M. (2003). Absolute memory distortions: Alcohol placebos influence the misinformation effect. *Psychological Science, 14,* 77–80.

Astin, S. (August, 2004). After the storm: My mother taught me to turn pain into strength. *Reader's Digest.* Retrieved February 12, 2007, from http://www.rd.com/content/openContent.do? contentId=27665

Athanasselis, T., Bakamadis, S., Dologlou, I., Cowie, R., Douglas-Cowie, E., & Cox, C. (2005). ASR for emotional speech: Clarifying the issues and enhancing performance. *Neural Networks, 18,* 437–444.

Atkinson, R. C., & Shiffrin, R. M. (1968). Human memory: A proposed system and its controlled processes. In K. W. Spence & J. T. Spence (Eds.), *The psychology of learning and motivation* (Vol. 2, pp. 89–195). New York: Academic.

Augestad, L. B. (2000). Prevalence and gender differences in eating attitudes and physical activity among Norwegians. *Eating and Weight Disorders: Studies on Anorexia, Bulimia, and Obesity, 5,* 62–72.

Austenfeld, J., & Stanton, A. (2004). Coping through emotional approach: A new look at emotion, coping, and health-related outcomes. *Journal of Personality, 72,* 1335–1363.

Avraham, K. (2001). Modifying with mitochondria. *Nature Genetics, 27,* 136–137.

Axel, R. (1995, October). The molecular logic of smell. *Scientific American, 273,* 154–159.

Ayllon, T., & Azrin, N. (1965). The measurement and reinforcement of behavior of psychotics. *Journal of the Experimental Analysis of Behavior, 8,* 357–383.

Ayllon, T., & Azrin, N. (1968). *The token economy: A motivational system for therapy and rehabilitation.* New York: Appleton-Century-Crofts.

Azar, B. (2000). A web of research. *Monitor on Psychology, 31* [Online version]. Retrieved March 13, 2002, from http://www.apa.org/monitor/

Azrin, N. H., & Holz, W. C. (1966). Punishment. In W. K. Honig (Ed.), *Operant behavior: Areas of research and application* (pp. 380–447). New York: Appleton-Century-Crofts.

Babor, T. (2004). Brief treatments for cannabis dependence: Findings from a randomized multisite trial. *Journal of Consulting & Clinical Psychology, 72,* 455–466.

Bach, P., & Hayes, S. (2002). The use of acceptance and commitment therapy to prevent the rehospitalization of psychotic patients: A randomized controlled trial. *Journal of Consulting and Clinical Psychology, 70,* 1129–1139.

Baddeley, A. (1998). *Human memory: Theory and practice.* Boston, MA: Allyn & Bacon.

Baddeley, A. D. (1990). *Human memory.* Boston, MA: Allyn & Bacon.

Baddeley, A. D. (1992). Working memory. *Science, 255,* 556–559.

Baddeley, A. D. (1995) Working memory. In M. S. Gazzaniga (Ed.), *The cognitive neurosciences.* Cambridge, MA: MIT Press.

Baer, J. (1996). The effects of task-specific divergent-thinking training. *Journal of Creative Behavior, 30,* 183–187.

Baer, L., Rauch, S. L., Ballantine, T., Jr., Martuza, R., Cosgrove, R., Cassem, E., et al. (1995). Cingulotomy for intractable obsessive-compulsive disorder. *Archives of General Psychiatry, 52,* 384–392.

Bagley, C., & Tremblay, P. (1998). On the prevalence of homosexuality and bisexuality in a random community survey of 750 men aged 18 to 27. *Journal of Homosexuality, 36,* 1–18.

Bahrick, H. P., Bahrick, P. O., & Wittlinger, R. P. (1975). Fifty years of memory for names and faces: A cross-sectional approach. *Journal of Experimental Psychology: General, 104,* 54–75.

Bahrick, H. P., Hall, L. K., & Berger, S. A. (1996). Accuracy and distortion in memory for high school grades. *Psychological Science, 7,* 265–271.

Bailey, J. M., & Pillard, R. C. (1991). A genetic study of male sexual orientation. *Archives of General Psychiatry, 48,* 1089–1096.

Bailey, J. M., & Pillard, R. C. (1994). The innateness of homosexuality. Harvard Mental Health Letter, 10(7), 4–6.

Bailey, J. M., Pillard, R. C., Neale, M. C., & Agyei, Y. (1993). Heritable factors influence sexual orientation in women. *Archives of General Psychiatry, 50,* 217–223.

Baker, M., & Bendabis, S. (2005). Narcolepsy. Retrieved December 16, 2006, from http://www.emedicine.com/neuro/topic522.htm

Baldwin, J. D., & Baldwin, J. I. (1997). Gender differences in sexual interest. *Archives of Sexual Behavior, 26,* 181–210.

Ball, S. G., Baer, L., & Otto, M. W. (1996). Symptom subtypes of obsessive-compulsive disorder in behavioral treatment studies: A quantitative review. *Behaviour Research and Therapy, 34,* 47–51.

Ballenger, J. C., Pecknold, J., Rickels, K., & Sellers, E. M. (1993). Medication discontinuation in panic disorder. *Journal of Clinical Psychiatry, 54*(10, Suppl.), 15–21.

Baltes, P., & Baltes, M. (1990). Psychological perspectives on successful aging: The model of selective optimization with compensation. In P. Baltes & M. Baltes (Eds.), *Successful aging* (pp. 1–34). Cambridge, U.K.: Cambridge University Press.

Baltes, P. B., Reese, H. W., & Lipsitt, L. P. (1980). Lifespan developmental psychology. *Annual Review of Psychology, 31,* 65–110.

Baltimore, D. (2000). Our genome unveiled. *Nature, 409,* 814–816.

Bandura, A. (1969). *Principles of behavior modification.* New York: Holt, Rinehart & Winston.

Bandura, A. (1973). *Aggression: A social learning analysis.* Englewood Cliffs, NJ: Prentice-Hall.

Bandura, A. (1976). On social learning and aggression. In E. P. Hollander & R. C. Hunt (Eds.), *Current perspectives in social psychology* (4th ed., pp. 116–128). New York: Oxford University Press.

Bandura, A. (1977). *Social learning theory.* Englewood Cliffs, NJ: Prentice-Hall.

Bandura, A. (1986). *Social functions of thought and action: A social-cognitive theory.* Englewood Cliffs, NJ: Prentice-Hall.

Bandura, A. (1989). Social cognitive theory. *Annals of Child Development, 6,* 1–60.

Bandura, A. (1997a, March). Self-efficacy. *Harvard Mental Health Letter, 13*(9), 4–6.

Bandura, A. (1997b). *Self-efficacy: The exercise of control.* New York: Freeman.

Bandura, A., Adams, N. E., & Beyer, J. (1977). Cognitive processes mediating behavioral change. *Journal of Personality and Social Psychology, 35,* 125–139.

Bandura, A., Jeffery, R. W., & Gajdos, E. (1975). Generalizing change through participant modeling with self-directed mastery. *Behaviour Research and Therapy, 13,* 141–152.

Bandura, A., Ross, D., & Ross, S. A. (1961). Transmission of aggression through imitation of aggressive models. *Journal of Abnormal and Social Psychology, 63,* 575–582.

Bandura, A., Ross, D., & Ross, S. A. (1963). Imitation of film-mediated aggressive models. *Journal of Abnormal and Social Psychology, 66,* 3–11.

Barbarich, N., McConaha, C., Gaskill, J., La Via, M., Frank, G., Achenbach, S., Plotnicov, K., & Kaye, W. (2004). An open trial of olanzapine in anorexia nervosa. *Journal of Clinical Psychiatry, 65,* 1480–1482.

Bard, P. (1934). The neurohumoral basis of emotional reactions. In C. A. Murchison (Ed.), *Handbook of general experimental psychology* (pp. 264–311). Worcester, MA: Clark University Press.

Bargmann, C. (1996). From the nose to the brain. *Nature, 384,* 512–513.

Barker, L. (2006). Teaching evolutionary psychology: An interview with David M. Buss. *Teaching of Psychology, 33,* 69–76.

Barlow, D. H. (1997). Cognitive-behavioral therapy for panic disorder: Current status. *Journal of Clinical Psychiatry, 58*(6, Suppl.), 32–36.

Barrick, M., Mount, M., & Judge, T. (2001). Personality and performance at the beginning of the new millennium: What do we know and where do we go next? *International Journal of Selection and Assessment, 9,* 9–30.

Barsh, G. S., Farooqi, I. S., & O'Rahilly, S. (2000). Genetics of body-weight regulation. *Nature, 404,* 644–651.

Barsky, A. J. (1993, August). How does hypochondriasis differ from normal concerns about health? *Harvard Mental Health Letter, 10*(3), 8.

Bartlett, A. (2002). Current perspectives on the goals of psychoanalysis. *Journal of the American Psychoanalytic Association, 50,* 629–638.

Bartlett, F. C. (1932). *Remembering: A study in experimental and social psychology.* London: Cambridge University Press.

Bartoshuk, L. M., & Beauchamp, G. K. (1994). Chemical senses. *Annual Review of Psychology, 45,* 419–449.

Bartzokis, G., Sultzer, D., Lu, P., Huechterlein, K., Mintz, J., & Cummings, J. (2004). Heterogeneous age-related breakdown of white matter structural integrity: Implications for cortical "disconnection" in aging and Alzheimer's disease. *Neurobiology of Aging, 25,* 843–851.

Bassili, J. N. (1995). Response latency and the accessibility of voting intentions: What contributes to accessibility and how it affects vote choice. *Personality and Social Psychology Bulletin, 21,* 686–695.

Bateson, G. (1982). Totemic knowledge in New Guinea. In U. Neisser (Ed.), *Memory observed: Remembering in natural contexts* (pp. 269–273). San Francisco: W. H. Freeman.

Batson, C. D., Batson, J. G., Griffitt, C. A., Barrientos, S., Brandt, J. R., Sprengelmeyer, P., et al. (1989). Negative-state relief and the empathy-altruism hypothesis. *Journal of Personality and Social Psychology, 56,* 922–933.

Bauchowitz, A., Gonder-Frederick, L., Olbrisch, M., Azarbad, L., Ryee, M., Woodson, M., et al. (2005). Psychosocial evaluation of bariatric surgery candidates: A survey of present practices. *Psychosomatic Medicine, 67,* 825–832.

Baumgardner, A. H., Heppner, P. P., & Arkin, R. M. (1986). Role of causal attribution in personal problem solving. *Journal of Personality and Social Psychology, 50,* 636–643.

Baumrind, D. (1967). Child care practices anteceding three patterns of preschool behavior. *Genetic Psychology Monographs, 75,* 43–88.

Baumrind, D. (1971). Current patterns of parental authority. *Developmental Psychology Monographs, 4*(1, Pt. 2).

Baumrind, D. (1980). New directions in socialization research. *American Psychologist, 35,* 639–652.

Baumrind, D. (1991). The influence of parenting style on adolescent competence and substance use. *Journal of Early Adolescence, 11,* 56–95.

Bavelier, D., Tomann, A., Hutton, C., Mitchell, T., Corina, D., Liu, G., & Neville, H. (2000). Visual attention to the periphery is enhanced in congenitally deaf individuals. *Journal of Neuroscience, 20,* 1–6.

Bazan, S. (1998). Enhancing decision-making effectiveness in problem-solving teams. *Clinical Laboratory Management Review, 12,* 272–276.

Bean, P., Loomis, C., Timmel, P., Hallinan, P., Moore, S., Mammel, J., et al. (2004). Outcome variables for anorexic males and females one year after discharge from residential treatment. *Journal of Addictive Diseases, 23,* 83–94.

Bean, R., Perry, B., & Bedell, T. (2002). Developing culturally competent marriage and family therapists: Treatment guidelines for non-African American therapists working with African American families. *Journal of Marital & Family Therapy, 28,* 153–164.

Beare, P., Severson, S., & Brandt, P. (2004). The use of a positive procedure to increase engagement on-task and decrease challenging behavior. *Behavior Modification, 28,* 28–44.

Beck, A. T. (1976). *Cognitive therapy and the emotional disorders.* New York: New American Library.

Beck, A. T. (1991). Cognitive therapy: A 30-year retrospective. *American Psychologist, 46,* 368–375.

Beck, A. T. (1993). Cognitive therapy: Past, present, and future. *Journal of Consulting and Clinical Psychology, 61,* 194–198.

Beede, K., & Kass, S. (2006). Engrossed in conversation: The impact of cell phones on simulated driving performance. *Accident Analysis & Prevention, 38,* 415–421.

Beirut, L., Dinwiddie, S., Begleiter, H., Crowe, R., Hesselbrock, V., Nurnberger, J., et al. (1998). Familial transmission of substance dependence: Alcohol, marijuana, cocaine, and habitual smoking: A report from the collaborative study on the genetics of alcoholism. *Archives of General Psychiatry, 55,* 982–988.

Békésy, G. von. (1957). The ear. *Scientific American, 197,* 66–78.

Belcourt-Dittloff, A., & Stewart, J. (2000). Historical racism: Implications for Native Americans. *American Psychologist, 55,* 1164–1165.

Bell, A. P., Weinberg, M. S., & Hammersmith, S. K. (1981). *Sexual preference: Its development in men and women.* Bloomington: Indiana University Press.

Belsky, J., & Fearon, R. (2002). Infant-mother attachment security, contextual risk, and early development: A moderational analysis. *Development & Psychopathology, 14,* 293–310.

Bem, D., & Honorton, C. (1994). Does psi exist? Replicable evidence for an anomalous process of information transfer. *Psychological Bulletin, 115,* 4–18.

Bem, S. L. (1981). Gender schema theory: A cognitive account of sex typing. *Psychological Review, 88,* 354–364.

Benes, F. M. (2000). Emerging principles of altered neural circuitry in schizophrenia. *Brain Research Reviews, 31,* 251–269.

Benjafield, J. G. (1996). *A history of psychology.* Boston: Allyn & Bacon.

Benjamin, L., & Crouse, E. (2002). The American Psychological Association's response to Brown v. Board of Education: The case of Kenneth B. Clark. *American Psychologist, 57,* 38–50.

Benjamin, L. T. (2000). The psychology laboratory at the turn of the 20th century. *American Psychologist, 55,* 318–321.

Bennett, S. K. (1994). The American Indian: A psychological overview. In W. J. Lonner & R. Malpass (Eds.), *Psychology and culture* (pp. 35–39). Boston: Allyn & Bacon.

Bennett, W. I. (1990, November). Boom and doom. *Harvard Health Letter, 16,* 1–4.

Ben-Porath, Y. S., & Butcher, J. N. (1989). The comparability of MMPI and MMPI–2 scales and profiles. *Psychological Assessment: A Journal of Consulting and Clinical Psychology, 1,* 345–347.

Beran, M. (2004). Long-term retention of the differential values of Arabic numerals by chimpanzees (Pan troglodytes). *Animal Cognition, 7,* 86–92.

Beran, M., & Rumbaugh, D. (2001). "Constructive" enumeration by chimpanzees (Pan troglodytes) on a computerized task. *Animal Cognition, 4,* 81–89.

Berckmoes, C., & Vingerhoets, G. (2004). Neural foundations of emotional speech processing. *Current Directions in Psychological Science, 13,* 182–185.

Berenbaum, S. A., Korman, K., & Leveroni, C. (1995). Early hormones and sex differences in cognitive abilities. *Learning and Individual Differences, 7,* 303–321.

Berenbaum, S. A., & Snyder, E. (1995). Early hormonal influences on childhood sex-typed activity and playmate preferences: Implications for the development of sexual orientation. *Developmental Psychology, 31,* 31–42.

Berkowitz, L. (1983). Aversively stimulated aggression: Some parallels and differences in research with animals and humans. *American Psychologist, 38,* 1135–1144.

Berkowitz, L. (1988). Frustrations, appraisals, and aversively stimulated aggression. *Aggressive Behavior, 14,* 3–11.

Berkowitz, L. (1990). On the formation and regulation of anger and aggression: A cognitive-neoassociationistic analysis. *American Psychologist, 45,* 494–503.

Bernal, M. E., & Castro, F. G. (1994). Are clinical psychologists prepared for service and research with ethnic minorities? Report of a decade of progress. *American Psychologist, 49,* 797–805.

Bernardi, L., Sleight, P., Bandinelli, G., Cencetti, S., Fattorini, L., Wdowczyc-Szulc, J., & Lagi, A. (2001). Effect of rosary prayer and yoga mantras on autonomic cardiovascular rhythms: Comparative study. *BMJ: British Medical Journal, 323,* 1446–1449.

Bernat, E., Shevrin, H., & Snodgrass, M. (2001). Subliminal visual oddball stimuli evoke P300 component. *Clinical Neurophysiology, 112,* 159–171.

Berndt, E. R., Koran, L. M., Finkelstein, S. N., Gelenberg, A. J., Kornstein, S. G., Miller, I. M., et al. (2000). Lost human capital from early-onset chronic depression. *American Journal of Psychiatry, 157,* 940–947.

Berndt, T. J. (1992). Friendship and friends' influence in adolescence. *Current Directions in Psychological Science, 1,* 156–159.

Bernstein, I. L. (1985). Learned food aversions in the progression of cancer and its treatment. *Annals of the New York Academy of Sciences, 443,* 365–380.

Bernstein, I. L., Webster, M. M., & Bernstein, I. D. (1982). Food aversions in children receiving chemotherapy for cancer. *Cancer, 50,* 2961–2963.

Berscheid, E., Dion, K., Walster, E., & Walster, G. W. (1971). Physical attractiveness and dating choice: A test of the matching hypothesis. *Journal of Experimental Social Psychology, 7,* 173–189.

Besharat, M. (2001). Management strategies of sexual dysfunctions. *Journal of Contemporary Psychotherapy, 31,* 161–180.

Beyenburg, S., Watzka, M., Clusmann, H., Blümcke, I., Bidlingmaier, F., Stoffel-Wagner, et al. (2000). Androgen receptor mRNA expression in the human hippocampus. *Neuroscience Letters, 294,* 25–28.

Bhugra, D. (2005). The global prevalence of schizophrenia. *Public Library of Science, 5.* [Online only, no pages.] Retrieved July 18, 2006, from http://medicine.plosjournals.org/perlserv?request=getdocument&doi=10.1371/journal.pmed.0020151

Bialystok, E., Shenfield, T., & Codd, J. (2000). Languages, scripts, and the environment: Factors in developing concepts of print. *Developmental Psychology, 36,* 66–76.

Bierman, A., Fazio, & Milkie, M. (2006). A multifaceted approach to the mental health advantage of the married: Assessing how explanations vary by outcome measure and unmarried group. *Journal of Family Issues, 27,* 554–582.

Billiard, M., Pasquiré-Magnetto, V., Heckman, M., Carlander, B., Besset, A., Zachariev, Z., et al. (1994). Family studies in narcolepsy. *Sleep, 17,* S54–S59.

Biondi, M., & Picardi, A. (2003). Increased probability of remaining in remission from panic disorder with agoraphobia after drug treatment in patients who received concurrent cognitive-behavioural therapy: A follow-up study. *Psychotherapy & Psychosomatics, 72,* 34–42.

Bird, T. (2001). *Alzheimer overview* [Online brochure]. Retrieved March 25, 2002, from http://www.geneclincis.org.

Birren, J. E., & Fisher, L. M. (1995). Aging and speed of behavior: Possible consequences for psychological functioning. *Annual Review of Psychology, 46,* 329–353.

Bishop, J., & Lane, R. C. (2000). Father absence and the attitude of entitlement. *Journal of Contemporary Psychotherapy, 30,* 105–117.

Bishop, R. (2005). Cognitive psychology: Hidden assumptions. In B. Slife, J. Reber, & F. Richardson (Eds.), *Critical thinking about psychology: Hidden assumptions and plausible alternatives* (151–170). Washington, DC: American Psychological Association.

Bisiach, E. (1996). Unilateral neglect and the structure of space representation. *Current Directions in Psychological Science, 5,* 62–65.

Bjorklund, D. F., Cassel, W. S., Bjorklund, B. R., Brown, R. D., Park, C. L., Ernst, K., et al. (2000). Social demand characteristics in children's and adults' memory and suggestibility: The effect of different interviewers on free recall and recognition. *Applied Cognitive Psychology, 14,* 421–433.

Blascovich, J., Wyer, N. A., Swart, L. A., & Kibler, J. L. (1997). Racism and racial categorization. *Journal of Personality and Social Psychology, 72,* 1364–1372.

Blatt, S. J., Sanislow, C. A., III, Zuroff, D. C., & Pilkonis, P. A. (1996). Characteristics of effective therapists: Further analyses of data from the National Institute of Mental Health Treatment of Depression Collaborative Research Program. *Journal of Consulting and Clinical Psychology, 64,* 1276–1284.

Bliese, P. D., & Castro, C. A. (2000). Role clarity, work overload and organizational support: Multilevel evidence of the importance of support. *Work & Stress, 14,* 65–73.

Blinn-Pike, L., Berger, T., Hewett, J., & Oleson, J. (2004). Sexually abstinent adolescents: An 18-month follow-up. *Journal of Adolescent Research, 19,* 495–511.

Bliss, T. V., & Lomo, T. (2000). Plasticity in a monosynaptic cortical pathway. *Journal of Physiology, 207,* 61.

Bloom, B. S. (Ed.). (1985). *Developing talent in young people.* New York: Ballantine.

Bloomer, C. M. (1976). *Principles of visual perception.* New York: Van Nostrand Reinhold.

Blyth, D. A., Simmons, R. G., Bulcroft, R., Felt, D., VanCleave, E. F., & Bush, D. M. (1981). The effects of physical development on self-image and satisfaction with body-image for early adolescent males. In R. G. Simmons (Ed.), *Research in community and mental health* (Vol. 2 pp. 43–73). Greenwich, CT: JAI.

Bogen, J. E., & Vogel, P. J. (1963). Treatment of generalized seizures by cerebral commissurotomy. *Surgical Forum, 14*, 431.

Bohannon, J. N., III. (1988). Flashbulb memories for the Space Shuttle disaster: A tale of two theories. *Cognition, 29*, 179–196.

Boivin, D. B., Czeisler, C. A., Dijk, D-J., Duffy, J. F., Folkard, S., Minors, D. S., et al. (1997). Complex interaction of the sleep-wake cycle and circadian phase modulates mood in healthy subjects. *Archives of General Psychiatry, 54*, 145–152.

Bompas, A., & O'Regan, J. (2006). Evidence for a role of action in colour perception. *Perception, 35*, 65–78.

Bonanno, G. A., Keltner, D., Holen, A., & Horowitz, M. J. (1995). When avoiding unpleasant emotions might not be such a bad thing: Verbal-autonomic response dissociation and midlife conjugal bereavement. *Journal of Personality and Social Psychology, 69*, 975–989.

Bonson, K., Grant, S., Contoreggi, C., Links, J., Metcalfe, J., Weyl, H., et al. (2002). Neural systems and cue-induced cocaine craving. *Neuropsychopharmacology, 26*, 376–386.

Borbely, A. A., Achermann, P., Trachsel, L., & Tobler, I. (1989). Sleep initiation and initial sleep intensity: Interactions of homeostatic and circadian mechanisms. *Journal of Biological Rhythms, 4*, 149–160.

Bornstein, R. F. (1989). Exposure and affect: Overview and meta-analysis of research, 1968–1987. *Psychological Bulletin, 106*, 265–289.

Borzekowski, D., Fobil, J., & Asante, K. (2006). Online access by adolescents in Accra: Ghanaian teens' use of the Internet for health information. *Developmental Psychology, 42*, 450–458.

Bosse, R., Aldwin, C. M., Levenson, M. R., & Workman-Daniels, K. (1991). How stressful is retirement? *Journal of Gerontology, 46*, 9–14.

Bouchard, T. J., Jr. (1994). Genes, environment, and personality. *Science, 264*, 1700–1701.

Bouchard, T. J., Jr. (1997, September/October). Whenever the twain shall meet. *The Sciences, 37*, 52–57.

Bouchard, T. J., Jr., Lykken, D. T., McGue, M., Segal, N. L., & Tellegen, A. (1990). Sources of human psychological differences: The Minnesota study of twins reared apart. *Science, 250*, 223–228.

Bouchard, T. J., Jr., & McGue, M. (1981). Familial studies of intelligence: A review. *Science, 212*, 1055–1058.

Bouchard, T. (2004). Genetic influence on human psychological traits: A survey. *Current Directions in Psychological Science, 13*, 148–151.

Boul, L. (2003). Men's health and middle age. *Sexualities, Evolution, & Gender, 5*, 5–22.

Bourassa, M., & Vaugeois, P. (2001). Effects of marijuana use on divergent thinking. *Creativity Research Journal, 13*, 411–416.

Bowden, C., Lecrubier, Y., Bauer, M., Goodwin, G., Greil, W., Sachs, G., et al. (2000). Maintenance therapies for classic and other forms of bipolar disorder. *Journal of Affective Disorders, 59*(1), S57–S67.

Bowden, C., Myers, J., Grossman, F., & Xie, Y. (2004). Risperidone in combination with mood stabilizers: A 10-week continuation phase study in bipolar I disorder. *Journal of Clinical Psychiatry, 65*, 707–714.

Bowen-Reid, T., & Harrell, J. (2002). Racist experiences and health outcomes: An examination of spirituality as a buffer. *Journal of Black Psychology, 28*, 18–36.

Bower, G. H. (1973, October). How to . . . uh . . . remember! *Psychology Today*, 63–70.

Bower, G. H., Thompson-Schill, S., & Tulving, E. (1994). Reducing retroactive interference: An interference analysis. *Journal of Experimental Psychology: Learning, Memory, and Cognition, 20*, 51–66.

Bowers, K. S. (1992). Imagination and dissociative control in hypnotic responding. *International Journal of Clinical and Experimental Hypnosis, 40*, 253–275.

Bowers, K. S., & Farvolden, P. (1996). Revisiting a century-old Freudian slip—from suggestion disavowed to the truth repressed. *Psychological Bulletin, 119*, 355–380.

Bowers, K. S., & Woody, E. Z. (1996). Hypnotic amnesia and the paradox of intentional forgetting. *Journal of Abnormal Psychology, 105*, 381–390.

Brady, S., & Matthews, K. (2006). Effects of media violence on health-related outcomes among young men. *Archives of Pediatric Adolescent Medicine, 160*, 341–347.

Brain imaging and psychiatry—Part I. (1997, January). *Harvard Mental Health Letter, 13*(7), 1–4.

Braun, A., Balkin, T., Wesensten, N., Gwadry, F., Carson, R., Varga, M., et al. (1998). Dissociated pattern of activity in visual cortices and their projections during human rapid eye movement sleep. *Science, 279*, 91–95.

Braun, S. (1996). New experiments underscore warnings on maternal drinking. *Science, 273*, 738–739.

Brawman-Mintzer, O., & Lydiard, R. B. (1996). Generalized anxiety disorder: Issues in epidemiology. *Journal of Clinical Psychiatry, 57*(7, Suppl.), 3–8.

Brawman-Mintzer, O., & Lydiard, R. B. (1997). Biological basis of generalized anxiety disorder. *Journal of Clinical Psychiatry, 58*(3, Suppl.), 16–25.

Bray, G. A., & Tartaglia, L. A. (2000). Medicinal strategies in the treatment of obesity. *Nature, 404*, 672–677.

Brecht, M., Greenwell, L., & Anglin, M. (2007). Substance use pathways to methamphetamine use among treated users. *Addictive Behaviors, 32*, 24–38.

Breckler, S. J. (1984). Empirical validation of affect, behavior, and cognition as distinct attitude components. *Journal of Personality and Social Psychology, 47*, 1191–1205.

Brennan, P. A., Raine, A., Schulsinger, F., Kirkegaard-Sorensen, L., Knop, J., Hutchings, B., et al. (1997). Psychophysiological protective factors for male subjects at high risk for criminal behavior. *American Journal of Psychiatry, 154*, 853–855.

Brent, D. A., Bridge, J., Johnson, B. A., & Connolly, J. (1996). Suicidal behavior runs in families: A controlled family study of adolescent suicide victims. *Archives of General Psychiatry, 53*, 1145–1152.

Brent, D., Oquendo, M., Birmaher, B., Greenhill, L., Kolko, D., Stanley, B., et al. (2002). Familial pathways to early-onset suicide attempt. *Archives of General Psychiatry, 59,* 801.

Breslau, N., Davis, G. C., Peterson, E. L., & Schultz, L. (1997). Psychiatric sequelae of posttraumatic stress disorder in women. *Archives of General Psychiatry, 54,* 81–87.

Brickman, P., & Campbell, D. (1971). Hedonic relativism and planning the good society. In N. H. Appley (Ed.), *Adaptation level theory: A symposium* (pp. 287–302). New York: Academic Press.

Brieger, P., Ehrt, U., & Marneros, A. (2003). Frequency of comorbid personality disorders in bipolar and unipolar affective disorders. *Comprehensive Psychiatry, 44,* 28–34.

BBC World Service. (2007). *Figure it out: Winning the lottery—probability and coincidence.* Retrieved January 27, 2007, from http://www.bbc.co.uk/worldservice/sci_tech/features/figure_it_out/lottery.shtml

Britt, R. (2006). *Sound science: Pete Townshend blames headphones for hearing loss.* Retrieved December 13, 2006, from http://www.foxnews.com/story/0,2933.180844,00.html

Broadbent, D. E. (1958). *Perception and communication.* New York: Pergamon Press

Brody, A., Saxena, S., Fairbanks, L., Alborzian, S., Demaree, H., Maidment, K., & Baxter, L. (2000). Personality changes in adult subjects with major depressive disorder or obsessive-compulsive disorder treated with paroxetine. *Journal of Clinical Psychiatry, 61,* 349–355.

Brody, L. R. (1985). Gender differences in emotional development: A review of theories and research. *Journal of Personality, 53,* 102–149.

Brooks-Gunn, J. (2003). Do you believe in magic? What we can expect from early childhood intervention programs. *Social Policy Report, 17,* 3–14.

Brooks-Gunn, J., & Furstenberg, F. F. (1989). Adolescent sexual behavior. *American Psychologist, 44,* 249–257.

Brotman, A. W. (1994). What works in the treatment of anorexia nervosa? *Harvard Mental Health Letter, 10*(7), 8.

Broughton, W. A., & Broughton, R. J. (1994). Psychosocial impact of narcolepsy. *Sleep, 17,* S45–S49.

Brown, A. (1996, Winter). Mood disorders in children and adolescents. *NARSAD Research Newsletter,* 11–14.

Brown, A. (2004). The déjà vu illusion. *Current Directions in Psychological Science, 13,* 256–259.

Brown, G. W., Harris, T. O., & Hepworth, C. (1994). Life events and endogenous depression: A puzzle reexamined. *Archives of General Psychiatry, 51,* 525–534.

Brown, J. D., & Rogers, R. J. (1991). Self-serving attributions: The role of physiological arousal. *Personality and Social Psychology Bulletin, 17,* 501–506.

Brown, R. (1973). *A first language: The early stages.* Cambridge, MA: Harvard University Press.

Brown, R., Cazden, C., & Bellugi, U. (1968). The child's grammar from I to III. In J. P. Hill (Ed.), *Minnesota symposium on child psychology* (Vol. 2, pp. 28–73). Minneapolis: University of Minnesota Press.

Brown, R., & Kulik, J. (1977). Flashbulb memories. *Cognition, 5,* 73–99.

Brown, R., & McNeil, D. (1966). The "tip of the tongue" phenomenon. *Journal of Verbal Learning and Verbal Behavior, 5,* 325–337.

Brown, W. A. (1998, January). The placebo effect. *Scientific American, 278,* 90–95.

Bruch, M., Fallon, M., & Heimberg, R. (2003). Social phobia and difficulties in occupational adjustment. *Journal of Counseling Psychology, 50,* 109–117.

Brummett, B., Babyak, M., Williams, R., Barefoot, J., Costa, P., & Siegler, I. (2006). NEO personality domains and gender predict levels and trends in body mass index over 14 years during midlife. *Journal of Research in Personality, 40,* 222–236.

Brundage, S. (2002). *Preconception health care.* Retrieved November 30, 2006, from http://www.aafp.org/afp/20020615/2507.html

Brunetti, A., Carta, P., Cossu, G., Ganadu, M., Golosio, B., Mura, G., et al. (2002). A real-time classification system of thalassemic pathologies based on artificial neural networks. *Medical Decision Making, 22,* 18–26.

Brunila, T., Lincoln, N., Lindell, A., Tenovuo, O., & Haemelaeinen, H. (2002). Experiences of combined visual training and arm activation in the rehabilitation of unilateral visual neglect: A clinical study. *Neuropsychological Rehabilitation, 12,* 27–40.

Brydon, L., Magid, K., & Steptoe, A. (2006). Platelets, coronary heart disease, and stress. *Brain, Behavior, and Immunity, 20,* 113–119.

Buchert, R., Thomasius, R., Wilke, F., Petersen, K., Nebeling, B., Obrocki, J., Schulze, O., Schmidt, U., & Clausen, M. (2004). A voxel-based PET investigation of the long-term effects of "ecstasy" consumption on brain serotonin transporters. *American Journal of Psychiatry, 161,* 1181–1189.

Buck, L. B. (1996). Information coding in the vertebrate olfactory system. *Annual Review of Neuroscience, 19,* 517–544.

Buckingham, H. W., Jr., & Kertesz, A. (1974). A linguistic analysis of fluent aphasics. *Brain and Language, 1,* 29–42.

Buhusi, C., & Meck, W. (2002). Differential effects of methamphetamine and haloperidol on the control of an internal clock. *Behavioral Neuroscience, 116,* 291–297.

Buller, D. B., Burgoon, M., Hall, J. R., Levine, N., Taylor, A. M., Beach, B. H., et al. (2000). Using language intensity to increase the success of a family intervention to protect children from ultraviolet radiation: Predictions from language expectancy theory. *Preventive Medicine, 30,* 103–113.

Burchinal, M., Campbell, F., Bryant, D., Wasik, B., & Ramey, C. (1997). Early intervention and mediating processes in cognitive performance of children of low-income African American families. *Child Development, 68,* 935–954.

Burke, A., Heuer, F., & Reisberg, D. (1992). Remembering emotional events. *Memory and Cognition, 20,* 277–290.

Burt, D. B., Zembar, M. J., & Niederehe, G. (1995). Depression and memory impairment: A meta-analysis of the association, its pattern, and specificity. *Psychological Bulletin, 117,* 285–305.

Burton, D. (2003). Male adolescents: Sexual victimization and subsequent sexual abuse. *Child & Adolescent Social Work Journal, 20,* 277–296.

Busch, C. M., Zonderman, A. B., & Costa, P. T. (1994). Menopausal transition and psychological distress in a nationally representative sample: Is menopause associated with psychological distress? *Journal of Aging and Health, 6,* 209–228.

Bushman, B. (2002). Does venting anger feed or extinguish the flame? Catharsis rumination, distraction, anger and aggressive responding. *Personality & Social Psychology Bulletin, 28,* 724–731.

Bushman, B., & Huesmann, R. (2006). Short-term and long-term effects of violent media on aggression in children and adults. *Archives of Pediatric Adolescent Medicine, 160,* 348–352.

Bushman, B. J. (1995). Moderating role of trait aggressiveness in the effects of violent media on aggression. *Journal of Personality and Social Psychology, 69,* 950–960.

Bushman, B. J., & Cooper, H. M. (1990). Effects of alcohol on human aggression: An integrative research review. *Psychological Bulletin, 107,* 341–354.

Busnel, M. C., Granier-Deferre, C., & Lecanuet, J. P. (1992). Fetal audition. *Annals of the New York Academy of Sciences, 662,* 118–134.

Buss, D. M. (1984). Marital assortment for personality dispositions: Assessment with three different data sources. *Behavioral Genetics, 14,* 111–123.

Buss, D. M. (1994). The strategies of human mating. *American Scientist, 82,* 238–249.

Buss, D. M. (1999). *Evolutionary psychology: The new science of the mind.* Boston: Allyn & Bacon.

Buss, D. M. (2000a). *The dangerous passion: Why jealousy is as necessary as sex and love.* New York: Free Press.

Buss, D. M. (2000b). Desires in human mating. *Annals of the New York Academy of Sciences, 907,* 39–49.

Buss, D. M., Abbott, M., Angleitner, A., Asherian, A., Biaggio, A., Blanco-Villasenor, A., et al. (1990). International preferences in selecting mates: A study of 37 cultures. *Journal of Cross-Cultural Psychology, 21,* 5–47.

Buss, D. M., Shackelford, T., Kirkpatrick, L., & Larsen, R. (2001). A half century of mate preferences: The cultural evolution of values. *Journal of Marriage and the Family, 63,* 491–503.

Bussey, K., & Bandura, A. (1999). Social cognitive theory of gender development and differentiation. *Psychological Review, 106,* 676–713.

Butcher, J. N., Dahlstrom, W. G., Graham, J. R., Tellegen, A., & Kaemmer, B. (1989). *Manual for the restandardized Minnesota Multiphasic Personality Inventory: MMPI–2. An administrative and interpretive guide.* Minneapolis: University of Minnesota Press.

Butcher, J. N., & Graham, J. R. (1989). *Topics in MMPI–2 interpretation.* Minneapolis: Department of Psychology, University of Minnesota.

Butcher, J. N., & Rouse, S. V. (1996). Personality: Individual differences and clinical assessment. *Annual Review of Psychology, 47,* 89–111.

Butler, R., & Lewis, M. (1982). *Aging and mental health* (3rd ed.). St. Louis: Mosby.

Byne, W. (1993). *Sexual orientation and brain structure: Adding up the evidence.* Paper presented at the annual meeting of the International Academy of Sex Research. Pacific Grove, CA.

Cabýoglu, M., Ergene, N., & Tan, U. (2006). The mechanism of acupuncture and clinical applications. *International Journal of Neuroscience, 116,* 115–125.

Cahill, L., & McGaugh, J. (1995). A novel demonstration of enhanced memory associated with emotional arousal. *Consciousness & Cognition, 4,* 410–421.

Camerer, C. (2005). Three cheers—psychological, theoretical, empirical—for loss aversion. *Journal of Marketing Research, 42,* 129–133.

Camp, D. S., Raymond, G. A., & Church, R. M. (1967). Temporal relationship between response and punishment. *Journal of Experimental Psychology, 74,* 114–123.

Campbell, F., Pungello, E., Miller-Johnson, S., Burchinal, M., & Ramey, C. (2001). The development of cognitive and academic abilities: Growth curves from an early childhood educational experiment. *Developmental Psychology, 37,* 231–242.

Campbell, F., & Ramey, C. (1994). Effects of early intervention on intellectual and academic achievement: A follow-up study of children from low-income families. *Child Development, 65,* 684–698.

Campbell, P., & Dhand, R. (2000). Obesity. *Nature, 404,* 631.

Cannon, T. D., Kaprio, J., Lönnqvist, J., Huttunen, M., & Koskenvuo, M. (1998). The genetic epidemiology of schizophrenia in a Finnish twin cohort: A population-based modeling study. *Archives of General Psychiatry, 55,* 67–74.

Cannon, W. B. (1927). The James-Lange theory of emotions: A critical examination as an alternative theory. *American Journal of Psychology, 39,* 106–112.

Cannon, W. B. (1929). *Bodily changes in pain, hunger, fear and rage* (2nd ed.). New York: Appleton.

Cannon, W. B. (1935). Stresses and strains of homeostasis. *American Journal of Public Health, 189,* 1–14.

Capel, B. (2000). The battle of the sexes. *Mechanisms of Development, 92,* 89–103.

Cardoso, S. H., de Mello, L. C., & Sabbatini, R. M. E. (2000). How nerve cells work. Retrieved June 10, 2007 from http://www.cerebromente.org.br/n10/fundamentos/pot2_i.htm.org.br/cm/n09/fundamentos/transmissao/voo_i.htm

Carlat, D. J., Camargo, C. A., Jr., & Herzog, D. B. (1997). Eating disorders in males: A report on 135 patients. *American Journal of Psychiatry, 154,* 1127–1132.

Carlson, N. R. (1998). *Foundations of physiological psychology* (4th ed.). Boston: Allyn & Bacon.

Carlsson, I., Wendt, P. E., & Risberg, J. (2000). On the neurobiology of creativity. Differences in frontal activity between high and low creative subjects. *Neuropsychologia, 38,* 873–885.

Carnagey, N., & Anderson, C. (2004). Violent video game exposure and aggression: A literature review. *Minerva Psychiatrica, 45,* 1–18.

Carnagey, N., & Anderson, C. (2005). The effects of reward and punishment in violent video games on aggressive affect, cognition, and behavior. *Psychological Science, 16,* 882–889.

Carpenter, S. (2001, March). Everyday fantasia: The world of synesthesia. *APA Monitor on Psychology* [Online version], *32.*

Carpenter, S. (2001). Sights unseen. *Monitor on Psychology, 32* [Electronic version]. Retrieved May 13, 2003, from http://www.apa.org/monitor/apr01/blindness.html

Carpenter, W. T., Jr. (1996). Maintenance therapy of persons with schizophrenia. *Journal of Clinical Psychiatry, 57*(9, Suppl.), 10–18.

Carrier, J. (1980). Homosexual behavior in cross-cultural perspective. In J. Marmor (Ed.), *Homosexual behavior* (pp. 100–122). New York: Basic Books.

Carroll, K. M., Rounsaville, B. J., Nich, C., Gordon, L. T., Wirtz, P. W., & Gawin, F. (1994). One-year followup of psychotherapy and pharmacotherapy for cocaine dependence: Delayed emergence of psychotherapy effects. *Archives of General Psychiatry, 51,* 989–997.

Carskadon, M. A., & Dement, W. C. (1989). Normal human sleep: An overview. In M. H. Kryger, T. Roth, & W. C. Dement (Eds.), *Principles and practice of sleep medicine* (pp. 3–13). Philadelphia: W. B. Saunders.

Carskadon, M. A., & Rechtschaffen, A. (1989). Monitoring and staging human sleep. In M. H. Kryger, T. Roth, & W. C. Dement (Eds.), *Principles and practice of sleep medicine* (pp. 665–683). Philadelphia: W. B. Saunders.

Carson, R., Butcher, J., & Mineka, S. (2000). *Abnormal psychology and modern life* (11th ed.). Boston: Allyn & Bacon.

Carson, R. C. (1989). Personality. *Annual Review of Psychology, 40,* 227–248.

Carver, C. S., Pozo, C., Harris, S. D., Noriega, V., Scheier, M. F., Robinson, D. S., et al. (1993). How coping mediates the effect of optimism on distress: A study of women with early stage breast cancer. *Journal of Personality and Social Psychology, 65,* 375–390.

Case, A., & Paxson, C. (2004). Sex differences in morbidity and mortality. *National Bureau of Economic Research Working Paper No. 10653.* Retrieved July 7, 2006, from http://www.nber.org/papers/W10653

Case, R. (Ed.). (1992). *The mind's staircase: Exploring the conceptual underpinnings of children's thought and knowledge.* Hillsdale, NJ: Erlbaum.

Casey, D. E. (1996). Side effect profiles of new antipsychotic agents. *Journal of Clinical Psychiatry, 57*(11, Suppl.), 40–45.

Cash, T. F., & Janda, L. H. (1984, December). The eye of the beholder. *Psychology Today,* 46–52.

Caspi, A. (2000). The child is father of the man: Personality continuities from childhood to adulthood. *Journal of Personality & Social Psychology, 78,* 158–172.

Caspi, A., Lynam, D., Moffitt, T. E., & Silva, P. A. (1993). Unraveling girls' delinquency: Biological, dispositional, and contextual contributions to adolescent misbehavior. *Developmental Psychology, 29,* 19–30.

Cattapan-Ludewig, K., Ludewig, S., Jaquenoud, S., Etzensberger, M., & Hasler, F. (2005). Why do schizophrenic patients smoke? *Nervenarzt, 76,* 287–294.

Cattell, R. B. (1950). *Personality: A systematic, theoretical, and factual study.* New York: McGraw-Hill.

Cavanaugh, S. (2004). The sexual debut of girls in early adolescence: The intersection of race, pubertal timing, and friendship group. *Journal of Research on Adolescence, 14,* 285–312.

CBS News. (July 31, 2002). *Fear of public speaking.* Retrieved February 14, 2003, from http://www.cbsnews.com/stories/2002/07/30

Centers for Disease Control and Prevention (CDC). (1999). *Physical activity and health.* Retrieved January 29, 2003, from http://www.cdc.gov/needphp/sgr/ataglan.htm

Centers for Disease Control and Prevention (CDC). (2000). Youth risk behavior surveillance—United States, 1999. *Morbidity and Mortality Weekly Report, 49,* 1–96.

Centers for Disease Control and Prevention (CDC). (2002). Nonfatal self-inflicted injuries treated in hospital emergency departments—United States, 2000. *Morbidity & Mortality Weekly Report, 51,* 436–438.

Centers for Disease Control and Prevention (CDC). (2003a). *About minority health.* Retrieved August 8, 2003, from http://www.cdc.gov/omh/AMH/AMH.htm

Centers for Disease Control and Prevention (CDC). (2003b). Sexually transmitted disease surveillance, 2002. Retrieved August 18, 2004, from http://www.cdc.gov/std/stats/natoverview.htm

Centers for Disease Control and Prevention (CDC). (2004a). Surveillance summaries. *Morbidity & Mortality Weekly Report, 53,* 1–100.

Centers for Disease Control and Prevention (CDC). (2004b). *Syphilis and men who have sex with men.* Retrieved July 3, 2006, from http://www.cdc.gov/std/syphilis/STDFact-MSM&Syphilis.htm

Centers for Disease Control and Prevention (CDC). (2005a). *About minority health.* Retrieved February 2, 2005, from http://www.cdc.gov/omh/AMH/AMH.htm

Centers for Disease Control and Prevention (CDC). (2005b). *Trends in reportable sexually transmitted diseases in the United States, 2004.* Retrieved July 3, 2006, from http://www.cdc.gov/std/stats/04pdf/trends2004.pdf

Centers for Disease Control and Prevention (CDC). (2006a). *HPV Vaccine questions and answers.* Retrieved June 29, 2006, from http://www.cdc.gov/std/hpv/STDFact-HPV-vaccine.htm#vaccine

Centers for Disease Control and Prevention (CDC). (2006b). Growing stronger: Strength training for older adults. Retrieved July 7, 2006 from http://www.cdc.gov/nccdphp/dnpa/physical/growing_stronger/index.htm

Centers for Disease Control and Prevention (CDC). (2006c). National youth risk behavior survey

1991–2005. Retrieved June 13, 2006 from http://www.cdc.gov/healthyyouth/yrbs/pdf/trends/2005_YRBS_Sexual_Behaviors.pdf

Centers for Disease Control and Prevention (CDC). (2006d). *Nutrition topics.* Retrieved July 7, 2006, from http://www.cdc.gov/nccdphp/dnpa/nutrition/index.htm

Centers for Disease Control and Prevention (CDC). (2006e). Quick stats: General information on alcohol use and health. Retrieved July 7, 2006 from http://www.cdc.gov/alcohol/quickstats/general_info.htm

Chambless, D. L., & Goldstein, A. J. (1979). Behavioral psychotherapy. In R. J. Corsini (Ed.), *Current psychotherapies* (2nd ed., pp. 230–272). Itasca, IL: F. E. Peacock.

Chamorro-Premuzic, T., & Furnham, A. (2003). Personality predicts academic performance: Evidence from two longitudinal university samples. *Journal of Research in Personality, 37,* 319–338.

Chang, E., & Merzenich, M. (2003). Environmental noise retards auditory cortical development. *Science, 300,* 498–502.

Chao, R. (2001). Extending research on the consequences of parenting style for Chinese Americans and European Americans. *Child Development, 72,* 1832–1843.

Chaplin, W. F., Philips, J. B., Brown, J. D., Clanton, N. R., & Stein, J. L. (2000). Handshaking, gender, personality, and first impressions. *Journal of Personality and Social Psychology, 19,* 110–117.

Charles, S., Mather, M., & Carstensen, L. (2003). Aging and emotional memory: The forgettable nature of negative images for older adults. *Journal of Experimental Psychology, 132,* 310–324.

Charness, N. (1989). Age and expertise: Responding to Talland's challenge. In L. W. Poon, D. C. Rubin, & B. A. Wilson (Eds.), *Everyday cognition in adulthood and old age* (pp. 437–456). New York: Cambridge University Press.

Chase, M. H., & Morales, F. R. (1990). The atonia and myoclonia of active (REM) sleep. *Annual Review of Psychology, 41,* 557–584.

Chassin, L., Presson, C., Sherman, S., & Kim, K. (2003). Historical changes in cigarette smoking and smoking-related beliefs after 2 decades in a midwestern community. *Health Psychology, 22,* 347 353.

Chen-Sea, M.-J. (2000). Validating the Draw-A-Man Test as a personal neglect test. *American Journal of Occupational Therapy, 54,* 391–397.

Cherry, E. (1953). Some experiments on the recognition of speech with one and two ears. *Journal of the Acoustical Society of America, 25,* 975–979.

Chesney, T. (2006). The effect of communication medium on research participation decisions. *Journal of Computer-Mediated Communication, 11,* 877–883.

Chi, S., Park, C., Lim, S., Park, E., Lee, Y., Lee, K., et al. (2005). EEG and personality dimensions: A consideration based on the rain oscillatory systems. *Personality and Individual Differences, 39,* 669–681.

Chilosi, A., Cipriani, P., Bertuccelli, B., Pfanner, L., & Cioni, G. (2001). Early cognitive and communication development in children with focal brain lesions. *Journal of Child Neurology, 16,* 309–316.

"Children spend more time playing video games than watching TV, MSU survey shows." (2004, April 4). Retrieved July 23, 2005, from http://www.newsroom.msu.edu/site/indexer/1943/content.htm

Cho, K. (2001). Chronic "jet lag" produces temporal lobe atrophy and spatial cognitive deficits. *Nature Neuroscience, 4,* 567–568.

Cho, K., Ennaceur, A., Cole, J., & Kook Suh, C. (2000). Chronic jet lag produces cognitive deficits. *Journal of Neuroscience, 20,* RC66.

Choi, H., & Smith, S. (2005). Incubation and the resolution of tip-of-the-tongue states. *Journal of General Psychology, 132,* 365–376.

Choi, I., Dalal, R., Kim-Prieto, C., & Park, H. (2003). Culture and judgment of causal relevance. *Journal of Personality & Social Psychology, 84,* 46–59.

Choi, J., & Silverman, I. (2002). The relationship between testosterone and route-learning strategies in humans. *Brain & Cognition, 50,* 116–120.

Chollar, S. (1989). Conversation with the dolphins. *Psychology Today, 23,* 52–57.

Chomsky, N. (1957). *Syntactic structures.* The Hague: Mouton.

Chomsky, N. (1968). *Language and mind.* New York: Harcourt, Brace & World.

Chowdhury, R., Ferrier, I., & Thompson, J. (2003). Cognitive dysfunction in bipolar disorder. *Current Opinion in Psychiatry, 16,* 7–12.

Christakis, D., Zimmerman, F., DiGiuseppe, D., & McCarty, C. (2004). Early television exposure and subsequent attentional problems in children. *Pediatrics, 113,* 708–713.

Christensen, A., Atkins, D., Berns, S., Wheeler, J., Baucom, D., & Simpson, L. (2004). Traditional versus integrative behavioral couple therapy for significantly and chronically distressed married couples. *Journal of Consulting and Clinical Psychology, 72,* 176–191.

Christianson, S-Å. (1992). Emotional stress and eyewitness memory: A critical review. *Psychological Bulletin, 112,* 284–309.

Church, M., Elliot, A., & Gable, S. (2001). Perceptions of classroom enviornment, achievement goals, and achievement outcomes. *Journal of Educational Psychology, 93,* 43–54.

Church, R. M. (1963). The varied effects of punishment on behavior. *Psychological Review, 70,* 369–402.

Cialdini, R. B., Cacioppo, J. T., Basset, R., & Miller, J. A. (1978). Low-ball procedure for producing compliance: Commitment then cost. *Journal of Personality and Social Psychology, 36,* 463–476.

Cialdini, R. B., Vincent, J. E., Lewis, S. K., Catalan, J., Wheeler, D., & Darby, B. L. (1975). Reciprocal concessions procedure for inducing compliance: The door-in-the-face technique. *Journal of Personality and Social Psychology, 31,* 206–215.

Clark, D. M., & Teasdale, J. D. (1982). Diurnal variation in clinical depression and accessibility of memories of positive and negative experiences. *Journal of Abnormal Psychology, 91,* 87–95.

Clark, L., Watson, D., & Reynolds, S. (1995). Ciagnosis and classification of psychopathology: Challenges to the current system and future directions. *Annual Review of Psychology, 46,* 121–153.

Clark, M. L., & Ayers, M. (1992). Friendship similarity during early adolescence: Gender and racial patterns. *Journal of Psychology, 126,* 393–405.

Classen, J., Liepert, J., Wise, S., Hallett, M., & Cohen, L. (1998). Rapid plasticity of human cortical movement representation induced by practice. *Journal of Neurophysiology, 79,* 1117–1123.

Clay, R. (2003). Researchers replace midlife myths with facts. *APA Monitor on Psychology, 34,* 36.

Clayton, V. (2004, September 8). *What's to blame for the rise in ADHD?* Retrieved November 22, 2004, from http://www.msnbc.msn.com/id/5933775/

Clément, K., Vaisse, C., Lahlou, N., Cabrol, S., Pelloux, V., Cassuto, D., et al. (1998). A mutation in the human leptin receptor gene causes obesity and pituitary dysfunction. *Nature, 392,* 398–401.

Clifford, E. (2000). Neural plasticity: Merzenich, Taub, and Greenough. *Harvard Brain [Special Issue], 6,* 16–20.

Cloitre, M., Koenen, K., Cohen, L., & Han, H. (2002). Skills training in affective and interpersonal regulation followed by exposure: A phase-based treatment for PTSD related to childhood abuse. *Journal of Consulting and Clinical Psychology, 70,* 1067–1074.

Cloninger, C. R., Sigvardsson, S., Bohman, M., & von Knorring, A. L. (1982). Predispositions to petty criminality in Swedish adoptees, II. Cross-fostering analysis of gene-environment interaction. *Archives of General Psychiatry, 39,* 1242–1249.

CNN.com. (February 16, 2003). *Fatal shooting caught on tape.* Retrieved February 17, 2003, from http://www.cnn.com/2003/US/South/02/16/gas.shooting.ap/index.html

Cohen, L. L., & Shotland, R. L. (1996). Timing of first sexual intercourse in a relationship: Expectations, experiences, and perceptions of others. *Journal of Sex Research, 33,* 291–299.

Cohen, S., Doyle, W., & Baum, A. (2006). Socioeconomic status is associated with stress hormones. *Psychosomatic Medicine, 68,* 414–420.

Cohen, S., Doyle, W. J., Skoner, D. P., Rabin, B. S., & Gwaltney, J. M., Jr. (1997). Social ties and susceptibility to the common cold. *Journal of the American Medical Association, 277,* 1940–1944.

Cohen, S., & Herbert, T. B. (1996). Health psychology: Psychological factors and physical disease from the perspective of human psychoneuroimmunology. *Annual Review of Psychology, 47,* 113–142.

Cohen, S., & Williamson, G. M. (1991). Stress and infectious disease in humans. *Psychological Bulletin, 109,* 5–54.

Colby, A., Kohlberg, L., Gibbs, J., & Lieberman, M. (1983). A longitudinal study of moral judgment. *Monographs of the Society for Research in Child Development, 48*(1–2, Serial No. 200).

Cole, R., Smith, J., Alcala, Y., Elliott, J., & Kripke, D. (2002). Bright-light mask treatment of delayed sleep phase syndrome. *Journal of Biological Rhythms, 17,* 89–101.

Coleman, C., King, B., Bolden-Watson, C., Book, M., Segraves, R., Richard, N., et al. (2001). A placebo-controlled comparison of the effects on sexual functioning of bupropion sustained release and fluoxetine. *Clinical Therapeutics: The International Peer-Reviewed Journal of Drug Therapy, 23,* 1040–1058.

Collaer, M. L., & Hines, M. (1995). Human behavioral sex differences: A role for gonadal hormones during early development. *Psychological Bulletin, 118,* 55–107.

Colwell, J., & Payne, J. (2000). Negative correlates of computer game play in adolescents. *British Journal of Psychology, 91*(Pt. 3), 295–310.

Conca, A., Swoboda, E., König, P., Koppi, S., Beraus, W., Künz, A., et al. (2000). Clinical impacts of single transcranial magnetic stimulation (sTMS) as an add-on therapy in severely depressed patients under SSRI treatment. *Human Psychopharmacology: Clinical and Experimental, 15,* 429–438.

Condon, W. S., & Sander, L. W. (1974). Neonatal movement is synchronized with adult speech: Interactional participation and language acquisition. *Science, 183,* 99–101.

Coney, J., & Fitzgerald, J. (2000). Gender differences in the recognition of laterally presented affective nouns. *Cognition and Emotion, 14,* 325–339.

Conrad, P., & Leiter, V. (2004). Medicalization, markets, and consumers. *Journal of Health and Social Behavior, 45* (Supplement), 158–176.

Conroy, D., Poczwardowski, A., & Henschen, K. (2001). Evaluative criteria and consequences associated with failure and success for elite athletes and performing artists. *Journal of Applied Sport Psychology, 13,* 300–322.

Consumer Reports. (1995, November) Mental health: Does therapy help?, 734–739.

Coolidge, F., Thede, L., & Young, S. (2002). The heritability of gender identity disorder in a child and adolescent twin sample. *Behavior Genetics, 32,* 251–257.

Coons, P. M. (1994). Confirmation of childhood abuse in child and adolescent cases of multiple personality disorder and dissociative disorder not otherwise specified. *Journal of Nervous and Mental Disease, 182,* 461–464.

Cooper, R. (1994). Normal sleep. In R. Cooper (Ed.), *Sleep.* New York: Chapman & Hall.

Coplan, J. D., Papp, L. A., Pine, D., Marinez, J., Cooper, T., Rosenblum, L. A., et al. (1997). Clinical improvement with fluoxetine therapy and noradrenergic function in patients with panic disorder. *Archives of General Psychiatry, 54,* 643–648.

Corballis, M. C. (1989). Laterality and human evolution. *Psychological Review, 96,* 492–509.

Coren, S. (1996a). Accidental death and the shift to daylight savings time. *Perceptual and Motor Skills, 83,* 921–922.

Coren, S. (1996b). Daylight savings time and traffic accidents. *New England Journal of Medicine, 334,* 924.

Corenblum, B., & Meissner, C. (2006). Recognition of faces of ingroup and outgroup children and adults. *Journal of Experimental Child Psychology, 93*, 187–206.

Cornelius, M. D., Leech, S. L., Goldschmidt, L., & Day, N. L. (2000). Prenatal tobacco exposure: Is it a risk factor for early tobacco experimentation? *Nicotine & Tobacco Research, 2*, 45–52.

Cortina, L., & Magley, V. (2003). Raising voice, risking retaliation: Events following interpersonal mistreatment in the workplace. *Journal of Occupational Health Psychology, 8*, 247–265.

Cosmides, L., & Tooby, J. (2000). Evolutionary psychology and the emotions. In M. Lewis, Jr., & J. M. Haviland-Jones (Eds.), *Handbook of emotions* (2nd ed.) (pp. 91–115). New York: Guilford.

Costa, P. T., Jr., & McCrae, R. R. (1985). *The NEO Personality Inventory.* Odessa, FL: Psychological Assessment Resources.

Costa E Silva, J. A., Chase, M., Sartorius, N., & Roth, T. (1996). Special report from a symposium held by the World Health Organization and the World Federation of Sleep Research Societies: An overview of insomnias and related disorders—recognition, epidemiology, and rational management. *Sleep, 19*, 412–416.

Courage, M. L., & Adams, R. J. (1990). Visual acuity assessment from birth to three years using the acuity card procedures: Cross-sectional and longitudinal samples. *Optometry and Vision Science, 67*, 713–718.

Covey, S. (1989). *The 7 habits of highly effective people.* New York: Simon & Shuster.

Cowan, N. (1988). Evolving conceptions of memory storage, selective attention, and their mutual constraints within the human information-processing system. *Psychological Bulletin, 104*, 163–191.

Cowley, E. (2005). Views from consumers next in line: The fundamental attribution error in a service setting. *Journal of the Academy of Marketing Science, 33*, 139–152.

Coyle, J., & Draper, E. S. (1996). What is the significance of glutamate for mental health? *Harvard Mental Health Letter, 13*(6), 8.

Coyne, S. (2004). Indirect aggression on screen: A hidden problem? *The Psychologist, 17*, 688–690.

Coyne, S., Archer, J., & Eslea, M. (2004). Cruel intentions on television and in real life: Can viewing indirect aggression increase viewers' subsequent indirect aggression? *Journal of Experimental Child Psychology, 88*, 234–253.

Craig, I., & Plomin, R. (2006). Quantitative trait loci for IQ and other complex traits: Single-nucleotide polymorphism genotyping using pooled DNA and microarrays. *Genes, Brain & Behavior, 5*, 32–37.

Craik, F. I. M., & Lockhart, R. S. (1972). Levels of processing: A framework for memory research. *Journal of Verbal Learning and Verbal Behavior, 11*, 671–684.

Craik, F. I. M., & Tulving, E. (1975). Depth of processing and the retention of words in episodic memory. *Journal of Experimental Psychology: General, 104*, 268–294.

Criglington, A. (1998). Do professionals get jet lag? A commentary on jet lag. *Aviation, Space, & Environmental Medicine, 69*, 810.

Crits-Christoph, P. (1992). The efficacy of brief dynamic psychotherapy: A meta-analysis. *American Journal of Psychiatry, 149*, 151–158.

Crits-Christoph, P., Gibbons, M., Losardo, D., Narducci, J., Schamberger, M., & Gallop, R. (2004). Who benefits from brief psychodynamic therapy for generalized anxiety disorder? *Canadian Journal of Psychoanalysis, 12*, 301–324.

Crockenberg, S., & Leerkes, E. (2005). Infant temperament moderates associations between childcare type and quantity and externalizing and internalizing behaviors at 2 1/2 years. *Infant Behavior & Development, 28*, 20–35.

Crombag, H., & Robinson, T. (2004). Drugs, environment, brain, and behavior. *Current Directions in Psychological Science, 13*, 107–111.

Crone, E., Wendelken, C., Donohue, S., van Leijenhorst, L., & Bunge, S. (2006). Neurocognitive development of the ability to manipulate information in working memory. *Proceedings for the National Academy of Sciences, 103*, 9315–9320.

Crowder, R. G. (1992) Sensory memory. In L. R. Squire (Ed.), *Encyclopedia of learning and memory.* New York: Macmillan.

Crowe, L. C., & George, W. H. (1989). Alcohol and human sexuality: Review and integration. *Psychological Bulletin, 105*, 374–386.

Crowley, B., Hayslip, B., & Hobdy, J. (2003). Psychological hardiness and adjustment to life events in adulthood. *Journal of Adult Development, 10*, 237–248.

Crowther, J., Kichler, J., Shewood, N., & Kuhnert, M. (2002). The role of familial factors in bulimia nervosa. *Eating Disorders: The Journal of Treatment & Prevention, 10*, 141–151.

Csikszentmihalyi, M. (1996, July/August). The creative personality. *Psychology Today, 29*, 36–40.

Cui, X-J., & Vaillant, G. E. (1996). Antecedents and consequences of negative life events in adulthood: A longitudinal study. *American Journal of Psychiatry, 153*, 21–26.

Culbertson, F. M. (1997). Depression and gender: An international review. *American Psychologist, 52*, 25–31.

Cullen, M., Hardison, C., & Sackett, P. (2004). Using SAT-grade and ability-job performance relationships to test predictions derived from stereotype threat theory. *Journal of Applied Psychology, 89*, 220–230.

Cunningham, M. R., Roberts, A. R., Barbee, A. P., Druen, P. B., & Wu, C-H. (1995). "Their ideas of beauty are, on the whole, the same as ours": Consistency and variability in the cross-cultural perception of female physical attractiveness. *Journal of Personality and Social Psychology, 68*, 261–279.

Cupach, W. R., & Canary, D. J. (1995). Managing conflict and anger: Investigating the sex stereotype hypothesis. In P. J. Kalbfleisch & M. J. Cody (Eds.),

Gender, power, and communication in human relationships (pp. 233–252). Hillsdale, NJ: Erlbaum.

Curci, A., Luminet, O., Finkenauer, C., & Gisler, L. (2001). Flashbulb memories in social groups: A comparative test-retest study of the memory of French president Mitterrand's death in a French and a Belgian group. *Memory, 9*, 81–101.

Curran, P. J., Stice, E., & Chassin, L. (1997). The relation between adolescent alcohol use and peer alcohol use: A longitudinal random coefficients model. *Journal of Consulting and Clinical Psychology, 65*, 130–140.

Cyranowski, J. M., Frand, E., Young, E., & Shear, M. K. (2000). Adolescent onset of the gender difference in lifetime rates of major depression. *Archives of General Psychiatry, 57*, 21–27.

Cytowic, R. (1993). *The man who tasted shapes.* Cambridge, MA: MIT Press.

Cytowic, R. (2002). *Synesthesia: A union of the senses* (2nd ed.). Cambridge, MA: MIT Press

Dabbs, J. M., Jr., & Morris, R. (1990). Testosterone, social class, and antisocial behavior in a sample of 4,462 men. *Psychological Science, 1*, 209–211.

Dadds., M., Fraser, J., Frost, A., & Hawes, D. (2005). Disentangling the underlying dimensions of psychopathy and conduct problems in childhood: A community study. *Journal of Consulting and Clinical Psychology, 73*, 400–410.

Dahloef, P., Norlin-Bagge, E., Hedner, J., Ejnell, H., Hetta, J., & Haellstroem, T. (2002). Improvement in neuropsychological performance following surgical treatment for obstructive sleep apnea syndrome. *Acta Oto-Laryngologica, 122*, 86–91.

Dale, N., & Kandel, E. R. (1990). Facilitatory and inhibitory transmitters modulate spontaneous transmitter release at cultured *Aplysia* sensorimotor synapses. *Journal of Physiology, 421*, 203–222.

Dallard, I., Cathebras, P., & Sauron, C. (2001). Is cocoa a psychotropic drug? Psychopathological study of self-labeled "chocolate addicts." *Encephale, 27*, 181–186.

Damasio, A. R. (1994). *Descartes' error: Emotion, reason, and the human brain.* New York: Lyons Press.

Damasio, A. R. (1999). *The feeling of what happens: Body and emotion in the making of consciousness.* New York: Harcourt.

Dandy, J., & Nettelbeck, T. (2002). The relationship between IQ, homework, aspirations and academic achievement for Chinese, Vietnamese and Anglo-Celtic Australian school children. *Educational Psychology, 22*, 267–276.

Dantzker, M., & Eisenman, R. (2003). Sexual attitudes among Hispanic college students: Differences between males and females. *International Journal of Adolescence & Youth, 11*, 79–89.

Darley, J. M., & Latané, B. (1968a). Bystander intervention in emergencies: Diffusion of responsibility. *Journal of Personality and Social Psychology, 8*, 377–383.

Darley, J. M., & Latané, B. (1968b, December). When will people help in a crisis? *Psychology Today*, 54–57, 70–71.

Darwin, C. (1872/1965). *The expression of emotion in man and animals.* Chicago: University of Chicago Press. (Original work published 1872).

Dasen, P. R. (1994). Culture and cognitive development from a Piagetian perspective. In W. J. Lonner & R. Malpass (Eds.), *Psychology and culture* (pp. 145–149). Boston: Allyn & Bacon.

Dauringnac, E., Toga, A., Jones, D., Aronen, H., Hommer, D., Jernigan, T., Krystal, J., & Mathalon, D. (2005). Applications of morphometric and diffusion tensor magnetic resonance imaging to the study of brain abnormalities in the alcoholism spectrum. *Alcoholism: Clinical and Experimental Research, 29*, 159–166.

Davalos, D., Kisley, M., & Ross, R. (2002). Deficits in auditory and visual temporal perception in schizophrenia. *Cognitive Neuropsychiatry, 7*, 273–282.

Davidson, J. R. T. (1997). Use of benzodiazepines in panic disorder. *Journal of Clinical Psychiatry, 58*(2, Suppl.), 26–28.

Davies, L. (2003). Singlehood: Transitions within a gendered world. *Canadian Journal on Aging, 22*, 343–352.

Davis, S., Butcher, S. P., & Morris, R. G. M. (1992). The NMDA receptor antagonist D-2-amino-5-phospho-nopentanoate (D-AP5) impairs spatial learning and LTP in vivo at intracerebral concentrations comparable to those that block LTP in vitro. *Journal of Neuroscience, 12*, 21–34.

Day, S., & Schneider, P. (2002). Psychotherapy using distance technology: A comparison of face-to-face, video, and audio treatment. *Journal of Counseling Psychology, 49*, 499–503.

D'Azevedo, W. A. (1982). Tribal history in Liberia. In U. Neisser (Ed.), *Memory observed: Remembering in natural contexts* (258–268). San Francisco: W. H. Freeman.

DeCasper, A. J., & Spence, M. J. (1986). Prenatal maternal speech influences newborns' perception of speech sounds. *Infant Behavior and Development, 9*, 133–150.

Dedert, E., Studts, J., Weissbecker, I., Salmon, P., Banis, P., & Sephton, S. (2004). Religiosity may help preserve the cortisol rhythm in women with stress-related illness. *International Journal of Psychiatry in Medicine, 34*, 61–77.

Deinzer, R., Kleineidam, C., Stiller-Winkler, R., Idel, H., & Bach, D. (2000). Prolonged reduction of salivary immunoglobulin (sIgA) after a major academic exam. *International Journal of Psychophysiology, 37*, 219–232.

de Jong, P., & vander Leij, A. (2002). Effects of phonological abilities and linguistic comprehension on the development of reading. *Scientific Studies of Reading, 6*, 51–77.

de Lacoste, M., Horvath, D., & Woodward, J. (1991). Possible sex differences in the developing human fetal brain. *Journal of Clinical and Experimental Neuropsychology, 13*, 831.

Delgado, J. M. R., & Anand, B. K. (1953). Increased food intake induced by electrical stimulation of the lateral hypothalamus. *American Journal of Physiology, 172*, 162–168.

DeLongis, A., Folkman, S., & Lazarus, R. S. (1988). The impact of daily stress on health and mood: Psychological and social resources as mediators. *Journal of Personality and Social Psychology, 54*, 486–495.

De Martino, B., Kumaran, O., Seymour, B., & Dolan, R. (2006). Frames, biases, and rational decision-making in the human brain. *Science, 313*, 684–687.

Dement, W., & Kleitman, N. (1957). The relation of eye movements during sleep to dream activity: An objective method for the study of dreaming. *Journal of Experimental Psychology, 53*, 339–346.

Denollet, J. (1997). Personality, emotional distress and coronary heart disease. *European Journal of Personality, 11*, 343–357.

Deovell, L. Y., Bentin, S., & Soroker, N. (2000). Electrophysiological evidence for an early (pre-attentive) information processing deficit in patients with right hemisphere damage and unilateral neglect. *Brain, 123*, 353–365.

DePrince, A., & Freyd, J. (2004). Forgetting trauma stimuli. *Psychological Science, 15*, 488–492.

De Raad, B., & Kokkonen, M. (2000). Traits and emotions: A review of their structure and management. *European Journal of Personality, 14*, 477–496.

DeSpelder, L., & Strickland, A. (1983). *The last dance: Encountering death and dying.* Palo Alto, CA: Mayfield.

Devanand, D. P., Dwork, A. J., Hutchinson, M. S. E., Bolwig, T. G., & Sackeim, H. A. (1994). Does ECT alter brain structure? *American Journal of Psychiatry, 151*, 957–970.

Devine, P. G. (1989). Stereotypes and prejudice: Their automatic and controlled components. *Journal of Personality and Social Psychology, 56*, 5–18.

De Vos, S. (1990). Extended family living among older people in six Latin American countries. *Journal of Gerontology: Social Sciences, 45*, S87–S94.

Dewsbury, D. A. (2000). Introduction: Snapshots of psychology circa 1900. *American Psychologist, 55*, 255–259.

DeYoung, C., Peterson, J., & Higgins, D. (2002). Higher-order factors of the Big Five predict conformity: Are there neuroses of health? *Personality & Individual Differences, 33*, 533–552.

Dickens, W., & Flynn, R. (2001). Heritability estimates versus large environmental effects: The IQ paradox resolved. *Psychological Review, 108*, 346–369.

Dickey, M. (2005). Engaging by design: How engagement strategies in popular computer and video games can inform instructional design. *Educational Technology Research and Development, 53*, 67–83.

Diefendorff, J., & Richard, E. (2003). Antecedents and consequences of emotional display rule perceptions. *Journal of Applied Psychology, 88*, 284–294.

Diener, E., Lucas, R., & Scollon, C. (2006). Beyond the hedonic treadmill: Revising the adaptation theory of well-being. *American Psychologist, 61*, 305–314.

Dijkstra, M., Buijtels, H., & van Raaij, W. (2005). Separate and joint effects of medium type on consumer response: A comparison of television, print, and the Internet. *Journal of Business Research, 58*, 2005.

DiLalla, L. F., & Gottesman, I. I. (1991). Biological and genetic contributors to violence—Widom's untold tale. *Psychological Bulletin, 109*, 125–129.

Dillard, J., & Anderson, J. (2004). The role of fear in persuasion. *Psychology & Marketing, 21*, 909–926.

Din-Dzietham, R., Nembhard, W., Collins, R., & Davis, S. (2004). Perceived stress following race-based discrimination at work is associated with hypertension in African-Americans. *Social Science & Medicine, 58*, 449–461.

Dion, K., Berscheid, E., & Walster, E. (1972). What is beautiful is good. *Journal of Personality and Social Psychology, 24*, 285–290.

Dipboye, R. L., Fromkin, H. L., & Wilback, K. (1975). Relative importance of applicant sex, attractiveness, and scholastic standing in evaluation of job applicant resumes. *Journal of Applied Psychology, 60*, 39–43.

Dodge, K. A., Bates, J. E., & Pettit, G. S. (1990). Mechanisms in the cycle of violence. *Science, 250*, 1678–1683.

Dodson, C. S., Koutstaal, W., & Schacter, D. L. (2000). Escape from illusion: Reducing false memories. *Trends in Cognitive Sciences, 4*, 391–397.

Dohanich, G. (2003). Ovarian steroids and cognitive function. *Current Directions in Psychological Science, 12*, 57–61.

Dohrenwend, B. (2006). Inventorying stressful life events as risk factors for psychopathology: Toward resolution of the problem of intracategory variability. *Psychological Bulletin, 132*, 477–495.

Dollard, J., Doob, L. W., Miller, N., Mowrer, O. H., & Sears, R. R. (1939). *Frustration and aggression.* New Haven: Yale University Press.

Domjan, M., Cusato, B., & Krause, M. (2004). Learning with arbitrary versus ecological conditioned stimuli: Evidence from sexual conditioning. *Psychonomic Bulletin & Review, 11*, 232–246. [5]

Domino, G. (1984). California Psychological Inventory. In D. J. Keyser & R. C. Sweetland (Eds.), *Test Critiques* (Vol. 1, pp. 146–157). Kansas City, MO: Test Corporation of America.

Doob, L. W., & Sears, R. R. (1939). Factors determining substitute behavior and the overt expression of aggression. *Journal of Abnormal and Social Psychology, 34*, 293–313.

Dorz, S., Lazzarini, L., Cattelan, A., Meneghetti, F., Novara, C., Concia, E., et al. (2003). Evaluation of adherence to antiretroviral therapy in Italian HIV patients. *AIDS Patient Care & STDs, 17*, 33–41.

Downing, P., Jiang, Y., Shuman, M., & Kanwisher, N. (2001). A cortical area selective for visual processing of the human body. *Science, 293*, 2470–2473.

Doyle, J. A., & Paludi, M. A. (1995). *Sex and gender* (3rd ed.). Madison, WI: Brown & Benchmark.

Dreikurs, R. (1953). *Fundamentals of Adlerian psychology.* Chicago: Alfred Adler Institute.

Drevets, W., Neugebauer, V., Li, W., Bird, G., & Han, J. (2004). The amygdala and persistent pain. *Neuroscientist, 10*, 221–234.

Drevets, W. C., Price, J. L., Simpson, J. R., Jr., Todd, R. D., Reich, T., Vannier, M., et al. (1997). Subgenual prefrontal cortex abnormalities in mood disorders. *Nature, 386*, 824–827.

Druckman, D., & Bjork, R. A. (Eds.) (1994). *Learning, remembering, believing: Enhancing human performance.* Washington, DC: National Academy Press.

Drug Enforcement Administration. National Drug Intelligence Center. (2003). *National Drug Threat Assessment/2003.* Retrieved October 22, 2003, from http://www.usdoj.gov/ndic/pubs3/3300/pharm.htm

Drug Free Workplace. (2002, September). *Designer Drugs. National Medical Report* [Electronic version]. Retrieved May 25, 2003, from http://www.drugfreeworkplace.com/drugsofabuse/designer.htm

Drummond, S., Brown, G., Salamat, J., & Gillin, J. (2004). Increasing task difficulty facilitates the cerebral compensatory response to total sleep deprivation. *Sleep: Journal of Sleep & Sleep Disorders Research, 27,* 445–451.

Drummond, S. P. A., Brown, G. G., Gillin, J. C., Stricker, J. L., Wong, E. C., & Buxton, R. B. (2000). Altered brain response to verbal learning following sleep deprivation. *Nature, 403,* 655–657.

Duck, S. (1983). *Friends for life: The psychology of close relationships.* New York: St. Martin's Press.

Duckworth, A., & Seligman, M. (2006). Self-discipline gives girls the edge: Gender in self-discipline, grades, and achievement test scores. *Journal of Educational Psychology, 98,* 198–208.

Duke, P., & Hochman, G. (1992). *A brilliant madness: Living with manic-depressive illness.* New York: Bantam Books.

Duke, P., & Turan, K. (1987). *Call me Anna.* New York: Bantam Books.

Dunkel-Schetter, C., Feinstein, L. G., Taylor, S. E., & Falke, R. L. (1992). Patterns of coping with cancer. *Health Psychology, 11,* 79–87.

Dunn, J., Cutting, A., & Fisher, N. (2002). Old friends, new friends: Predictors of children's perspective on their friends at school. *Child Development, 73,* 621–635.

Durbin, C., & Klein, D. (2006). Ten-year stability of personality disorders among outpatients with mood disorders. *Journal of Abnormal Psychology, 115,* 75–84.

Durex. (2005). *Durex Global Sex Survey 2005.* Retrieved July 3, 2006, from http://www.durex.com/cm/gss2005results.asp

Duyme, M. (1988). School success and social class: An adoption study. *Developmental Psychology, 24,* 203–209.

Dyl, J., Kittler, J., Phillips, K., & Hunt, J. (2006). Body dysmorphic disorder and other clinically significant body image concerns in adolescent psychiatric inpatients: Prevalence and clinical characteristics. *Child Psychiatry and Human Development, 36,* 369–382.

Dywan, J., & Bowers, K. (1983). The use of hypnosis to enhance recall. *Science, 222,* 184–185.

Eagly, A. H., Ashmore, R. D., Makhijani, M. G., & Longo, L. L. (1991). What is beautiful is good . . .: A meta-analytic review of research on the physical attractiveness stereotype. *Psychological Bulletin, 110,* 109–128.

Eagly, A. H., & Carli, L. (1981). Sex of researchers and sex-typed communications as determinants of sex differences in influence-ability: A meta-analysis of social influence studies. *Psychological Bulletin, 90,* 1–20.

Eagly, A. H., & Wood, W. (1999). The origins of sex differences in human behavior: Evolved dispositions versus social roles. *American Psychologist, 54,* 408–423.

Earlandsson, L., & Eklund, M. (2003). The relationships among hassles and uplifts to experience of health in working women. *Women & Health, 38,* 19–37.

Ebbinghaus, H. (1913). *Memory* (H. A. Ruger & C. E. Bussenius, Trans.). New York: Teacher's College Press. (Original work published 1885)

Ebbinghaus, H. E. (1885/1964). *Memory: A contribution to experimental psychology* (H. A. Ruger & C. E. Bussenius, Trans.). New York: Dover. (Original work published 1885).

Edwards, B., Atkinson, G., Waterhouse, J., Reilly, T., Godfrey, R., & Budgett, R. (2000). Use of melatonin in recovery from jet-lag following an eastward flight across 10 time-zones. *Ergonomics, 43,* 1501–1513.

Edwards, K., & Smith, E. E. (1996). A disconfirmation bias in the evaluation of arguments. *Journal of Personality and Social Psychology, 71,* 5–24.

Egeth, H. E. (1993). What do we not know about eyewitness identification? *American Psychologist, 48,* 577–580.

Eichenbaum, H. (1997). Declarative memory: Insights from cognitive neurobiology. *Annual Review of Psychology, 48,* 547–572.

Eichenbaum, H., & Fortin, N. (2003). Episodic memory and the hippocampus: It's about time. *Current Directions in Psychological Science, 12,* 53–57.

Eichenbaum, H., & Otto, T. (1993). LTP and memory: Can we enhance the connection? *Trends in Neurosciences, 16,* 163.

Eidelson, R., & Eidelson, J. (2003). Dangerous ideas. *American Psychologist, 58,* 182–192.

Eisold, B. (2005). Notes on lifelong resilience: Perceptual and personality factors implicit in the creation of a particular adaptive style. *Psychoanalytic Psychology, 22,* 411–425.

Ekman, P. (1972). Universals and cultural differences in facial expression of emotion. In J. Cole (Ed.), *Nebraska symposium on motivation* (Vol. 19). Lincoln: University of Nebraska Press.

Ekman, P. (1993). Facial expression and emotion. *American Psychologist, 48,* 384–392.

Ekman, P., & Friesen, W. V. (1975). *Unmasking the face: A guide to recognizing emotions from facial clues.* Englewood Cliffs, NJ: Prentice-Hall.

Ekman, P., Levenson, R. W., & Friesen, W. V. (1983). Autonomic nervous system activity distinguishes among emotions. *Science, 221,* 1208–1210.

Elal, G., Altug, A., Slade, P., & Tekcan, A. (2000). Factor structure of the Eating Attitudes Test (EAT) in a Turkish university sample. *Eating and Weight Disorders: Studies on Anorexia, Bulimia, and Obesity, 5,* 46–50.

Elkin, I., Gibbons, R. D., Shea, M. T., Sotsky, S. M., Watkins, J. T., Pikonis, P. A., & Hedeker, D. (1995). Initial severity and differential treatment outcome in the National Institute of Mental Health Treatment of Depression Collaborative Research Program. *Journal of Consulting and Clinical Psychology, 63,* 841–847.

Elkin, I., Shea, M. T., Watkins, J. T., et al. (1989). National Institute of Mental Health Treatment of Depression Collaborative Research Program: General effectiveness of treatments. *Archives of General Psychology, 46,* 971–982.

Elkind, D. (1967). Egocentrism in adolescence. *Child Development, 38,* 1025–1034.

Elkind, D. (1974). *Children and adolescents: Interpretive essays on Jean Piaget* (2nd ed.). New York: Oxford University Press.

Ellason, J. W., & Ross, C. A. (1997). Two-year follow-up of inpatients with dissociative identity disorder. *American Journal of Psychiatry, 154,* 832–839.

Elliot, A. J., & Devine, P. G. (1994). On the motivational nature of cognitive dissonance: Dissonance as psychological discomfort. *Journal of Personality and Social Psychology, 67,* 382–394.

Ellis, A. (1961). *A guide to rational living.* Englewood Cliffs, NJ: Prentice-Hall.

Ellis, A. (1977). The basic clinical theory of rational-emotive therapy. In A. Ellis & R. Grieger (Eds.), *Handbook of rational-emotive therapy* (pp. 3–33). New York: Springer.

Ellis, A. (1993). Reflections on rational-emotive therapy. *Journal of Consulting and Clinical Psychology, 61,* 199–201.

Ellis, A. (2004a). Why I (really) became a therapist. *Journal of Rational-Emotive & Cognitive Behavior Therapy, 22,* 73–77.

Ellis, A. (2004b). Why rational-emotive behavior therapy is the most comprehensive and effective form of behavior therapy. *Journal of Rational-Emotive & Cognitive Behavior Therapy, 22,* 85–92.

Else-Quest, N., Hyde, J., Goldsmith, H., & Van Hulle, C. (2006). Gender differences in temperament: A meta-analysis. *Psychological Bulletin, 132,* 33–72.

Engel, G. L. (1977). The need for a new medical model: A challenge for biomedicine. *Science, 196,* 126–129.

Engel, G. L. (1980). The clinical application of the biopsychosocial model. *American Journal of Psychiatry, 137,* 535–544.

Engels, G. I., Garnefski, N., & Diekstra, R. F. W. (1993). Efficacy of rational-emotive therapy: A quantitative analysis. *Journal of Consulting and Clinical Psychology, 61,* 1083–1090.

Engen, T. (1982). *The perception of odors.* New York: Academic Press.

Epstein, J. (1983). Examining theories of adolescent friendships. In J. Epstein & N. Karweit (Eds.), *Friends in school* (pp. 39–61). New York: Academic Press.

Epstein, J., Stern, E., & Silbersweig, D. (2001). Neuropsychiatry at the millennium: The potential for mind/brain integration through emerging interdisciplinary research strategies. *Clinical Neuroscience Research, 1,* 10–18.

Equifax. (2006). *How lenders see you.* Retrieved November 29, 2006, from https://www.econsumer.equifax.com/consumer/sitepage.ehtml?forward=cps_hlsysample

Erdogan, A., Kocabasoglu, N., Yalug, I., Ozbay, G., & Senturk, H. (2004). Management of marked liver enzyme increase during clozapine treatment: A case report and review of the literature. *International Journal of Psychiatry in Medicine, 34,* 83–89.

Erikson, E. (1968). *Identity, youth, and crisis.* (New York: W. W. Norton & Company.

Erikson, E., & Erikson, K. (1957). The confirmation of the delinquent. *Chicago Review, 10,* 15–23.

Erikson, E. H. (1980). *Identity and the life cycle.* New York: Norton.

Erlenmeyer-Kimling, L., & Jarvik, L. F. (1963). Genetics and intelligence: A review. *Science, 142,* 1477–1479.

Eron, L. D. (1987). The development of aggressive behavior from the perspective of a developing behaviorism. *American Psychologist, 42,* 435–442.

Eronen, M., Hakola, P., & Tiihonen, J. (1996). Mental disorders and homicidal behavior in Finland. *Journal of Personality and Social Psychology, 53,* 497–501.

Estes, W. K. (1994). *Classification and cognition.* New York: Oxford University Press.

Etcoff, N., Ekman, P., Magee, J., & Frank, M. (2000). Lie detection and language comprehension. *Nature, 405,* 139.

Evans, D., & Zarate, O. (2000). *Introducing evolutionary psychology.* New York: Totem Books.

Evans, G. W., & Lepore, S. J. (1993). Household crowding and social support: A quasiexperimental analysis. *Journal of Personality and Social Psychology, 65,* 308–316.

Evans, S., Huxley, P., Gately, C., Webber, M., Mears, A., Pajak, S., Medina, J., Kendall, T., & Katona, C. (2006). Mental health, burnout and job satisfaction among mental health social workers in England and Wales. *British Journal of Psychiatry, 188,* 75–80.

Everson, S. A., Goldberg, D. E., Kaplan, G. A., Cohen, R. D., Pukkala, E., Tuomilehto, J., et al. (1996). Hopelessness and risk of mortality and incidence of myocardial infarction and cancer. *Psychosomatic Medicine, 58,* 113–121.

Exner, J. E. (1993). *The Rorschach: A comprehensive system: Vol. 1. Basic foundations* (3rd ed.). New York: Wiley.

Eysenbach, G., Powell, J., Kuss, O., & Sa, E. (2002). Empirical studies of health information for consumers on the World Wide Web: A systematic review. *JAMA: Journal of the American Medical Association, 287,* 2691–2700.

Eysenck, H. J. (1990). Genetic and environmental contributions to individual differences: The three major dimensions of personality. *Journal of Personality, 58,* 245–261.

Eysenck, H. J. (1994). The outcome problem in psychotherapy: What have we learned? *Behaviour Research and Therapy, 32,* 477–495.

Fackelmann, K. (1997). Marijuana on trial: Is marijuana a dangerous drug or a valuable medicine? *Science News, 151,* 178–179, 183.

Fagot, B. (1995). Observations of parent reactions to sex-stereotyped behavior: Age and sex effects. *Child Development, 62,* 617–628.

Faisal-Cury, A., Tedesco, J., Kahhale, S., Menezes, P., & Zugaib, M. (2004). Postpartum depression: In relation to life events and patterns of coping. *Archives of Women's Mental Health, 7,* 123–131.

Famighetti, R. (Ed.). (1997). *The world almanac and book of facts 1998.* Mahwah, NJ: World Almanac Books.

Fang, C., & Myers, H. (2001). The effects of racial stressors and hostility on cardiovascular reactivity in African American and Caucasian men. *Health Psychology, 20,* 64–70.

Fanous, A., Gardner, C., Prescott, C., Cancro, R., & Kendler, K. (2002). Neuroticism, major depression and gender: A population-based twin study. *Psychological Medicine, 32,* 719–728.

Fantz, R. L. (1961). The origin of form perception. *Scientific American, 204,* 66–72.

Farde, L. (1996). The advantage of using positron emission tomography in drug research. *Trends in Neurosciences, 19,* 211–214.

Farrer, L. A., & Cupples, A. (1994). Estimating the probability for major gene Alzheimer disease. *American Journal of Human Genetics, 54,* 374–383.

Fauerbach, J., Lawrence, J., Haythornthwaite, J., & Richter, L. (2002). Coping with the stress of a painful medical procedure. *Behaviour Research & Therapy, 40,* 1003–1015.

Faunce, G. (2002). Eating disorders and attentional bias: A review. *Eating Disorders: The Journal of Treatment & Prevention, 10,* 125–139.

Fazio, R. H. (1989). On the power and functionality of attitudes: The role of attitude accessibility. In A. R. Pratkanis, S. J. Breckler, & A. G. Greenwald (Eds.), *Attitude structure and function* (pp. 153–179). Hillsdale, NJ: Erlbaum.

Fazio, R. H., & Williams, C. J. (1986). Attitude accessibility as a moderator of the attitude perception and attitude-behavior relations: An investigation of the 1984 presidential election. *Journal of Personality and Social Psychology, 51,* 505–514.

Federal Interagency Forum on Aging—Related Statistics (FIFARS). (2000). *Older Americans 2000: Key indicators of well-being.* Retrieved July 30, 2003, from http://www.agingstats.gov

Federal Interagency Forum on Aging—Related Statistics (FIFARS). (2004). *Older Americans 2004: Key indicators of well-being.* Retrieved January 27, 2005, from http://www.agingstats.gov/chartbook2004/default.htm

Feingold, A. (1988). Matching for attractiveness in romantic partners and same-sex friends: A meta-analysis and theoretical critique. *Psychological Bulletin, 104,* 226–235.

Fenn, K., Nusbaum, H., & Margoliash, D. (2003). Consolidation during sleep of perceptual learning of spoken language. *Nature, 425,* 614–616.

Fenton, W. S., & McGlashan, T. H. (1991). Natural history of schizophrenia subtypes: I. Longitudinal study of paranoid, hebephrenic, and undifferentiated schizophrenia. *Archives of General Psychiatry, 48,* 969–977.

Fenton, W. S., & McGlashan, T. H. (1994). Antecedents, symptom progression, and long-term outcome of the deficit syndrome in schizophrenia. *American Journal of Psychiatry, 151,* 351–356.

Fernald, A. (1993). Approval and disapproval: Infant responsiveness to vocal affect in familiar and unfamiliar languages. *Child Development, 64,* 637–656.

Ferreira, S., de Mello, M., Pompeia, S., & de Souza-Formigoni, M. (2006). Effects of energy drink ingestion on alcohol intoxication. *Alcoholism: Clinical and Experimental Research, 30,* 598.

Festinger, L. (1957). *A theory of cognitive dissonance.* Evanston, IL: Row, Peterson.

Festinger, L., & Carlsmith, J. M. (1959). Cognitive consequences of forced compliance. *Journal of Abnormal and Social Psychology, 58,* 203–210.

Fiatarone, M. A., Morley, J. E., Bloom, E. T., Benton, D., Makinodan, T., & Solomon, G. F. (1988). Endogenous opioids and the exercise-induced augmentation of natural killer cell activity. *Journal of Laboratory and Clinical Medicine, 112,* 544–552.

Fiatarone, M. A., O'Neill, E. F., Ryan, N. D., Clements, K. M., Solares, G. R., Nelson, M. E., et al. (1994). Exercise training and nutritional supplementation for physical frailty in very elderly people. *New England Journal of Medicine, 330,* 1769–1775.

Field, M., & Duka, T. (2002). Cues paired with a low dose of alcohol acquire conditioned incentive properties in social drinkers. *Psychopharmacology, 159,* 325–334.

Field, T. (2002). Infants' need for touch. *Human Development, 45,* 100–103.

Field, T., Schanberg, S. M., Scfidi, F., Bauer, C. R., Vega-Lahr, N., Garcia, R., et al. (1986, May). Tactile/kinesthetic stimulation effects on preterm neonates. *Pediatrics, 77,* 654–658.

Field, T. M., Cohen, D., Garcia, R., & Greenberg, R. (1984). Mother–stranger face discrimination by the newborn. *Infant Behavior and Development, 7,* 19–25.

Fields, J., Walton, K., & Schneider, R. (2002). Effect of a multimodality natural medicine program on carotid atherosclerosis in older subjects: A pilot trial of Maharishi Verdic Medicine. *American Journal of Cardiology, 89,* 952–958.

Finch, A. E., Lambert, M. J., & Brown, G. (2000). Attacking anxiety: A naturalistic study of a multimedia self-help program. *Journal of Clinical Psychology, 56,* 11–21.

Fink, B., & Penton-Voak, I. (2002). Evolutionary psychology of facial attractiveness. *Current Directions in Psychological Science, 11,* 154–158.

Fischbach, G. D. (1992). Mind and brain. *Scientific American, 267,* 48–56.

Fischer, K., & Rose, S. (1994). Dynamic development of coordination of components in brain and behavior: A framework for theory and research. In K. Fischer & G. Dawson (Eds.), *Human Behavior and the Developing Brain* (pp. 3–66). New York: Guilford Press.

Fivush, R., & Nelson, K. (2004). Culture and language in the emergence of autobiographical memory. *Psychological Science, 15,* 573–577.

Fixx, J. F. (1978). *Solve It! A perplexing profusion of puzzles.* New York: Doubleday.

Flavell, J. H. (1985). *Cognitive development.* Englewood, NJ: Prentice-Hall.

Flavell, J. H. (1992). Cognitive development: Past, present, and future. *Developmental Psychology, 28,* 998–1005.

Flavell, J. H. (1996). Piaget's legacy. *Psychological Science, 7,* 200–203.

Fleck, D., Hendricks, W., DelBellow, M., & Strakowski, S. (2002). Differential prescription of maintenance antipsychotics to African American and White patients with new-onset bipolar disorder. *Journal of Clinical Psychiatry, 63,* 658–664.

Fleming, J. D. (1974, July). Field report: The state of the apes. *Psychology Today,* pp. 31–46.

Fleshner, M., & Laudenslager, M. (2004). Psychoneuroimmunology: Then and now. *Behavioral & Cognitive Neuroscience Reviews, 3,* 114–130.

Fletcher, J. M., Page, B., Francis, D. J., Copeland, K., Naus, M. J., Davis, C. M., Morris, R., Krauskopf, D., & Satz, P. (1996). Cognitive correlates of long-term cannabis use in Costa Rican men. *Archives of General Psychiatry, 53,* 1051–1057.

Flynn, J. (1999). Searching for justice: The discovery of IQ gains over time. *American Psychologist, 54,* 5–20.

Flynn, J. R. (1987). Race and IQ: Jensen's case refuted. In S. Modgil, & C. Modgil (Eds.), *Arthur Jensen: Consensus and controversy* (221–232). New York: Palmer Press.

Foa, E. B. (1995). How do treatments for obsessive-compulsive disorder compare? *Harvard Mental Health Letter, 12*(1), 8.

Foley, D. J., Monjan, A. A., Brown, S. L., Simonsick, E. M., Wallace, R. B., & Blazer, D. G. (1995). Sleep complaints among elderly persons: An epidemiologic study of three communities. *Sleep, 18,* 425–432.

Folkman, S. (1984). Personal control and stress and coping processes: A theoretical analysis. *Journal of Personality and Social Psychology, 46,* 839–852.

Folkman, S., Chesney, M., Collette, L., Boccellari, A., & Cooke, M. (1996). Postbereavement depressive mood and its prebereavement predictors in HIV+ and HIV− gay men. *Journal of Personality and Social Psychology, 70,* 336–348.

Folkman, S., & Lazarus, R. S. (1980). An analysis of coping in a middle-aged community sample. *Journal of Health and Social Behavior, 21,* 219–239.

Ford, C. S., & Beach, F. A. (1951). *Patterns of sexual behavior.* New York: Harper & Row.

Foulkes, D. (1996). Sleep and dreams: Dream research: 1953–1993. *Sleep, 19,* 609–624.

Fourkas, A., Ionta, S., & Aglioti, S. (2006). Influence of imagined posture and imagery modality on corti-cospinal excitability. *Behavioural Brain Research, 168,* 190–196.

Fox, N. A., & Bell, M. A. (1990). Electrophysiological indices of frontal lobe development: Relations to cognitive and affective behavior in human infants over the first year of life. *Annals of the New York Academy of Sciences, 608,* 677–698.

Francis-Smythe, J., & Smith, P. (1997). The psychological impact of assessment in a development center. *Human Relations, 50,* 149–167.

Francks, C., DeLisi, L., Fisher, S., Laval, S., Rue, J., Stein, J., et al. (2003). Confirmatory evidence for linkage of relative hand skill to 2p12-q11. *American Journal of Human Genetics, 72,* 499–502.

Frank, E., Anderson, B., Reynolds, C. F., III, Ritenour, A., & Kupfer, D. J. (1994). Life events and the research diagnostic criteria endogenous subtype. *Archives of General Psychiatry, 51,* 519–524.

Frank, E., Kupfer, D. J., Wagner, E. F., McEachran, A. B., & Cornes, C. (1991). Efficacy of interpersonal psychotherapy as a maintenance treatment of recurrent depression: Contributing factors. *Archives of General Psychiatry, 48,* 1053–1059.

Franklin, A., Pilling, M., & Davies, I. (2005). The nature of infant colour categorization: Evidence from eye-movements on a target detection task. *Journal of Experimental Child Psychology, 91,* 227–248.

Franks, P., Gold, M., & Fiscella, K. (2003). Sociodemographics, self-rated health, and mortality in the U. S. *Social Science & Medicine, 56,* 2505–2514.

Frantz, K., Hansson, K., Stouffer, D., & Parsons, L. (2002). 5-HT-sub-6 receptor antagonism potentiates the behavioral and neurochemical effects of amphetamine but not cocaine. *Neuropharmacology, 42,* 170–180.

Frazer, A. (1997). Antidepressants. *Journal of Clinical Psychiatry, 58*(6, Suppl.), 9–25.

Frazer, N., Larkin, K., & Goodie, J. (2002). Do behavioral responses mediate or moderate the relation between cardiovascular reactivity to stress and parental history of hypertension? *Health Psychology, 21,* 244–253.

Fredricks, J., & Eccles, J. (2002). Children's competence and value beliefs from childhood through adolescence growth trajectories in two male-sex-typed domains. *Developmental Psychology, 38,* 519–533.

Fredrickson, B. (2001). The role of positive emotions in positive psychology. *American Psychologist, 56,* 218–226.

Fredrikson, M., Annas, P., Fischer, H., & Wik, G. (1996). Gender and age differences in the prevalence of specific fears and phobias. *Behaviour Research and Therapy, 34,* 33–39.

Freedman, J. L., & Fraser, S. C. (1966). Compliance without pressure: The foot-in-the-door technique. *Journal of Personality and Social Psychology, 4,* 195–202.

Freeman, C. (2004). Trends in educational equity of girls & women. Retrieved July 3, 2006 from http://nces.ed.gov/pubs2005/2005016.pdf

Freeman, W. J. (1991). The physiology of perception. *Scientific American, 264,* 78–85.

Freud, S. (1900/1953a). The interpretation of dreams. In J. Strachey (Ed. and trans.), *The standard edition of the complete psychological works of Sigmund Freud* (Vols. 4 and 5). London: Hogarth Press. (Original work published 1900).

Freud, S. (1905/1953b). Three essays on the theory of sexuality. In J. Strachey (Ed. and Trans.), *The standard edition of the complete psychological works of Sigmund Freud* (Vol. 7). London: Hogarth Press. (Original work published 1905).

Freud, S. (1920/1963b). *A general introduction to psychoanalysis* (J. Riviere, Trans.). New York: Simon & Schuster. (Original work published 1920).

Freud, S. (1922). *Beyond the pleasure principle.* London: International Psychoanalytic Press.

Freud, S. (1925/1963a). *An autobiographical study* (J. Strachey, Trans.). New York: W.W. Norton. (Original work published 1925).

Freud, S. (1930/1962). *Civilization and its discontents* (J. Strachey, Trans.). New York: W. W. Norton. (Original work published 1930).

Freud, S. (1933/1965). *New introductory lectures on psychoanalysis* (J. Strachey, Trans.). New York: W. W. Norton. (Original work published 1933).

Freudenberger, H., & Richelson, G. (1981). *Burnout.* New York: Bantam Books.

Frey, K. P., & Eagly, A. H. (1993). Vividness can undermine the persuasiveness of messages. *Journal of Personality and Social Psychology, 65,* 32–44.

Frey, M., & Detterman, D. (2004). Scholastic assessment or *g?* The relationship between the scholastic assessment test and general cognitive ability. *Psychological Science, 15,* 373–378.

Frick, P., Cornell, A., Bodin, S., Dane, H., Barry, C., & Loney, B. (2003). Callous-unemotional traits and developmental pathways to severe conduct problems. *Developmental Psychology, 39,* 246–260.

Friedland, N., Keinan, G., & Regev, Y. (1992). Controlling the uncontrollable: Effects of stress on illusory perceptions of controllability. *Journal of Personality and Social Psychology, 63,* 923–931.

Friedman, J. M. (1997). The alphabet of weight control. *Nature, 385,* 119–120.

Friedman, J. M. (2000). Obesity in the new millennium. *Nature, 404,* 632–634.

Friedman, M., & Rosenman, R. H. (1974). *Type A behavior and your heart.* New York: Fawcett.

Friedman, M. I., Tordoff, M. G., & Ramirez, I. (1986). Integrated metabolic control of food intake. *Brain Research Bulletin, 17,* 855–859.

Fujita, F., Diener, E., & Sandvik, E. (1991). Gender differences in negative affect and well-being: The case for emotional intensity. *Journal of Personality and Social Psychology, 61,* 427–434.

Gadea, M., Martinez-Bisbal, M., Marti-Bonmati, Espert, R., Casanova, B., Coret, F., & Celda, B. (2004). Spectroscopic axonal damage of the right locus coeruleus relates to selective attention impairment in early stage relapsing-remitting multiple sclerosis. *Brain, 127,* 89–98.

Galambos, N., Turner, P., & Tilton-Weaver, L. (2005). Chronological and subjective age in emerging adulthood: The crossover effect. *Journal of Adolescent Research, 20,* 538–556.

Gallagher, M., & Rapp, P. R. (1997). The use of animal models to study the effects of aging on cognition. *Annual Review of Psychology, 48,* 339–370.

Gallo, L., Troxel, W., Matthews, K., Jansen-McWilliams, L., Kuller, L., & Suton-Tyrrell, K. (2003). Occupation and subclinical carotid artery disease: Are clerical workers at greater risk? *Health Psychology, 22,* 19–29.

Gallup, G. (1970). Chimpanzees: Self-recognition. *Science, 167,* 86–87.

Gallup, G., Anderson, J., & Shillito, D. (2002). The mirror test. In M. Bekoff, C. Allen, & G. Burghardt (Eds.), *The cognitive animal: Empirical and theoretical perspectives on animal cognition* (pp. 325–334). Cambridge, MA: MIT Press.

Gallup, G., Jr., & Hugick, L. (1990). Racial tolerance grows, progress on racial equality less evident. *Gallup Poll Monthly, 297,* 23–32.

Gao, J-H., Parsons, L. M., Bower, J. M., Xiong, J., Li, J., & Fox, P. T. (1996). Cerebellum implicated in sensory acquisition and discrimination rather than motor control. *Science, 272,* 545–547.

Ganellen, R. J. (1996). Comparing the diagnostic efficiency of the MMPI, MCMI-II, and Rorschach: A review. *Journal of Personality Assessment, 67,* 219–243.

Garavan, H., Morgan, R. E., Levitsky, D. A., Hermer-Vasquez, L., & Strupp, B. J. (2000). Enduring effects of early lead exposure: Evidence for a specific deficit in associative ability. *Neurotoxicology and Teratology, 22,* 151–164.

Garcia, J., & Koelling, A. (1966). Relation of cue to consequence in avoidance learning. *Psychonomic Science, 4,* 123–124.

Gardner, H. (1983). *Frames of mind: The theory of multiple intelligences.* New York: Basic Books.

Gardner, H., & Hatch, T. (1989). Multiple intelligences go to school: Educational implication of the theory of multiple intelligences. *Educational Researcher, 18*(8), 6.

Gardner, R. A., & Gardner, B. T. (1969). Teaching sign language to a chimpanzee. *Science, 165,* 664–672.

Garfield, C. (1986). *Peak performers: The new heroes of American business.* New York: Morrow.

Garma, L., & Marchand, F. (1994). Non-pharmacological approaches to the treatment of narcolepsy. *Sleep, 17,* S97–S102.

Garmon, L. C., Basinger, K. S., Gregg, V. R., & Gibbs, J. C. (1996). Gender differences in stage and expression of moral judgment. *Merrill-Palmer Quarterly, 42,* 418–437.

Garrett, M., Garrett, J., & Brotherton, D. (2001). Inner circle/outer circle: A group technique based on Native American healing circles. *Journal for Specialists in Group Work, 26,* 17–30.

Garry, M., & Loftus, E. F. (1994). Pseudomemories without hypnosis. *International Journal of Clinical and Experimental Hypnosis, 42,* 363–373.

Gartner, J., & Whitaker-Azimitia, P. M. (1996). Developmental factors influencing aggression: Animal models and clinical correlates. *Annals of the New York Academy of Sciences, 794,* 113–120.

Gavin, J., Scott, A., & Duffield, J. (2006). *Passion, intimacy and commitment in online dating: Time versus channel effects.* Paper presented at the International Association for Relationship Research Conference. July, 2006, University of Crete, Greece.

Gawin, F. H. (1991). Cocaine addiction: Psychology and neurophysiology. *Science, 251,* 1580–1586.

Gawronski, B., Alshut, E., Grafe, J., Nespethal, J., Ruhmland, A., & Schulz, L. (2002). Processes of judging known and unknown persons. *Zeitschrift fuer Sozialpsychologie, 33,* 25–34.

Gazzaniga, M. (1970). *The bisected brain.* New York: Appleton- Century-Crofts.

Gazzaniga, M. (1989). Organization of the human brain. *Science, 245,* 947–952.

Gazzola, N., & Stalikas, A. (2004). Therapist interpretations and client processes in three therapeutic modalities: Implications for psychotherapy integration. *Journal of Psychotherapy Integration, 14,* 397–418.

Ge, X., Brody, G., Conger, R., Simons, R., & Murry, V. (2002). Contextual amplification of pubertal transition effects on deviant peer affiliation and externalizing behavior among African American children. *Developmental Psychology, 38,* 42–54.

Geary, D. C. (1996). Sexual selection and sex differences in mathematical abilities. *Behavioral and Brain Sciences, 19,* 229–284.

Geary, N. (2004). Endocrine controls of eating: CCK, leptin, and ghrelin. *Physiology & Behavior, 81,* 719–733.

Geen, R. G. (1984). Human motivation: New perspectives on old problems. In A. M. Rogers & C. J. Scheier (Eds.), *The G. Stanley Hall lecture series* (Vol. 4, pp. 9–57). Washington, DC: American Psychological Association.

Gehart, D., & Lyle, R. (2001). Client experience of gender in therapeutic relationships: An interpretive ethnography. *Family Process, 40,* 443–458.

Gehring, D. (2003). Couple therapy for low sexual desire: A systematic approach. *Journal of Sex & Marital Therapy, 29,* 25–38.

Geiselman, R. E., Schroppel, T., Tubridy, A., Konishi, T., & Rodriguez, V. (2000). Objectivity bias in eye witness performance. *Applied Cognitive Psychology, 14,* 323–332.

George, M. S., Ketter, T. A., & Post, R. M. (1993). SPECT and PET imaging in mood disorders. *Journal of Clinical Psychiatry, 54*(11, Suppl.), 6–13.

George, T., & Vessicchio, J. (2001). Nicotine addiction and schizophrenia. *Psychiatric Times.* Retrieved February 12, 2007, from http://www.psychiatrictimes.com/p010239.html

German, T., & Barrett, H. (2005). Functional fixedness in a technologically sparse culture. *Psychological Science, 16,* 1–5.

Gerrits, M., Petromilli, P., Westenberg, H., Di Chiara, G., & van Ree, J. (2002). Decrease in basal dopamine levels in the nucleus accumbens shell during daily drug-seeking behavior in rats. *Brain Research, 924,* 141–150.

Gevins, A., Leong, H., Smith, M. E., Le, J., & Du, R. (1995). Mapping cognitive brain function with modern high-resolution electroencephalography. *Trends in Neurosciences, 18,* 429–436.

Gibbons, A. (1991). Déjà vu all over again: Chimp-language wars. *Science, 251,* 1561–1562.

Gibson, E., & Walk, R. D. (1960). The "visual cliff." *Scientific American, 202,* 64–71.

Gibson, J. (1994). The visual perception of objective motion and subjective motion. *Psychological Review, 101,* 318–323.

Giedd, J. N., Rapoport, J. L., Garvey, M. A., Perlmutter, S., & Swedo, S. E. (2000). MRI assessment of children with obsessive-compulsive disorder or tics associated with streptococcal infection. *American Journal of Psychiatry, 157,* 2281–2283.

Gigerenzer, G. (2004). Dread risk, September 11, and fatal traffic accidents. *Psychological Science, 15,* 286–287.

Gilbert, D. (2006). *Stumbling on happiness.* New York: Alfred A. Knopf.

Gilbert, D. T., & Malone, P. S. (1995). The correspondence bias. *Psychological Bulletin, 117,* 21–38.

Gilligan, C. (1982). *In a different voice: Psychological theory and women's development.* Cambridge, MA: Harvard University Press.

Gingell, C., Nicolosi, A., Buvat, J., Glasser, D., Simsek, F., Hartmann, U., et al. (2003). *Sexual activity and dysfunction among men and women aged 40 to 80 years.* Poster presented at the XVIIIth Congress of the European Association of Urology. Madrid, March, 2003.

Ginty, D. D., Kornhauser, J. M., Thompson, M. A., Bading, H., Mayo, K. E., Takahashi, J. S., et al. (1993). Regulation of CREB phosphorylation in the suprachiasmatic nucleus by light and a circadian clock. *Science, 260,* 238–241.

Ginzburg, K., Solomon, Z., & Bleich, A. (2002). Repressive coping style, acute stress disorder, and post-traumatic stress disorder after myocardial infarction. *Journal of the American Psychosomatic Society, 64,* 748–757.

Giraud, A., Price, C., Graham, J., & Frackowisk, R. (2001). Functional plasticity of language-related brain areas after cochlear implantation. *Neuropsychopharmacology, 124,* 1307–1316.

Girolamo, G., & Bassi, M. (2003). Community surveys of mental disorders: Recent achievements and works in progress. *Current Opinion in Psychiatry, 16,* 403–411.

Glannon, W. (2006). Neuroethics. *Bioethics, 20,* 37–52.

Glantz, L. A., & Lewis, D. A. (2000). Decreased dendritic spine density on prefrontal cortical pyramidal neurons in schizophrenia. *Archives of General Psychiatry, 57,* 65–73.

Glass, D. C., & Singer, J. E. (1972). *Urban stress: Experiments in noise and social stressors.* New York: Academic Press.

Glazer, W. M., Morgenstern, H., & Doucette, J. T. (1993). Predicting the long-term risk of tardive dyskinesia in outpatients maintained on neuroleptic medications. *Journal of Clinical Psychiatry, 54,* 133–139.

Gleaves, D. J. (1996). The sociocognitive model of dissociative identity disorder: A reexamination of the evidence. *Psychological Bulletin, 120,* 42–59.

Global Fund to Fight AIDS, Tuberculosis, and Malaria, (2005). *Global Fund ARV factsheet.* Retrieved July 3, 2006, from http://www.theglobalfund.org/en/files/publications/factsheets/aids/ARV_Factsheet_2006.pdf

Glover, J. A., & Corkill, A. J. (1987). Influence of paraphrased repetitions on the spacing effect. *Journal of Educational Psychology, 79,* 198–199.

Gluck, M. A., & Myers, C. E. (1997). Psychobiological models of hippocampal function in learning and memory. *Annual Review of Psychology, 48,* 481–514.

Godden, D. R., & Baddeley, A. D. (1975). Context-dependent memory in two natural environments: On land and underwater. *British Journal of Psychology, 66,* 325–331.

Goeders, N. (2004). Stress, motivation, and drug addiction. *Current Directions in Psychological Science, 13,* 33–35.

Gökcebay, N., Cooper, R., Williams, R. L., Hirshkowitz, M., & Moore, C. A. (1994). Function of sleep. In R. Cooper (Ed.), *Sleep* (pp. 47–59). New York: Chapman & Hall.

Gogtay, N., Giedd, J., Lusk, L., Hayashi, K., Greenstein, D., Vaituzis, A., et al. (2004). Dynamic mapping of human cortical development during childhood through early adulthood. *Proceedings of the National Academy of Science, 101,* 8174–8179.

Goldberg, L. (1993). The structure of phenotypic personality traits. *American Psychologist, 48,* 26–34.

Goldstein, D. & Gigerenzer, G. (2002). Models of ecological rationality: The recognition heuristic. *Psychological Review, 109,* 75–90.

Goleman, D., Kaufman, P., & Ray, M. (1992). *The creative spirit.* New York: Dutton.

Gollan, T., & Brown, A. (2006). From tip-of-the-tongue (TOT) data to theoretical implications in two steps: When more TOTs means better retrieval. *Journal of Experimental Psychology: General, 135,* 462–483.

Gollan, T., & Silverberg, N. (2001). Tip-of-the-tongue states in Hebrew-English bilinguals. *Bilingualism: Language and Cognition, 4,* 63–83.

Gonsalves, B., Reber, P., Gitelman, D., Parrish, T., Mesulam, M., & Paller, K. (2004). Neural evidence that vivid imagining can lead to false remembering. *Psychological Science, 15,* 655–660.

Gonzalez, R., Ellsworth, P. C., & Pembroke, M. (1993). Response biases in lineups and showups. *Journal of Personality and Social Psychology, 64,* 525–537.

Good, C., Aronson, J., & Inzlicht, M. (2003). Improving adolescents' standardized test performance: An intervention to reduce the effects of stereotype threat. *Applied Developmental Psychology, 24,* 645–662.

Goodglass, H. (1993). *Understanding aphasia.* San Diego, CA: Academic Press.

Goodman, E., McEwen, B., Huang, B., Dolan, L., & Adler, N. (2005). Social inequalities in biomarkers of cardiovascular risk in adolescence. *Psychosomatic Medicine, 67,* 9–15.

Goodwin, G. M. (1996). How do antidepressants affect serotonin receptors? The role of serotonin receptors in the therapeutic and side effect profile of the SSRIs. *Journal of Clinical Psychiatry, 57*(4, Suppl.), 9–13.

Goodwin, R., & Fitzgibbon, M. (2002). Social anxiety as a barrier to treatment for eating disorders. *International Journal of Eating Disorders, 32,* 103–106.

Goodwin, R., & Gotlib, I. (2004). Gender differences in depression: The role of personality factors. *Psychiatry Research, 126,* 135–142.

Gordon, H. (2002). Early environmental stress and biological vulnerability to drug abuse. *Psychoneuroendocrinology, 27,* 115–126.

Gorman, C. (1996, Fall). Damage control. *Time* [Special Issue], 31–35.

Gottesman, I. I. (1991). *Schizophrenia genesis: The origins of madness.* New York: W. H. Freeman.

Gottesmann, C. (2000). Hypothesis for the neurophysiology of dreaming. *Sleep Research Online, 3,* 1–4.

Gough, H. (1987). *California Psychological Inventory: Administrator's Guide.* Palo Alto: Consulting Psychologists Press.

Gould, E. R., Reeves, A. J., Graziano, M. S. A., & Gross, C. (1999). Neurogenesis in the neocortex of adult primates. *Science, 286,* 548.

Gow, A., Whiteman, M., Pattie, A., & Deary, I. (2005). Goldberg's IPIP Big-Five factor markers: Internal consistency and concurrent validation in Scotland. *Personality and Individual Differences, 39,* 317–329.

Granic, I., & Patterson, G. (2006). Toward a comprehensive model of antisocial development: A dynamic systems approach. *Psychological Review, 113,* 101–131.

Grant, D., & Harari, E. (2005). Psychoanalysis, science and the seductive theory of Karl Popper. *Australian and New Zealand Journal of Psychiatry, 39,* 446–452.

Greden, J. F. (1994). Introduction Part III. New agents for the treatment of depression. *Journal of Clinical Psychiatry, 55*(2, Suppl.), 32–33.

Green, B. L., Lindy, J. D., & Grace, M. C. (1985). Post-traumatic stress disorder: Toward DSM-IV. *Journal of Nervous and Mental Disorders, 173,* 406–411.

Green, J., & Shellenberger, R. (1990). *The dynamics of health and wellness: A biopsychosocial approach.* Fort Worth: Holt, Rinehart & Winston.

Green, J. P., & Lynn, S. J. (2000). Hypnosis and suggestion-based approaches to smoking cessation: An examination of the evidence. *International Journal of Clinical Experimental Hypnosis, 48,* 195–224.

Green, L. R., Richardson, D. R., & Lago, T. (1996). How do friendship, indirect, and direct aggression relate? *Aggressive Behavior, 22,* 81–86.

Greenwald, A. (1992). New look 3: Unconscious cognition reclaimed. *American Psychologist, 47,* 766–779.

Greenwald, A., Spangenberg, E., Pratkanis, A., & Eskenazi, J. (1991). Double-blind tests of subliminal self-help audiotapes. *Psychological Science, 2,* 119–122.

Greer, M. (2005). Keeping them hooked in. *APA Monitor on Psychology, 36,* 60.

Gregory, R. J. (1996). *Psychological testing: History, principles, and applications* (2nd ed.). Boston: Allyn & Bacon.

Greist, J. H. (1992). An integrated approach to treatment of obsessive compulsive disorder. *Journal of Clinical Psychiatry, 53*(4, Suppl.), 38–41.

Greist, J. H. (1995). The diagnosis of social phobia. *Journal of Clinical Psychiatry, 56*(5, Suppl.), 5–12.

Griffiths, M. (2003). Communicating risk: Journalists have responsibility to report risks in context. *British Medical Journal, 327,* 1404.

Grigorenko, E. (2003). Epistasis and the genetics of complex traits. In R. Plomin, J. DeFries, I. Craig, & P. McGuffin (Eds.), *Behavioral genetics in the postgenomic era* (pp. 247–266). Washington, DC: American Psychological Association.

Grigorenko, E., Jarvin, L., & Sternberg, R. (2002). School-based tests of the triarchic theory of intelligence: Three settings, three samples, three syllabi. *Contemporary Educational Psychology, 27,* 167–208.

Grigorenko, E., Meier, E., Lipka, J., Mohatt, G., Yanez, E., & Sternberg, R. (2004). Academic and practical intelligence: A case study of the Yup'ik in Alaska. *Learning & Individual Differences, 14,* 183–207.

Grinker, J. A. (1982). Physiological and behavioral basis for human obesity. In D. W. Pfaff (Ed.), The physiological mechanisms of motivation. New York: Springer-Verlag.

Grochowicz, P., Schedlowski, M., Husband, A., King, M., Hibberd, A., & Bowen, K. (1991). Behavioral conditioning prolongs heart allograft survival in rats. *Brain, Behavior, and Immunity, 5,* 349–356.

Gron, G., Wunderlich, A. P., Spitzer, M., Tomczrak, R., & Riepe, M. W. (2000). Brain activation during human navigation: Gender-different neural networks as substrate of performance. *Nature Neuroscience, 3,* 404–408.

Gross, J. (2002). Emotion regulation: Affective, cognitive, and social consequences. *Psychophysiology, 39,* 281–291.

Grossenbacher, P., & Lovelace, C. (2001). Mechanisms of synesthesia: Cognitive and physiological constraints. *Trends in Cognitive Sciences, 5,* 36–41.

Grossman, H. J. (Ed.). (1983). *Manual on terminology and classification in mental retardation.* Washington, DC: American Association on Mental Deficiency.

Grossman, J., & Ruiz, P. (2004). Shall we make a leap-of-faith to disulfiram (Antabuse)? *Addictive Disorders & Their Treatment, 3,* 129–132.

Grossman, M., & Wood, W. (1993). Sex differences in intensity of emotional experience: A social role interpretation. *Journal of Personality and Social Psychology, 65,* 1010–1022.

Grünbaum, A. (2006). Is Sigmund Freud's psychoanalytic edifice relevant to the 21st century? *Psychoanalytic Psychology, 23,* 257–284.

Guadagno, R., & Cialdini, R. (2007). Persuade him by email, but see her in person: Online persuasion revisited. *Computers in Human Behavior, 23,* 99–1015.

Guenole, N., & Chernyshenko, O. (2005). The suitability of Goldberg's Big Five IPIP personality markers in New Zealand: A dimensionality, bias, and criterion validity evaluation. *New Zealand Journal of Psychology, 34,* 86–96.

Guilford, J. P. (1967). *The nature of human intelligence.* New York: McGraw-Hill.

Guilleminault, C. (1993). Amphetamines and narcolepsy: Use of the Stanford database. *Sleep, 16,* 199–201.

Gur, R., Gunning-Dixon, F., Bilker, W., & Gur, R. (2002). Sex differences in temporolimbic and frontal brain volumes of healthy adults. *Cerebral Cortex, 12,* 998–1003.

Gur, R. C., Turetsky, B., Mastsui, M., Yan, M. Bilker, W., Hughett, P., & Gur, R. E. (1999). Sex differences in brain gray and white matter in healthy young adults: correlations with cognitive performance. *Journal of Neuroscience, 19,* 4067–4072.

Gurin, J. (1989, June). Leaner, not lighter. *Psychology Today,* 32–36.

Guthrie, R. (2004). *Even the rat was white* (classic ed.). Boston, MA: Allyn & Bacon.

Haag, L., & Stern, E. (2003). In search of the benefits of learning Latin. *Journal of Educational Psychology, 95,* 174–178.

Habel, U., Kuehn, E., Salloum, J., Devos, H., & Schneider, F. (2002). Emotional processing in psychopathic personality. *Aggressive Behavior, 28,* 394–400.

Haber, R. N. (1980). How we perceive depth from flat pictures. *American Scientist, 68,* 370–380.

Haberlandt, D. (1997). *Cognitive psychology* (2nd ed.). Boston: Allyn & Bacon.

Hackel, L. S., & Ruble, D. N. (1992). Changes in the marital relationship after the first baby is born: Predicting the impact of expectancy disconfirmation. *Journal of Personality and Social Psychology, 62,* 944–957.

Hada, M., Porjesz, B., Begleiter, H., & Polich, J. (2000). Auditory P3a assessment of male alcoholics. *Biological Psychiatry, 48,* 276–286.

Hada, M., Porjesz, B., Chorlian, D., Begleiter, H., & Polich, J. (2001). Auditory P3a deficits in male subjects at high risk for alcoholism. *Biological Psychiatry, 49,* 726–738.

Häkkänen, H., & Summala, H. (1999). Sleepiness at work among commercial truck drivers. *Sleep, 23,* 49–57.

Hakuta, K., Bialystok, E., & Wiley, E. (2003). Critical evidence: A test of the critical-period hypothesis for second-language acquisition. *Psychological Science, 14,* 31–38.

Halaas, J. L., Gajiwala, K. S., Maffei, M., Cohen, S. L., Chait, B. T., Rabinowitz, D., et al. (1995). Weight-reducing effects of the plasma protein encoded by the obese gene. *Science, 269,* 543–546.

Halama, P., & Strízenec, M. (2004). Spiritual, existential or both? Theoretical considerations on the nature of "higher" intelligences. *Studia Psychologica, 46,* 239–253.

Halaris, A. (2003). Neurochemical aspects of the sexual response cycle. *CNS Spectrums, 8,* 211–216.

Halford, G. S. (1989). Reflections on 25 years of Piagetian cognitive developmental psychology, 1963–1988. *Human Development, 32,* 325–327.

Halligan, P. W., & Marshall, J. C. (1994). Toward a principled explanation of unilateral neglect. *Cognitive Neuropsychology, 11,* 167–206.

Hallon, S., Stewart, M., & Strunk, D. (2006). Enduring effects for cognitive therapy in the treatment of depression and anxiety. *Annual Review of Psychology, 57,* 285–316.

Hallschmid, M., Benedict, C., Born, J., Fehm, H., & Kern, W. (2004). Manipulating central nervous mechanisms of food intake and body weight regulation by intranasal administration of neuropeptides in man. *Physiology & Behavior, 83,* 55–64.

Halmi, K. A. (1996). Eating disorder research in the past decade. *Annals of the New York Academy of Sciences, 789,* 67–77.

Ham, P. (2003). Suicide risk not increased with SSRI and antidepressants. *Journal of Family Practice, 52,* 587–589.

Hamilton, C. S., & Swedo, S. E. (2001). Autoimmune-mediated, childhood onset obsessive-compulsive disorder and tics: A review. *Clinical Neuroscience Research, 1,* 61–68.

Hampson, S., Goldberg, L., Vogt, T., & Dubanoski, J. (2006). Forty years on: Teachers' assessments of children's personality traits predict self-reported health behaviors and outcomes at midlife. *Health Psychology, 25,* 57–64.

Hancock, P., & Ganey, H. (2003). From the inverted-u to the extended-u: The evolution of a law of psychology. *Journal of Human Performance in Extreme Environments, 7,* 5–14.

Hanley, S., & Abell, S. (2002). Maslow and relatedness: Creating an interpersonal model of self-actualization. *Journal of Humanistic Psychology, 42,* 37–56.

Hannover, B., & Kuehnen, U. (2002). "The clothing makes the self" via knowledge activation. *Journal of Applied Social Psychology, 32,* 2513–2525.

Hanoch, Y., & Vitouch, O. (2004). When less is more: Information, emotional arousal and the ecological reframing of the Yerkes-Dodson law. *Theory & Psychology, 14,* 427–452.

Harackiewicz, A., Barron, A., Pintrich, A., Elliot, A., & Thrash, A. (2002). Revision of achievement goal theory: Necessary and illuminating. *Journal of Educational Psychology, 94,* 638–645.

Hare, R. (1998). The Hare PCL-R: Some issues concerning its use and misuse. *Legal and Criminological Psychology, 3,* 99–119.

Hargadon, R., Bowers, K. S., & Woody, E. Z. (1995). Does counterpain imagery mediate hypnotic analgesia? *Journal of Abnormal Psychology, 104,* 508–516.

Harlow, H. F., & Harlow, M. K. (1962). Social deprivation in monkeys. *Scientific American, 207,* 137–146.

Harlow, J. M. (1848). Passage of an iron rod through the head. *Boston Medical and Surgical Journal, 39,* 389–393.

Harms, P., Roberts, B., & Winter, D. (2006). Becoming the Harvard Man: Person–environment fit, personality development, and academic success. *Personality and Social Psychology Bulletin, 32,* 851–865.

Harp, S., & Mayer, R. (1998). How seductive details do their damage: A theory of cognitive interest in science learning. *Journal of Educational Psychology, 90,* 414–434.

Harris, J. A., Rushton, J. P., Hampson, E., & Jackson, D. N. (1996). Salivary testosterone and self-report aggressive and pro-social personality characteristics in men and women. *Aggressive Behavior, 22,* 321–331.

Harris, R. A., Brodie, M. S., & Dunwiddie, T. V. (1992). Possible substrates of ethanol reinforcement: GABA and dopamine. *Annals of the New York Academy of Sciences, 654,* 61–69.

Harrison, Y., & Horne, J. A. (2000). Sleep loss and temporal memory. *Journal of Experimental Psychology, 53,* 271–279.

Hart, J., Karau, S., Stasson, M., & Kerr, N. (2004). Achievement motivation, expected coworker performance, and collective task motivation: Working hard or hardly working? *Journal of Applied Social Psychology, 34,* 984–1000.

Haslam, S. A., & Reicher, S. (2006). Stressing the group: Social identity and the unfolding dynamics of responses to stress. *Journal of Applied Psychology, 91,* 1037–1052.

Hatashita-Wong, M., Smith, T., Silverstein, S., Hull, J., & Willson, D. (2002). Cognitive functioning and social problem-solving skills in schizophrenia. *Cognitive Neuropsychiatry, 7,* 81–95.

Hauser, M., Li, Y., Xu, H., Noureddine, M., Shao, Y., Gullans, S., et al. (2005). Expression profiling of substantia nigra in Parkinson disease, progressive supranuclear palsy, and frontotemporal dementia with Parkinsonism. *Archives of Neurology, 62,* 917–921.

Hauser, M. D. (1993). Right hemisphere dominance for the production of facial expression in monkeys. *Science, 261,* 475–477.

Hawley, K., & Weisz, J. (2003). Child, parent and therapist (dis)agreement on target problems in outpatient therapy: The therapist's dilemma and its implications. *Journal of Consulting & Clinical Psychology, 71,* 62–70.

Haxby, J., Gobbini, M., Furey, M., Ishai, A., Schouten, J., & Pietrini, P. (2001). Distributed and overlapping representations of faces and objects in ventral temporal cortex. *Science, 293,* 2425–2430.

Hay, D. F. (1994). Prosocial development. *Journal of Child Psychology and Psychiatry, 35,* 29–71.

Hazlett-Stevens, H., Craske, M., Roy-Byrne, P., Sherbourne, C., Stein, M., & Bystritsky, A. (2002). Predictors of willingness to consider medication and psychosocial treatment for panic disorder in primary care patients. *General Hospital Psychology, 24,* 316–321.

HCF Nutrition Foundation. (2003). *The benefits of fiber.* Retrieved January 29, 2003, from http://www.hcf-nutrition.org/fiber/fiberben_article.html

He, Y., Colantonio, A., & Marshall, V. (2003). Later-life career disruption and self-rated health: An analysis of General Social Survey data. *Canadian Journal on Aging, 22,* 45–57.

Heatherton, T., Macrae, N., & Kelley, W. (2004). What the social brain sciences can tell us about the self. *Current Directions in Psychological Science, 13,* 190–193.

Hebb, D. O. (1949). *The organization of behavior.* New York: John Wiley & Sons.

Hébert, S., Béland, R., Dionne-Fournelle, O., Crête, M., & Lupien, S. (2005). Physiological stress response to video-game playing: The contribution of built-in music. *Life Sciences, 76,* 2371–2380.

Hecht, S., Shlaer, S., & Pirenne, M. H. (1942). Energy, quanta, and vision. *Journal of General Physiology, 25,* 819.

Heckhausen, J., & Brian, O. (1997). Perceived problems for self and others: Self-protection by social downgrading throughout adulthood. *Psychology & Aging, 12,* 610–619.

Hedges, L. B., & Nowell, A. (1995). Sex differences in mental test scores, variability, and numbers of high-scoring individuals. *Science, 269,* 41–45.

Heil, M., Rolke, B., & Pecchinenda, A. (2004). Automatic semantic activation is no myth. *Psychological Science, 15,* 852–857.

Heiman, J. (2002). Psychologic treatments for female sexual dysfunction: Are they effective and do we need them? *Archives of Sexual Behavior, 31,* 445–450.

Heitjtz, R., Kolb, B., & Forssberg, H. (2003). Can a therapeutic dose of amphetamine during pre-adolescence modify the pattern of synaptic organization in the brain? *European Journal of Neuroscience, 18,* 3394–3399.

Held, R. (1993). What can rates of development tell us about underlying mechanisms? In C. E. Granrud (Ed.), *Visual perception and cognition in infancy* (pp. 75–89). Hillsdale, NJ: Erlbaum.

Hellige, J. B. (1990). Hemispheric asymmetry. *Annual Review of Psychology, 41,* 55–80.

Hellstrom, Y., & Hallberg, I. (2004). Determinants and characteristics of help provision for elderly people living at home and in relation to quality of life. *Scandinavian Journal of Caring Sciences, 18,* 387–395.

Hendin, H., & Haas, A. P. (1991). Suicide and guilt as manifestations of PTSD in Vietnam combat veterans. *American Journal of Psychiatry, 148,* 586–591.

Henkel, L. A., Franklin, N., & Johnson, M. K. (2000). Cross-modal source monitoring confusions between perceived and imagined events. *Journal of Experimental Psychology: Learning, Memory, and Cognition, 26,* 321–335.

Herbert, T. B., & Cohen, S. (1993). Depression and immunity: A meta-analytic review. *Psychological Bulletin, 113,* 472–486.

Herek, G. (2002). Gender gaps in public opinion about lesbians and gay men. *Public Opinion Quarterly, 66,* 40–66.

Herkenham, M. (1992). Cannabinoid receptor localization in brain: Relationship to motor and reward systems. *Annals of the New York Academy of Sciences, 654,* 19–32.

Herman, L. (1981). Cognitive characteristics of dolphins. In L. Herman (Ed.), *Cetacean behavior* (pp. 363–430). New York: Wiley.

Hernandez, L., & Hoebel, B. G. (1989). Food intake and lateral hypothalamic self-stimulation covary after medial hypothalamic lesions or ventral midbrain 6-hydroxydopamine injections that cause obesity. *Behavioral Neuroscience, 103,* 412–422.

Herness, S. (2000). Coding in taste receptor cells: The early years of intracellular recordings. *Physiology and Behavior, 69,* 17–27.

Herpertz., S., Kielmann, R., Wolf, A., Hebebrand, J., & Senf, W. (2004). Do psychosocial variables predict weight loss or mental health after obesity surgery? A systematic review. *Obesity Research, 12,* 1554–1569.

Hershberger, S., & Segal, N. (2004). The cognitive, behavioral, and personality profiles of a male monozygotic triplet set discordant for sexual orientation. *Archives of Sexual Behavior, 33,* 497–514.

Hertzog, C. (1991). Aging, information processing speed, and intelligence. In K. W. Schaie & M. P. Lawton (Eds.), *Annual Review of Gerontology and Geriatrics* (Vol. 11, pp. 55–79). New York: Springer Publishing Company.

Hetherington, A. W., & Ranson, S. W. (1940). Hypothalamic lesions and adiposity in the rat. *Anatomical Record, 78,* 149–172.

Heyman, G., Gee, C., & Giles, J. (2003). Preschool children's reasoning about ability. *Child Development, 74,* 516–534.

Hickman, J., & Geller, E. (2003). A safety self-management intervention for mining operations. *U.S. Journal of Safety Research, 34,* 299–308.

Higbee, K. L. (1977). *Your memory: How it works and how to improve it.* Englewood Cliffs, NJ: Prentice-Hall.

Higgins, A. (1995). Educating for justice and community: Lawrence Kohlberg's vision of moral education. In W. M. Kurtines & J. L. Gerwirtz (Eds.), *Moral development: An introduction* (pp. 49–81). Boston: Allyn & Bacon.

Hilgard, E. R. (1975). Hypnosis. *Annual Review of Psychology, 26,* 19–44.

Hilgard, E. R. (1986). *Divided consciousness: Multiple controls in human thought and action.* New York: Wiley.

Hilgard, E. R. (1992). Dissociation and theories of hypnosis. In E. Fromm & M. R. Nash (Eds.), *Contemporary hypnosis research* (pp. 69–101). New York: Guilford.

Hill, M., & Augoustinos, M. (2001). Stereotype change and prejudice reduction: Short- and long-term evaluation of a cross-cultural awareness programme. *Journal of Community & Applied Social Psychology, 11,* 243–262.

Hillebrand, J. (2000). New perspectives on the manipulation of opiate urges and the assessment of cognitive effort associated with opiate urges. *Addictive Behaviors, 25,* 139–143.

Hobson, C., & Delunas, L., (2001). National norms and life-event frequencies for the revised Social Readjustment Rating Scale. *International Journal of Stress Management, 8,* 299–314.

Hobson, J. A. (1988). *The dreaming brain.* New York: Basic Books.

Hobson, J. A. (1989). *Sleep.* New York: Scientific American Library.

Hobson, J. A., & McCarley, R. W. (1977). The brain as a dream state generator: An activation-synthesis hypothesis of the dream process. *American Journal of Psychiatry, 134,* 1335–1348.

Hodgins, S., Mednick, S. A., Brennan, P. A., Schulsinger, F., & Engberg, M. (1996). Mental disorder and crime: Evidence from a Danish birth cohort. *Journal of Personality and Social Psychology, 53,* 489–496.

Hofer, H., Carroll, J., Neitz, J., Neitz, M., & Williams, D. (2005). Organization of the human trichromatic cone mosaic. *Journal of Neuroscience, 25,* 9669–9679.

Hofstede, G. (1980). *Culture's consequences: International differences in work-related values.* Beverly Hills, CA: Sage.

Hofstede, G. (1983). Dimensions of national cultures in fifty countries and three regions. In J. Deregowski, S. Dzuirawiec, and R. Annis (Eds.), *Explications in cross-cultural psychology* (pp. 335–355). Lisse, The Netherlands: Swets and Zeitlinger.

Hogan, E., & McReynolds, C. (2004). An overview of anorexia nervosa, bulimia nervosa, and binge eating disorders: Implications for rehabilitation professionals. *Journal of Applied Rehabilitation Counseling, 35,* 26–34.

Holden, C. (1996). Sex and olfaction. *Science, 273,* 313.

Holland, J. L. (1973). *Making vocational choices: A theory of careers.* Englewood Cliffs, NJ: Prentice Hall.

Holland, J. L. (1992). *Making vocational choices: A theory of vocational personalities and work environments* (2nd ed.). Odessa, FL: Psychological Assessment Resources.

Hollon, S., Thase, M., & Markowitz, J. (2002). Treatment and prevention of depression. *Psychological Science in the Public Interest, 3,* 39–77.

Holmes, T. H., & Masuda, M. (1974). Life change and illness susceptibility. In B. S. Dohrenwend & B. P. Dohrenwend (Eds.), *Stressful life events: Their nature and effects* (pp. 45–72). New York: Wiley.

Holmes, T. H., & Rahe, R. H (1967). The social readjustment rating scale. *Journal of Psychosomatic Research, 11,* 213–218.

Holt-Lunstad, J., Uchino, B., Smith, T., Olson-Cerny, C., & Nealey-Moore, J. (2003). Social relationships and ambulatory blood pressure: Structural and qualitative predictors of cardiovascular function during everyday social interactions. *Health Psychology, 22,* 388–397.

Home, S., & Biss, W. (2005). Sexual satisfaction as more than a gendered concept: The roles of psychological well-being and sexual orientation. *Journal of Constructivist Psychology, 18,* 25–38.

Hooten, W., Wolter, T., Ames, S., Hurt, R., Viciers, K., Offord, K., & Hays, J. (2005). Personality correlates related to tobacco abstinence following treatment. *International Journal of Psychiatry in Medicine, 35,* 59–74.

Hopkins, W., & Cantalupo, C. (2004, in press). Handedness in chimpanzees (*Pan troglodytes*) is associated with asymmetries of the primary motor cortex but not with homologous language areas. *Behavioral Neuroscience, 118,* 1176–1183.

Horberry, T., Anderson, J., Regan, M., Triggs, T., & Brown, J. (2006). Driver distraction: The effects of concurrent in-vehicle tasks, road environment complexity and age on driving performance. *Accident Analysis & Prevention, 38,* 185–191.

Horn, J. L. (1982). The theory of fluid and crystallized intelligence in relation to concepts of cognitive psychology and aging in adulthood. In F. I. M. Craik & S. Trehub (Eds.), *Aging and cognitive processes* (pp. 201–238). New York: Plenum Press.

Horn, L. J., & Zahn, L. (2001). *From bachelor's degree to work: Major field of study and employment outcomes of 1992–93 bachelor's degree recipients who did not enroll in graduate education by 1997* (NCES 2001–165). Retrieved March 7, 2002, from http://nces.ed.gov/pubs2001/quarterly/spring/q5_2.html

Horney, K. (1937). *The neurotic personality of our time.* New York: W. W. Norton.

Horney, K. (1939). *New ways in psychoanalysis.* New York: W. W. Norton.

Horney, K. (1945). *Our inner conflicts.* New York: W. W. Norton.

Horney, K. (1950). *Neurosis and human growth.* New York: W. W. Norton.

Horney, K. (1967). *Feminine psychology.* New York: W. W. Norton.

Hoshi, R., Pratt, H., Mehta, S., Bond, A., & Curran, H. (2006). An investigation into the sub-acute effects of ecstasy on aggressive interpretive bias and aggressive mood—Are there gender differences? *Journal of Psychopharmacology, 20,* 291–301.

Houzel, D. (2004). The psychoanalysis of infantile autism. *Journal of Child Psychotherapy, 30,* 225–237.

Hovland, C. I., Lumsdaine, A. A., & Sheffield, F. D. (1949). *Experiments on mass communication.* Princeton, NJ: Princeton University Press.

Howard, A. D., Feighner, S. D., Cully, D. F., Arena, J. P., Liberator, P. A., Rosenblum, C. I., et al. (1996). A receptor in pituitary and hypothalamus that functions in growth hormone release. *Science, 273,* 974–977.

Hrushesky, W. J. M. (1994, July/August). Timing is everything. *The Sciences,* pp. 32–37.

Hubel, D. H. (1963). The visual cortex of the brain. *Scientific American, 209,* 54–62.

Hubel, D. H. (1995). *Eye, brain, and vision.* New York: Scientific American Library.

Hubel, D. H., & Wiesel, T. N. (1959). Receptive fields of single neurons in the cat's striate cortex. *Journal of Physiology, 148,* 547–591.

Hubel, D. H., & Wiesel, T. N. (1979). Brain mechanisms of vision. *Scientific American, 241,* 130–144.

Hudson, J. I., Carter, W. P., & Pope, H. G., Jr. (1996). Antidepressant treatment of binge-eating disorder: Research findings and clinical guidelines. *Journal of Clinical Psychiatry, 57*(8, Suppl.), 73–79.

Huesman, L., Moise-Titus, J., Podolski, C., & Eron, L. (2003). Longitudinal relations between children's exposure to television violence and their aggressive and violent behavior in young adulthood. *Developmental Psychology, 39,* 201–221.

Huesmann, L. R., & Moise, J. (1996, June). Media violence: A demonstrated public health threat to children. *Harvard Mental Health Letter, 12*(12), 5–7.

Hughes, S., Harrison, M., & Gallup, G. (2004). Sex differences in mating strategies: Mate guarding, infidelity and multiple concurrent sex partners. *Evolution & Gender, 6,* 3–13.

Hull, C. L. (1943). *Principles of behavior.* New York: Appleton-Century-Crofts.

Hultsch, D. F., & Dixon, R. A. (1990). Learning and memory in aging. In J. E. Birren & K. W. Schaie (Eds.), *Handbook of the psychology of aging* (3rd ed., pp. 359–374). San Diego: Academic Press.

Hunton, J., & Rose, J. (2005). Cellular telephones and driving performance: The effects of attentional demands on motor vehicle crash risk. *Risk Analysis, 25,* 855–866.

Huttenlocher, P. (1994). Synaptogenesis, synapse elimination, and neural plasticity in human cerebral cortex. In C. Nelson (Ed.), *The Minnesota symposia on child psychology* (Vol. 27, pp. 35–54). Hillsdale, NJ: Erlbaum.

Hyde, J. (2005). The gender similarities hypothesis. *American Psychologist, 60,* 581–592.

Hyman, I. E., Jr., Husband, T. H., & Billings, E. J. (1995). False memories of childhood. *Applied Cognitive Psychology, 9,* 181–197.

Hyman, I. E., Jr., & Pentland, J. (1996). The role of mental imagery in the creation of false childhood memories. *Journal of Memory and Language, 35,* 101–117.

Insel, T. R. (1990). Phenomenology of obsessive compulsive disorder. *Journal of Clinical Psychiatry, 51*(2, Suppl.), 4–8.

Intons-Peterson, M. J., & Fournier, J. (1986). External and internal memory aids: When and how often do we use them? *Journal of Experimental Psychology: General, 115,* 267–280.

Isaksson, K., Johansson, G., Bellaagh, K., & Sjöberg, A. (2004). Work values among the unemployed: Changes over time and some gender differences. *Scandinavian Journal of Psychology, 45,* 207–214.

Ishii, K., Reyes, J., & Kitayama, S. (2003). Spontaneous attention to word content versus emotional tone: Differences among three cultures. *Psychological Science, 14,* 39–46.

Ito, T. A., Miller, N., & Pollock, V. E. (1996). Alcohol and aggression: A meta-analysis on the moderating effects of inhibitory cues, triggering events, and self-focused attention. *Psychological Bulletin, 120,* 60–82.

Izard, C. E. (1971). *The face of emotion.* New York: Appleton-Century-Crofts.

Izard, C. E. (1977). *Human emotions.* New York: Plenum Press.

Izard, C. E. (1990). Facial expressions and the regulation of emotions. *Journal of Personality and Social Psychology, 58,* 487–498.

Izard, C. E. (1992). Basic emotions, relations among emotions, and emotion-cognition relations. *Psychological Review, 99,* 561–565.

Izard, C. E. (1993). Four systems for emotion activation: Cognitive and noncognitive processes. *Psychological Review, 100,* 68–90.

Jacklin, C. N. (1989). Female and male: Issues of gender. *American Psychologist, 44,* 127–133.

Jackson, S. (2002). A study of teachers' perceptions of youth problems. *Journal of Youth Studies, 5,* 313–322.

James, W. (1884). What is an emotion? *Mind, 9,* 188–205.

Jamieson, D. W., & Zanna, M. P. (1989). Need for structure in attitude formation and expression. In A. R. Pratkanis, S. J. Breckler, & A. G. Greenwald (Eds.), *Attitude structure and function* (pp. 383–406). Hillsdale, NJ: Erlbaum.

Janis, I. L. (1982). *Groupthink: Psychological studies of policy decisions and fiascoes* (2nd ed.). Boston: Houghton Mifflin.

Janssen, T., & Carton, J. (1999). The effects of locus of control and task difficulty on procrastination. *Journal of Genetic Psychology, 160,* 436–442.

Jansz, J. (2005). The emotional appeal of violent video games for adolescent males. *Communication Theory, 15,* 219–241.

Jansz, J., & Martens, L. (2005). Gaming at a LAN event: The social context of playing video games. *New Media & Society, 7,* 333–355.

Jefferson, J. W. (1995). Social phobia: A pharmacologic treatment overview. *Journal of Clinical Psychiatry, 56*(5, Suppl.), 18–24.

Jefferson, J. W. (1997). Antidepressants in panic disorder. *Journal of Clinical Psychiatry, 58*(2, Suppl.), 20–24.

Jelicic, M., & Bonke, B. (2001). Memory impairments following chronic stress? A critical review. *European Journal of Psychiatry, 15,* 225–232.

Jellinek, E. M. (1960). *The disease concept of alcoholism.* New Brunswick, NJ: Hillhouse Press.

Jenike, M. A. (1990, April). Obsessive-compulsive disorder. *Harvard Medical School Health Letter, 15,* 4–8.

Jenkins, J. J., Jimenez-Pabon, E., Shaw, R. E., & Sefer, J. W. (1975). *Schuell's aphasia in adults: Diagnosis, prognosis, and treatment* (2nd ed.). Hagerstown, MD: Harper & Row.

Jimerson, D. C., Wolfe, B. E., Metzger, E. D., Finkelstein, D. M., Cooper, T. B., & Levine, J. M. (1997). Decreased serotonin function in bulimia nervosa. *Archives of General Psychiatry, 54,* 529–534.

Jing, L., (2004). Neural correlates of insight. *Acta Psychologica Sinica, 36,* 219–234.

John, L. (2004). Subjective well-being in a multicultural urban population: Structural and multivariate analyses of the Ontario Health Survey well-being scale. *Social Indicators Research, 68,* 107–126.

Johnson, J., Simmons, C., Trawalter, S., Ferguson, T., & Reed, W. (2003). Variation in Black anti-White bias and target distancing cues: Factors that influence perceptions of "ambiguously racist" behavior. *Personality & Social Psychology Bulletin, 29,* 609–622.

Johnson, M. P., Duffy, J. F., Dijk, D-J., Ronda, J. M., Dyal, C. M., & Czeisler, C. A. (1992). Short-term memory, alertness and performance: A reappraisal of their relationship to body temperature. *Journal of Sleep Research, 1,* 24–29.

Johnson, W. G., Tsoh, J. Y., & Varnado, P. J. (1996). Eating disorders: Efficacy of pharmacological and psychological interventions. *Clinical Psychology Review, 16,* 457–478.

Johnston, D. (2000). A series of cases of dementia presenting with PTSD symptoms in World War II combat veterans. *Journal of the American Geriatrics Society, 48,* 70–72.

Johnston, L. E., O'Malley, P. M., & Bachman, J. G. (2001). *Monitoring the future national results on adolescent drug use: Overview of key findings, 2000* (NIH Publication No. 01-4923). Rockville MD: National Institute on Drug Abuse.

Jolicoeur, D., Richter, K., Ahgluwalia, J., Mosier, M., & Resnicow, K. (2003). Smoking cessation, smoking reduction, and delayed quitting among smokers given nicotine patches and a self-help pamphlet. *Substance Abuse, 24,* 101–106.

Jonas, J. M., & Cohon, M. S. (1993). A comparison of the safety and efficacy of alprazolam versus other agents in the treatment of anxiety, panic, and depression: A review of the literature. *Journal of Clinical Psychiatry, 54*(10, Suppl.), 25–45.

Jones, E. E. (1976). How do people perceive the causes of behavior? *American Scientist, 64,* 300–305.

Jones, E. E. (1990). *Interpersonal perception.* New York: Freeman.

Jones, E. E., & Nisbett, R. E. (1971). *The actor and the observer: Divergent perceptions of the causes of behavior.* New York: General Learning.

Jones, H. E., Herning, R. I., Cadet, J. L., & Griffiths, R. R. (2000). Caffeine withdrawal increases cerebral blood flow velocity and alters quantitative electroencephalography (EEG) activity. *Psychopharmacology, 147,* 371–377.

Jones, M. C. (1924). A laboratory study of fear: The case of Peter. *Pedagogical Seminary, 31,* 308–315.

Jones, P. (2005). The American Indian Church and its sacramental use of pcyote: A review for professionals in the mental-health arena. *Mental Health, Religion, & Culture, 8,* 227–290.

Jones, R. (2003). Listen and learn. *Nature Reviews Neuroscience, 4,* 699.

Jones, S. (2003). *Let the games begin: Gaming technology and entertainment among college students.* Washington, DC: Pew Internet and American Life Project. Retrieved May 17, 2006, from http://www.pewinternet.org/PPF/r/93/report_display.asp

Jorgensen, G. (2006). Kohlberg and Gilligan: Duet or duel? *Journal of Moral Education, 35,* 179–196.

Jorgensen, M., & Keiding, N. (1991). Estimation of spermarche from longitudinal spermaturia data. *Biometrics, 47,* 177–193.

Josephs, R., Newman, M., Brown, R., & Beer, J. (2003). Status, testosterone, and human intellectual performance. *Psychological Science, 14,* 158–163.

Joynt, R. (2000). Chapter 42: Aging and the nervous system. In T. Beers (Ed.) *Merck Manual of Geriatrics* (3rd Ed.). [Online edition] Retrieved October 12, 2006, from http://www.merck.com/mrkshared/mmg/sec6/ch42/ch42a.jsp

Joyce, P., Mulder, R., Luty, S., McKenzie, J., Sullivan, P., & Cloninger, R. (2003). Borderline personality disorder in major depression: Symptomatology, temperament, character, differential drug response, and 6-month outcome. *Comprehensive Psychiatry, 44,* 35–43.

Judd, L. L., Akiskal, H. S., Zeller, P. J., Paulus, M., Leon, A. C., Maser, J. D., et al. (2000). Psychosocial disability during the long-term course of unipolar major depressive disorder. *Archives of General Psychiatry, 57,* 375–380.

Juengling, F., Schmahl, C., Heblinger, B., Ebert, D., Bremner, J., Gostomzyk, J., et al. (2003). Positron emission tomography in female patients with borderline personality disorder. *Journal of Psychiatric Research, 37,* 109–115.

Juliano, S. L. (1998). Mapping the sensory mosaic. *Science, 279,* 1653–1654.

Julien, R. M. (1995). *A primer of drug action* (7th ed.). New York: W.H. Freeman.

Jung, C. G. (1933). *Modern man in search of a soul.* New York: Harcourt Brace Jovanovich.

Kagan, J. (2003). Foreword: A behavioral science perspective. In R. Plomin, J. DeFries, I. Craig, & P. McGuffin (Eds.), *Behavioral genetics in the postgenomic era* (pp. xvii–xxiii). Washington, DC: American Psychological Association.

Kahneman, D., & Tversky, A. (1984). Choices, values, and frames. *American Psychologist, 39,* 341–350.

Kail, R. (2000). Speed of information processing: Developmental change and links to intelligence. *Journal of School Psychology, 38,* 51–61.

Kalidindi, S., & McGuffin, P. (2003). The genetics of affective disorders: Present and future. In R. Plomin, J. Defries, I. Craig, & P. McGuffin (Eds.), *Behavioral genetics in the postgenomic era* (pp. 481–502). Washington, DC: American Psychological Association.

Kalish, H. I. (1981). *From behavioral science to behavior modification.* New York: McGraw-Hill.

Kaltiala-Heino, R., Rimpelae, M., Rissanen, A., & Rantanen, P. (2001). Early puberty and early sexual activity are associated with bulimic-type eating pathology in middle adolescence. *Journal of Adolescent Health, 28,* 346–352.

Kamarajan, C., Porjesz, B., Jones, K., Chorlian, D., Padmanabhapillai, A., Rangaswamy, M., et al. (2006). Event-related oscillations in offspring of alcoholics: Neurocognitive disinhibition as a risk for alcoholism. *Biological Psychiatry, 59,* 625–634.

Kampman, M., Keijsers, G., Hoogduin, C., & Hendriks, G. (2002). A randomized, double-blind, placebo-controlled study of the effects of adjunctive paroxetine in panic disorder patients unsuccessfully treated with cognitive-behavioral therapy alone. *Journal of Clinical Psychiatry, 63,* 772–777.

Kane, J. M. (1996). Treatment-resistant schizophrenic patients. *Journal of Clinical Psychiatry, 57*(9, Suppl.), 35–40.

Kanner, A. D., Coyne, J. C., Schaefer, C., & Lazarus, R. S. (1981). Comparison of two modes of stress measurement: Daily hassles and uplifts versus major life events. *Journal of Behavioral Medicine, 4,* 1–39.

Karau, S. J., & Williams, K. D. (1993). Social loafing; a meta-analytic review and theoretical integration. *Journal of Personality and Social Psychology, 65,* 681–706.

Karni, A., Tanne, D., Rubenstein, B. S., Askenasy, J. J. M., & Sagi, D. (1994). Dependence on REM sleep of overnight improvement of a perceptual skill. *Science, 265,* 679–682.

Kastenbaum, R. (1992). *The psychology of death.* New York: Springer-Verlag.

Katerndahl, D., Burge, S., & Kellogg, N. (2005). Predictors of development of adult psychopathology in female victims of childhood sexual abuse. *Journal of Nervous and Mental Disease, 193,* 258–264.

Katzell, R. A., & Thompson, D. E. (1990). Work motivation: Theory and practice. *American Psychologist, 45,* 144–153.

Kawanishi, Y., Tachikawa, H., & Suzuki, T. (2000). Pharmacogenomics and schizophrenia. *European Journal of Pharmacology, 410,* 227–241.

Kazdin, A., & Benjet, C. (2003). Spanking children: Evidence and issues. *Current Directions in Psychological Science, 12,* 99–103.

Keating, C. R. (1994). World without words: Messages from face and body. In W. J. Lonner & R. Malpass (Eds.), *Psychology and culture* (pp. 175–182). Boston: Allyn & Bacon.

Keenan, J., Gallup, G., & Falk, D. (2003). *The face in the mirror: The search for the origins of consciousness.* New York: HarperCollins.

Keenan, J., Wheeler, M., Gallup, G., & Pascual-Leone, A. (2000). Self-recognition and the right prefrontal cortex. *Trends in Cognitive Sciences, 4,* 338–344.

Keitner, G. I., Ryan, C. E., Miller, I. W., & Norman, W. H. (1992). Recovery and major depression: Factors associated with twelve-month outcome. *American Journal of Psychiatry, 149,* 93–99.

Kellett, S., Newman, D., Matthews, L., & Swift, A. (2004). Increasing the effectiveness of large group format CBT via the application of practice-based evidence. *Behavioural & Cognitive Psychotherapy, 32,* 231–234.

Kelly, C., & McCreadie, R. (2000). Cigarette smoking and schizophrenia. *Advances in Psychiatric Treatment, 6,* 327–331.

Kelner, K. L. (1997). Seeing the synapse. *Science, 276,* 547.

Kendler, K. S., & Diehl, S. R. (1993). The genetics of schizophrenia: A current genetic-epidemiologic perspective. *Schizophrenia Bulletin, 19,* 261–285.

Kendler, K. S., MacLean, C., Neale, M., Kessler, R., Heath, A., & Eaves, L. (1991). The genetic epidemiology of bulimia nervosa. *American Journal of Psychiatry, 148,* 1627–1637.

Kendler, K. S., Neale, M. C., Kessler, R. C., Heath, A. C., & Eaves, L. J. (1992). The genetic epidemiology of phobias in women. *Archives of General Psychiatry, 49,* 273–281.

Kendler, K. S., Neale, M. C., Kessler, R. C., Heath, A. C., & Eaves, L. J. (1993). The lifetime history of major depression in women: Reliability of diagnosis and heritability. *Archives of General Psychiatry, 50,* 863–870.

Kennedy, Q., Mather, M., & Carstensen, L. (2004). The role of motivation in the age-related positivity effect in autobiographical memory. *Psychological Science, 15,* 208–214.

Kenney-Benson, G., Pomerantz, E., Ryan, A., & Patrick, H. (2006). Sex differences in math performance: The role of children's approach to schoolwork. *Developmental Psychology, 42,* 11–26.

Kenwright, M., & Marks, I. (2004). Computer-aided self-help for phobia/panic via Internet at home: A pilot study. *British Journal of Psychiatry, 184,* 448–449.

Kessler, R., Berglund, P., Demler, O., Jin, R., & Walters, E. (2005a). Lifetime prevalence and age-of-onset distributions of DSM-IV disorders in the National Comorbidity Survey Replication. *Archives of General Psychiatry, 62,* 593–602.

Kessler, R., Chiu, W., Demler, O., & Walters, E. (2005b). Prevalence, severity, and comorbidity of 12-month DSM-IV disorders in the National Comorbidity Survey replication. *Archives of General Psychiatry, 62,* 617–627.

Kessler, R. C., Stein, M. B., & Berglund, P. (1998). Social phobia subtypes in the National Comorbidity Survey. *American Journal of Psychiatry, 155,* 613–619.

Kiecolt-Glaser, J. (2000). *Friends, lovers, relaxation, and immunity: How behavior modifies health. Cortisol and the language of love: Text analysis of newlyweds' relationship stories.* Paper presented at the annual meeting of the American Psychological Association, Washington, DC.

Kiecolt-Glaser, J. K., Fisher, L. D., Ogrocki, P., Stout, J., Speicher, C. E., & Glaser, R. (1987). Marital quality, marital disruption, and immune function. *Psychosomatic Medicine, 49,* 13–34.

Kiecolt-Glaser, J. K., Glaser, R., Gravenstein, S., Malarkey, W. B., & Sheridan, J. (1996). Chronic stress alters the immune response to influenza virus vaccine in older adults. *Proceedings of the National Academy of Science, 93,* 3043–3047.

Kihlstrom, J. F. (1985). Hypnosis. *Annual Review of Psychology, 26,* 557–591.

Kihlstrom, J. F. (1986). Strong inferences about hypnosis. *Behavioral and Brain Sciences, 9,* 474–475.

Kihlstrom, J. F., & Barnhardt, T. M. (1993). The self-regulation of memory: For better and for worse, with and without hypnosis. In D. M. Wegner & J. W. Pennebaker (Eds.), *Handbook of mental control*. Englewood Cliffs, NJ: Prentice Hall.

Kilbride, J. E., & Kilbride, P. L. (1975). Sitting and smiling behavior of Baganda infants. *Journal of Cross-Cultural Psychology, 6*, 88–107.

Kilpatrick, D., Ruggiero, K., Acierno, R., Saunders, B., Resnick, H., & Best, C. (2003). Violence and risk of PTSD, major depression, substance abuse/dependence, and comorbidity: Results from the National Survey of Adolescents. *Journal of Consulting and Clinical Psychology, 71*, 692–700.

Kim, H., & Chung, R. (2003). Relationship of recalled parenting style to self-perception in Korean American college students. *Journal of Genetic Psychology, 164*, 481–492.

Kim, J. J., Mohamed, S., Andreasen, N. C., O'Leary, D. S., Watkins, L., Ponto, L. L. B., et al. (2000). Regional neural dysfunctions in chronic schizophrenia studied with positron emission tomography. *American Journal of Psychiatry, 157*, 542–548.

Kim, K. H. S., Relkin, N. R., Lee, K-M., & Hirsch, J. (1997). Distinct cortical areas associated with native and second languages. *Nature, 388*, 171–174.

Kimura, D. (1992). Sex differences in the brain. *Scientific American, 267*, 118–125.

Kimura, D. (2000). *Sex and cognition*. Cambridge, MA: MIT Press.

King, B. (2006). The rise, fall, and resurrection of the ventromedial hypothalamus in the regulation of feeding behavior and body weight. *Physiology & Behavior, 87*, 221–244.

Kinnunen, T., Zamansky, H. S., & Block, M. L. (1994). Is the hypnotized subject lying? *Journal of Abnormal Psychology, 103*, 184–191.

Kinomura, S., Larsson, J., Gulyás, B., & Roland, P. E. (1996). Activation by attention of the human reticular formation and thalamic intralaminar nuclei. *Science, 271*, 512–515.

Kinsey, A. C., Pomeroy, W. B., & Martin, C. E. (1948). *Sexual behavior in the human male*. Philadelphia: W. B. Saunders.

Kinsey, A. C., Pomeroy, W. B., Martin, C. E., & Gebhard, P. H. (1953). *Sexual behavior in the human female*. Philadelphia: W. B. Saunders.

Kirchner, T., & Sayette, M. (2003). Effects of alcohol on controlled and automatic memory processes. *Experimental & Clinical Psychopharmacology, 11*, 167–175.

Kirkcaldy, B., Shephard, R., & Furnham, A. (2002). The influence of Type A behavior and locus of control upon job satisfaction and occupational health. *Personality & Individual Differences, 33*, 1361–1371.

Kirsch, I., & Lynn, S. J. (1995). The altered state of hypnosis: Changes in the theoretical landscape. *American Psychologist, 50*, 846–858.

Kisilevsky, B., Hains, S., Lee, K., Xie, X., Huang, H., Ye, H., et al. (2003). Effects of experience on fetal voice recognition. *Psychological Science, 14*, 220–224.

Kitayama, S., & Markus, H. R. (2000). The pursuit of happiness and the realization of sympathy: Cultural patterns of self, social relations, and well-being. In E. Diener & E. M. Suh (Eds.), *Subjective well-being across cultures* (pp. 113–164). Cambridge, MA: MIT Press.

Kite, M. E., Deaux, K., & Miele, M. (1991). Stereotypes of young and old: Does age outweigh gender? *Psychology and Aging, 6*, 19–27.

Kittler, J., Menard, W., & Phillips, K. (2007). Weight concerns in individuals with body dysmorphic disorder. *Eating Behavior, 8*, 115–120.

Kiyatkin, E., & Wise, R. (2002). Brain and body hyperthermia associated with heroin self-administration in rats. *Journal of Neuroscience, 22*, 1072–1080

Klaczynski, P., Fauth, J, & Swanger, A. (1998). Adolescent identity: Rational vs. experiential processing, formal operations, and critical thinking beliefs. *Journal of Youth & Adolescence, 17*, 185–207.

Klar, A. (2003). Human handedness and scalp hair-whorl direction develop from a common genetic mechanism. *Genetics, 165*, 269–276.

Klatzky, R. L. (1980). *Human memory: Structures and processes* (2nd ed.). New York: W. H. Freeman.

Klatzky, R. L. (1984). *Memory and awareness: An information-processing perspective*. New York: W. H. Freeman.

Kleinman, A., & Cohen, A. (1997, March). Psychiatry's global challenge. *Scientific American, 276*, 86–89.

Klerman, G. L., Weissman, M. N., Rounsaville, B. J., & Chevron, E. S. (1984). *Interpersonal therapy of depression*. New York: Academic Press.

Kliegman, R. (1998). Fetal and neonatal medicine. In R. Behrman & R. Kliegman (Eds.), *Nelson essentials of pediatrics* (3rd ed., pp. 167–225). Philadelphia: W. B. Saunders.

Kline, G., Stanley, S., Markan, H., Olmos-Gallo, P., St. Peters, M., Whitton, S., et al. (2004). Timing is everything: Pre-engagement cohabitation and increased risk for poor marital outcomes. *Journal of Family Psychology, 18*, 311–318.

Kluft, R. P. (1984). An introduction to multiple personality disorder. *Psychiatric Annals, 14*, 19–24.

Kobasa, S. (1979). Stressful life events, personality, and health: An inquiry into hardiness. *Journal of Personality and Social Psychology, 37*, 1–11.

Kobasa, S. C., Maddi, S. R., & Kahn, S. (1982). Hardiness and health: A prospective study. *Journal of Personality and Social Psychology, 42*, 168–177.

Kochanska, G. (1993). Toward a synthesis of parental socialization and child temperament in early development of conscience. *Child Development, 64*, 325–347.

Kochavi, D., Davis, J., & Smith, G. (2001). Corticotropin-releasing factor decreases meal size by decreasing cluster number in Koletsky (LA/N) rats with and without a null mutation of the leptin receptor. *Physiology & Behavior, 74*, 645–651.

Koehler, T., Tiede, G., & Thoens, M. (2002). Long and short-term forgetting of word associations: An experimental study of the Freudian concepts of resistance and repression. *Zeitschrift fuer Klinische Psychologie, Psychiatrie und Psychotherapie, 50,* 328–333.

Koerner, B. (2002, July/August). Disorders made to order. *Mother Jones.* [Online, no pages specified.] Retrieved July 25, 2006, from http://www.motherjones.com/news/feature/2002/07/disorders.html

Kohlberg, L. (1966). A cognitive-developmental analysis of children's sex-role concepts and attitudes. In E. E. Maccoby (Ed.), *The development of sex differences* (pp. 82–173). Palo Alto, CA: Stanford University Press.

Kohlberg, L. (1968, September). The child as a moral philosopher. *Psychology Today,* 24–30.

Kohlberg, L. (1969). *Stages in the development of moral thought and action.* New York: Holt, Rinehart & Winston.

Kohlberg, L., & Ullian, D. Z. (1974). In R. C. Friedman, R. M. Richart, & R. L. Vande Wiele (Eds.), *Sex differences in behavior* (pp. 209–222). New York: Wiley.

Köhler, W. (1925). *The mentality of apes* (E. Winter, Trans.). New York: Harcourt Brace Jovanovich.

Koltz, C. (1983, December). Scapegoating. *Psychology Today,* 68–69.

Kon, M. A., & Plaskota, L. (2000). Information complexity of neural networks. *Neural Networks, 13,* 365–375.

Konishi, M. (1993). Listening with two ears. *Scientific American, 268,* 66–73.

Kopinska, A., & Harris, L. (2003). Spatial representation in body coordinates: Evidence from errors in remembering positions of visual and auditory targets after active eye, head, and body movements. *Canadian Journal of Experimental Psychology, 57,* 23–37.

Kopp, C. P., & Kaler, S. R. (1989). Risk in infancy: Origins and implications. *American Psychologist, 44,* 224–230.

Korobov, N., & Thorne, A. (2006). Intimacy and distancing: Young men's conversations about romantic relationships. *Journal of Adolescent Research, 21,* 27–55.

Kosslyn, S. M. (1988). Aspects of a cognitive neuroscience of mental imagery. *Science, 240,* 1621–1626.

Kovacs, D., Mahon, J., & Palmer, R. (2002). Chewing and spitting out food among eating-disordered patients. *International Journal of Eating Disorders, 32,* 112–115.

Kowatch, R., Suppes, T., Carmody, T., Bucci, J., Hume, J., Kromelis, M., et al. (2000). Effect size of lithium, divalproex sodium, and carbamazepine in children and adolescents with bipolar disorder. *Journal of the American Academy of Child & Adolescent Psychiatry, 39,* 713–720.

Kozak, M. J., Foa, E. B., & McCarthy, P. R. (1988). Obsessive-compulsive disorder. In C. G. Last & M. Herson (Eds.), *Handbook of anxiety disorders* (pp. 87–108). New York: Pergamon Press.

Kozel, F., Padgett, T., & George, M. (2004). A replication study of the neural correlates of deception. *Behavioral Neuroscience, 118,* 852–856.

Krantz, D. S., Grunberg, N. E., & Baum, A. (1985). Health psychology. *Annual Review of Psychology, 36,* 349–383.

Kranzler, H. R. (1996). Evaluation and treatment of anxiety symptoms and disorders in alcoholics. *Journal of Clinical Psychiatry, 57*(6, Suppl.).

Kraus, S. J. (1995). Attitudes and the prediction of behavior: A meta-analysis of the empirical literature. *Personality and Social Psychology Bulletin, 21,* 58–75.

Krcmar, M., & Cooke, M. (2001). Children's moral reasoning and their perceptions of television violence. *Journal of Communication, 51,* 300–316.

Krebs, D., & Denton, K. (2005). Toward a more pragmatic approach to morality: A critical evaluation of Kohlberg's model. *Psychological Review, 112,* 629–649.

Kripke, D., Garfinkel, L., Wingard, D., Klauber, M., & Marler, M. (2002). Mortality associated with sleep duration. *Archives of General Psychiatry, 59,* 131–136.

Kripke, D., Youngstedt, S., Elliott, J., Tuunainen, A., Rex, K., Hauger, R., et al. (2005). Circadian phase in adults of contrasting ages. *Chronobiology International, 22,* 695–709.

Kroll, N. E. A., Ogawa, K. H., & Nieters, J. E. (1988). Eyewitness memory and the importance of sequential information. *Bulletin of the Psychonomic Society, 26,* 395–398.

Krueger, J. M., & Takahashi, S. (1997). Thermoregulation and sleep: Closely linked but separable. *Annals of the New York Academy of Sciences, 813,* 281–286.

Krueger, R., & Johnson, W. (2004). Genetic and environmental structure of adjectives describing the domains of the Big Five model of personality: A nationwide U.S. twin study. *Journal of Research in Personality, 38,* 448–472.

Krueger, W. C. F. (1929). The effect of overlearning on retention. *Journal of Experimental Psychology, 12,* 71–81.

Kruk, M., Meelis, W., Halasz, J., & Haller, J. (2004). Fast positive feedback between the adrenocortical stress response and a brain mechanism involved in aggressive behavior. *Behavioral Neuroscience, 118,* 1062–1070

Kübler-Ross, E. (1969). *On death and dying.* New York: Macmillan.

Kubzansky, L., Cole, S., Kawachi, I., Vokonas, P., & Sparrow, D. (2006). Shared and unique contributions of anger, anxiety, and depression to coronary heart disease: A prospective study in the normative aging study. *Annals of Behavioral Medicine, 31,* 21–29.

Kucharska-Pietura, K., & Klimkowski, M. (2002). Perception of facial affect in chronic schizophrenia and right brain damage. *Acta Neurobiologiae Experimentalis, 62,* 33–43.

Kuhn, D. (1984). *Cognitive development.* In M. H. Bernstein & M. E. Lamb (Eds.), *Developmental psychology.* Hillsdale, NJ: Erlbaum.

Kuhn, D., & Lao, J. (1996). Effects of evidence on attitudes: Is polarization the norm? *Psychological Science, 7,* 115–120.

Kumar, R., O'Malley, P., Johnston, L., Schulenberg, J., & Bachman, J. (2002). Effects of school-level norms on student substance abuse. *Prevention Science, 3,* 105–124.

Kumpfer, K., Alvarado, R., Smith, P., & Ballamy, N. (2002). Cultural sensitivity and adaptation in family-based prevention interventions. *Prevention Science, 3,* 241–246.

Kunda, Z., & Oleson, K. C. (1995). Maintaining stereotypes in the face of disconfirmation: Construction grounds for subtyping deviants. *Journal of Personality and Social Psychology, 68*, 565–579.

Kunz, D., & Herrmann, W. M. (2000). Sleep-wake cycle, sleep-related disturbances, and sleep disorders: A chronobiological approach. *Comparative Psychology, 41*(2, Suppl. 1), 104–105.

Kuo, C., & Tsaur, C. (2004). Locus of control, supervisory support and unsafe behavior: The case of the construction industry in Taiwan. *Chinese Journal of Psychology, 46*, 392–405.

Kuroda, K. (2002). An image retrieval system by impression words and specific object names-IRIS. *Neurocomputing: An International Journal, 43*, 259–276.

Kurup, R., & Kurup, P. (2002). Detection of endogenous lithium in neuropsychiatric disorders. *Human Psychopharmacology: Clinical & Experimental, 17*, 29–33.

Lal, S. (2002). Giving children security: Mamie Phipps Clark and the racialization of child psychology. *American Psychologist, 57*, 20–28.

Lam, L., & Kirby, S. (2002). Is emotional intelligence an advantage? An exploration of the impact of emotional and general intelligence on individual performance. *Journal of Social Psychology, 142*, 133–143.

Lambe, E. K., Katzman, D. K., Mikulis, D. J., Kennedy, S. H., & Zipursky, R. B. (1997). Cerebral gray matter volume deficits after weight recovery from anorexia nervosa. *Archives of General Psychiatry, 54*, 537–542.

Lamberg, L. (1996). Narcolepsy researchers barking up the right tree. *Journal of the American Medical Association, 276*, 265–266.

Lambert, M. (2003). Suicide risk assessment and management: Focus on personality disorders. *Current Opinion in Psychiatry, 16*, 71–76.

Lamborn, S. D., Mounts, N. S., Steinberg, L., & Dornbusch, S. M. (1991). Patterns of competence and adjustment among adolescents from authoritative, authoritarian, indulgent, and neglectful families. *Child Development, 62*, 1049–1065.

Lambright, L. (2004). *Lessons from Vietnam.* Paper presented at International Intercultural Education Conference, St Louis, MO, April, 2004.

Landry, D. W. (1997, February). Immunotherapy for cocaine addiction. *Scientific American, 276*, 42–45.

Lang, A., Craske, M., Brown, M., & Ghaneian, A. (2001). Fear-related state dependent memory. *Cognition & Emotion, 15*, 695–703.

Lang, A. R., Goeckner, D. J., Adesso, V. J., & Marlatt, G. A. (1975). Effects of alcohol on aggression in male social drinkers. *Journal of Abnormal Psychology, 84*, 508–518.

Lange, C. G., & James, W. (1922). *The emotions* (I. A. Haupt, Trans.). Baltimore: Williams and Wilkins.

Langer, E. J., & Rodin, J. (1976). The effects of choice and enhanced personal responsibility for the aged: A field experiment in an institutional setting. *Journal of Personality and Social Psychology, 34*, 191–198.

Langer, P., Holzner, B., Magnet, W., & Kopp, M. (2005). Hands-free mobile phone conversation impairs the peripheral visual system to an extent comparable to an alcohol level of 4–5g/100 ml. *Human Psychopharmacology: Clinical and Experimental, 20*, 65–66.

Langevin, B., Sukkar, F., Léger, P., Guez, A., & Robert, D. (1992). Sleep apnea syndromes (SAS) of specific etiology: Review and incidence from a sleep laboratory. *Sleep, 15*, S25–S32.

Langlois, J. H., Kalakanis, L., Rubenstein, A. J., Larson, A., Hallam, M., & Smoot, M. (2000). Maxims or myths of beauty? A meta-analytic and theoretical review. *Psychological Bulletin, 126*, 390–423.

Lao, J., & Kuhn, D. (2002). Cognitive engagement and attitude development. *Cognitive Development, 17*, 1203–1217.

Larson, M. (2003). Gender, race, and aggression in television commercials that feature children. *Sex Roles, 48*, 67–75.

Larsson, H., Andershed, H., & Lichtenstein, P. (2006). A genetic factor explains most of the variation in the psychopathic personality. *Journal of Abnormal Psychology, 115*, 221–230.

Latané, B., Williams, K., & Harkins, S. (1979). Many hands make light the work: The causes and consequences of social loafing. *Journal of Personality and Social Psychology, 37*, 822–832.

Latham, G., & Pinder, C. (2005). Work motivation theory and research at the dawn of the twenty-first century. *Annual Review of Psychology, 56*, 485–516.

Latner, J., & Wilson, T. (2004). Binge eating and satiety in bulimia nervosa and binge eating disorder: Effects of macronutrient intake. *International Journal of Eating Disorders, 36*, 402–415.

Laumann, E. O., Gagnon, J. H., Michael, R. T., & Michaels, S. (1994). *The social organization of sexuality.* Chicago: University of Chicago Press.

Laurent, J., Swerdik, M., & Ryburn, M. (1992). Review of validity research on the Stanford-Binet Intelligence Scale: Fourth Edition. *Psychological Assessment, 4*, 102–112.

Lauriello, J., McEvoy, J., Rodriguez, S., Bossie, C., & Lasser, R. (2005). Long-acting risperidone vs. placebo in the treatment of hospital inpatients with schizophrenia. *Schizophrenia Research, 72*, 249–258.

Lavie, P., Herer, P., Peled, R., Berger, I., Yoffe, N., Zomer, J., et al. (1995). Mortality in sleep apnea patients: A multivariate analysis of risk factors. *Sleep, 18*, 149–157.

Lawton, B. (2001). *Damage to human hearing by airborne sound of very high frequency or ultrasonic frequency.* Contract Research Report No. 343/2001. Highfield, Southampton, U.K.: Institution of Sound and Vibration Research, University of Southampton/Highfield. Retrieved December 13, 2006, from http://www.compoundsecurity.co.uk/download/HSE. pdf

Layton, L., Deeny, K., Tall, G., & Upton, G. (1996). Researching and promoting phonological awareness in the nursery class. *Journal of Research in Reading, 19*, 1–13.

Lazarus, R. S. (1966). *Psychological stress and the coping process.* New York: McGraw-Hill.

Lazarus, R. S. (1984). On the primacy of cognition. *American Psychologist, 39,* 124–129.

Lazarus, R. S. (1991a). Cognition and motivation in emotion. *American Psychologist, 46,* 352–367.

Lazarus, R. S. (1991b). Progress on a cognitive-motivational-relational theory of emotion. *American Psychologist, 46,* 819–834.

Lazarus, R. S. (1995). Vexing research problems inherent in cognitive-mediational theories of emotion—and some solutions. *Psychological Inquiry, 6,* 183–187.

Lazarus, R. S., & DeLongis, A. (1983). Psychological stress and coping in aging. *American Psychologist, 38,* 245–253.

Lazarus, R. S., & Folkman, S. (1984). *Stress, appraisal, and coping.* New York: Springer.

Lebow, J. L., & Gurman, A. S. (1995). Research assessing couple and family therapy. *Annual Review of Psychology, 46,* 27–57.

Lecomte, T., & Lecomte, C. (2002). Toward uncovering robust principles of change inherent to cognitive-behavioral therapy for psychosis. *American Journal of Orthopsychiatry, 72,* 50–57.

LeDoux, J. E. (1994). Emotion, memory, and the brain. *Scientific American, 270,* 50–57.

LeDoux, J. E. (1995). Emotion: clues from the brain. *Annual Review of Psychology, 46,* 209–235.

LeDoux, J. E. (1996). *The emotional brain: The mysterious underpinnings of emotional life.* New York: Simon & Schuster.

LeDoux, J. E. (2000). Emotion circuits in the brain. *Annual Review of Neuroscience, 23,* 155–184.

Lee, I., & Kesner, R. (2002). Differential contribution of NMDA receptors in hippocampal subregions to spatial working memory. *Nature Neuroscience, 5,* 162–168.

Lee, J., Kelly, K., & Edwards, J. (2006). A closer look at the relationships among trait procrastination, neuroticism, and conscientiousness. *Personality and Individual Differences, 40,* 27–37.

Lefebvre, P., & Merrigan, P. (1998). *Family background, family income, maternal work and child development.* Human Resources Development Canada Report #@-98-12E. Retrieved November 28, 2006 from http://www.hrsdc.gc.ca/en/cs/sp/sdc/pkrf/publications/research/1998-002345/page01.shtml

Leichtman, M. D., & Ceci, S. J. (1995). The effects of stereotypes and suggestions on preschoolers' reports. *Developmental Psychology, 31,* 568–578.

Leitenberg, H., & Henning, K. (1995). Sexual fantasy. *Psychological Bulletin, 117,* 469–496.

Lenneberg, E. (1967). *Biological foundations of language.* New York: Wiley.

Leon, M. (1992). The neurobiology of filial learning. *Annual Review of Psychology, 43,* 337–398.

Leonardo, E., & Hen, R. (2006). Genetics of affective and anxiety disorders. *Annual Review of Psychology* (Vol. 57, pp. 117–138). Palo Alto, CA: Annual Reviews.

Lerman, D. C., & Iwata, B. A. (1996). Developing a technology for the use of operant extinction in clinical settings: An examination of basic and applied research. *Journal of Applied Behavior Analysis, 29,* 345–382.

Lesch, K. (2003). Neuroticism and serotonin: A developmental genetic perspective. In R. Plomin, J. DeFries, I. Craig, & P. McGuffin (Eds.), *Behavioral genetics in the postgenomic era* (pp. 389–423). Washington, DC: American Psychological Association.

Lester, B., Hoffman, J., & Brazelton, T. (1985). The rhythmic structure of mother-infant interaction in term and preterm infants. *Child Development, 56,* 15–27.

Leuchter, A., Cook, I., Witte, E., Morgan, M., & Abrams, M. (2002). Changes in brain function of depressed subjects during treatment with placebo. *American Journal of Psychiatry, 159,* 122–129.

LeVay, S. (1991). A difference in hypothalamic structure between heterosexual and homosexual men. *Science, 253,* 1034–1037.

Levenson, R. W., Ekman, P., & Friesen, W. (1990). Voluntary facial action generates emotion-specific autonomic nervous system activity. *Psychophysiology, 27,* 363–385.

Levy, J. (1985, May). Right brain, left brain: Fact and fiction. *Psychology Today,* pp. 38–44.

Levy-Shiff, R., Lerman, M., Har-Even, D., & Hod, M. (2002). Maternal adjustment and infant outcome in medically defined high-risk pregnancy. *Developmental Psychology, 38,* 93–103.

Lewald, J. (2004). Gender-specific hemispheric asymmetry in auditory space perception. *Cognitive Brain Research, 19,* 92–99.

Lewinsohn, P. M., & Rosenbaum, M. (1987). Recall of parental behavior by acute depressives, remitted depressives, and nondepressives. *Journal of Personality and Social Psychology, 52,* 611–619.

Lewis, D. O., Pincus, J. H., Feldman, M., Jackson, L., & Bard, B. (1986). Psychiatric, neurological, and psychoeducational characteristics of 15 death row inmates in the United States. *American Journal of Psychiatry, 143,* 838–845.

Leyens, J-P., Yzerbyt, V., & Olivier, C. (1996). The role of applicability in the emergence of the overattribution bias. *Journal of Personality and Social Psychology, 70,* 219–229.

Li, J. (2003). U.S. and Chinese cultural beliefs about learning. *Journal of Educational Psychology, 95,* 258–267.

Lidz, C., & Macrine, S. (2001). An alternative approach to the identification of gifted culturally and linguistically diverse learners: The contribution of dynamic assessment. *School Psychology International, 22,* 74–96.

Lieblum, S. (2002). After sildenafil: Bridging the gap between pharmacologic treatment and satisfying sexual relationships. *Journal of Clinical Psychiatry, 63,* 17–22.

Liepert, J., Terborg, C., & Weiller, C. (1999). Motor plasticity induced by synchronized thumb and foot movements. *Experimental Brain Research, 125,* 435–439.

Lievens, F., Coetsier, P., De Fruyt, F., & De Maeseneer, J. (2002). Medical students' personality characteristics and academic performance: A five-factor model perspective. *Medical Education, 36,* 1050–1056.

Lijtmaer, R. (2001). Splitting and nostalgia in recent immigrants: Psychodynamic considerations. *Journal of the American Academy of Psychoanalysis, 29,* 427–438.

Lim, V. (2002). The IT way of loafing on the job: Cyberloafing, neutralizing and organizational justice. *Journal of Organizational Behavior, 23,* 675–694.

Lindenberger, U., Mayr, U., & Kliegl, R. (1993). Speed and intelligence in old age. *Psychology and Aging, 8,* 207–220.

Lindsay, D., Hagen, L., Read, J., Wade, K., & Garry, M. (2004). True photographs and false memories. *Psychological Science, 15,* 149–154.

Linville, P. W., Fischer, G. W., & Salovey, P. (1989). Perceived distributions of the characteristics of in-group and out-group members: Empirical evidence and a computer simulation. *Journal of Personality and Social Psychology, 57,* 165–188.

Liossi, C. (2006). Hypnosis in cancer care. *Contemporary Hypnosis, 23,* 47–57.

Lishman, W. A. (1990). Alcohol and the brain. *British Journal of Psychiatry, 156,* 635–644.

Little, J., McFarlane, J., & Ducharme, H. (2002). ECT use delayed in the presence of comorbid mental retardation: A review of clinical and ethical issues. *Journal of ECT, 18,* 218–222.

Little, R. E., Anderson, K. W., Ervin, C. H., Worthington-Roberts, B., & Clarren, S. K. (1989). Maternal alcohol use during breast-feeding and infant mental and motor development at one year. *New England Journal of Medicine, 321,* 425–430.

Liu, B., & Lee, Y. (2006). In-vehicle workload assessment: Effects of traffic situations and cellular telephone use. *Journal of Safety Research, 37,* 99–105.

Livingston, E., Huerta, S., Arthur, D., Lee, S., De Shields, S., & Heber, D. (2002). Male gender is a predictor of morbidity and age a predictor of mortality for patients undergoing gastric bypass surgery. *Annals of Surgery, 236,* 576–582.

Lock, C. (2004). Deception detection: Psychologists try to learn how to spot a liar. *Science News, 166,* 72.

Loeber, R., & Hay, D. (1997). Key issues in the development of aggression and violence from childhood to early adulthood. *Annual Review of Psychology, 48,* 371–410.

Loehlin, J. C. (1992). *The limits of family influence: Genes, experience, and behavior.* New York: Guilford.

Loehlin, J. C., Horn, J. M., & Willerman, L. (1990). Heredity, environment, and personality change: Evidence from the Texas Adoption Project. *Journal of Personality, 58,* 221–243.

Loehlin, J. C., Lindzey, G., & Spuhler, J. N. (1975). *Race differences in intelligence.* San Francisco: Freeman.

Loehlin, J. C., Willerman, L., & Horn, J. M. (1987). Personality resemblance in adoptive families: A 10-year follow-up. *Journal of Personality and Social Psychology, 53,* 961–969.

Loehlin, J. C., Willerman, L., & Horn, J. M. (1988). Human behavior genetics. *Annual Review of Psychology, 39,* 101–133.

Loftus, E. (2003). Our changeable memories: Legal and practical implications. *Nature Reviews: Neuroscience, 4,* 231–234.

Loftus, E. (2004). Memories of things unseen. *Current Directions in Psychological Science, 13,* 145–147.

Loftus, E., & Bernstein, D. (2005). Rich false memories: The royal road to success. In A. Healy (Ed.), *Experimental cognitive psychology and its applications* (pp. 101–113). Washington, DC: American Psychological Association.

Loftus, E. F. (1979). *Eyewitness testimony.* Cambridge, MA: Harvard University Press.

Loftus, E. F. (1993). Psychologists in the eyewitness world. *American Psychologist, 48,* 550–552.

Loftus, E. F. (1997). Creating false memories. *Scientific American, 277,* 71–75.

Loftus, E. F., & Hoffman, H. G. (1989). Misinformation and memory: The creation of new memories. *Journal of Experimental Psychology: General, 118,* 100–104.

Loftus, E. F., & Loftus, G. R. (1980). On the permanence of stored information in the human brain. *American Psychologist, 35,* 409–420.

Loftus, E. F., & Pickrell, J. (1995). The formation of false memories. *Psychiatric Annals, 25,* 720–725.

London, E. D., Ernst, M., Grant, S., Bonson, K., & Weinstein, A. (2000). Orbitofrontal cortex and human drug abuse: Functional imaging. *Cerebral Cortex, 10,* 334–342.

Long, D., & Baynes, K. (2002). Discourse representation in the two cerebral hemispheres. *Journal of Cognitive Neuroscience, 14,* 228–242.

Long, G. M., & Crambert, R. F. (1990). The nature and basis of age-related changes in dynamic visual acuity. *Psychology and Aging, 5,* 138–143.

Lott, B., & Saxon, S. (2002). The influence of ethnicity, social class and context on judgments about U.S. women. *Journal of Social Psychology, 142,* 481–499.

Lotze, M., Montoya, P., Erb, M., Hulsmann, E., Flor, H., Klose, U., Birbaumer, N., & Grodd, W. (1999). Activation of cortical and cerebellar motor areas during executed and imagined hand movements: An fMRI study. *Journal of Cognitive Neuroscience, 11,* 491–501.

Lubart, T. (2003). In search of creative intelligence. In R. Sternberg, J. Lautrey, & T. Lubart (Eds.), *Models of intelligence: International perspective* (pp. 279–292). Washington, DC: American Psychological Association.

Luchins, A. S. (1957). Experimental attempts to minimize the impact of first impressions. In C. I. Hovland (Ed.), *Yale studies in attitude and communication: Vol. 1. The order of presentation in persuasion* (pp. 62–75). New Haven, CT: Yale University Press.

Luo, S., & Klohnen, E. (2005). Assortative mating and marital quality in newlyweds: A couple-centered approach. *Journal of Personality & Social Psychology, 88,* 304–326.

Lustig, C., & Hasher, L. (2002). Working memory span: The effect of prior learning. *American Journal of Psychology, 115,* 89–101.

Lustig, C., Konkel, A., & Jacoby, L. (2004). Which route to recovery? Controlled retrieval and accessibility bias in retroactive interference. *Psychological Science, 15,* 729–735.

Lutchmaya, S., Baron-Cohen, S., & Raggatt, P. (2002). Foetal testosterone and vocabulary size in 18- and 24-month-old infants. *Infant Behavior & Development, 24,* 418–424.

Lutz, A., Greischar, L., Rawlings, N., Ricard, M., & Davidson, R. (2004). Long-term meditators self-induce high-amplitude gamma synchrony during mental practice. *Proceedings of the National Academy of Sciences, 101,* 16369–16373.

Lydiard, R. B., Brawman-Mintzer, O., & Ballenger, J. C. (1996). Recent developments in the psychopharmacology of anxiety disorders. *Journal of Consulting and Clinical Psychology, 64,* 660–668.

Lynn, R. (2006). *Race differences in intelligence: An evolutionary analysis.* Atlanta, GA: Washington Summit Books.

Lynn, S. J., Kirsch, I., Barabasz, A., Cardena, E., & Patterson, D. (2000). Hypnosis as an empirically supported clinical intervention: The state of the evidence and a look to the future. *International Journal of Clinical Experimental Hypnosis, 48,* 239–259.

Lynn, S. J., & Nash, M. R. (1994). Truth in memory: Ramifications for psychotherapy and hypnotherapy. *American Journal of Clinical Hypnosis, 36,* 194–208.

Lyvers, M. (2000). "Loss of control" in alcoholism and drug addiction: A neuroscientific interpretation. *Experimental and Clinical Psychopharmacology, 8,* 225–245.

Maccoby, E. E. (1992). The role of parents in the socialization of children: An historical overview. *Developmental Psychology, 28,* 1006–1017.

Maccoby, E. E., & Martin, J. A. (1983). Socialization in the context of the family: Parent-child interaction. In P. H. Mussen (Ed.), *Handbook of child psychology* (4th ed., Vol. 4. pp. 1–101). New York: John Wiley.

MacDonald, A., Pogue-Geile, M., Johnson, M., & Carter, C. (2003). A specific deficit in context processing in the unaffected siblings of patients with schizophrenia. *Archives of General Psychiatry, 60,* 57–65.

Macey, P., Henderson, L., Macey, K., Alger, J., Frysinger, R., Woo, M., et al. (2002). Brain morphology associated with obstructive sleep apnea. *American Journal of Respiratory and Critical Care Medicine, 166,* 1382–1387.

Mack, A. (2003). Inattentional blindness: Looking without seeing. *Current Directions in Psychological Science, 12,* 180–184.

Mack, A., & Rock, I. (1998). *Inattentional blindness.* Cambridge, MA: MIT Press.

MacWhinney, B. (2005). Language development. In M. Bornstein & M. Lamb, (Eds.), *Developmental science: An advanced textbook* (5th ed., pp. 359–387). Hillsdale, NJ: Lawrence Erlbaum Associates.

Madden, M., & Lenhart, A. (2006). *Pew Internet and American life project: Online dating.* Retrieved July 3, 2006 from http://www.pewinternet.org/pdfs/PIP_Online_Dating.pdf

Maguire, E., Spiers, H., Good, C., Hartley, T., Frackowiak, R., & Burgess, N. (2003). Navigation expertise and the human hippocampus: A structural brain imaging analysis. *Hippocampus, 13,* 208–217.

Maguire, E. A., Gadian, D. G., Johnsrude, I. S., Good, C. D., Ashburner, J., Frackowiak, R. S. J., & Frith, C. D. (2000). Navigation-related structural change in the hippocampi of taxi drivers. *Proceedings of the National Academy of Science, 97,* 4398–4403.

Mahler, H., Kulik, J., Gibbons, F., Gerrard, M., & Harrell, J. (2003). Effects of appearance-based intervention on sun protection intentions and self-reported behaviors. *Health Psychology, 22,* 199–209.

Maiden, R., Peterson, S., Caya, M., & Hayslip, B. (2003). Personality changes in the old-old: A longitudinal study. *Journal of Adult Development, 10,* 31–39.

Maier, S. F., & Laudenslager, M. (1985, August). Stress and health: Exploring the links. *Psychology Today,* 44–49.

Main, M., & Solomon, J. (1990). Procedures for identifying infants as disorganized/disoriented during the Ainsworth Strange Situation. In M. Greenberg, D. Cicchetti, & M. Cummings (Eds.), *Attachment in the preschool years: Theory, research, and intervention* (pp. 121–160). Chicago: University of Chicago Press.

Maj, M. (1990). Psychiatric aspects of HIV–1 infection and AIDS. *Psychological Medicine, 20,* 547–563.

Malik, A., & D'Souza, D. (2006). Gone to pot: The association between cannabis and psychosis. *Psychiatric Times, 23.* Retrieved May 15, 2006 from http://www.psychiatrictimes.com/article/showArticle.jhtml?articleId=185303874.

Malkoff, S. B., Muldoon, M. F., Zeigler, Z. R., & Manuck, S. B. (1993). Blood platelet responsivity to acute mental stress. *Psychosomatic Medicine, 55,* 477–482.

Maltz, W. (1991). *The sexual healing journey: A guide for survivors of sexual abuse.* New York: HarperCollins.

Mancini, J., Lethel, V., Hugonenq, C., & Chabrol, B. (2001). Brain injuries in early foetal life: Consequences for brain development. *Developmental Medicine & Child Neurology, 43,* 52–60.

Manderscheid, R., & Henderson, M. (2001). *Mental health, United States, 2000.* Rockville, MD: Center for Mental Health Services. Retrieved January 14, 2003, from http://www.mentalhealth.org/publications/allpubs/SMA01-3537/

Mandler, J. M. (1990). A new perspective on cognitive development in infancy. *American Scientist, 78*(3), 236–243.

Manhal-Baugus, M. (2001). E-therapy: Practical, ethical, and legal issues. *CyberPsychology and Behavior, 4,* 551–563.

Manton, K. G., Siegler, I. C., & Woodbury, M. A. (1986). Patterns of intellectual development in later life. *Journal of Gerontology, 41,* 486–499.

Manzardo, A., Stein, L., & Belluzi, J. (2002). Rats prefer cocaine over nicotine in a two-level self-administration choice test. *Brain Research, 924,* 10–19.

Maratsos, M., & Matheny, L. (1994). Language specificity and elasticity: Brain and clinical syndrome studies. *Annual Review of Psychology, 45,* 487–516.

Marcia, J. (2002). Identity and psychosocial development in adulthood. *Identity, 2,* 7–28.

Marcus, G. F. (1996). Why do children say "breaked"? *Current Directions in Psychological Science, 5,* 81–85.

Marder, S. R. (1996). Clinical experience with risperidone. *Journal of Clinical Psychiatry, 57*(9, Suppl.), 57–61.

Mares, M., & Woodard, E. (2005). Positive effects of television on children's social interactions: A meta-analysis. *Media Psychology, 7,* 301–322.

Marks, I. (1987). The development of normal fear: A review. *Journal of Child Psychology and Psychiatry, 28,* 667–697.

Marks, I. M. (1972). Flooding (implosion) and allied treatments. In W. S. Agras (Ed.), *Behavior modification* (pp. 151–211). New York: Little, Brown.

Marriott, L., & Wenk, G. (2004). Neurobiological consequences of long-term estrogen therapy. *Current Directions in Psychological Science, 13,* 173–176.

Marsh, A., Elfenbein, H., & Ambady, N. (2003). Nonverbal "accents": Cultural differences in facial expressions of emotion. *Psychological Science, 14,* 373–376.

Marshall, R. D., Schneier, F. R., Fallon, B. A., Feerick, J., & Liebowitz, M. R. (1994). Medication therapy for social phobia. *Journal of Clinical Psychiatry, 56*(6, Suppl.), 33–37.

Marshall, W. L., & Segal, Z. (1988). Behavior therapy. In C. G. Last & M. Hersen (Eds.), *Handbook of anxiety disorders* (pp. 338–361). New York: Pergamon.

Martikainen, P., & Valkonen, R. (1996). Mortality after the death of a spouse: Rates and causes of death in a large Finnish cohort. *American Journal of Public Health, 86,* 1087–1093.

Martin, C., & Ruble, D. (2002). Cognitive theories of early gender development. *Psychological Bulletin, 128,* 903–933.

Martin, C. L., & Little, J. K. (1990). The relation of gender understanding to children's sex-typed preferences and gender stereotypes. *Child Development, 61,* 1427–1439.

Martinez, C. (1986). Hispanics: Psychiatric issues. In C. B. Wilkinson (Ed.), *Ethnic psychiatry* (pp. 61–88). New York: Plenum.

Martinez, C. (2006). Abusive family experiences and object relation disturbances: A case study. *Clinical Case Studies, 5,* 209–219.

Martinez, I. (2002). The elder in the Cuban American family: Making sense of the real and ideal. *Journal of Comparative Family Studies, 33,* 359–375.

Martinez, J. L., Jr., & Derrick, B. E. (1996). Long-term potentiation and learning. *Annual Review of Psychology, 47,* 173–203.

Martinez, M., & Belloch, A. (2004). The effects of a cognitive-behavioural treatment for hypochondriasis on attentional bias. *International Journal of Clinical & Health Psychology, 4,* 299–311.

Masataka, N. (1996). Perception of motherese in a signed language by 6-month-old deaf infants. *Developmental Psychology, 32,* 874–879.

Masland, R. H. (1996). Unscrambling color vision. *Science, 271,* 616–617.

Mason, B., Goodman, A., Chabac, S., & Lehert, P. (2006). Effect of oral acamprosate on abstinence in patients with alcohol dependence in a double-blind, placebo-controlled trial: The role of patient motivation. *Journal of Psychiatric Research, 40,* 383–393.

Mason, R., & Just, M. (2004). How the brain processes causal inferences in text: A theoretical account of generation and integration component processes utilizing both cerebral hemispheres. *Psychological Science, 15,* 1–7.

Massey Cancer Center. (2006). *Familial cancer: Genetic counseling and consultation services.* Retrieved November 30, 2006, from http://www.massey.vcu.edu/discover/?pid=1888

Masters, W. H., & Johnson, V. E. (1966). *Human sexual response.* Boston: Little, Brown.

Mathew, R. J., & Wilson, W. H. (1991). Substance abuse and cerebral blood flow. *American Journal of Psychiatry, 148,* 292–305.

Mathy, R. (2002). Suicidality and sexual orientation in five continents: Asia, Australia, Europe, North America, and South America. *International Journal of Sexuality & Gender Studies, 7,* 215–225.

Matlin, M. W. (1989). *Cognition* (2nd ed.). New York: Holt, Rinehart & Winston.

Matlin, M. W., & Foley, H. J. (1997). *Sensation and perception* (4th ed.). Boston: Allyn & Bacon.

Matsuda, L., Lolait, S. J., Brownstein, M. J., Young, A. C., & Bonner, T. I. (1990). Structure of a cannabinoid receptor and functional expression of the cloned CDNA. *Nature, 346,* 561–564.

Matsunami, H., Montmayeur, J-P., & Buck, L. B. (2000). A family of candidate taste receptors in human and mouse. *Nature, 404,* 601–604.

Matta, D., & Knudson-Martin, C. (2006). Father responsivity: Couple processes and the coconstruction of fatherhood. *Family Process, 45,* 19–37.

Matthews, K. A. (1992). Myths and realities of the menopause. *Psychosomatic Medicine, 54,* 1–9.

Matthews, K. A., Shumaker, S. A., Bowen, D. J., Langer, R. D., Hunt, J. R., Kaplan, R. M., et al. (1997). Women's health initiative: Why now? What is it? What's new? *American Psychologist, 52,* 101–116.

Matthiesen, S., & Einarsen, S. (2004). Psychiatric distress and symptoms of PTSD among victims of bullying at work. *British Journal of Guidance and Counseling, 32,* 335–356.

Matz, D., & Wood, W. (2005). Cognitive dissonance in groups: The consequences of disagreement. *Journal of Personality & Social Psychology, 88,* 22–37.

Mayer, R., Heiser, J., & Lonn, S. (2001). Cognitive constraints on multimedia learning: When presenting more material results in less understanding. *Journal of Educational Psychology, 93,* 187–198.

Mayo Clinic. (2005). *Weight loss: 6 strategies for success*. Retrieved June 16, 2006, from https://www.mayoclinic.com/health/weight-loss/HQ01625

Mayo Clinic. (2006a). *Hearing loss: MP3 players can pose risk*. Retrieved December 13, 2006, from http://mayoclinic.com/health/hearing-loss/GA00046

Mayo Clinic. (2006b). *Sleep tips for the perpetually awake*. Retrieved December 16, 2006, from http://mayoclinic.com/health/sleep/HQ01387

Mazzoni, G., & Memon, A. (2003). Imagination can create false autobiographical memories. *Psychological Science, 14*, 186–188.

McAdams, D. P. (1992). The five-factor model in personality: A critical appraisal. *Journal of Personality, 60*, 329–361.

McCall, W., Dunn, A., & Rosenquist, P. (2004). Quality of life and function after electroconvulsive therapy. *British Journal of Psychiatry, 185*, 405–409.

McClearn, G. E., Johansson, B., Berg, S., Pedersen, N. L., Ahern, F., Petrill, S. A., et ak. (1997). Substantial genetic influence on cognitive abilities in twins 80 or more years old. *Science, 276*, 1560–1563.

McClelland, D. C. (1961). *The achieving society*. Princeton, NJ: Van Nostrand.

McClelland, D. C. (1985). *Human motivation*. New York: Cambridge University Press.

McClelland, D. C., Atkinson, J. W., Clark, R. W., & Lowell, E. L. (1953). *The achievement motive*. New York: Appleton-Century-Crofts.

McClelland, J. L., McNaughton, B. L., & O'Reilly, R. C. (1995). Why there are complementary learning systems in the hippocampus and neocortex: Insights from the successes and failures of connectionist models of learning and memory. *Psychological Bulletin, 102*, 419–457.

McCormick, C. B., & Kennedy, J. H. (2000). Father–child separation, retrospective and current views of attachment relationship with father and self-esteem in late adolescence. *Psychological Reports, 86*, 827–834.

McCrae, R. (1984). Situational determinants of coping responses: Loss, threat, and challenge. *Journal of Personality and Social Psychology, 46*, 919–928.

McCrae, R. (2002). The maturation of personality psychology: Adult personality development and psychological well-being. *Journal of Research in Personality, 36*, 307–317.

McCrae, R. R. (1993). Moderated analyses of longitudinal personality stability. *Journal of Personality and Social Psychology, 65*, 577–583.

McCrae, R. R., & Costa, P. T., Jr. (1990). *Personality in adulthood*. New York: Guilford.

McCrae, R. R., Costa, P. T., Jr., Ostendorf, F., Angleitner, A., Hrebickova, M., Avia, S. J., et al. (2000). Nature over nurture: Temperament, personality, and life span development. *Journal of Personality & Social Psychology, 78*, 173–186.

McCue, J. M., Link, K. L., Eaton, S. S., & Freed, B. M. (2000). Exposure to cigarette tar inhibits ribonucleotide reductase and blocks lymphocyte proliferation. *Journal of Immunology, 165*, 6771–6775.

McCullough, M. E., Hoyt, W. T., Larson, D. B., Koenig, H. G., & Thoresen, C. (2000). Religious involvement and mortality: A meta-analytic review. *Health Psychology, 19*, 211–222.

McDonald, A. D., Armstrong, B. G., & Sloan, M. (1992). Cigarette, alcohol, and coffee consumption and prematurity. *American Journal of Public Health, 82*, 87–90.

McDonald, J. L. (1997). Language acquisition: The acquisition of linguistic structure in normal and special populations. *Annual Review of Psychology, 48*, 215–241.

McDowell, C., & Acklin, M. W. (1996). Standardizing procedures for calculating Rorschach interrater reliability: Conceptual and empirical foundations. *Journal of Personality Assessment, 66*, 308–320.

McElree, B., Jia, G., & Litvak, A. (2000). The time course of conceptual processing in three bilingual populations. *Journal of Memory & Language, 42*, 229–254.

McElwain, N., & Volling, B. (2004). Attachment security and parental sensitivity during infancy: Associations with friendship quality and false-belief understanding at age 4. *Journal of Social & Personal Relationships, 21*, 639–667.

McGlashan, T. H., & Hoffman, R. E. (2000). Schizophrenia as a disorder of developmentally reduced synaptic connectivity. *Archives of General Psychiatry, 57*, 637–648.

McGuire, W. J. (1985). Attitudes and attitude change. In G. Lindzey & E. Aronson (Ed.), *Handbook of social psychology* (Vol. 2, 3rd ed.). New York: Random House.

McKelvie, S. (1984). Relationship between set and functional fixedness: A replication. *Perceptual and Motor Skills, 58*, 996–998.

McNally, R., Lasko, N., Clancy, S., Macklin, M., Pitman, R., & Orr, S. (2004). Psychophysiological responding during script-driven imagery in people reporting abduction by space aliens. *Psychological Science, 15*, 493–497.

Medina, J. H., Paladini, A. C., & Izquierdo, I. (1993). Naturally occurring benzodiazepines and benzodiazepine-like molecules in brain. *Behavioural Brain Research, 58*, 1–8.

Mednick, S. A., Brennan, P., & Kandel, E. (1988). Predisposition to violence. *Aggressive Behavior, 14*, 25–33.

Mednick, S. A., & Mednick, M. T. (1967). *Examiner's manual, Remote Associates Test*. Boston: Houghton-Mifflin.

Meltzer, H., Alphs, L., Green, A., Altamura, A., Anand, R., Bertoldi, A., et al. (2003). Clozapine treatment for suicidality in schizophrenia: International suicide prevention trial. *Archives of General Psychiatry, 60*, 82–91.

Meltzer, H. Y., Rabinowitz, J., Lee, M. A., Cola, P. A., Ranjan, R., Findling, R. L., et al. (1997). Age at onset and gender of schizophrenic patients in relation to neuroleptic resistance. *American Journal of Psychiatry, 154*, 475–482.

Melzack, R., & Wall, P. D. (1965). Pain mechanisms: A new theory. *Science, 150*, 971–979.

Melzack, R., & Wall, P. D. (1983). *The challenge of pain.* New York: Basic Books.

Merck Manual of Diagnosis and Therapy. (2005). *Anxiolitics and sedatives.* Retrieved December 16, 2006, from http://www.merck.com/mmpe/sec15/ch198/ch198e.html

Meschyan, G., & Hernandez, A. (2002). Is native-language decoding skill related to second-language learning? *Journal of Educational Psychology, 94,* 14–22.

Meyer, A. (1997, March/April). Patching up testosterone. *Psychology Today,* 30, 54–57, 66–70.

Meyer, P. (1972). If Hitler asked you to electrocute a stranger, would you? In R. Greenbaum & H. A. Tilker (Eds.), *The challenge of psychology* (pp. 456–465). Englewood Cliffs, NJ: Prentice-Hall.

Meyers, L. (2006). Still wearing the "kick me" sign. *APA Monitor on Psychology, 37,* 68–69.

Michaels, J. W., Bloomel, J. M., Brocato, R. M., Linkous, R. A., & Rowe, J. S. (1982). Social facilitation and inhibition in a natural setting. *Replications in Social Psychology, 2,* 21–24.

Middlebrooks, J. C., & Green, D. M. (1991). Sound localization by human listeners. *Annual Review of Psychology, 42,* 135–159.

Miles, D. R., & Carey, G. (1997). Genetic and environmental architecture of human aggression. *Journal of Personality and Social Psychology, 72,* 207–217.

Miles, J., & Hempel, S. (2004). The Eysenck Personality Scales: The Eysenck Personality Questionnaire-Revised (EPQ-R) and the Eysenck Personality Profiler (EPP). In M. Hilsenroth & D. Segal (Eds.), *Comprehensive handbook of psychological assessment, personality assessment* (Vol. 2, pp. 99–107). New York: John Wiley & Sons.

Miles, R. (1999). A homeostatic switch. *Nature, 397,* 215–216.

Milgram, S. (1963). Behavioral study of obedience. *Journal of Abnormal and Social Psychology, 67,* 371–378.

Milgram, S. (1965). Liberating effects of group pressure. *Journal of Personality and Social Psychology, 1,* 127–134.

Miller, B., Norton, M., Curtis, T., Hill, E., Schvaneveldt, P., & Young, M. (1998). The timing of sexual intercourse among adolescents: Family, peer, and other antecedents: Erratum. *Youth & Society, 29,* 390.

Miller, G., Cohen, S., & Ritchey, A. (2002). Chronic psychological stress and the regulation of pro-inflammatory cytokines: A glucocorticoid-resistance model. *Health Psychology, 21,* 531–541.

Miller, G. A. (1956). The magical number seven, plus or minus two: Some limits on our capacity for processing information. *Psychological Review, 63,* 81–97.

Miller, J., Lynam, D., Zimmerman, R., Logan, T., Leukefeld, C., & Clayton, R. (2004). The utility of the Five Factor Model in understanding risky sexual behavior. *Personality and Individual Differences, 36,* 1611–1626.

Miller, J. G., Bersoff, D. M., & Harwood, R. L. (1990). Perceptions of social responsibilities in India and in the United States: Moral imperatives or personal decisions? *Journal of Personality and Social Psychology, 58,* 33–47.

Miller, L. (1989, November). What biofeedback does (and doesn't) do. *Psychology Today,* pp. 22–23.

Miller, N. E. (1941). The frustration-aggression hypothesis. *Psychological Review, 48,* 337–342.

Miller, N. E. (1985, February). Rx: Biofeedback. *Psychology Today,* pp. 54–59.

Miller, N. S., & Gold, M. S. (1994). LSD and Ecstasy: Pharmacology, phenomenology, and treatment. *Psychiatric Annals, 24,* 131–133.

Miller, T. Q., Smith, T. W., Turner, C. W., Guijarro, M. L., & Hallet, A. J. (1996). A meta-analytic review of research on hostility and physical health. *Psychological Bulletin, 119,* 322–348.

Miller, W., & Thoresen, C. (2003). Spirituality, religion, and health: An emerging research field. *American Psychologist, 58,* 24–35.

Millman, R. (2005). Excessive sleepiness in adolescents and young adults: Causes, consequences, and treatment strategies. *Pediatrics, 115,* 1774–1786.

Milner, B. (1966). Amnesia following operation on the temporal lobes. In C. W. M. Whitty & O. L. Zangwill (Eds.), *Amnesia* (pp. 109–133). London: Butterworth.

Milner, B., Corkin, S., & Teuber, H. L. (1968). Further analysis of the hippocampal amnesic syndrome: 14-year follow-up study of H. M. *Neuropsychologia, 6,* 215–234.

Milos, G., Spindler, A., Ruggiero, G., Klaghofer, R., & Schnyder, U. (2002). Comorbidity of obsessive-compulsive disorders and duration of eating disorders. *International Journal of Eating Disorders, 31,* 284–289.

Milos, G., Spindler, A., & Schnyder, U. (2004). Psychiatric comorbidity and Eating Disorder Inventory (EDI) profiles in eating disorder patients. *Canadian Journal of Psychiatry, 49,* 179–184.

Milton, J., & Wiseman, R. (2001). Does psi exist? Reply to Storm and Ertel (2001). *Psychological Bulletin, 127,* 434–438.

Mischel, W. (1966). A social-learning view of sex differences in behavior. In E. E. Maccoby (Ed.), *The development of sex differences* (pp. 56–81). Palo Alto, CA: Stanford University Press.

Mischel, W. (1968). *Personality and assessment.* New York: Wiley.

Mischel, W. (1973). Toward a cognitive social learning reconceptualization of personality. *Psychological Review, 80,* 252–283.

Mischel, W. (1977). The interaction of person and situation. In D. Magnusson & N. S. Endler (Eds.), *Personality at the crossroads: Current issues in interactional psychology* (pp. 333–352). Hillsdale, NJ: Lawrence Erlbaum.

Mischel, W. (2004). Toward an integrative science of the person. *Annual Review of Psychology, 55,* 1–22.

Mishra, R. (1997). Cognition and cognitive development. In J. Berry, P. Dasen, & T. Saraswathi (Eds.), *Handbook of cross-cultural psychology* (Vol. 2). Boston, MA: Allyn & Bacon.

Mishra, R., & Singh, T. (1992). Memories of Asur children for locations and pairs of pictures. *Psychological Studies, 37,* 38–46.

Mistry, J., & Rogoff, B. (1994). Remembering in cultural context. In W. J. Lonner & R. Malpass (Eds.), *Psychology and culture* (pp. 139–144). Boston: Allyn & Bacon.

Mitler, M. M., Aldrich, M. S., Koob, G. F., & Zarcone, V. P. (1994). Narcolepsy and its treatment with stimulants. *Sleep, 17,* 352–371.

Mitsis, E. M., Halperin, J. M., & Newcorn, J. H. (2000). Serotonin and aggression in children. *Current Psychiatry Reports, 2,* 95–101.

Mogg, K., Baldwin, D., Brodrick, P., & Bradley, B. (2004). Effect of short-term SSRI treatment on cognitive bias in generalised anxiety disorder. *Psychopharmacology, 176,* 466–470.

Mohan, J. (2006). Cardiac psychology. *Journal of the Indian Academy of Applied Psychology, 32,* 214–220.

Mohanty, A., & Perregaux, C. (1997). Language acquisition and bilingualism. In J. Berry, P. Dasen, & T. Saraswathi (Eds.), *Handbook of cross-cultural psychology* (pp. 217–254). Boston: Allyn & Bacon.

Mohr, D., Goodkin, D., Nelson, S., Cox, D., & Weiner, M. (2002). Moderating effects of coping on the relationship between stress and the development of new brain lesions in multiple sclerosis. *Psychosomatic Medicine, 64,* 803–809.

Molnar, M., Potkin, S., Bunney, W., & Jones, E. (2003). MRNA expression patterns and distribution of white matter neurons in dorsolateral prefrontal cortex of depressed patients differ from those in schizophrenia patients. *Biological Psychiatry, 53,* 39–47.

Mombereau, C., Kaupmann, K., Froestl, W., Sansig, G., van der Putten, H., & Cryan, J. (2004). Genetic and pharmaceutical evidence of a role for GABA-sub(b) receptors in the modulation of anxiety- and antidepressant-like behavior. *Neuropsychopharmacology, 29,* 1050–1062.

Mondloch, C., & Maurer, D. (2004). Do small white balls squeak? Pitch-object correspondences in young children. *Cognitive, Affective, & Behavioral Neuroscience, 4,* 133–136.

Monk, T. H. (1989). Circadian rhythms in subjective activation, mood, and performance efficiency. In M. H. Kryger, T. Roth, & W. C. Dement (Eds.), *Principles and practice of sleep medicine* (pp. 163–172). Philadelphia: W. B. Saunders.

Montejo, A., Llorca, G., Izquierdo, J., & Rico-Villademoros, F. (2001). Incidence of sexual dysfunction associated with antidepressant agents: A prospective multicenter study of 1022 outpatients. *Journal of Clinical Psychiatry, 62,* 10–21.

Montgomery, G. (2003). Color blindness: More prevalent among males. *Seeing, Hearing, and Smelling the World.* Retrieved May 13, 2003, from http://www.hhmi.org/senses/b130.html

Montgomery, G., Weltz, C., Seltz, M., & Bovbjerg, D. (2002). Brief presurgery hypnosis reduces distress and pain in excisional breast biopsy patients. *International Journal of Clinical & Experimental Hypnosis, 50,* 17–32.

Montgomery, G. H., DuHamel, K. N., & Redd, W. H. (2000). A meta-analysis of hypnotically induced analgesia: How effective is hypnosis? *International Journal of Clinical Experimental Hypnosis, 48,* 138–153.

Moran, M. G., & Stoudemire, A. (1992). Sleep disorders in the medically ill patient. *Journal of Clinical Psychiatry, 53*(6, Suppl.), 29–36.

Moreno, R., Mayer, R. E., Spires, H., & Lester, J. (2001). The case for social agency in computer-based teaching: Do students learn more deeply when they interact with animated pedagogical agents? *Cognition and Instruction, 19,* 177–213.

Morgan, C. D., & Murray, H. A. (1935). A method for investigating fantasies: The Thematic Apperception Test. *Archives of Neurology and Psychiatry, 34,* 289–306.

Morgan, C. D., & Murray, H. A. (1962). Thematic Apperception Test. In H. A. Murray et al. (Eds.), *Explorations in personality: A clinical and experimental study of fifty men of college age* (pp. 530–545). New York: Science Editions.

Morgan, C. L. (1996). Odors as cues for the recall of words unrelated to odor. *Perceptual and Motor Skills, 83,* 1227–1234.

Morgan, R., & Flora, D. (2002). Group psychotherapy with incarcerated offenders: A research synthesis. *Group Dynamics: Theory, Research, and Practice, 6,* 203–218.

Morgan, R. E., Levitsky, D. A., & Strupp, B. J. (2000). Effects of chronic lead exposure on learning and reaction time in a visual discrimination task. *Neurotoxicology and Teratology, 22,* 337–345.

Morofushi, M., Shinohara, K., Funabashi, T., & Kimura, F. (2000). Positive relationship between menstrual synchrony and ability to smell 5alpha-androst-16-en-3alpha-ol. *Chemical Senses, 25,* 407–411.

Morris, J. S., Frith, C. D., Perrett, D. I., Rowland, D., Young, A. W., Calder, A. J., & Dolan, R. J. (1996). A differential neural response in the human amygdala to fearful and happy facial expressions. *Nature, 383,* 812–815.

Mościcki, E. K. (1995). Epidemiology of suicidal behavior. *Suicide and Life-Threatening Behavior, 25,* 22–31.

Moser, G., & Robin, M. (2006). Environmental annoyances: An urban-specific threat to quality of life? *European Review of Applied Psychology, 56,* 35–41.

Most, S., Simons, D., Scholl, B., Jimenez, R., Clifford, E., & Chabris, C. (2001). How not to be seen: The contribution of similarity and selective ignoring to sustained inattentional blindness. *Psychological Science, 12,* 9–17.

Mourtazaev, M. S., Kemp, B., Zwinderman, A. H., & Kamphuisen, H. A. C. (1995). Age and gender affect different characteristics of slow waves in the sleep EEG. *Sleep, 18,* 557–564.

Moynihan, J., Larson, M., Treanor, J., Duberstein, P., Power, A., Shre, B., et al. (2004). Psychosocial factors and the response to influenza vaccination in older adults. *Psychosomatic Medicine, 66,* 950–953.

Moynihan, R., & Cassels, A. (2005). *Selling sickness: How the world's biggest pharmaceutical companies are turning us all into patients.* New York: Nation Books.

Mufson, L., Gallagher, T., Dorta, K., & Young, J. (2004). A group adaptation of interpersonal psychotherapy for depressed adolescents. *American Journal of Psychotherapy, 58,* 220–237.

Mühlberger, A., Weik, A., Pauli, P., & Wiedemann, G. (2006). One-session virtual reality exposure treatment for fear of flying: 1-year follow-up and graduation flight accompaniment effects. *Psychotherapy Research, 16,* 26–40.

Mukerjee, M. (1997). Trends in animal research. *Scientific American, 276,* 86–93.

Mukherjee, R., & Turk, J. (2004). Fetal alcohol syndrome. *Lancet, 363,* 1556.

Muller, L. (2002). Group counseling for African American males: When all you have are European American counselors. *Journal for Specialists in Group Work, 27,* 299–313.

Müller, M., Regenbogen, B., Sachse, J., Eich, F., Härtter, S., & Hiemke, C. (2006). Gender aspects in the clinical treatment of schizophrenic inpatients with amisulpride: A therapeutic drug monitoring study. *Pharmacopsychiatry, 39,* 41–46.

Mumtaz, S., & Humphreys, G. (2002). The effect of Urdu vocabulary size on the acquisition of single word reading in English. *Educational Psychology, 22,* 165–190.

Munarriz, R., Talakoub, L., Flaherty, E., Gioia, M., Hoag, L., Kim, N., et al. (2002). Androgen replacement therapy with dehydroepiandrosterone for androgen insufficiency and female sexual dysfunction: Androgen and questionnaire results. *Journal of Sex & Marital Therapy, 28,* 165–173.

Munroe, R. H., Shimmin, H. S., & Munroe, R. L. (1984). Gender role understanding and sex role preference in four cultures. *Developmental Psychology, 20,* 673–682.

Munzar, P., Li, H., Nicholson, K., Wiley, J., & Balster, R. (2002). Enhancement of the discriminative stimulus effects of phencyclidine by the tetracycline antibiotics doxycycline and minocycline in rats. *Psychopharmacology, 160,* 331–336.

Murphy, E. (2003). Being born female is dangerous to your health. *American Psychologist, 58,* 205–210.

Murray, B. (2002). Finding the peace within us. *APA Monitor on Psychology, 33,* 56–57.

Murray, H. (1938). *Explorations in personality.* New York: Oxford University Press.

Murray, J., Liotti, M., Ingmundson, P., Mayburg, H., Pu, Y., Zamarripa, F., et al. (2006). Children's brain activations while viewing televised violence revealed by fMRI. *Media Psychology, 8,* 24–37.

Mustanski, B., Chivers, M., & Bailey, J. (2002). A critical review of recent biological research on human sexual orientation. *Annual Review of Sex Research, 13,* 89–140.

Myers, D. G., & Bishop, G. D. (1970). Discussion effects on racial attitudes. *Science, 169,* 778–779.

Nader, K. 2003. Re-recording human memories. *Nature, 425,* 571–572.

Nadon, R., Hoyt, I. P., Register, P. A., & Kilstrom, J. F. (1991). Absorption and hypnotizability: Context effects reexamined. *Journal of Personality and Social Psychology, 60,* 144–153.

Namie, G., & Namie, R. (2000). Naperville, IL: Sourcebooks.

Narita, M., Kaneko, C., Miyoshi, K., Nagumo, Y., Kuzumaki, N., Nakajima, M., et al. (2006). Chronic pain induces anxiety with concomitant changes in opioidergic function in the amygdala. *Neuropsychopharmacology, 31,* 739–750.

Narvaez, D. (2002). Does reading moral stories build character? *Educational Psychology Review, 14,* 155–171.

Nash, M. (1987). What, if anything, is regressed about hypnotic age regression? A review of the empirical literature. *Psychological Bulletin, 102,* 42–52.

Nash, M., & Baker, E. (1984, February). Trance encounters: Susceptibility to hypnosis. *Psychology Today,* pp. 18, 72–73.

Nash, M. R. (1991). Hypnosis as a special case of psychological regression. In S. J. Lynn & J. W. Rhue (Eds.), *Theories of hypnosis: Current models and perspectives* (pp. 171–194). New York: Guilford.

National Alliance for Mental Illness (NAMI). (2003). *Panic disorder.* Retrieved July 19, 2006, from http://www.nami.org/Template.cfm?Section=By_Illness&Template=/TaggedPage/TaggedPageDisplay.cfm&TPLID=54&ContentID=23050

National Cancer Institute. (2000). *Questions and answers about smoking cessation.* Retrieved January 29, 2003, from http://cis.nci.nih.gov/fact/8_13.htm

National Center for Chronic Disease Prevention and Health Promotion. (2006). *The health consequences of involuntary exposure to tobacco smoke: A report of the surgeon general.* Retrieved July 7, 2006, from http://www.cdc.gov/TOBACCO/sgr/sgr_2006/index.htm

National Center for Education Statistics (NCES). (2006). *Digest of Education Statistics, 2005.* Retrieved November 28, 2006 from http://nces.ed.gov/fastfacts/display.asp?id=98

National Center for Health Statistics (NCHS). (2000). *Health, United States, 2000 with adolescent health chartbook.* Retrieved June 10, 2007 from http://www.cdc.gov/nchs/data/hus/hus00.pdf

National Center for Health Statistics (NCHS). (2002). *Fast stats A to Z: Mental health.* [Online fact sheet]. Retrieved November 9, 2002, from http://www.cdc.gov/nchs/fastats/mental.htm

National Center for Health Statistics (NCHS). (2004a). *Health in the U.S. 2004.* Retrieved February 1, 2005, from http://www.cdc.gov/nchs/hus.htm

National Center for Health Statistics (NCHS). (2004b). *Prevalence of overweight and obesity among adults: United States, 1999–2002.* Retrieved February 1, 2005, from http://www.cdc.gov/nchs/products/pubs/pubd/hestats/obese/obse99.htm

National Center for Health Statistics (NCHS). (2005). *Health, United States, 2005.* Retrieved July 5, 2006, from http://www.cdc.gov/nchs/data/hus/hus05.pdf#053

National Center for Health Statistics (NCHS). (2006a). *Health, United States, 2006.* Retrieved February 12, 2007, from http://www.cdc.gov/nchs/data/hus/hus06.pdf#046

National Center for Health Statistics (NCHS). (2006b). *Teen births.* Retrieved January 28, 2007, from http://www.cdc.gov/nchs/fastats/teenbrth.htm

National Highway and Traffic Safety Administration (NHTSA). (2007). *Alcohol poisoning.* Retrieved February 7, 2007, from http://www.nhtsa.dot.gov/PEOPLE/outreach/safesobr/15qp/web/idalc.html

National Institute of Mental Health. (1999b). *The invisible disease—depression.* Retrieved June 10, 2007 from http://www.nimh.nih.gov/publicat/invisible.cfm

National Institute of Mental Health (NIMH). (2001). *The numbers count: Mental disorders in America (NIMH Report No. 01–4584).* Washington, DC: Author.

National Institute of Neurological Disorders and Stroke rt-PA Stroke Study Group. (1995). Tissue plasminogen activator for acute ischemic stroke. *New England Journal of Medicine, 333,* 1581–1587.

National Institute on Aging. (2001). Progress report on Alzheimer's Disease: Taking the next steps. Silver Spring, MD: Alzheimer's Disease Education and Referral Center (ADEAR) of the National Institute on Aging.

National Institute on Drug Abuse (NIDA). (2001). *Ecstasy: What we know and don't know about MDMA: A scientific review.* Retrieved October 17, 2003, from http://www.nida.nih.gov/Meetings/MDMA/MDMAExSummary.html

National Science Foundation (NSF). (2000a). *Characteristics of scientists and engineers in the United States: 1999.* Washington, DC: Author. Retrieved April 25, 2006, from http://srsstats.sbe.nsf.gov/preformatted-tables/1999/DST1999.html

National Science Foundation (NSF). (2002). *Science and engineering: Indicators 2002.* Retrieved January 29, 2003, from http://www.nsf.gov/sbc/srs/seind02/toc.htm

Nawrot, M., Nordenstrom, B., & Olson, A. (2004). Disruption of eye movements by ethanol intoxication affects perception of depth from motion parallax. *Psychological Science, 15,* 858–865.

Needleman, H. L., Riess, J. A., Tobin, M. J., Biesecker, G. E., & Greenhouse, J. B. (1996). Bone lead levels and delinquent behavior. *Journal of the American Medical Association, 275,* 363–369.

Neimark, E. D. (1981). Confounding with cognitive style factors: An artifact explanation for the apparent nonuniversal incidence of formal operations. In I. Sigel, D. Brodzinsky, & R. Golinkoff (Eds.), *New directions in Piagetian research and theory.* Hillsdale, NJ: Erlbaum.

Neisser, U., Boodoo, G., Bouchard, T. J., Jr., Boykin, A. W., Brody, N., Ceci, S. J., et al. (1996). Intelligence: Knowns and unknowns. *American Psychologist, 51,* 77–101.

Neisser, U., & Harsch, N. (1992). Phantom flashbulbs: False recollections of hearing the news about *Challenger.* In E. Winograd & U. Neisser (Eds.), *Affect and accuracy in recall: Studies of "flashbulb" memories* (pp. 9–31). New York: Cambridge University Press.

Neitz, J., Neitz, M., & Kainz, M. (1996). Visual pigment gene structure and the severity of color vision defects. *Science, 274,* 801–804.

Neitz, M., & Neitz, J. (1995). Numbers and ratios of visual pigment genes for normal red-green color vision. *Science, 267,* 1013–1016.

Nelson, J. C. (1997). Safety and tolerability of the new antidepressants. *Journal of Clinical Psychiatry, 58*(6, Suppl.), 26–31.

Nelson, T. (1996). Consciousness and metacognition. *American Psychologist, 51,* 102–116.

Nestadt, G., Samuels, J., Riddle, M., Bienvenu, J., Liang, K., LaBuda, M., Walkup, J., Grados, M., & Hoehn-Saric, R. (2000). A family study of obsessive-compulsive disorder. *Archives of General Psychiatry, 57,* 358–363.

Nestor, P., Graham, K., Bozeat, S., Simons, J., & Hodges, J. (2002). Memory consolidation and the hippocampus: Further evidence from studies of autobiographical memory in semantic dementia and frontal variant frontotemporal dementia. *Neuropsychologia, 40,* 633–654.

Newberg, A., Alavi, A. Baime, M., Pourdehnad, M., Santanna, J. d'Aquili. E. (2001). The measurement of cerebral blood flow during the complex cognitive task of meditation: A preliminary SPECT study. *Psychiatry Research: Neuroimaging, 106,* 113–122.

Newell, B., & Shanks, D. (2003). Take the best or look at the rest? Factors influencing "one-reason" decision making. *Journal of Experimental Psychology: Learning, Memory, and Cognition, 29,* 53–65.

Newell, B., & Shanks, D. (2004). On the role of recognition in decision making. *Journal of Experimental Psychology: Learning, Memory and Cognition, 30,* 923–935.

Newell, P., & Cartwright, R. (2000). Affect and cognition in dreams: A critique of the cognitive role in adaptive dream functioning and support for associative models. *Psychiatry: Interpersonal & Biological Processes, 63,* 34–44.

Nguyen, P. V., Abel, T., & Kandel, E. R. (1994). Requirement of a critical period of transcription for induction of a late phase of LTP. *Science, 265,* 1104–1107.

Nickerson, R. S., & Adams, M. J. (1979). Long-term memory for a common object. *Cognitive Psychology, 11,* 287–307.

Nicol, S. E., & Gottesman, I. I. (1983). Clues to the genetics and neurobiology of schizophrenia. *American Scientist, 71,* 398–404.

Nisbett, R. E., & Wilson, T. D. (1977). The halo effect: Evidence for unconscious alteration of judgments. *Journal of Personality and Social Psychology, 35,* 250–256.

Nogrady, H., McConkey, K. M., & Perry, C. (1985). Enhancing visual memory: Trying hypnosis, trying imagination, and trying again. *Journal of Abnormal Psychology, 94,* 195–204.

Noise Pollution Council. (2003). *Comparing standards for safe noise exposure.* Retrieved May 16, 2003, from http://www.nonoise.org/hearing/exposure/standardschart.htm

Nordentoft, M., Lou, H. C., Hansen, D., Nim, J., Pryds, O., Rubin, P., et al. (1996). Intrauterine growth retardation and premature delivery: The influence of maternal smoking and psychosocial factors. *American Journal of Public Health, 86,* 347–354.

Noriko, S. (2004). Identity development pre- and post-empty nest women. *Japanese Journal of Developmental Psychology, 15,* 52–64.

Norman, S., Norman, G., Rossi, J., & Prochaska, J. (2006). Identifying high- and low-success smoking cessation subgroups using signal detection analysis. *Addictive Behaviors, 31,* 31–41.

Norman, W. (1963). Toward an adequate taxonomy of personality attributes: Replicated factor structure in peer nomination personality ratings. *Journal of Abnormal & Social Psychology, 66,* 574–583.

Norris, J. E., & Tindale, J. A. (1994). *Among generations: The cycle of adult relationships.* New York: Freeman.

Norton, M., Moniu, B., Cooper, J., & Hogg, M. (2003). Vicarious dissonance: Attitude change from the inconsistency of others. *Journal of Personality & Social Psychology, 85,* 47–62.

Noyes, R., Jr., Burrows, G. D., Reich, J. H., Judd, F. K., Garvey, M. J., Norman, T. R., et al. (1996). Diazepam versus alprazolam for the treatment of panic disorder. *Journal of Clinical Psychiatry, 57,* 344–355.

Nunn, J., Gregory, L., Brammer, M., Williams, S., Parslow, D., Morgan, M., Morris, R., Bullmore, E., Baron-Cohen, S., & Gray, J. (2002). Functional magnetic resonance imaging of synesthesia: Activation of V4/V8 by spoken words. *Nature Neuroscience, 5,* 371–375.

Nutt, D. (2000). Treatment of depression and concomitant anxiety. *European Neuropsychopharmacology, 10* (Suppl. 4), S433–S437.

Nyberg, L., Eriksson, J., Larsson, A., & Marklund, P. (2006). Learning by doing versus learning by thinking. An fMRI study of motor and mental training. *Neuropsychologia, 44,* 711–717.

O'Brien, C. P. (1996). Recent developments in the pharmacotherapy of substance abuse. *Journal of Consulting and Clinical Psychology, 64,* 677–686.

Ogawa, A., Mizuta, I., Fukunaga, T., Takeuchi, N., Honaga, E., Sugita, Y., Mikami, A., Inoue, Y., & Takeda, M. (2004). Electrogastrography abnormality in eating disorders. *Psychiatry & Clinical Neurosciences, 58,* 300–310.

Ohman, A., & Mineka, S. (2003). The malicious serpent: Snakes as a prototypical stimulus for an evolved module of fear. *Current Directions in Psychological Science, 12,* 5–8.

O'Kane, G., Kensinger, E., & Corkin, S. (2004). Evidence for semantic learning in profound amnesia: An investigation with patient H. M. *Hippocampus, 14,* 417–425.

Okura, Y., Akira, M., Kuniko, K., Park, I., Matthias, S., & Matsumoto, Y. (2006). Nonviral amyloid-beta DNA vaccine therapy against Alzheimer's disease: Long-term effects and safety. *Proceedings of the National Academy of Sciences, 103,* 9619–9624.

Olatunji, B., Lohr, J, Sawchuk, C., & Tolin, D. (2007). Multimodal assessment of disgust in contamination-related obsessive-compulsive disorder. *Behaviour Research and Therapy, 45,* 263–276.

O'Leary, K. D., & Smith, D. A. (1991). Marital interactions. *Annual Review of Psychology, 42,* 191–212.

Oliver, J. E. (1993). Intergenerational transmission of child abuse: Rates, research, and clinical implications. *American Journal of Psychiatry, 150,* 1315–1324.

Olson, M., Krantz, D., Kelsey, S., Pepine, C., Sopko, G., Handberg, E., Rogers, W., Gierach, G., McClure, C., & Merz, C. (2005). Hostility scores are associated with increased risk of cardiovascular events in women undergoing coronary angiography: A report from the NHLBI-sponsored WISE study. *Psychosomatic Medicine, 67,* 546–552.

Ono, H. (2003). Women's economic standing, marriage timing and cross-national contexts of gender. *Journal of Marriage & Family, 65,* 275–286.

Oquendo, M., Placidi, G., Malone, K., Campbell, C., Kelp, J., Brodsky, B., et al. (2003). Positron emission tomography of regional brain metabolic responses to a serotonergic challenge and lethality of suicide attempts in major depression. *Archives of General Psychiatry, 60,* 14–22.

Orman, M. (1996). *How to conquer public speaking fear.* Retrieved February 15, 2003, from http://www.stresscure.com/jobstress/speak.html

Ortega-Alvaro, A., Gilbert-Rahola, J., & Micó, J. (2006). Influence of chronic treatment with olanzapine, clozapine, and scopolamine on performance of a learned 8-arm radial maze task in rats. *Progress in Neuro-Psychopharmacology & Biological Psychiatry, 30,* 104–111.

Osborn, D., Fletcher, A., Smeeth, L., Sitrling, S., Bulpitt, C., Breeze, E., et al. (2003). Factors associated with depression in a representative sample of 14,217 people aged 75 and over in the United Kingdom: Results from the MRC trial of assessment and management of older people in the community. *International Journal of Geriatric Psychiatry, 18,* 623–630.

Öst, L-G., & Westling, B. E. (1995). Applied relaxation vs. cognitive behavior therapy in the treatment of panic disorder. *Behavior Research and Therapy, 33,* 145–158.

Ostrom, T. M., Carpenter, S. L., Sedikides, C., & Li, F. (1993). Differential processing of in-group and out-group information. *Journal of Personality and Social Psychology, 64,* 21–34.

Otto, M. W., Pollack, M. H., Sachs, G. S., Reiter, S. R., Meltzer-Brody, S., & Rosenbaum, J. F. (1993). Discontinuation of benzodiazepine treatment: Efficacy of cognitive-behavioral therapy for patients with panic disorder. *American Journal of Psychiatry, 150,* 1485–1490.

Overby, K. (2002). Pediatric health supervision. In A. Rudolph, R. Kamei, & K. Overby (Eds.), *Rudolph's fundamentals of pediatrics* (3rd ed., pp. 1–69). New York: McGraw-Hill.

Overmeier, J. B., & Seligman, M. E. P. (1967). Effects of inescapable shock upon subsequent escape and avoidance responding. *Journal of Comparative and Physiological Psychology, 67,* 28–33.

Owen, M., & O'Donovan, M. (2003). Schizophrenia and genetics. In R. Plomin, J. Defries, I. Craig, & P. McGuffin (Eds.), *Behavioral genetics in the postgenomic era* (pp. 463–480). Washington, DC: American Psychological Association.

Paivio, S. C., & Greenberg, L. S. (1995). Resolving "unfinished business": Efficacy of experiential therapy using empty-chair dialogue. *Journal of Consulting and Clinical Psychology, 63,* 419–425.

Pal, S. (2005). Prevalence of chronic pain and migraine. *U.S. Pharmacist, 3,* 12–15.

Palinscar, A. S., & Brown, A. L. (1984). Reciprocal teaching of comprehension-fostering and comprehension-monitoring activities. *Cognition and Instruction, 1,* 117–175.

Pansu, P., & Gilibert, D. (2002). Effect of causal explanations on work-related judgments. *Applied Psychology: An International Review, 51,* 505–526.

Papousek, I., & Schulter, G. (2002). Covariations of EEG asymmetries and emotional states indicate that activity at frontopolar locations is particularly affected by state factors. *Psychophysiology, 39,* 350–360.

Paquette, D. (2004). Dichotomizing paternal and maternal functions as a means to better understand their primary contributions. *Human Development, 47,* 237–238.

Paraherakis, A., Charney, D., & Gill, K. (2001). Neuropsychological functioning in substance-dependent patients. *Substance Use & Misuse, 36,* 257–271.

Parke, R. D. (1977). Some effects of punishment on children's behavior–revisited. In E. M. Hetherington, E. M. Ross, & R. D. Parke (Eds.), *Contemporary readings in child psychology.* New York: McGraw-Hill.

Parkinson, W. L., & Weingarten, H. P. (1990). Dissociative analysis of ventromedial hypothalamic obesity syndrome. *American Journal of Physiology, 259,* 829–835.

Partinen, M., Hublin, C., Kaprio, J., Koskenvuo, M., & Guilleminault, C. (1994). Twin studies in narcolepsy. *Sleep, 17,* S13–S16.

Parvizi, J., & Damasio, A. (2001). Consciousness and the brainstem. *Cognition, 79,* 135–159.

Pascual-Leone, A., Dhuna, A., Altafullah, I., & Anderson, D. C. (1990). Cocaine-induced seizures. *Neurology, 40,* 404–407.

Pastore, N. (1950). The role of arbitrariness in the frustration-aggression hypothesis. *Journal of Abnormal and Social Psychology, 47,* 728–731.

Patterson, C. J. (1995). Sexual orientation and human development: An overview. *Developmental Psychology, 31,* 3–11.

Patterson, D. (2004). Treating pain with hypnosis. *Current Directions in Psychological Science, 13,* 252–255.

Paul, T., Schroeter, K., Dahme, B., & Nutzinger, D. (2002). Self-injurious behavior in women with eating disorders. *American Journal of Psychiatry, 159,* 408–411.

Paul, W. E. (1993). Infectious diseases and the immune system. *Scientific American, 269,* 90–99.

Paulhus, D., Harms, P., Bruce, M., & Lysy, D. (2003). The over-claiming technique: Measuring self-enhancement independent of ability. *Journal of Personality & Social Psychology, 84,* 890–904.

Paulus, P. B., Cox, V. C., & McCain, G. (1988). *Prison crowding: A psychological perspective.* New York: Springer-Verlag.

Paunonen, S. V., Keinonen, M., Trzebinski, J., Forsterling, F., Grishenko-Roze, N., Kouznetsova, L., et al. (1996). The structure of personality in six cultures. *Journal of Cross-Cultural Psychology, 27,* 339–353.

Pause, B. (2004). Are androgen steroids acting as pheromones in humans? *Physiology & Behavior, 83,* 21–29.

Payami, H., Montee, K., & Kaye, J. (1994). Evidence for familial factors that protect against dementia and outweigh the effect of increasing age. *American Journal of Human Genetics, 54,* 650–657.

Pavlov, I. P. (1927/1960). *Conditioned reflexes: An investigation of the physiological activity of the cerebral cortex* (G. V. Anrep, Trans.). New York: Dover. (Original translation published 1927).

Pedersen, D. M., & Wheeler, J. (1983). The Müller-Lyer illusion among Navajos. *Journal of Social Psychology, 121,* 3–6.

Pedersen, S., & Denollet, J. (2003). Type D personality, cardiac events, and impaired quality of life: A review. *European Journal of Cardiovascular Prevention and Rehabilitation, 10,* 241–248.

Pedersen, S., Van Domburg, R., & Theuns, D. (2004). Type D personality is associated with increased anxiety and depressive symptoms in patients with an implantable cardioverter defibrillator and their partners. *Psychosomatic Medicine, 66,* 714–719.

Penfield, W. (1969). Consciousness, memory, and man's conditioned reflexes. In K. Pribram (Ed.), *On the biology of learning* (pp. 129–168). New York: Harcourt Brace Jovanovich.

Pennebaker, J., & Seagal, J. (1999). Forming a story: The health benefits of narrative. *Journal of Clinical Psychology, 55,* 1243–1254.

Pennisi, E. (1997). Tracing molecules that make the brain–body connection. *Science, 275,* 930–931.

Peplau, L. (2003). Human sexuality: How do men and women differ? *Current Directions in Psychological Science, 12,* 37–40.

Pepperberg, I. (2006). Grey parrot *(Psittacus erithacus)* numerical abilities: Addition and further experiments on a zero-like concept. *Journal of Comparative Psychology, 120,* 1–11.

Pepperberg, I. M. (1991, Spring). Referential communication with an African grey parrot. *Harvard Graduate Society Newsletter,* 1–4.

Pepperberg, I. M. (1994a). Numerical competence in an African grey parrot (Psittacus erithacus). *Journal of Comparative Psychology, 108,* 36–44.

Pepperberg, I. M. (1994b). Vocal learning in grey parrots (Psittacus erithacus): Effects of social interaction, reference, and context. *The Auk, 111,* 300–314.

Perls, F. S. (1969). *Gestalt therapy verbatim.* Lafayette, CA: Real People Press.

Perry, S., Wallace, N., & Wilhelm, I. (2005). Donations for victims of Katrina reach $404 million. *Chronicle of Philanthropy.* [Online edition] Retrieved October 29, 2006, from http://philanthropy.com/free/update/2005/09/2005090201.htm.

Pesonen, A., Raeikkoenen, K., Keskivaara, P., & Keltikangas-Jaervinen, L. (2003). Difficult temperament in childhood and adulthood: Continuity from maternal perceptions to self-ratings over 17 years. *Personality & Individual Differences, 34,* 19–31.

Peters, A., Leahu, D., Moss, M. B., & McNally, J. (1994). The effects of aging on area 46 of the frontal cortex of the rhesus monkey. *Cerebral Cortex, 6,* 621–635.

Peterson, A. C. (1987, September). Those gangly years. *Psychology Today,* 28–34.

Peterson, L. R., & Peterson, M. J. (1959). Short-term retention of individual verbal items. *Journal of Experimental Psychology, 58,* 193–198.

Petry, N. (2002). Psychosocial treatments for pathological gambling: Current status and future directions. *Psychiatric Annals, 32,* 192–196.

Petry, N., Tedford, J., Austin, M., Nich, C., Carroll, K., & Rounsaville, B. (2004). Prize reinforcement contingency management for treating cocaine users: How low can we go, and with whom? *Addiction, 99,* 349–360.

Pettus, A. (2006). Psychiatry by prescription. *Harvard Magazine,* 108, 38–44, 90–91. Retrieved July 8, 2006, from http://www.harvardmagazine.com/on-line/070646.html

Petty, R. E., Wegener, D. T., & Fabrigar, L. R. (1997). Attitudes and attitude change. *Annual Review of Psychology, 48,* 609–647.

Pew Research Center. (2006). *Global gender gaps.* Retrieved June 29, 2006, from http://pewglobal.org/commentary/display.php? AnalysisID=90

Phillips, K., Fulker, D. W., Carey, G., & Nagoshi, C. T. (1988). Direct marital assortment for cognitive and personality variables. *Behavioral Genetics, 18,* 347–356.

Phillips, S. T., & Ziller, R. C. (1997). Toward a theory and measure of the nature of nonprejudice. *Journal of Personality and Social Psychology, 72,* 420–434.

Piaget, J. (1927/1965). *The moral judgment of the child.* New York: Free Press.

Piaget, J. (1963). *Psychology of intelligence.* Patterson, NJ: Littlefield, Adams.

Piaget, J. (1964). *Judgment and reasoning in the child.* Patterson, NJ: Littlefield, Adams.

Piaget, J., & Inhelder, B. (1969). *The psychology of the child.* New York: Basic Books.

Pich, E. M., Pagliusi, S. R., Tessari, M., Talabot-Ayer, D., van Huijsduijnen, R. H., & Chiamulera, C. (1997). Common neural substrates for the addictive properties of nicotine and cocaine. *Science, 275,* 83–86.

Pieringer, W., Fazekas, C., & Pieringer, C. (2005). Schizophrenia: An existential disease. *Fortschritte der Neurologie, Psychiatrie, 73,* S25–S31.

Pigott, T. A. (1996). OCD: Where the serotonin selectivity story begins. *Journal of Clinical Psychiatry, 57*(6, Suppl.), 11–20.

Pihl, R. O., Lau, M. L., & Assaad, J-M. (1997). Aggressive disposition, alcohol, and aggression. *Aggressive Behavior, 23,* 11–18.

Pilcher, J. J., Lambert, B. J., & Huffcutt, A. I. (2000). Differential effects of permanent and rotating shifts on self-report sleep length: A meta-analytic review. *Sleep, 23,* 155–163.

Pillemer, D. B. (1990). Clarifying the flashbulb memory concept: Comment on McCloskey, Wible, and Cohen (1988). *Journal of Experimental Psychology: General, 119,* 92–96.

Pillow, D. R., Zautra, A. J., & Sandler, I. (1996). Major life events and minor stressors: Identifying mediational links in the stress process. *Journal of Personality and Social Psychology, 70,* 381–394.

Pillsworth, E., Haselton, M., & Buss, D. (2004). Ovulatory shifts in female sexual desire. *Journal of Sex Research, 41,* 55–65.

Pinel, J. (2007). *Basics of Biopsychology.* Boston: Allyn & Bacon.

Pinel, J. P. L. (2000). *Biopsychology* (4th ed.). Boston: Allyn & Bacon.

Pinikahana, J., Happell, B., & Keks, N. (2003). Suicide and schizophrenia: A review of literature for the decade (1990–1999) and implications for mental health nursing. *Issues in Mental Health Nursing, 24,* 27–43.

Pinker, S. (1994). *The language instinct: How the mind creates language.* New York: Morrow.

Pinquart, M., & Sörensen, S. (2000). Influences of socioeconomic status, social network, and competence on subjective well-being in later life: A meta-analysis. *Psychology and Aging, 15,* 187–224.

Pittenger, D. J. (1993). The utility of the Myers-Briggs Type Indicator. *Review of Educational Research, 63,* 467–488.

Plaks, J., Grant, H., & Dweck, C. (2005). Violations of implicit theories and the sense of prediction and control: Implications for motivated person perception. *Journal of Personality & Social Psychology, 88,* 245–262.

Platek, S., Loughead, J., Gur, R., Busch, S., Ruparel, K., Phend, N., et al. (2006). Neural substrates for functionally discriminating self-face from personally familiar faces. *Human Brain Mapping, 27,* 91–98.

Platek, S., Thomson, J., & Gallup, G. (2004). Cross-modal self-recognition: The role of visual, auditory, and olfactory primes. *Consciousness and Cognition: An International Journal, 13,* 197–210.

Plomin, R., Defries, J., Craig, I., & McGuffin, P. (2003). *Behavioral genetics in the postgenomic era.* Washington, DC: American Psychological Association.

Plomin, R., DeFries, J. C., & Fulker, D. W. (1988). *Nature and nurture during infancy and early childhood.* New York: Cambridge University Press.

Plomin, R., DeFries, J. C., McClearn, G. E., & Rutter, M. (1997). *Behavioral genetics* (3rd ed.). New York: Freeman.

Plomin, R., Owen, M. J., & McGuffin, P. (1994). The genetic basis of complex human behaviors. *Science, 264,* 1733–1739.

Plotnik, J., de Waal, F., & Reiss, D. (2006). Self-recognition in an Asian elephant. *Proceedings of the National Academy of Science, 103,* 17053–17057.

Plumer, B. (2005, July). Licensed to ill. *Mother Jones.* [Online. No pages specified.] Retrieved July 25, 2006, from http://www.motherjones.com/commentary/columns/2005/07/selling_sickness.html

Poldrack, R., & Wagner, A. (2004). What can neuroimaging tell us about the mind? Insights from prefrontal cortex. *Current Directions in Psychological Science, 13,* 177–181.

Pontieri, F. C., Tanda, G., Orzi, F., & Di Chiara, G. (1996). Effects of nicotine on the nucleus accumbens and similarity to those of addictive drugs. *Nature, 382,* 255–257.

Poponoe, D., & Whitehead, B. D. (2000). Sex without strings, relationships without rings: Today's young singles talk about mating and dating. In *National Marriage Project, The State of Our Unions, 2000.* Retrieved June 10, 2007 from http://marriage.rutgers.edu/Publications/SOOU/NMPAR2000.pdf.

Porjesz, B., Begleiter, H., Reich, T., Van Eerdewegh, P., Edenberg, H., Foroud, T., et al. (1998). Amplitude of visual P3 event-related potential as a phenotypic marker for a predisposition to alcoholism: Preliminary results from the COGA project. *Alcoholism: Clinical & Experimental Research, 22,* 1317–1323.

Porrino, L. J., & Lyons, D. (2000). Orbital and medial prefrontal cortex and psychostimulant abuse: Studies in animal models. *Cerebral Cortex, 10,* 326–333.

Porte, H. S., & Hobson, J. A. (1996). Physical motion in dreams: One measure of three theories. *Sleep, 105,* 3329–3335.

Porter, F. L., Porges, S. W., & Marshall, R. E. (1988). Newborn pain cries and vagal tone: Parallel changes in response to circumcision. *Child Development, 59,* 495–505.

Posada, G., Jacobs, A., Richmond, M., Carbonell, O., Alzate, G., Bustamante, M., et al. (2002). Maternal caregiving and infant security in two cultures. *Developmental Psychology, 38,* 67–78.

Posner, M. I. (1996, September). Attention and psychopathology. *Harvard Mental Health Letter, 13*(3), 5–6.

Postman, L., & Phillips, L. W. (1965). Short-term temporal changes in free recall. *Quarterly Journal of Experimental Psychology, 17,* 132–138.

Potts, N. L. S., Davidson, J. R. T., & Krishman, K. R. R. (1993). The role of nuclear magnetic resonance imaging in psychiatric research. *Journal of Clinical Psychiatry, 54*(12, Suppl.), 13–18.

Powell, C., & Van Vugt, M. (2003). Genuine giving or selfish sacrifice? The role of commitment and cost level upon willingness to sacrifice. *European Journal of Social Psychology, 33,* 403–412.

Powell, L., Shahabi, L., & Thoresen, C. (2003). Religion and spirituality: Linkages to physical health. *American Psychologist, 58,* 36–52.

Power, F. C., Higgins, A., & Kohlberg, L. (1989). *Lawrence Kohlberg's approach to moral education.* New York: Columbia University Press.

Power, K. G., Sharp, D. M., Swanson, V., & Simpson, R. J. (2000). Therapist contact in cognitive behaviour therapy for panic disorder and agoraphobia in primary care. *Clinical Psychology & Psychotherapy, 7,* 37–46.

Powlishta, K. K. (1995). Intergroup processes in childhood: Social categorization and sex role development. *Developmental Psychology, 31,* 781–788.

Pöysti, L., Rajalin, S., & Summala, H. (2005). Factors influencing the use of cellular (mobile) phone during driving and hazards while using it. *Accident Analysis & Prevention, 37,* 47–51.

Poznanski, M., & Thagard, P. (2005). Changing personalities: Towards realistic virtual characters. *Journal of Experimental & Theoretical Artificial Intelligence, 17,* 221–241.

Prabhu, V., Porjesz, B., Chorlian, D., Wang, K., Stimus, A., & Begleiter, H. (2001). Visual P3 in female alcoholics. *Alcoholism: Clinical & Experimental Research, 25,* 531–539.

Pratkanis, A. R. (1989). The cognitive representation of attitudes. In A. R. Pratkanis, S. J. Breckler, & A. G. Greenwald (Eds.), *Attitude structure and function* (pp. 71–93). Hillsdale, NJ: Erlbaum.

Premack, D. (1971). Language in chimpanzees. *Science, 172,* 808–822.

Premack, D., & Premack, A. J. (1983). *The mind of an ape.* New York: Norton.

Prien, R. F., & Kocsis, J. H. (1995). Long-term treatment of mood disorders. In F. E. Bloom & D. J. Kupfer (Eds.), *Psychopharmacology: The fourth generation of progress* (pp. 1067–1079). New York: Raven.

Prigerson, H. G., Bierhals, A. J., Kasl, S. V., Reynolds, C. F., III, Shear, M. K., Day, N., et al. (1997). Traumatic grief as a risk factor for mental and physical mortality. *American Journal of Psychiatry, 154,* 616–623.

Prinz, P. N., Vitiello, M. V., Raskind, M. A., & Thorpy, M. J. (1990). Geriatrics: Sleep disorders and aging. *New England Journal of Medicine, 323,* 520–526.

Pryke, S., Lindsay, R. C. L., & Pozzulo, J. D. (2000). Sorting mug shots: Methodological issues. *Applied Cognitive Psychology, 14,* 81–96.

Public Agenda Online. (2002). *The issues: Race.* Retrieved November 13, 2002, from http://www.publicagenda.com/issues/overview.dfm?issue_type=race

Public Health Agency of Canada. (2006). *Hearing loss infosheet for seniors.* Retrieved December 13, 2006, from http://www.phac-aspc.gc.ca/seniors-aines/pubs/info_sheets/hearing_loss/index.htm

Putnam, F. W. (1989). *Diagnosis and treatment of multiple personality disorder.* New York: Guilford Press.

Putnam, F. W. (1992). Altered states: Peeling away the layers of a multiple personality. *The Sciences, 32,* 30–36.

Quaid, K., Aschen, S., Smiley, C., Nurnberger, J. (2001). Perceived genetic risks for bipolar disorder in patient population: An exploratory study. *Journal of Genetic Counseling, 10,* 41–51.

Querido, J., Warner, T., & Eyberg, S. (2002). Parenting styles and child behavior in African American families of preschool children. *Journal of Clinical Child & Adolescent Psychology, 31,* 272–277.

Quesnel, C., Savard, J., Simard, S., Ivers, H., & Morin, C. (2003). Efficacy of cognitive-behavioral therapy for insomnia in women treated for nonmetastatic breast cancer. *Journal of Consulting & Clinical Psychology, 71,* 189–200.

Quiroga, T., Lemos-Britton, Z., Mostafapour, E., Abbott, R., & Berninger, V. (2002). Phonological awareness and beginning reading in Spanish-speaking ESL first graders: Research into practice. *Journal of School Psychology, 40,* 85–111.

Rabinowitz, P. (2000). Noise-induced hearing loss. *American Family Physician, 61,* 1053.

Rachman, S. J., & Wilson, G. T. (1980). *The effects of psychological therapy* (2nd ed.). New York: Pergamon.

Raeikkoenen, K., Matthews, K., & Salomon, K. (2003). Hostility predicts metabolic syndrome risk factors in children and adolescents. *Health Psychology, 22,* 279–286.

Rahe, R. J., Meyer, M., Smith, M., Kjaer, G., & Holmes, T. H. (1964). Social stress and illness onset. *Journal of Psychosomatic Research, 8,* 35–44.

Rahman, Q. (2005). Fluctuating asymmetry, second to fourth finger length ratios and human sexual orientation. *Psychoneuroendocrinology, 30,* 382–391.

Rahman, Q., & Wilson, G. (2003). Born gay? The psychobiology of human sexual orientation. *Personality and Individual Differences, 34,* 1337–1382.

Raine, A. (1996). Autonomic nervous system factors underlying disinhibited, antisocial, and violent behavior: Biosocial perspectives and treatment implications. *Annals of the New York Academy of Sciences, 794,* 46–59.

Ralph, M. R. (1989, November/December). The rhythm maker: Pinpointing the master clock in mammals. *The Sciences, 29,* 40–45.

Ramey, C. (1993). A rejoinder to Spitz's critique of the Abecedarian experiment. *Intelligence, 17,* 25–30.

Ramey, C., & Campbell, F. (1987). The Carolina Abecedarian project. An educational experiment concerning human malleability. In J. J. Gallagher & C. T. Ramey (Eds.), *The malleability of children* (pp. 127–140). Baltimore: Brookes.

Ramey, C., & Ramey, S. (2004). Early learning and school readiness: Can early intervention make a difference? 471–491.

Ramsay, D. S., & Woods, S. C. (1997). Biological consequences of drug administration: Implications for acute and chronic tolerance. *Psychological Review, 104,* 170–193.

Ramsey, J., Langlois, J., Hoss, R., Rubenstein, A., & Griffin, A. (2004). Origins of a stereotype: Categorization of facial attractiveness by 6-month-old infants. *Developmental Science, 7,* 201–211.

Ranjan, A., & Gentili, A. (2005). Primary insomnia. Retrieved December 16, 2006, from http://www.emedicine.com/med/topic3128.htm

Rantanen, J., Pulkkinen, L., & Kinnunen, U. (2005). The Big Five personality dimensions, work-family conflict, and psychological distress: A longitudinal view. *Journal of Individual Differences, 26,* 155–166.

Rapp, S., Espeland, M., Shumaker, S., Henderson, V., Brunner, R., Manson, J., et al. (2003). Effect of estrogen plus progestin on global cognitive function in postmenopausal women: The Women's Health Initiative Memory Study: A randomized controlled trial. *Journal of the American Medical Association (JAMA), 289,* 2663–2672.

Rasmussen, S. A., & Eisen, J. L. (1990). Epidemiology of obsessive compulsive disorder. *Journal of Clinical Psychiatry, 51*(2, Suppl.), 10–13.

Ratty, H., Vaenskae, J., Kasanen, K., & Kaerkkaeinen, R. (2002). Parents' explanations of their child's performance in mathematics and reading: A replication and extension of Yee and Eccles. *Sex Roles, 46,* 121–128.

Ray, S., & Bates, M. (2006). Acute alcohol effects on repetition priming and word recognition memory with equivalent memory cues. *Brain and Cognition, 60,* 118–127.

Raz, A., Deouell, L., & Bentin, S. (2001). Is pre-attentive processing compromised by prolonged wakefulness? Effects of total sleep deprivation on the mismatch negativity. *Psychophysiology, 38,* 787–795.

Raz, N., Lindenberger, U., Rodrigue, K., Kennedy, K., Head, D., Williamson, A., Dahle, C., Gerstorf, D., & Acker, J. (2006). Regional brain changes in aging healthy adults: General trends, individual differences and modifiers. *Cerebral Cortex, 15,* 1679–1689.

Razoumnikova, O. M. (2000). Functional organization of different brain areas during convergent and divergent thinking: An EEG investigation. *Cognitive Brain Research, 10,* 11–18.

Rebs, S., & Park, S. (2001). Gender differences in high-achieving students in math and science. *Journal for the Education of the Gifted, 25,* 52–73.

Reicher, S., & Haslam, A. (2004). The banality of evil: Thoughts on the psychology of atrocity. *Anthropology News, 45,* 14–15.

Reichle, B., & Gefke, M. (1998). Justice of conjugal divisions of labor—you can't always get what you want. *Social Justice Research, 11,* 271–287.

Reis, H. T., Wilson, I. M., Monestere, C., Bernstein, S., Clark, K., Seidl, E., et al. (1990). What is smiling is beautiful and good. *European Journal of Social Psychology, 20,* 259–267.

Reiss, D., & Marino, L. (2001). Mirror self-recognition in the bottlenose dolphin: A case of cognitive convergence. *Proceedings of the National Academy of Science, 98,* 5937–5942.

Reite, M., Buysse, D., Reynolds, C., & Mendelson, W. (1995). The use of polysomnography in the evaluation of insomnia. *Sleep, 18,* 58–70.

Reitman, D., Murphy, M., Hupp, S., & O'Callaghan, P. (2004). Behavior change and perceptions of change: Evaluating the effectiveness of a token economy. *Child & Family Behavior Therapy, 26,* 17–36.

Reneman, L., Booij, J., Schmand, B., van den Brink, W., & Gunning, B. (2000). Memory disturbances in "Ecstasy" users are correlated with an altered brain serotonin neurotransmission. *Psychopharmacology, 148*, 322–324.

Rentfrow, P., & Gosling, S. (2003). The do re mi's of everyday life: The structure and personality correlates of music preferences. *Journal of Personality & Social Psychology, 84*, 1236–1256.

Rescorla, R. A. (1967). Pavlovian conditioning and its proper control procedures. *Psychological Review, 74*, 71–80.

Rescorla, R. A. (1968). Probability of shock in the presence and absence of CS in fear conditioning. *Journal of Comparative and Physiological Psychology, 66*, 1–5.

Rescorla, R. A. (1988). Pavlovian conditioning: It's not what you think it is. *American Psychologist, 43*, 151–160.

Rescorla, R. A., & Wagner, A. R. (1972). A theory of Pavlovian conditioning: Variations in the effectiveness of reinforcement and nonreinforcement. In A. Black & W. F. Prokasy (Eds.), *Classical conditioning: II. Current research and theory* (pp. 64–99). New York: Appleton.

Restak, R. (1988). *The mind.* Toronto: Bantam.

Restak, R. (1993, September/October). Brain by design. *The Sciences*, pp. 27–33.

Reuters News Service. (2006, June 30). *Japan elderly population ratio now world's highest.* Retrieved July 3, 2006, from http://today.reuters.co.uk/news/newsArticle.aspx?type=worldNews&storyID=2006-06-30T084625Z_01_T83766_RTRUKOC_0_UKJAPANPOPULATION.xml&archived=False

Revensuo, A. (2000). The reinterpretation of dreams: An evolutionary hypothesis of the function of dreaming. *Behavioral & Brain Science, 23*.

Reyna, V. (2004). How people make decisions that involve risk: A dual-processes approach. *Current Directions in Psychological Science, 13*, 60–66.

Reyna, V., & Adam, M. (2003). Fuzzy-trace theory, risk communication, and product labeling in sexually transmitted diseases. *Risk Analysis, 23*, 325–342.

Reyner, A., & Horne, J. A. (1995). Gender- and age-related differences in sleep determined by home-recorded sleep logs and actimetry from 400 adults. *Sleep, 18*, 127–134.

Rhéaume, J., & Ladouceur, R. (2000). Cognitive and behavioural treatments of checking behaviours: An examination of individual cognitive change. *Clinical Psychology & Psychotherapy, 7*, 118–127.

Rhodes, N., & Wood, W. (1992). Self-esteem and intelligence affect influenceability: The medicating role of message reception. *Psychological Bulletin, 111*, 156–171.

Rich, L. (2004). Along with increased surgery, a growing need for support. *APA Monitor on Psychology, 35*, 54.

Richter, W., Somorjai, R., Summers, R., Jarmasz, M., Ravi, S., Menon, J. S., et al. (2000). Motor area activity during mental rotation studied by time-resolved single-trial fMRI. *Journal of Cognitive Neuroscience, 12*, 310–320.

Rickels, K., Schweizer, E., Weiss, S., & Zavodnick, S. (1993). Maintenance drug treatment for panic disorder II. Short- and long-term outcome after drug taper. *Archives of General Psychiatry, 50*, 61–68.

Riedel, G. (1996). Function of metabotropic glutamate receptors in learning and memory. *Trends in Neurosciences, 19*, 219–224.

Riegle, R. (2005). Viewpoint: Online courses as video games. *Campus Technology*, June 15, 2005. Retrieved May 5, 2006, from http://www.campus-technology.com

Rieker, P., & Bird, C. (2005). Rethinking gender differences in health: Why we need to integrate social and biological perspectives. *The Journals of Gerontology Series B: Psychological Sciences and Social Sciences, 60*, S40–S47.

Rini, C., Manne, S., DuHamel, K., Austin, J., Ostroff, J., Boulad, F., et al. (2004). Mothers' perceptions of benefit following pediatric stem cell transplantation: A longitudinal investigation of the roles of optimism, medical risk, and sociodemographic resources. *Annals of Behavioral Medicine, 28*, 132–141.

Ritz, S. (2006). The bariatric psychological evaluation: A heuristic for determining the suitability of the morbidly obese patient for weight loss surgery. *Bariatric Nursing and Surgical Patient Care, 1*, 97–105.

Roan, S. (2000, March 6). *Cyberanalysis.* Retrieved June 10, 2007 from http://www.doctorchase.com/html/cyberanalysis.html.

Roberts, B., Chernyshenko, O., Stark, S., & Goldberg, L. (2005). The structure of conscientiousness: An empirical investigation based on seven major personality questionnaires. *Personnel Psychology, 58*, 103–139.

Roberts, B. W., & DelVecchio, W. F. (2000). The rank-order consistency of personality traits from childhood to old age: A quantitative review of longitudinal studies. *Psychological Bulletin, 126*, 3–25.

Roberts, J., & Bell, M. (2000). Sex differences on a mental rotation task: Variations in electroencephalogram hemispheric activation between children and college students. *Developmental Neuropsychology, 17*, 199–223.

Roberts, P., & Moseley, B. (1996, May/June). Fathers' time. *Psychology Today, 29*, 48–55, 81.

Robins, C. J., & Hayes, A. M. (1993). An appraisal of cognitive therapy. *Journal of Consulting and Clinical Psychology, 61*, 205–214.

Robins, R. W., Gosling, S. D., & Craik, K. H. (1999). An empirical analysis of trends in psychology. *American Psychologist, 54*, 117–128.

Robinson, D., Phillips, P. Budygin, E., Trafton, B., Garris, P., & Wightman, R. (2001). Sub-second changes in accumbal dopamine during sexual behavior in male rats. *Neuroreport: For Rapid Communication of Neuroscience Research, 12*, 2549–2552.

Robinson, F. (1970). *Effective study* (4th ed.). New York: Harper & Row.

Robinson, M., & Tamir, M. (2005). Neuroticism as mental noise: A relation between neuroticism and reaction time standard deviations. *Journal of Personality and Social Psychology, 89*, 107–114.

Robles, T., Glaser, R., & Kiecolt-Glaser, J. (2005). Out of balance: A new look at chronic stress, depression, and immunity. *Current Directions in Psychological Science, 14,* 111–115.

Rock, I., & Palmer, S. (1990). The legacy of Gestalt psychology. *Scientific American, 263,* 84–90.

Rodin, J., & Salovey, P. (1989). Health psychology. *Annual Review of Psychology, 40,* 533–579.

Rodin, J., Wack, J., Ferrannini, E., & DeFronzo, R. A. (1985). Effect of insulin and glucose on feeding behavior. *Metabolism, 34,* 826–831.

Rodríguez, C., & Church, A. (2003). The structure and personality correlates of affect in Mexico: Evidence of cross-cultural comparability using the Spanish language. *Journal of Cross-Cultural Psychology, 34,* 211–223.

Roediger, H. L., III. (1980). The effectiveness of four mnemonics in ordering recall. *Journal of Experimental Psychology: Human Learning and Memory, 6,* 558–567.

Roehrich, L., & Kinder, B. N. (1991). Alcohol expectancies and male sexuality: Review and implications for sex therapy. *Journal of Sex and Marital Therapy, 17,* 45–54.

Roesch, S. C., & Amirkhan, J. H. (1997). Boundary condition for self-serving attributions: Another look at the sports pages. *Journal of Applied Social Psychology, 27,* 245–261.

Rogers, C. R. (1951). *Client-centered therapy: Its current practice, implications, and theory.* Boston: Houghton Mifflin.

Rogge, R., Bradbury, T., Hahlweg, K., Engl, J., & Thurmaier, F. (2006). Predicting marital distress and dissolution: Refining the two-factor hypothesis. *Journal of Family Psychology, 20,* 156–159.

Rogoff, B. (1990). *Apprenticeship in thinking: Cognitive development in social context.* New York: Oxford University Press.

Roisman, G., Masten, A., Coatsworth, J., & Tellegen, A. (2004). Salient and emerging developmental tasks in the transition to adulthood. *Child Development, 75,* 123–133.

Romach, M., Busto, U., Somer, G., Kaplan, A., et al. (1995). Clinical aspects of chronic use of alprazolam and lorazepam. *American Journal of Psychiatry, 152,* 1161–1167.

Rönnqvist, L., & Domellöf, E. (2006). Quantitative assessment of right and left reaching movements in infants: A longitudinal study from 6 to 36 months. *Developmental Psychobiology, 48,* 444–459.

Roorda, A., & Williams, D. R. (1999). The arrangement of the three cone classes in the living human eye. *Nature, 397,* 520–521.

Rosch, E. & Lloyd, B. (1978). *Cognition and categorization.* Hillsdale, NJ: Erlbaum.

Rosch, E. H. (1973). Natural categories. *Cognitive Psychology, 4,* 328–350.

Rosch, E. H. (1987). Linguistic relativity. *Et Cetera, 44,* 254–279.

Rose, J., (2006). Nicotine and nonnicotine factors in cigarette addiction. *Psychopharmacology, 184,* 274–285.

Rose, R. J., Koskenvuo, M., Kaprio, J., Sarna, S., & Langinvainio, H. (1988). Shared genes, shared experiences, and similarity of personality: Data from 14,288 adult Finnish co-twins. *Journal of Personality and Social Psychology, 54,* 161–171.

Rosekind, M. R. (1992). The epidemiology and occurrence of insomnia. *Journal of Clinical Psychiatry, 53*(6, Suppl.), 4–6.

Roselli, C., Larkin, K., Schrunk, J., & Stormshak, F. (2004). Sexual partner preference, hypothalamic morphology and aromatase in rams. *Physiology & Behavior, 83,* 233–245.

Rosenbloom, T. (2006). Sensation seeking and pedestrian crossing compliance. *Social Behavior and Personality, 34,* 113–122.

Rosenbluth, R., Grossman, E. S., & Kaitz, M. (2000). Performance of early-blind and sighted children on olfactory tasks. *Perception, 29,* 101–110.

Rosengren, A., Tibblin, G., & Wilhelmsen, L. (1991). Self-perceived psychological stress and incidence of coronary artery disease in middle-aged men. *American Journal of Cardiology, 68,* 1171–1175.

Rosenhan, D. L. (1973). On being sane in insane places. *Science, 179,* 250–258.

Rosenvinge, J. H., Matinussen, M., & Ostensen, E. (2000). The comorbidity of eating disorders and personality disorders: A meta-analytic review of studies published between 1983 and 1998. *Eating and Weight Disorders: Studies on Anorexia, Bulimia, and Obesity, 5,* 52–61.

Rosenzweig, M. R. (1961). Auditory localization. *Scientific American, 205,* 132–142.

Ross, C. A., Norton, G. R., & Wozney, K. (1989). Multiple personality disorder: An analysis of 236 cases. *Canadian Journal of Psychiatry, 34,* 413–418.

Ross, J., Baldessarini, R. J., & Tondo, L. (2000). Does lithium treatment still work? Evidence of stable responses over three decades. *Archives of General Psychiatry, 57,* 187–190.

Rossow, I., & Amundsen, A. (1997). Alcohol abuse and mortality: A 40-year prospective study of Norwegian conscripts. *Social Science & Medicine, 44,* 261–267.

Roth, T. (1996). Social and economic consequences of sleep disorders. *Sleep, 19,* S46–S47.

Rotter, J. B. (1966). Generalized expectancies for internal versus external control of reinforcement. *Psychological Monographs, 80*(1, Whole No. 609).

Rotter, J. B. (1971, June). External control and internal control. *Psychology Today,* 37–42, 58–59.

Rotter, J. B. (1990). Internal versus external control of reinforcement: A case history of a variable. *American Psychologist, 45,* 489–493.

Rotton, J., & Cohn, E. G. (2000). Violence is a curvilinear function of temperature in Dallas: A replication. *Journal of Personality & Social Psychology, 78,* 1074–1082.

Rotton, J., Frey, J., Barry, T., Milligan, M., & Fitzpatrick, M. (1979). The air pollution experience and physical aggression. *Journal of Applied Social Psychology, 9,* 397–412.

Rowe, D. (2003). Assessing genotype-environment interactions and correlations in the postgenomic era. In R. Plomin, J. DeFries, I. Craig, & P. McGuffin (Eds.), *Behavioral genetics in the postgenomic era* (pp. 71–86). Washington, DC: American Psychological Association.

Rowe, D. C. (1987). Resolving the person-situation debate: Invitation to an interdisciplinary dialogue. *American Psychologist, 42,* 218–227.

Rowe, J., & Kahn, R. (1998). *Successful aging.* New York: Pantheon.

Rozell, E., Pettijohn, C., & Parker, R. (2002). An empirical evaluation of emotional intelligence: The impact on management development. *Journal of Management Development, 21,* 272–289.

Rubinstein, G. (2001). Sex-role reversal and clinical judgment of mental health. *Journal of Sex & Marital Therapy, 27,* 9–19.

Ruby, N., Dark, J., Burns, D., Heller, H., & Zucker, I. (2002). The suprachiasmatic nucleus is essential for circadian body temperature rhythms in hibernating ground squirrels. *Journal of Neuroscience, 22,* 357–364.

Rudman, L., Ashmore, R., & Gary, M. (2001). "Unlearning" automatic biases: The malleability of implicit prejudice and stereotypes. *Journal of Personality & Social Psychology, 81,* 856–868.

Ruggero, M. A. (1992). Responses to sound of the basilar membrane of the mammalian cochlea. *Current Opinion in Neurobiology, 2,* 449–456.

Rumbaugh, D. (1977). *Language learning by a chimpanzee: the Lana project.* New York: Academic Press.

Ruscio, J. (2001). Administering quizzes at random to increase students' reading. *Teaching of Psycholog, 28,* 204–206.

Rushton, J., & Jensen, A. (2003). African–White IQ differences from Zimbabwe on the Wechsler Intelligence Scale for Children-Revised are mainly on the g factor. *Personality & Individual Differences, 34,* 177–183.

Rushton, J. P., Fulker, D. W., Neale, M. C., Nias, D. K. B., & Eysenck, H. J. (1986). Altruism and aggression: The heritability of individual differences. *Journal of Personality and Social Psychology, 50,* 1192–1198.

Russell, T., Rowe, W., & Smouse, A. (1991). Subliminal self-help tapes and academic achievement: An evaluation. *Journal of Counseling and Development, 69,* 359–362.

Ryan, R., Kim, Y., & Kaplan, U. (2003). Differentiating autonomy from individualism and independence: A self-determination theory perspective on internalization of cultural orientations and well-being. *Journal of Personality and Social Psychology, 84,* 97–110.

Sachs, G., Grossman, F., Ghaemi, S., Okamoto, A., & Bosden, C. (2002). Combination of a mood stabilizer with risperidone or haloperidol for treatment of acute mania: A double-blind, placebo-controlled comparison of efficacy and safety. *American Journal of Psychiatry, 159,* 1146–1154.

Sackeim, H. A., Luber, B., Katzman, G. P., Moeller, J. R., Prudic, J., Devanand, D. P., et al. (1996). The effects of electroconvulsive therapy on quantitative electroencephalograms. *Archives of General Psychiatry, 53,* 814–824.

Sackeim, H. A., Prudic, J., Devanand, D. P., Nobler, M. S., Lisanby, S. H., Peyser, S., et al. (2000). A prospective, randomized, double-blind comparison of bilateral and right unilateral electroconvulsive therapy at different stimulus intensities. *Archives of General Psychiatry, 57,* 425–434.

Sackett, P., Hardison, C., & Cullen, M. (2004). On interpreting stereotype threat as accounting for African American-White differences on cognitive tests. *American Psychologist, 59,* 7–13.

Sacks, O. (1984). *A leg to stand on.* New York: Harper & Row.

Sacks, O. (1995). An anthropologist on Mars. New York: Macmillan.

Saczynski, J., Willis, S., & Schaie, K. W. (2002). Strategy use in reasoning training with older adults. *Aging, Neuropsychology, & Cognition, 9,* 48–60.

Sadeh, A., Gruber, R., & Raviv, A. (2003). The effect of sleep restriction and extension on school-age children: What a difference an hour makes. *Child Development, 74,* 444–455.

Sahoo, F., Sahoo, K., & Harichandan, S. (2005). Big Five factors of personality and human happiness. *Social Science International, 21,* 20–28.

Salat, D., van der Kouwe, A., Tuch, D., Quinn, B., Fischl, A., & Corkin, S. (2006). Neuroimaging H. M.: A 10-year follow-up examination. *Hippocampus, 16,* 936–945.

Salisch, M. (2001). Children's emotional development: Challenges in their relationships to parents, peers, and friends. *International Journal of Behavioural Development, 25,* 310–319.

Salmon, J., Owen, N., Crawford, D., Bauman, A., & Sallis, J. (2003). Physical activity and sedentary behavior: A population-based study of barriers, enjoyment, and preference. *Health Psychology, 22,* 178–188.

Salovey, P., & Pizarro, D. (2003). The value of emotional intelligence. In R. Sternberg, J. Lautrey, & T. Lubart (Eds.), *Models of intelligence: International perspective* (pp. 263–278). Washington, DC: American Psychological Association.

Salthouse, T. (2004). What and when of cognitive aging. *Current Directions in Psychological Science, 13,* 140–144.

Salthouse, T. A. (1996). The processing-speed theory of adult age differences in cognition. *Psychological Review, 103,* 403–428.

Sample, J. (2004). The Myers-Briggs type indicator and OD: Implications for practice from research. *Organization Development Journal, 22,* 67–75.

Sanbonmatsu, D. M., & Fazio, R. H. (1990). The role of attitudes in memory-based decision making. *Journal of Personality and Social Psychology, 59,* 614–622.

Sanes, J. N., & Donoghue, J. P. (2000). Plasticity and primary motor cortex. *Annual Review of Neuroscience, 23,* 393–415.

Sanes, J. N., Donoghue, J. P., Thangaraj, V., Edelman, R. R., & Warach, S. (1995). Shared neural substrates controlling hand movements in human motor cortex. *Science, 268,* 1775.

Santiago-Rivera, A., & Altarriba, J. (2002). The role of language in therapy with the Spanish-English bilingual client. *Professional Psychology: Research & Practice, 33,* 30–38.

Saper, C., Scammell, T., & Lu, J. (2005). Hypothalamic regulation of sleep and circadian rhythms. *Nature, 437,* 1257–1263.

Sarrio, M., Barbera, E., Ramos, A., & Candela, C. (2002). The glass ceiling in the professional promotion of women. *Revista de Psicologia Social, 17,* 167–182.

Sastry, R., Lee, D., & Har-El, G. (1997). Palate perforation from cocaine abuse. *Otolaryngol Head Neck Surgery, 116,* 565–566.

Sateia, M. J., Doghramji, K., Hauri, P. J., & Morin, C. M. (2000). Evaluation of chronic insomnia. An American Academy of Sleep Medicine review. *Sleep, 23,* 243–308.

Sattler, J., & Dumont, R. (2004). *Assessment of children: WISC-IV and WPPSI-III supplement.* San Diego, CA: Jerome M. Sattler, Publisher.

Saudino, K. (2005). Special article: Behavioral genetics and child temperament. *Journal of Developmental & Behavioral Pediatrics, 26,* 214–223.

Savage, M., & Holcomb, D. (1999). Adolescent female athletes' sexual risk-taking behaviors. *Journal of Youth and Adolescence, 28,* 583–594.

Savage-Rumbaugh, E. S. (1986). *Ape language.* New York: Columbia University Press.

Savage-Rumbaugh, E. S. (1990). Language acquisition in a nonhuman species: Implications for the innateness debate. *Developmental Psychology, 26,* 599–620.

Savage-Rumbaugh, E. S. (1993). Language learnability in man, ape, and dolphin. In H. L. Roitblat, L. M. Herman, & P. E. Nachtigall (Eds.), *Language and communication: Comparative perspectives. Comparative cognition and neuroscience* (pp. 457–484). Hillsdale, NJ: Erlbaum.

Savage-Rumbaugh, E. S., Sevcik, R. A., Brakke, K. E., & Rumbaugh, D. M. (1992). Symbols: Their communicative use, communication, and combination by bonobos (Pan paniscus). In L. P. Lipsitt & C. Rovee-Collier (Eds.). *Advances in infancy research* (Vol. 7, pp. 221–278). Norwood, NJ: Ablex.

Scarr, S., & Weinberg, R. (1976). The influence of "family background" on intellectual attainment. *American Sociological Review, 43,* 674–692.

Schachter, S., & Singer, J. E. (1962). Cognitive, social, and physiological determinants of emotional state. *Psychological Review, 69,* 379–399.

Schaie, K. (2005). *Developmental influences on adult intelligence: The Seattle longitudinal study.* New York: Oxford University Press.

Schauer, P., Ikramuddin, S., Gourash, W., Ramanathan, R., & Luketich, J. (2000). Outcomes after laparoscopic roux-en-Y gastric bypass for morbid obesity. *Annals of Surgery, 232,* 515–529.

Schellenberg, E. (2004). Music lessons enhance IQ. *Psychological Science, 15,* 511–514.

Schenck, C. H., & Mahowald, M. W. (2000). Parasomnias. Managing bizarre sleep-related behavior disorders. *Postgraduate Medicine, 107,* 145–156.

Scherer, K. R., & Wallbott, H. G. (1994). Evidence for universality and cultural variation of differential emotion response patterning. *Journal of Personality and Social Psychology, 66,* 310–328.

Schieber, M. H., & Hibbard, L. S. (1993). How somatotopic is the motor cortex hand area? *Science, 261,* 489–492.

Schiff, M., & Lewontin, R. (1986). *Education and class: The irrelevance of IQ genetic studies.* Oxford, England: Clarendon.

Schizophrenia.com. (2006). *Brain disorders, smoking and nicotine addiction: A special report.* Retrieved February 12, 2007, from http://www.schizophrenia.com/smok-erreport.htm

Schlosberg, S. (2004). *The curse of the singles table: A true tale of 1001 nights without sex.* New York: Warner Books.

Schmidt, P., Murphy, J., Haq, N., Rubinow, D., & Danaceau, M. (2004). Stressful life events, personal losses, and perimenopause-related depression. *Archives of Women's Mental Health, 7,* 19–26.

Schneider, E., Lang, A., Shin, M., & Bradley, S. (2004). Death with a story: How story impacts emotional, motivational, and physiological responses to first-person shooter video games. *Human Communication Research, 30,* 361–375.

Schofield, J. W., & Francis, W. D. (1982). An observational study of peer interaction in racially mixed "accelerated" classrooms. *Journal of Educational Psychology, 74,* 722–732.

Scholz, U., Dona, B., Sud, S., & Schwarzer, R. (2002). Is general self-efficacy a universal construct? Psychometric findings from 25 countries. *European Journal of Psychological Assessment, 18,* 242–251.

Schou, M. (1997). Forty years of lithium treatment. *Archives of General Psychiatry, 54,* 9–13.

Schuckit, M., Edenberg, H., Kalmijn, J., Flury, L., Smith, T., Reich, T., Beirut, L., Goate, A., & Foroud, T. (2001). A genome-wide search for gens that relate to a low level of response to alcohol. *Alcoholism: Clinical & Experimental Research, 25,* 323–329.

Schultz, W. (2006). Behavioral theories and the neurophysiology of reward. In S. Fiske, A. Kazdin, & D. Schacter (Eds.). *Annual Review of Psychology* (Vol. 57, pp. 87–116). Palo Alto, CA: Annual Reviews.

Schwartz, G. E. (1982). Testing the biopsychosocial model: The ultimate challenge facing behavioral medicine? *Journal of Consulting and Clinical Psychology, 50,* 1040–1052.

Schwartz, S., & Maquet, P. (2002). Sleep imaging and the neuro-psychological assessment of dreams. *Trends in Cognitive Sciences, 6,* 23–30.

Scott, S. K., Young, A. W., Calder, A. J., Hellawell, D. J., Aggleton, J. P., & Johnson, M. (1997). Impaired auditory recognition of fear and anger following bilateral amygdala lesions. *Nature, 385,* 254–257.

Scully, J., Tosi, H., & Banning, K. (2000). Life event checklists: Revisiting the Social Readjustment Rating Scale after 30 years. *Educational & Psychological Measurement, 60,* 864–876.

Sedikides, C., Gaertner, L., & Toguchi, Y. (2003). Pancultural self-enhancement. *Journal of Personality & Social Psychology, 84,* 60–79.

Seegert, C. (2004). Token economies and incentive programs: Behavioral improvement in mental health inmates housed in state prisons. *Behavior Therapist, 26,* 210–211.

Seeman, T., Dubin, L., & Seeman, M. (2003). Religiosity/spirituality and health. *American Psychologist, 58,* 53–63.

Seenoo, K., & Takagi, O. (2003). The effect of helping behaviors on helper: A case study of volunteer work for local resident welfare. *Japanese Journal of Social Psychology, 18,* 106–118.

Segal, Z., Williams, M., & Teasdale, J. (2001). *Mindfulness-based cognitive therapy for depression.* New York: Guilford Press.

Segall, M. H. (1994). A cross-cultural research contribution to unraveling the nativist/empiricist controversy. In J. Lonner & R. Malpass (Eds.), *Psychology and culture* (pp. 135–138). Boston: Allyn & Bacon.

Segall, M. H., Campbell, D. T., & Herskovitz, M. J. (1966). *The influence of culture on visual perception.* Indianapolis: Bobbs-Merrill.

Seger, C. A., Desmond, J. E., Glover, G. H., & Gabrieli, J. D. E. (2000). Functional magnetic resonance imaging evidence for right-hemisphere involvement in processing unusual semantic relationships. *Neuropsychology, 14,* 361–369.

Seidman, S. (2002). Exploring the relationship between depression and erectile dysfunction in aging men. *Journal of Clinical Psychiatry, 63,* 5–12.

Self, M., & Zeki, S. (2005). The integration of colour and motion by the human visual brain. *Cerebral Cortex, 15,* 1270–1279.

Seligman, M., & Csikszentmihalyi, M. (2000). Positive psychology: An introduction. *American Psychologist, 55,* 5–14.

Seligman, M., Steen, T., Park, N., & Peterson, C. (2005). Positive psychology progress: Empirical validation of interventions. *American Psychologist, 60,* 410–421.

Seligman, M. E. P. (1970). On the generality of the laws of learning. *Psychological Review, 77,* 406–418.

Seligman, M. E. P. (1972). Phobias and preparedness. In M. E. P. Seligman & J. L. Hager (Eds.), *Biological boundaries of learning* (pp. 307–320). Englewood Cliffs, NJ: Prentice Hall.

Seligman, M. E. P. (1975). *Helplessness: On depression, development and death.* San Francisco: Freeman.

Seligman, M. E. P. (1990). *Learned optimism: How to change your mind and your life.* New York: Simon & Schuster.

Seligman, M. E. P. (1991). *Learned optimism.* New York: Knopf.

Seligman, M. E. P. (1995). The effectiveness of psychotherapy: The *Consumer Reports* Study. *American Psychologist, 50,* 965–974.

Seligman, M. E. P. (1996). Science as an ally of practice. *American Psychologist, 51,* 1072–1079.

Selye, H. (1956). *The stress of life.* New York: McGraw-Hill.

Sensky, T., Turkington, D., Kingdon, D., Scott, J. L., Scott, J., Siddle, R., O'Carroll, M., & Barnes, T. R. E. (2000). A randomized controlled trial of cognitive-behavioral therapy for persistent symptoms in schizophrenia resistant to medication. *Archives of General Psychiatry, 57,* 165–172.

Sentenac, J. (2007). *Anger erupts over insurance company's IQ test for weight-loss surgery.* Retrieved January 25, 2007, from http://www.foxnews.com/story/0,2933,246519,00.html

Serido, J., Almeida, D., & Wethington, E. (2004). Chronic stressors and daily hassles: Unique and interactive relationships with psychological distress. *Journal of Health and Social Behavior, 45,* 17–33.

Serpell R., & Hatano, G. (1997). Education, schooling, and literacy. In J. Berry, P. Dasen, & T. Sarswthi (Eds.), *Handbook of cross-cultural psychology* (Vol. 2, pp. 339–376). Boston: Allyn & Bacon.

Shackelford, T., Schmitt, T., & Buss, D. (2005). Universal dimensions of human mate preferences. *Personality and Individual Differences, 39,* 447–458.

Shackelford, T., Voracek, M., Schmitt, D., Buss, D., Weekes-Shackelford, V., & Michalski, R. (2004). Romantic jealousy in early adulthood and in later life. *Human Nature, 15,* 283–300.

Shaffer, D., Gould, M. S., Fisher, P., Trautman, P., Moreau, D., Kleinman, M., et al. (1996). Psychiatric diagnosis in child and adolescent suicide. *Archives of General Psychiatry, 53,* 339–348.

Sharma, S. (2006). Parasomnias. Retrieved December 16, 2006, from http://www.emedicine.com/med/topic3131.html

Sharp, D., Cole, M., & Lave, C. (1979). Education and cognitive development: The evidence from experimental research. *Monographs of the Society for Research in Child Development, 44*(1–2, Serial No. 178).

Shaunessy, E., Karnes, F., & Cobb, Y. (2004). Assessing potentially gifted students from lower socioeconomic status with nonverbal measures of intelligence. *Perceptual & Motor Skills, 98,* 1129–1138.

Shaw, J. I., & Steers, W. N. (2001). Gathering information to form an impression: Attribute categories and information valence. *Current Research in Social Psychology, 6,* 1–21.

Shaw, J. S., III. (1996). Increases in eyewitness confidence resulting from postevent questioning. *Journal of Experimental Psychology: Applied, 2,* 126–146.

Shaw, V. N., Hser, Y.-I., Anglin, M. D., & Boyle, K. (1999). Sequences of powder cocaine and crack use among arrestees in Los Angeles County. *American Journal of Drug and Alcohol Abuse, 25,* 47–66.

Shears, J., Robinson, J., & Emde, R. (2002). Fathering relationships and their associations with juvenile delinquency. *Infant Mental Health Journal, 23,* 79–87.

Sheehan, D. V., & Raj, A. B. (1988). Monoamine oxidase inhibitors. In C. G. Last & M. Hersen (Eds.), *Handbook of anxiety disorders* (pp. 478–506). New York: Pergamon.

Shelton, J., & Richeson, J. (2005). Intergroup contact and pluralistic ignorance. *Journal of Personalty & Social Psychology, 88,* 91–107.

Shepperd, J. (2001). The desire to help and behavior in social dilemmas: Exploring responses to catastrophes. *Group Dynamics, 5,* 304–314.

Sher, A. E., Schechtman, K. B., & Piccirillo, J. F. (1996). The efficacy of surgical modifications of the upper airway in adults with obstructive sleep apnea syndrome. *Sleep, 19,* 156–177.

Sher, L. (2004a). Hypothalamic-pituitary-adrenal function and preventing major depressive episodes. *Canadian Journal of Psychiatry, 49,* 574–575.

Sher, L. (2004b). Type D personality, cortisol and cardiac disease. *Australian and New Zealand Journal of Psychiatry, 38,* 652–653.

Sherif, M. (1956). Experiments in group conflict. *Scientific American, 195,* 53–58.

Sherif, M. (1958). Superordinate goals in the reduction of intergroup conflict. *American Journal of Sociology, 63,* 349–358.

Sherif, M., & Sherif, C. W. (1967). The Robbers' Cave study. In J. F. Perez, R. C. Sprinthall, G. S. Grosser, & P. J. Anastasiou, *General psychology: Selected readings* (pp. 411–421). Princeton, NJ: D. Van Nostrand.

Shimamura, A. P., Berry, J. M., Mangela, J. A., Rusting, C. L., & Jurica, P. J. (1995). Memory and cognitive abilities in university professors: Evidence for successful aging. *Psychological Science, 6,* 271–277.

Shinar, D., Tractinsky, N., & Compton, R. (2005). Effects of practice, age, and task demands, on interference from a phone task while driving. *Accident Analysis & Prevention, 37,* 315–326.

Shiner, R. (2000). Linking childhood personality with adaptation: Evidence for continuity and change across time into late adolescence. *Journal of Personality and Social Psychology, 78,* 310–325.

Shneidman, E. (1989). The Indian summer of life: A preliminary study of septuagenarians. *American Psychologist, 44,* 684–694.

Shneidman, E. S. (1994). Clues to suicide, reconsidered. *Suicide and Life-Threatening Behavior, 24,* 395–397.

Shumaker, S., Legault, C., Rapp, S., Thal, L., Wallace, R., Ockene, J., et al. (2003). Estrogen plus progestin and the incidence of dementia and mild cognitive impairment in postmenopausal women: The Women's Health Initiative Memory Study: A randomized controlled trial. *Journal of the American Medical Association (JAMA), 289,* 2651–2662.

Siegel, R. (2005). *Intoxication: The universal drive for mind-altering substances.* Rochester, VT: Park Street Press.

Siegler, R. S. (1991). *Children's thinking* (2nd ed.). Englewood Cliffs, NJ: Prentice-Hall.

Siegrist, J., Peter, R., Junge, A., Cremer, P., & Seidel, D. (1990). Low status control, high effort at work and is-chemic heart disease: Prospective evidence from blue-collar men. *Social Science and Medicine, 31,* 1127–1134.

Silva, C. E., & Kirsch, I. (1992). Interpretive sets, expectancy, fantasy proneness, and dissociation as predictors of hypnotic response. *Journal of Personality and Social Psychology, 63,* 847–856.

Simon, G., Cherkin, D., Sherman, K., Eisenberg, D., Deyo, R., & Davis, R. (2004). Mental health visits to complementary and alternative medicine providers. *General Hospital Psychiatry, 26,* 171–177.

Simon, H. (1956). Rational choice and the structure of the environment. *Psychological Review, 63,* 129–138.

Simon, H. B. (1988, June). Running and rheumatism. *Harvard Medical School Health Letter, 13,* 2–4.

Simons, D. & Chabris, C. (1999). Gorillas in our midst: Sustained inattentional blindness for dynamic events. *Perception, 28,* 1059–1074.

Simons, D., & Rensink, R. (2005). Change blindness: Past, present, and future. *Trends in Cognitive Sciences, 9,* 16–20.

Simons, J., & Carey, K. (2002). Risk and vulnerability for marijuana use problems. *Psychology of Addictive Behaviors, 16,* 72–75.

Simpson, P., & Stroh, L. (2004). Gender differences: Emotional expression and feelings of personal inauthenticity. *Journal of Applied Psychology, 89,* 715–721.

Singer, M. I., Miller, D. B., Guo, S., Flannery, D. J., Frierson, T., & Slovak, K. (1999). Contributors to violent behavior among elementary and middle school children. *Pediatrics, 104*(Pt. 1), 878–884.

Singh, B. (1991). Teaching methods for reducing prejudice and enhancing academic achievement for all children. *Educational Studies, 17,* 157–171.

Singh, I. (2004). Doing their jobs: Mothering with Ritalin in a culture of mother-blame. *Social Science & Medicine, 59,* 1193–1205.

Singh, S., & Darroch, J. (2000). Adolescent pregnancy and childbearing: Levels and trends in industrialized countries. *Family Planning Perspectives, 32,* 14–23.

Sivacek, J., & Crano, W. D. (1982). Vested interest as a moderator of attitude-behavior consistency. *Journal of Personality and Social Psychology, 43,* 210–221.

Skinner, B. F. (1953). *Science and human behavior.* New York: Macmillan.

Skinner, B. F. (1957). *Verbal behavior.* New York: Appleton Century.

Skrabalo, A. (2000). Negative symptoms in schizophrenia(s): The conceptual basis. *Harvard Brain, 7,* 7–10.

Slawinski, E. B., Hartel, D. M., & Kline, D. W. (1993). Self-reported hearing problems in daily life throughout adulthood. *Psychology and Aging, 8,* 552–561.

Slobin, D. (1972, July). Children and language: They learn the same all around the world. *Psychology Today,* 71–74, 82.

Sluzki, C. (2004). House taken over by ghosts: Culture, migration, and the developmental cycle of a Moroccan family invaded by hallucination. *Families, Systems, & Health, 22,* 321–337.

Small, G. (2005). *Effects of a 14-day healthy aging lifestyle program on brain function.* Paper presented at the 44th

Annual Meeting of the American College of Neuropsychopharmacology. December 11–15, 2005. Waikoloa, Hawaii.

Smith, M. L., Glass, G. V., & Miller, T. I. (1980). *The benefits of psychotherapy.* Baltimore, MD: Johns Hopkins University Press.

Smith, N., Young, A., & Lee, C. (2004). Optimism, health-related hardiness and well-being among older Australian women. *Journal of Health Psychology, 9,* 741–752.

Smith, S. M., Glenberg, A., & Bjork, R. A. (1978). Environmental context and human memory. *Memory & Cognition, 6,* 342–353.

Smith, T., & Ruiz, J. (2002). Psychosocial influences on the development and course of coronary heart disease: Current status and implications for research and practice. *Journal of Consulting and Clinical Psychology, 70,* 548–568.

Smolar, A. (1999). Bridging the gap: Technical aspects of the analysis of an Asian immigrant. *Journal of Clinical Psychoanalysis, 8,* 567–594.

Snarey, J. R. (1985). Cross-cultural universality of social-moral development: A critical review of Kohlbergian research. *Psychological Bulletin, 97,* 202–232.

Snarey, J. R. (1995). In communitarian voice: The sociological expansion of Kohlbergian theory, research, and practice. In W. M. Kurtines & J. L. Gewirtz (Eds.), *Moral development: An introduction* (pp. 109–134). Boston: Allyn & Bacon.

Snow, C. E. (1993). Bilingualism and second language acquisition. In J. B. Gleason & N. B. Ratner (Eds.), *Psycholinguistics* (pp. 391–416). Fort Worth, TX: Harcourt.

Snyder, D., Castellani, A., & Whisman, M. (2006). Current status and future directions in couple therapy. *Annual Review of Psychology, 57,* 317–344.

Sobin, C., & Sackeim, H. A. (1997). Psychomotor symptoms of depression. *American Journal of Psychiatry, 154,* 4–17.

Sokolov, E. N. (2000). Perception and the conditioning reflex: Vector encoding. *International Journal of Psychophysiology, 35,* 197–217.

Solano, L., Donati, V., Pecci, F., Perischetti, S., & Colaci, A. (2003). Postoperative course after papilloma resection: Effects of written disclosure of the experience in subjects with different alexithymia levels. *Psychosomatic Medicine, 65,* 477–484.

Solomon, S., Rothblum, E, & Balsam, K. (2004). Pioneers in partnership: Lesbian and gay male couples in civil unions compared with those not in civil unions and married heterosexual siblings. *Journal of Family Psychology, 18,* 275–286.

Sonnentag, S. (2003). Recovery, work engagement, and proactive behaviour: A new look at the interface between work and non-work. *Journal of Applied Psychology, 88,* 518–528.

Sotres-Bayon, F., Bush, D., & LeDoux, J. (2004). Emotional perseveration: An update on prefrontal–amygdala interactions in fear extinction. *Learning & Memory, 11,* 525–535.

Soussignan, R. (2002). Duchenne smile, emotional experience, and autonomic reactivity: A test of the facial feedback hypothesis. *Emotion, 2,* 52–74.

Spangler, D. L., Simons, A. D., Monroe, S. M., & Thase, M. E. (1996). Gender differences in cognitive diathesis-stress domain match: Implications for differential pathways to depression. *Journal of Abnormal Psychology, 105,* 653–657.

Spanos, N. P. (1986). Hypnotic behavior: A social-psychological interpretation of amnesia, analgesia, and "trance logic." *Behavioral and Brain Sciences, 9,* 499–502.

Spanos, N. P. (1991). A sociocognitive approach to hypnosis. In S. J. Lynn & J. W. Rhue (Eds.), *Theories of hypnosis: Current models and perspectives* (pp. 324–361). New York: Guilford.

Spanos, N. P. (1994). Multiple identity enactments and multiple personality disorder: A sociocognitive perspective. *Psychological Bulletin, 116,* 143–165.

Spataro, L., Sloane, E., Milligan, E., Wieseler-Frank, J., Schoeniger, D., Jakich, B., et al. (2004). Spinal gap junctions: Potential involvement in pain facilitation. *Journal of Pain, 5,* 392–405.

Spearman, C. (1927). *The abilities of man.* New York: Macmillan.

Spencer, R., Zelaznik, H., Diedrichsen, J., & Ivry, R. (2003). Disrupted timing of discontinuous but not continuous movements by cerebellar lesions. *Science, 300,* 1437–1439.

Sperling, G. (1960). The information available in brief visual presentations. *Psychological Monographs: General and Applied 74* (Whole No. 498), 1–29.

Sperry, R. W. (1964). The great cerebral commissure. *Scientific American, 210,* 42–52.

Sperry, R. W. (1968). Hemisphere deconnection and unity in conscious experience. *American Psychologist, 23,* 723–733.

Spiers, H., Maguire, E., & Burgess, N. (2001). Hippocampal amnesia. *Neurocase, 7,* 357–382.

Spitzer, M. W., & Semple, M. N. (1991). Interaural phase coding in auditory midbrain: Influence of dynamic stimulus features. *Science, 254,* 721–724.

Sporer, S. L., Penrod, S., Read, D., & Cutler, B. (1995). Choosing, confidence, and accuracy: A meta-analysis of the confidence-accuracy relation in eyewitness identification studies. *Psychological Bulletin, 118,* 315–327.

Spreen, O., Risser, A., & Edgell, D. (1995). *Developmental neuropsychology.* New York: Oxford University Press.

Squire, L. R., Knowlton, B., & Musen, G. (1993). The structure and organization of memory. *Annual Review of Psychology, 44,* 453–495.

Srivastava, S., John, O., Gosling, S., & Potter, J. (2003). Development of personality in early and middle adulthood: Set like plaster or persistent change? *Journal of Personality & Social Psychology, 84,* 1041–1053.

Stea, R. A., & Apkarian, A. V. (1992). Pain and somatosensory activation. *Trends in Neurosciences, 15,* 250–251.

Steblay, N. M. (1992). A meta-analytic review of the weapon focus effect. *Law and Human Behavior, 16,* 413–424.

Steele, C., & Aronson, J. (1995). Stereotype threat and the intellectual test performance of African Americans. *Journal of Personality & Social Psychology, 69,* 797–811.

Steele, J., & Mayes, S. (1995). Handedness and directional asymmetry in the long bones of the human upper limb. *International Journal of Osteoarchaeology, 5,* 39–49.

Steeves, R. (2002). The rhythms of bereavement. *Family & Community Health, 25,* 1–10.

Steffens, A. B., Scheurink, A. J., & Luiten, P. G. (1988). Hypothalamic food intake regulating areas are involved in the homeostasis of blood glucose and plasma FFA levels. *Physiology and Behavior, 44,* 581–589.

Steffensen, M., & Calker, L. (1982). Intercultural misunderstandings about health care: Recall of descriptions of illness and treatments. *Social Science and Medicine, 16,* 1949–1954.

Stein, M. B., & Kean, Y. M. (2000). Disability and quality of life in social phobia: Epidemiologic findings. *American Journal of Psychiatry, 157,* 1606–1613.

Stein-Behrens, B., Mattson, M. P., Chang, I., Yeh, M., & Sapolsky, R. (1994). Stress exacerbates neuron loss and cytoskeletal pathology in the hippocampus. *Journal of Neuroscience, 14,* 5373–5380.

Steinberg, L. (1990). Autonomy, conflict, and harmony in the family relationship. In S. S. Feldman & R. E. Glen (Eds.). *At the threshold: The developing adolescent* (pp. 255–276). Cambridge, MA: Harvard University Press.

Steinberg, L., Blatt-Eisengart, I., & Cauffman, E. (2006). Patterns of competence and adjustment among adolescents from authoritative, authoritarian, indulgent, and neglectful homes: A replication in a sample of serious juvenile offenders. *Journal of Research on Adolescence, 16,* 47–58.

Steinberg, L., & Dornbusch, S. (1991). Negative correlates of part-time employment during adolescence: Replication and elaboration. *Developmental Psychology, 27,* 304–313.

Steinberg, L., Elman, J. D., & Mounts, N. S. (1989). Authoritative parenting, psychosocial maturity, and academic success among adolescents. *Child Development, 60,* 1424–1436.

Steinberg, L., Lamborn, S. D., Darling, N., Mounts, N. S., & Dornbusch, S. M. (1994). Over-time changes in adjustment and competence among adolescents from authoritative, authoritarian, indulgent, and neglectful families. *Child Development, 65,* 754–770.

Steinman, L. (1993). Autoimmune disease. *Scientific American, 269,* 106–114.

Stelmachowicz, P., Beauchaine, K., Kalberer, A., & Jesteadt, W. (1989). Normative thresholds in the 8- to 20-kHz range as a function of age. *Journal of the Acoustical Society of America, 86,* 1384–1391.

Stephan, K. M., Fink, G. R., Passingham, R. E., Silbersweig, D., Ceballos-Baumann, A. O., Frith, C. D., et al. (1995). Functional anatomy of the mental representation of upper extremity movements in healthy subjects. *Journal of Neurophysiology, 73,* 373–386.

Stephenson, M. T., & Witte, K. (1998). Fear, threat, and perceptions of efficiency from frightening skin cancer messages. *Public Health Review, 26,* 147–174.

Steptoe, A. (2000). Stress, social support and cardiovascular activity over the working day. *International Journal of Psychophysiology, 37,* 299–308.

Steriade, M. (1996). Arousal: Revisiting the reticular activating system. *Science, 272,* 225–226.

Sternberg, R. (2003a). Issues in the theory and measurement of successful intelligence: A reply to Brody. *Intelligence, 31,* 331–337.

Sternberg, R. (2003b). Our research program validating the triarchic theory of successful intelligence: Reply to Gottfredson. *Intelligence, 31,* 399–413.

Sternberg, R., Castejon, J., Prieto, M., Hautamacki, J., & Grigorenko, E. (2001). Confirmatory factor analysis of the Sternberg Triarchic Abilities Test in three international samples: An empirical test of the triarchic theory of intelligence. *European Journal of Psychological Assessment, 17,* 1–16.

Sternberg, R. J. (1985). *Beyond IQ: A triarchic theory of human intelligence.* New York: Cambridge University Press.

Sternberg, R. J. (1986a). *Intelligence applied: Understanding and increasing your intellectual skills.* San Diego: Harcourt Brace Jovanovich.

Sternberg, R. J. (1986b). A triangular theory of love. *Psychological Review, 93,* 119–135.

Sternberg, R. J. (1987). Liking versus loving: A comparative evaluation of theories. *Psychological Bulletin, 102,* 331–345.

Sternberg, R. J. (2000). The holey grail of general intelligence. *Science, 289,* 399–401.

Sternberg, R. J., Wagner, R. K., Williams, W. M., & Horvath, J. A. (1995). Testing common sense. *American Psychologist, 50,* 912–927.

Stevenson, H. W. (1992). Learning from Asian schools. *Scientific American, 267,* 70–76.

Stewart, G., Fulmer, I., & Barrick, M. (2005). An exploration of member roles as a multilevel linking mechanism for individual traits and team outcomes. *Personnel Psychology, 58,* 343–365.

Stigler, J., & Stevenson, H. (1991). How Asian teachers polish each lesson to perfection. *American Educator, 12–20,* 43–47.

Still, C. (2001). *Health benefits of modest weight loss.* Retrieved January 29, 2003, from http://abcnews.go.com/sections/living/Healthology/weightloss_benefits011221. html

Stilwell, N., Wallick, M., Thal, S., & Burleson, J. (2000). Myers-Briggs type and medical specialty choice: A new look at an old question. *Teaching & Learning in Medicine, 12,* 14–20.

Stockhorst, U., Gritzmann, E., Klopp, K., Schottenfeld-Naor, Y., Hübinger, A., Berresheim, H., Stingrüber, H., & Gries, F. (1999). Classical conditioning of insulin effects in healthy humans. *Psychosomatic Medicine, 61,* 424–435.

Stone, J. (2003). Self-consistency for low self-esteem in dissonance processes: The role of self-standards. *Personality & Social Psychology Bulletin, 29,* 846–858.

Stone, K., Karem, K., Sternberg, M., McQuillan, G., Poon, A., Unger, E., & Reeves, W. (2002). Seroprevalence of human papillomavirus type 16 infection in the United States. *Journal of Infectious Diseases, 186,* 1396–1402.

Strack, F., Martin, L. L., & Stepper, S. (1988). Inhibiting and facilitating conditions of facial expressions: A nonobtrusive test of the facial feedback hypothesis. *Journal of Personality and Social Psychology, 54,* 768–777.

Strange, B., Hurlemann, R., & Dolan, R. (2003). An emotion-induced retrograde amnesia in humans is amygdala- and β-adrenergic-dependent. *Proceedings of the National Academy of Science, 100,* 13626–13631.

Strayer, D., & Drews, F. (2004). Profiles in driver distraction: Effects of cell phone conversations on younger and older drivers. *Human Factors, 46,* 640–649.

Strickland, B. R. (1995). Research on sexual orientation and human development: A commentary. *Developmental Psychology, 31,* 137–140.

Stroebe, M., & Schut, H. (1999). The dual process model of coping with bereavement: Rationale and description. *Death Studies, 23,* 197–224.

Strohmetz, D., Rind, B., Fisher, R., & Lynn, M. (2002). Sweetening the till: The use of candy to increase restaurant tipping. *Journal of Applied Social Psychology, 32,* 300–309.

Stromeyer, C. F., III. (1970, November). Eidetikers. *Psychology Today,* pp. 76–80.

Stubbs, P. (2005). *A consumer's guide to online mental health care.* Retrieved June 10, 2007 from http://www.m-a-h.net/hip/index.html.

Stuss, D. T., Gow, C. A., & Hetherington, C. R. (1992). "No longer Gage": Frontal lobe dysfunction and emotional changes. *Journal of Consulting and Clinical Psychology, 60,* 349–359

Suarez, M. G. (1983). *Implications of Spanish-English bilingualism in the TAT stories.* Unpublished doctoral dissertation, University of Connecticut.

Sugita, M., & Shiba, Y. (2005). Genetic tracing shows segregation of taste neuronal circuitries for bitter and sweet. *Science, 309,* 781–785.

Sullivan, A., Maerz, J., & Madison, D. (2002). Anti-predator response of red-backed salamanders (Plethodon cinereus) to chemical cues from garter snakes (Thamnophis sirtalis): Laboratory and field experiments. *Behavioral Ecology & Sociobiology, 51,* 227–233.

Sullivan, A. D., Hedberg, K., & Fleming, D. W. (2000). Legalized physician-assisted suicide in Oregon—The second year. *New England Journal of Medicine, 342,* 598–604.

Sullivan, M. J. L., Bishop, S. R., & Pivik, J. (1995). The pain catastrophizing scale: Development and validation. *Psychological Assessment, 7,* 524–532.

Summerfeldt, L., Kloosterman, P., Antony, M., & Parker, J. (2006). Emotional intelligence, and interpersonal adjustment. *Journal of Psychopathology and Behavioral Assessment, 28,* 57–68.

Sun, W., & Rebec, G. (2005). The role of prefrontal cortex D1-like and D2-like receptors in cocaine-seeking behavior in rats. *Psychopharmacology, 177,* 315–323.

Sung, K-T. (1992). Motivations for parent care: The case of filial children in Korea. *International Journal of Aging and Human Development, 34,* 109–124.

Super, C. W. (1981). Behavioral development in infancy. In R. H. Munroe, R. L. Munroe, & B. B. Whiting (Eds.), *Handbook of cross-cultural human development* (pp. 181–269). Chicago: Garland.

Super, D. (1971). A theory of vocational development. In N. H. J. Peters & J. C. Hansen (Eds.), *Vocational guidance and career development* (pp. 111–122). New York: MacMillan.

Super, D. (1986). Life career roles: Self-realization in work and leisure. In D. T. H. & Associates (Eds.), *Career development in organizations* (pp. 95–119). San Francisco: Jossey-Bass.

"Survey: Four in 10 American adults play video games." (2006, May 9). Retrieved May 12, 2006, from http://www.foxnews.com

Sussman, S., & Dent, C. W. (2000). One-year prospective prediction of drug use from stress-related variables. *Substance Use & Misuse, 35,* 717–735.

Swanson, L. W. (1995). Mapping the human brain: past, present, and future. *Trends in Neurosciences, 18,* 471–474.

Swanson, N. G. (2000). Working women and stress. *Journal of the American Medical Women's Association, 55,* 276–279.

Sweatt, J. D., & Kandel, E. R. (1989). Persistent and transcriptionally dependent increase in protein phosphorylation in long-term facilitation of *Aplysia* sensory neurons. *Nature, 339,* 51–54.

Swedo, S., & Grant, P. (2004). PANDAS: A model for autoimmune neuropsychiatric disorders. *Primary Psychiatry, 11,* 28–33.

Sweller, J., & Levine, M. (1982). Effects of goal specificity on means-end analysis and learning. *Journal of Experimental Psychology: Learning, Memory, and Cognition, 8,* 463–474.

Symister, P., & Friend, R. (2003). The influence of social support and problematic support on optimism and depression in chronic illness: A prospective study evaluating self-esteem as a mediator. *Health Psychology, 22,* 123–129.

Tamminga, C., & Vogel, M. (2005). Images in neuroscience: The cerebellum. *American Journal of Psychiatry, 162,* 1253.

Tamminga, C. A. (1996, Winter). The new generation of antipsychotic drugs. *NARSAD Research Newsletter, 4*–6.

Tamminga, C. A., & Conley, R. R. (1997). The application of neuroimaging techniques to drug development. *Journal of Clinical Psychiatry, 58*(10, Suppl.), 3–6.

Tanda, G., Pontieri, F. E., & Di Chiara, G. (1997). Cannabinoid and heroin activation of mesolimbic dopamine transmission by a common μ1 opioid receptor mechanism. *Science, 276,* 2048–2050.

Tanner, J. M. (1990). *Fetus into man* (2nd ed.). Cambridge MA: Harvard University Press.

Tate, D., Paul, R., Flanigan, T., Tashima, K., Nash, J., Adair, C., et al. (2003). The impact of apathy and depression on quality of life in patients infected with HIV. *AIDS Patient Care & STDs, 17,* 117–120.

Taub, G., Hayes, B., Cunningham, W., & Sivo, S. (2001). Relative roles of cognitive ability and practical intelligence in the prediction of success. *Psychological Reports, 88*, 931–942.

Tay, C., Ang, S., & Dyne, L. (2006). Personality, biographical characteristics, and job interview success: A longitudinal study of the mediating effects of interviewing self-efficacy and the moderating effects of internal locus of causality. *Journal of Applied Psychology, 91*, 446–454.

Taylor, C., & Luce, K. (2003). Computer- and Internet-based psychotherapy interventions. *Current Directions in Psychological Science, 12*, 18–22.

Taylor, S. E. (1991). *Health psychology* (2nd ed.). New York: McGraw-Hill.

Taylor, S. E., & Repetti, R. L. (1997). Health psychology: What is an unhealthy environment and how does it get under the skin? *Annual Review of Psychology, 48*, 411–447.

Tchanturia, K., Serpell, L., Troop, N., & Treasure, J. (2001). Perceptual illusions in eating disorders: Rigid and fluctuating styles. *Journal of Behavior Therapy & Experimental Psychiatry, 32*, 107–115.

Teachman, J. (2003). Premarital sex, premarital cohabitation and the risk of subsequent marital dissolution among women. *Journal of Marriage and Family, 65*, 444-455.

Teitelbaum, P. (1957). Random and food-directed activity in hyperphagic and normal rats. *Journal of Comparative and Physiological Psychology, 50*, 486–490.

Tellegen, A., Lykken, D. T., Bouchard, T. J., Jr., Wilcox, K. J., Segal, N. L., & Rich, S. (1988). Personality similarity in twins reared apart and together. *Journal of Personality and Social Psychology, 54*, 1031–1039.

Tennant, C. (2002). Life events, stress and depression: A review of the findings. *Australian & New Zealand Journal of Psychiatry, 36*, 173–182.

Tepper, B., & Ullrich, N. (2002). Influence of genetic taste sensitivity to 6-n-propylthiouracil (PROP), dietary restraint and disinhibition on body mass index in middle-aged women. *Physiology & Behavior, 75*, 305–312.

Tercyak, K., Johnson, S., Roberts, S., & Cruz, A. (2001). Psychological response to prenatal genetic counseling and amniocentesis. *Patient Education & Counseling, 43*, 73–84.

Terlecki, M., & Newcombe, N. (2005). How important is the digital divide? The relation of computer and videogame usage to gender differences in mental rotation ability. *Sex Roles, 53*, 433–441.

Terman, L. M. (1925). *Genetic studies of genius, Vol. 1: Mental and physical traits of a thousand gifted children.* Palo Alto, CA: Stanford University Press.

Terman, L. M., & Oden, M. H. (1947). *Genetic studies of genius, Vol. 4: The gifted child grows up.* Palo Alto, CA: Stanford University Press.

Terman, L. M., & Oden, M. H. (1959). *Genetic studies of genius, Vol. 5: The gifted group at mid-life.* Palo Alto, CA: Stanford University Press.

Terrace, H. (1979, November). How Nim Chimpski changed my mind. *Psychology Today*, 65–76.

Terrace, H. S. (1981). A report to an academy. *Annals of the New York Academy of Sciences, 364*, 115–129.

Terrace, H. S. (1985). In the beginning was the "name." *American Psychologist, 40*, 1011–1028.

Terrace, H. S. (1986). *Nim: A chimpanzee who learned sign language.* New York: Columbia University Press.

Tew, J. D., Mulsant, B. H., Haskett, R. F., Prudic, J., Thase, M. E., Crowe, R. R., et al. (1999). Acute efficacy of ECT in the treatment of major depression in the old-old. *American Journal of Psychiatry, 156*, 1865–1870.

Tham, K., Borell, L., & Gustavsson, A. (2000). The discovery of disability: A phenomenological study of unilateral neglect. *American Journal of Occupational Therapy, 54*, 398–406.

Thase, M. E., Frank, E., Mallinger, A. G., Hammer, T., & Kupfer, D. J. (1992). Treatment of imipramine-resistant recurrent depression, III: Efficacy of monoamine oxidise inhibitors. *Journal of Clinical Psychiatry, 53*(1, Suppl.), 5–11.

Thase, M. E., & Kupfer, D. J. (1996). Recent developments in the pharmacotherapy of mood disorders. *Journal of Consulting and Clinical Psychology, 64*, 646–659.

Thirthalli, J., & Benegal, V. (2006). Psychosis among substance users. *Current Opinion in Psychiatry, 19*, 239–245.

Thomas, A., Chess, S., & Birch, H. G. (1970). The origin of personality. *Scientific American, 223*, 102–109.

Thomas, S., & Jordan, T. (2004). Contributions of oral and extraoral facial movement to visual and audiovisual speech perception. *Journal of Experimental Psychology: Human Perception & Performance, 30*, 873–888.

Thompson, P., Vidal, C., Giedd, J., Gochman, P., Blumenthal, J., Nicolson, R., et al. (2001). Mapping adolescent brain change reveals dynamic wave of accelerated gray matter loss in very early-onset schizophrenia. *Proceedings of the National Academy of Sciences, 98*, 11650–11655.

Thompson, R., Emmorey, K., & Gollan, T. (2005). "Tip of the fingers" experiences by deaf signers. *Psychological Science, 16*, 856–860.

Thompson, S. C., Sobolew-Shubin, A., Galbraith, M. E., Schwankovsky, L., & Cruzen, D. (1993). Maintaining perceptions of control: Finding perceived control in low-control circumstances. *Journal of Personality and Social Psychology, 64*, 293–304.

Thorndike, E. (1898). Some experiments on animal intelligence. *Science, 7*(181), 818–824.

Thorndike, E. L. (1911/1970). *Animal intelligence: Experimental studies.* New York: Macmillan. (Original work published 1911).

Thorne, B. (2000). Extra credit exercise: A painless pop quiz. *Teaching of Psychology, 27*, 204–205.

Thurstone, L. L. (1938). *Primary mental abilities.* Chicago: University of Chicago Press.

Tidey, J., O'Neill, S., & Higgins, S. (2002). Contingent monetary reinforcement of smoking reductions, with and without transferal nicotine, in outpatients with schizophrenia. *Experimental and Clinical Psychopharmacology, 10*, 241–247.

Tiedemann, J. (2000). Parents' gender stereotypes and teachers' beliefs as predictors of children's concept of their mathematical ability in elementary school. *Journal of Educational Psychology, 92,* 144–151.

Tiihonen, J., Isohanni, M., Räsänen, P., Koiranen, M., & Moring, J. (1997). Specific major mental disorders and criminality: A 26-year prospective study of the 1966 northern Finland birth cohort. *American Journal of Psychiatry, 154,* 840–845.

Toastmasters International. (2003). *Ten tips for successful public speaking.* Retrieved November 25, 2003, from http://www.toastmasters.org/pdfs/top10.pdf

Todorov, A., & Bargh, J. (2002). Automatic sources of aggression. *Aggression & Violent Behavior, 7,* 53–68.

Tolman, E. C. (1932). *Purposive behavior in animals and men.* New York: Appleton-Century-Crofts.

Tolman, E. C., & Honzik, C. H. (1930). Introduction and removal of reward, and maze performance in rats. *University of California Publications in Psychology, 4,* 257–275.

Toot, J., Dunphy, G., Turner, M., & Ely, D. (2004). The SHR Y-chromosome increases testosterone and aggression, but decreases serotonin as compared to the SKY Y-chromosome in the rat model. *Behavior Genetics, 34,* 515–524.

Tori, C., & Bilmes, M. (2002). Multiculturalism and psychoanalytic psychology: The validation of a defense mechanism's measure in an Asian population. *Psychoanalytic Psychology, 19,* 701–721.

Torrey, E. (1992). *Freudian fraud: The malignant effect of Freud's theory on American thought and culture.* New York: Harper Collins.

Tourangeau, R., Smith, T. W., & Rasinski, K. A. (1997). Motivation to report sensitive behaviors on surveys: Evidence from a bogus pipeline experiment. *Journal of Applied Social Psychology, 27,* 209–222.

Traverso, A., Ravera, G., Lagattolla, V., Testa, S., & Adami, G. F. (2000). Weight loss after dieting with behavioral modification for obesity: The predicting efficiency of some psychometric data. *Eating and Weight Disorders: Studies on Anorexia, Bulimia, and Obesity, 5,* 102–107.

Triandis, H. C. (1994). *Culture and social behavior.* New York: McGraw-Hill.

Trijsburg, R., Perry, J., & Semeniuk, T. (2004). An empirical study of the differences in interventions between psychodynamic therapy and cognitive-behavioural therapy for recurrent major depression. *Canadian Journal of Psychoanalysis, 12,* 325–345.

Triplett, N. (1898). The dynamogenic factors in pacemaking and competition. *American Journal of Psychology, 9,* 507–533.

Trivedi, M. J. (1996). Functional neuroanatomy of obsessive-compulsive disorder. *Journal of Clinical Psychiatry, 57*(8, Suppl.), 26–36.

Troglauer, T., Hels, T., & Christens, P. (2006). Extent and variations in mobile phone use among drivers of heavy vehicles in Denmark. *Accident Analysis & Prevention, 38,* 105–111.

Troxel, W., Matthews, K., Bromberger, J., & Sutton-Tyrrell, K. (2003). Chronic stress burden, discrimination, and subclinical carotid artery disease in African American and Caucasian women. *Health Psychology, 22,* 300–309.

Trull, T., Stepp, S., & Durrett, C. (2003). Research on borderline personality disorder: An update. *Current Opinion in Psychiatry, 16,* 77–82.

Tsai, J., Knutson, B., & Fung, H. (2006). Cultural variation in affect valuation. *Journal of Personality and Social Psychology, 90,* 288–307.

Tsai, S., Kuo, C., Chen, C., & Lee, H. (2002). Risk factors for completed suicide in bipolar disorder. *Journal of Clinical Psychiatry, 63,* 469–476.

Tulving, E. (1995). Organization of memory: Quo vadis? In M. S. Gazzaniga (Ed.), *The cognitive neurosciences* (pp. 839–847). Cambridge, MA: MIT Press.

Tulving, E. (2002). Episodic memory: From mind to brain. *Annual Review of Psychology, 53,* 1–25.

Tulving, E., & Thompson, D. M. (1973). Encoding specificity and retrieval processes in episodic memory. *Psychological Review, 80,* 352–373.

Turner, J. C., Hogg, M. A., Oakes, P. J., Reicher, S. D., & Wetherell, M. S. (1987). *Rediscovering the social group: A self-categorization theory.* Oxford, England: Blackwell.

Tversky, A. (1972). Elimination by aspects: A theory of choice. *Psychological Review, 79,* 281–299.

Tweed, R., & Lehman, D. (2002). Learning considered within a cultural context: Confucian and Socratic approaches. *American Psychologist, 57,* 89–99.

Uchino, B. N., Cacioppo, J. T., & Kiecolt-Glaser, J. K. (1996). The relationship between social support and physiological processes: A review with emphasis on underlying mechanisms and implications for health. *Psychological Bulletin, 119,* 488–531.

Umberson, D., Williams, K., Powers, D., Liu, H., & Needham, B. (2006). You make me sick: Marital quality and health over the life course. *Journal of Health and Social Behavior, 47,* 1–16.

Underwood, B. J. (1957). Interference and forgetting. *Psychological Review, 64,* 49–60.

Underwood, B. J. (1964). Forgetting. *Scientific American, 210,* 91–99.

University of Michigan Transportation Research Institute (UMTRI). (2003). Ready for the road: Software helps teens drive safely. *UMTRI Research Review, 34,* 1–2.

Urry, H., Nitschke, J., Dolski, I., Jackson, D., Dalton, K., Mueller, C., Rosenkranz, M., Ryff, C., Singer, B., & Davidson, R. (2004). Making a life worth living: Neural correlates of well-being. *Psychological Science, 15,* 367–372.

U.S. Census Bureau. (2001). *Statistical abstract of the United States.* Washington, DC: U.S. Government Printing Office.

U.S. Census Bureau. (2004). Income 2003: Press release. Retrieved July 5, 2006, from http://www.census.gov/Press-release/www/releases/archives/income_wealth/002484.html

U. S. Census Bureau. (2006). *2005 American community survey*. Retrieved November 19, 2006, from http://www.census.gov/acs/www/index.html

U.S. Department of Energy. (2003). *International consortium completes Human Genome Project*. Retrieved January 16, 2005, from http://www.ornl.gov/sci/techresources/Human_Genome/

U.S. Department of Health and Human Services. (2000). *Reducing tobacco use: A report of the Surgeon General—executive summary*. Atlanta: Department of Health and Human Services, Centers for Disease Control and Prevention, National Center for Chronic Disease Prevention and Health Promotion, Office on Smoking and Health.

U.S. Department of Health and Human Services. (2001). *Ecstasy: Teens speak out* [Online factsheet]. Retrieved October 22, 2003, from http://www.health.org/govpubs/prevalert/v4/8.aspx

U.S. Food and Drug Administration (FDA). (2004, October 15). *Suicidality in children and adolescents being treated with antidepressant medication*. Retrieved May 12, 2005, from http://www.fda.gov/cder/drug/antidepressants/SSRIPHA200410.htm.

U.S. Food and Drug Administration (FDA). (2006a, April 20). Interagency advisory regarding claims that smoked marijuana is a medicine. Retrieved May 15, 2006, from http://www.fda.gov/bbs/topics/NEWS/2006/NEW01362.html

U.S. Food and Drug Administration (FDA). (2006b). *Prozac patient information sheet*. Retrieved July 26, 2006, from http://www.fda.gov/cder/drug/InfoSheets/patient/fluoxetinePIS.htm

Ushikubo, M. (1998). A study of factors facilitating and inhibiting the willingness of the institutionalized disabled elderly for rehabilitation: A United States–Japanese comparison. *Journal of Cross-Cultural Gerontology, 13*, 127–157.

Utsey, S., Chae, M., Brown, C., & Kelly, D. (2002). Effect of ethnic group membership on ethnic identity, race-related stress and quality of life. *Cultural Diversity & Ethnic Minority Psychology, 8*, 367–378.

Vaccarino, V., Abramson, J., Veledar, E., & Weintraub, W. (2002). Sex differences in hospital mortality after coronary artery bypass surgery: Evidence for a higher mortality in younger women. *Circulation, 105*, 1176.

Van Assema, P., Martens, M., Ruiter, A., & Brug, J. (2002). Framing of nutrition education messages in persuading consumers of the advantages of a healthy diet. *Journal of Human Nutrition & Dietetics, 14*, 435–442.

Van Boven, L., White, K., Kamada, A., & Gilovich, T. (2003). Intuitions about situational correction in self and others. *Journal of Personality & Social Psychology, 85*, 249–258.

Van Cauter, E. (2000). Slow-wave sleep and release of growth hormone. *Journal of the American Medical Association, 284*, 2717–2718.

Van der Elst, W., Van Boxtel, M., Van Breukelen, G., & Jolles, J. (2006). The Stroop color-word test: Influence of age, sex, and education; and normative data for a large sample across the adult age range. *Assessment, 13*, 62–79.

Van der Zee, K., Thijs, M., & Schakel, L. (2002). The relationship of emotional intelligence with academic intelligence and the Big Five. *European Journal of Personality, 16*, 103–125.

van Elst, L. T., Woermann, F. G., Lemieux, L., Thompson, P. J., & Trimble, M. R. (2000). Affective aggression in patients with temporal lobe epilepsy. *Brain, 123*, 234–243.

Van Groen, T., Kadish, I., & Wyss, J. (2002). The role of the laterodorsal nucleus of the thalamus in spatial learning and memory in the rat. *Behavior and Brain Research, 136*, 329–337.

Van Lancker, D. (1987, November). Old familiar voices. *Psychology Today*, pp. 12–13.

Van Lommel, S., Laenen, A., & d'Ydewalle, G. (2006). Foreign-grammar acquisition while watching subtitled television programmes. *British Journal of Educational Psychology, 76*, 243–258.

van Vianen, A., & Fischer, A. (2002). Illuminating the glass ceiling: The role of organizational culture preferences. *Journal of Occupational & Organizational Psychology, 75*, 315–337.

Vargha-Khadem, F., Gadian, D. G., Watkins, D. E., Connelly, A., Van Paesschen, W., & Mishkin, M. (1997). Differential effects of early hippocampal pathology on episodic and semantic memory. *Science, 277*, 376–380.

Varley, A., & Blasco, M. (2003). Older women's living arrangements and family relationships in urban Mexico. *Women's Studies International Forum, 26*, 525–539.

Vasterling, J., Duke, L., Brailey, K., Constans, J., Allain, A., & Sutker, P. (2002). Attention, learning, and memory performances and intellectual resources in Vietnam veterans: PTSD and no disorder comparisons. *Neuropsychology, 16*, 5–14.

Verdejo-García, A., López-Torrecillas, F., Aguilar de Arcos, F., & Pérez-García, M. (2005). Differential effects of MDMA, cocaine, and cannabis use severity on distinctive components of the executive functions in polysubstance users: A multiple regression analysis. *Addictive Behaviors, 30*, 89–101.

Verhaeghen, P., Marcoen, A., & Goossens, L. (1993). Facts and fiction about memory aging. A quantitative integration of research findings. *Journal of Gerontology, 48*, 157–171.

Vetulani, J., & Nalepa, I. (2000). Antidepressants: Past, present and future. *European Journal of Pharmacology, 405*, 351–363.

Viding, E., Blair, R., Moffitt, T., & Plomin, R. (2005). Evidence of substantial genetic risk for psychopathy in 7-year-olds. *Journal of Child Psychology and Psychiatry, 46*, 592–597.

Viemerö, V. (1996). Factors in childhood that predict later criminal behavior. *Aggressive Behavior, 22*, 87–97.

Vieta, E. (2003). Atypical antipsychotics in the treatment of mood disorders. *Current Opinion in Psychiatry, 16*, 23–27.

Villegas, A., Sharps, M., Satterthwaite, B., & Chisholm, S. (2005). Eyewitness memory for vehicles. *Forensic Examiner, 14*, 24–28.

Vincent, M., & Pickering, M. R. (1988). Multiple personality disorder in childhood. *Canadian Journal of Psychiatry, 33*, 524–529.

Visser, P., & Mirabile, R. (2004). Attitudes in the social context: The impact of social network composition on individual-level attitude strength. *Journal of Personality & Social Psychology, 87*, 779–795.

Visser, P. S., & Krosnick, J. A. (1998). Development of attitude strength over the life cycle: Surge and decline. *Journal of Personality & Social Psychology, 75*, 1389–1410.

Vitello, P. (2006, June 12). A ring tone meant to fall on deaf ears. *New York Times* [Online]. Retrieved December 13, 2006, from http://www.nytimes.com/06/12/technology/12ring.html?ex_1307764899&en_2a80

Vitousek, K., & Manke, F. (1994). Personality variables and disorders in anorexia nervosa and bulimia nervosa. *Journal of Abnormal Psychology, 103*, 137–147.

Volis, C., Ashburn-Nardo, L., & Monteith, M. (2002). Evidence of prejudice-related conflict and associated affect beyond the college setting. *Group Processes & Intergroup Relations, 5*, 19–33.

Volkow, N. D., & Fowler, J. S. (2000). Addiction, a disease of compulsion and drive: Involvement of the orbitofrontal cortex. *Cerebral Cortex, 10*, 318–325.

Votruba, S., Horvitz, M., & Schoeller, D. (2000). The role of exercise in the treatment of obesity. *Nutrition, 16*, 179–188.

Voyer, D., & Rodgers, M. (2002). Reliability of laterality effects in a dichotic listening task with nonverbal material. *Brain & Cognition, 48*, 602–606.

Vygotsky, L. (1926/1992). *Educational psychology.* Boca Raton, FL: St. Lucie Press.

Vygotsky, L. S. (1936/1986). *Thought and language* (A. Kozulin, Trans.). Cambridge, MA: MIT Press. (Original work published 1936).

Wacker, J., Chavanon, M., & Stemmler, G. (2006). Investigating the dopaminergic basis of extraversion in humans: A multilevel approach. *Journal of Personality and Social Psychology, 91*, 171–187.

Wade, T., & DiMaria, C. (2003). Weight halo effects: Individual differences in personality evaluations as a function of weight. *Sex Roles, 48*, 461–465.

Wagner, D., Wenzlaff, R., & Kozak, M. (2004). Dream rebound: The return of suppressed thoughts in dreams. *Psychological Science, 15*, 232–236.

Wald, G. (1964). The receptors of human color vision. *Science, 145*, 1007–1017.

Wald, G., Brown, P. K., & Smith, P. H. (1954). Iodopsin. *Journal of General Physiology, 38*, 623–681.

Waldron, S., & Helm, F. (2004). Psychodynamic features of two cognitive-behavioural and one psychodynamic treatment compared using the analytic process scales. *Canadian Journal of Psychoanalysis, 12*, 346–368,

Walitzer, K., & Demen, K. (2004). Alcohol-focused spouse involvement and behavioral couples therapy: Evaluation of enhancements to drinking reduction treatment for male problem drinkers. *Journal of Consulting & Clinical Psychology, 72*, 944–955.

Walker, E., Kestler, L., Bollini, A., & Hochman, K. (2004). Schizophrenia: Etiology and course. *Annual Review of Psychology, 55*, 401–430.

Walker, I., & Crogan, M. (1998). Academic performance, prejudice and the jigsaw classroom: New pieces to the puzzle. *Journal of Community & Applied Social Psychology, 8*, 381–393.

Walker, L. (1989). A longitudinal study of moral reasoning. *Child Development, 60*, 157–166.

Walker, M., Brakefield, T., Hobson, J., & Stickgold, R. (2003). Dissociable stages of human memory consolidation and reconsolidation. *Nature, 425*, 616–620.

Walker, M., & Stickgold, R. (2006). Sleep, memory, and plasticity. *Annual Review of Psychology: 57*, 139–166.

Walsh, B., Seidman, S., Sysko, R., & Gould, M. (2002). Placebo response in studies of major depression: Variable, substantial, and growing. *JAMA: Journal of the American Medical Association, 287*, 1840–1847.

Walsh, D., Gentile, D., VanOverbeke, M., & Chasco, E. (2002). *MediaWise video game report card.* National Institute on Media and the Family. Retrieved May 18, 2006, from http://www.mediafamily.org/research/report_vgrc_2002-2.shtml

Walster, E., & Walster, G. W. (1969). The matching hypothesis. *Journal of Personality and Social Psychology, 6*, 248–253.

Walters, C. C., & Grusec, J. E. (1977). *Punishment.* San Francisco: Freeman.

Wang, P., & Li, J. (2003). An experimental study on the belief bias effect in syllogistic reasoning. *Psychological Science (China), 26*, 1020–1024.

Wang, X., & Perry, A. (2006). Metabolic and physiologic responses to video game play in 7- to 10-year-old boys. *Archives of Pediatric Adolescent Medicine, 160*, 411–415.

Wang, Z., & Chen, M. (2002). Managerial competency modeling: A structural equation testing. *Psychological Science (China), 25*, 513–516.

Warburton, J., McLaughlin, D., & Pinsker, D. (2006). Generative acts: Family and community involvement of older Australians. *International Journal of Aging & Human Development, 63*, 115–137.

Ward, C. (1994). Culture and altered states of consciousness. In W. J. Lonner & R. Malpass (Eds.), *Psychology and culture* (pp. 59–64). Boston: Allyn & Bacon.

Wark, G. R., & Krebs, D. L. (1996). Gender and dilemma differences in real-life moral judgment. *Developmental Psychology, 32*, 220–230.

Warshaw, M. G., & Keller, M. B. (1996). The relationship between fluoxetine use and suicidal behavior in 654 subjects with anxiety disorders. *Journal of Clinical Psychiatry, 57*, 158–166.

Washington University School of Medicine. (2003). *Epilepsy surgery* [Online factsheet]. Retrieved September 29, 2003, from http://neurosurgery.wustl.edu/clinprog/epilepsysurg.htm

Waterman, A. (1985). Identity in the context of adolescent psychology. *Child Development, 30,* 5–24.

Watson, D. (2002). Predicting psychiatric symptomatology with the Defense Style Questionnaire-40. *International Journal of Stress Management, 9,* 275–287.

Watson, J. B., & Rayner, R. (1920). Conditioned emotional reactions. *Journal of Experimental Psychology, 3,* 1–14.

Webb, R., Lubinski, D., & Benbow, C. (2002). Mathematically facile adolescents with math-science aspirations: New perspectives on their educational and vocational development. *Journal of Educational Psychology, 94,* 785–794.

Webb, W. (1995). The cost of sleep-related accidents: A reanalysis. *Sleep, 18,* 276–280.

Webb, W. B. (1975). *Sleep: The gentle tyrant.* Englewood Cliffs, NJ: Prentice-Hall.

Weber, R., Ritterfeld, U., & Mathiak, K. (2006). Does playing violent video games induce aggression? Empirical evidence of a functional magnetic resonance imaging study. *Media Psychology, 8,* 39–60.

Wechsler, D. (1939). *The measurement of adult intelligence.* Baltimore: Williams & Wilkins.

Weekes, J. R., Lynn, S. J., Green, J. P., & Brentar, J. T. (1992). Pseudomemory in hypnotized and task-motivated subjects. *Journal of Abnormal Psychology, 101,* 356–360.

Weeks, D. L., & Anderson, L. P. (2000). The interaction of observational learning with overt practice: Effects on motor skill learning. *Acta Psychologia, 104,* 259–271.

Weigman, O., & van Schie, E. G. (1998). Video game playing and its relations with aggressive and prosocial behaviour. *British Journal of Social Psychology, 37*(Pt. 3), 367–378.

Weiner, I. (2004). Monitoring psychotherapy with performance-based measures of personality functioning. *Journal of Personality Assessment, 83,* 323–331.

Weiner, I. B. (1996). Some observations on the validity of the Rorschach Inkblot Method. *Psychological Assessment, 8,* 206–213.

Weiner, I. B. (1997). Current status of the Rorschach Inkblot Method. *Journal of Personality Assessment, 68,* 5–19.

Weissman, M. M., Bland, R. C., Canino, G. J., Faravelli, C., Greenwald, S., Hwu, H-G., et al. (1996). Cross-national epidemiology of major depression and bipolar disorder. *Journal of the American Medical Association, 276,* 293–299.

Wells, D. L., & Hepper, P. G. (2000). The discrimination of dog odours by humans. *Perception, 29,* 111–115.

Wells, G. L. (1993). What do we know about eyewitness identification? *American Psychologist, 48,* 553–571.

Wells, G. L., Malpass, R. S., Lindsay, R. C., Fisher, R. P., Turtle, J. W., & Fulero, S. M. (2000). From the lab to the police station. A successful application of eyewitness research. *American Psychologist, 55,* 6581–6598.

Wertheimer, M. (1912). Experimental studies of the perception of movement. *Zeitschrift fuer Psychologie, 61,* 161–265.

Wesensten, N., Balenky, G., Kautz, M., Thorne, D., Reichardt, R., & Balkin, T. (2002). Maintaining alertness and performance during sleep deprivation: Modafinil versus caffeine. *Psychopharmacology, 159,* 238–247.

Westerhof, G., Katzko, M., Dittmann-Kohli, F., & Hayslip, B. (2001). Life contexts and health-related selves in old age: Perspectives from the United States, India and Congo-Zaire. *Journal of Aging Studies, 15,* 105–126.

Wetherell, J., Gatz, M., & Craske, M. (2003). Treatment of generalized anxiety disorder in older adults. *Journal of Consulting & Clinical Psychology, 71,* 31–40.

Wheeler, M., & McMillan, C. (2001). Focal retrograde amnesia and the episodic-semantic distinction. *Cognitive, Affective & Behavioral Neuroscience, 1,* 22–36.

Whisenhunt, B. L., Williamson, D. A., Netemeyer, R. G., & Womble, L. G. (2000). Reliability and validity of the Psychosocial Risk Factors Questionnaire (PRFQ). *Eating and Weight Disorders: Studies on Anorexia, Bulimia, and Obesity, 5,* 1–6.

Whitam, F. L., Diamond, M., & Martin, J. (1993). Homosexual orientation in twins: A report on 61 pairs and three triplet sets. *Archives of Sexual Behavior, 22,* 187–296.

White, D. P. (1989). Central sleep apnea. In M. H. Kryger, T. Roth, & W. C. Dement (Eds.), *Principles and practice of sleep medicine* (pp. 513–524). Philadelphia: W. B. Saunders.

White, S. D., & DeBlassie, R. R. (1992). Adolescent sexual behavior. *Adolescence, 27,* 183–191.

Whitehead, B., & Popenoe, D. (2005). *The state of our unions: The social health of marriage in America: 2005: What does the Scandinavian experience tell us?* Retrieved June 15, 2006, from http://marriage.rutgers.edu/Publications/SOOU/TEXTSOOU2005.htm

Whitehurst, G. J., Fischel, J. E., Caulfield, M. B., DeBaryshe, B. D., & Valdez-Menchaca, M. C. (1989). Assessment and treatment of early expressive language delay. In P. R. Zelazo & R. Barr (Eds.), *Challenges to developmental paradigms: Implications for assessment and treatment* (pp. 113–135). Hillsdale, NJ: Erlbaum.

Whorf, B. L. (1956). Science and linguistics. In J. B. Carroll (Ed.), *Language, thought, and reality: Selected writings of Benjamin Lee Whorf* (pp. 207–219). Cambridge, MA: MIT Press.

Wickelgren, I. (1996). For the cortex, neuron loss may be less than thought. *Science, 273,* 48–50.

Wicker, A. W. (1969). Attitudes versus action: The relationship of verbal and overt behavioral responses to attitude objects. *Journal of Social Issues, 25,* 41–78.

Widom, C. S. (1989). Does violence beget violence? A critical examination of the literature. *Psychological Bulletin, 106,* 3–28.

Widom, C. S., & Maxfield, M. G. (1996). A prospective examination of risk for violence among abused and neglected children. *Annals of the New York Academy of Sciences, 794,* 224–237.

Widom, C. S., & Morris, S. (1997). Accuracy of adult recollections of childhood victimization: Part 2. Childhood sexual abuse. *Psychological Bulletin, 9,* 34–46.

Wigboldus, D., Dijksterhuis, A., & Van Knippenberg, A. (2003). When stereotypes get in the way: Stereotypes obstruct stereotype-inconsistent trait inferences. *Journal of Personality & Social Psychology, 84*, 470–484.

Wilcox, D., & Hager, R. (1980). Toward realistic expectation for orgasmic response in women. *Journal of Sex Research, 16*, 162–179.

Wilhelm, K., Kovess, V., Rios-Seidel, C., & Finch, A. (2004). Work and mental health. *Social Psychiatry & Psychiatric Epidemiology, 39*, 866–873.

Wilken, J. A., Smith, B. D., Tola, K., & Mann, M. (2000). Trait anxiety and prior exposure to non-stressful stimuli: Effects on psychophysiological arousal and anxiety. *International Journal of Psychophysiology, 37*, 233–242.

Wilkinson, R. (2004). The role of parental and peer attachment in the psychological health and self-esteem of adolescents. *Journal of Youth & Adolescence, 33*, 479–493.

Williams, J. (2003). Dementia and genetics. In R. Plomin, J. de Fries, I. Craig, & P. McGuffin (Eds.), *Behavioral genetics in the postgenomic era* (pp. 503–528). Washington, DC: APA.

Williams, K., Harkins, S. G., & Latané, B. (1981). Identifiability as a deterrent to social loafing: Two cheering experiments. *Journal of Personality and Social Psychology, 40*, 303–311.

Williams, L. M. (1994). Recall of childhood trauma: A prospective study of women's memories of child sexual abuse. *Journal of Consulting and Clinical Psychology, 62*, 1167–1176.

Wilson, F. R. (1998). *The hand: How its use shapes the brain, language, and human culture.* New York: Pantheon.

Wilson, M. A., & McNaughton, B. L. (1993). Dynamics of the hippocampal ensemble code for space. *Science, 261*, 1055–1058.

Wilson, W., Mathew, R., Turkington, T., Hawk, T., Coleman, R. E., & Provenzale, J. (2000). Brain morphological changes and early marijuana use: A magnetic resonance and positron emission tomography study. *Journal of Addictive Diseases, 19*, 1–22.

Winerman, L. (2006). Reaching out to Muslim and Arab Americans. *APA Monitor on Psychology, 37*, 54–55.

Winograd, E. (1988). Some observations on prospective remembering. In M. M. Gruneberg, P. E. Morris, & R. N. Sykes (Eds.), *Practical aspects of memory: Current research and issues: Vol. 1* (pp. 348–353). Chichester, England: John Wiley & Sons.

Winokur, G., Coryell, W., Keller, M., Endicott, J., & Akiskal, H. S. (1993). A prospective follow-up of patients with bipolar and primary unipolar affective disorder. *Archives of General Psychiatry, 50*, 457–465.

Witt, L., Burke, L., Barrick, M., & Mount, M. (2002). The interactive effects of conscientiousness and agreeableness on job performance. *Journal of Applied Psychology, 87*, 164–169.

Wolford, G., Miller, M. B., & Gazzaniga, M. (2000). The left hemisphere's role in hypothesis formation. *Journal of Neuroscience, 20*, 1–4.

Wolpe, J. (1958). *Psychotherapy by reciprocal inhibition.* Palo Alto, CA: Stanford University Press.

Wolpe, J. (1973). *The practice of behavior therapy* (2nd ed.). New York: Pergamon.

Wolsko, P., Eisenberg, D., Davis, R., & Phillips, R. (2004). Use of mind-body medical therapies: Results of a national survey. *Journal of General Internal Medicine, 19*, 43–50.

Wolters, C. (2003). Understanding procrastination from a self-regulated learning perspective. *Journal of Educational Psychology, 95*, 179–187.

Wolters, C. (2004). Advancing achievement goal theory using goal structures and goal orientations to predict students' motivation, cognition, and achievement. *Journal of Educational Psychology, 96*, 136–250.

Wood, J., Cowan, P., & Baker, B. (2002). Behavior problems and peer rejection in preschool boys and girls. *Journal of Genetic Psychology, 163*, 72–88.

Wood, J. M., Nezworski, M. T., & Stejskal, W. J. (1996). The Comprehensive System for the Rorschach: A critical examination. *Psychological Science, 7*, 3–10.

Wood, W., & Conway, M. (2006). Subjective impact, meaning making, and current and recalled emotions for self-defining memories. *Journal of Personality, 75*, 811–846.

Wood, W., Lundgren, S., Ovellette, J. A., Busceme, S., & Blackstone, T. (1994). Minority influence: A meta-analytic review of social influence processes. *Psychological Bulletin, 115*, 323–345.

Wood, W., Wong, F. Y., & Chachere, J. G. (1991). Effects of media violence on viewers' aggression in unconstrained social interaction. *Psychological Bulletin, 109*, 371–383.

Woodman, G., & Luck, S. (2003). Serial deployment of attention during visual search. *Journal of Experimental Psychology: Human Perception and Performance, 29*, 121–138.

Woodward, A. L., Markman, E. M., & Fitzsimmons, C. M. (1994). Rapid word learning in 13- and 18-month-olds. *Developmental Psychology, 30*, 553–566.

Woody, E. Z., & Bowers, K. S. (1994). A frontal assault on dissociated control. In S. J. Lynn & J. W. Rhue (Eds.), *Dissociation: Clinical, theoretical and research perspectives* (pp. 52–79). New York: Guilford.

Woolley, J., & Boerger, E. (2002). Development of beliefs about the origins and controllability of dreams. *Developmental Psychology, 38*, 24–41.

World Health Organization (WHO). (2000b). *Violence against women.* [Online report] Retrieved September 1, 2000, from http://www.who.int

Worrel, J. A., Marken, P. A., Beckman, S. E., & Ruehter, V. L. (2000). Atypical antipsychotic agents: A critical review. *American Journal of Health System Pharmacology, 57*, 238–255.

Worthen, J., & Wood, V. (2001). Memory discrimination for self-performed and imagined acts: Bizarreness effects in false recognition. *Quarterly Journal of Experimental Psychology, 54A*, 49–67.

Wright, J. C., & Mischel, W. (1987). A conditional approach to dispositional constructs: The local predictability of social behavior. *Journal of Personality and Social Psychology, 53,* 1159–1177.

Wright, K. (2002, September). Times of our lives. *Scientific American,* 58–65.

Wyrobek, A., Eskenazi, B., Young, S., Arnheim, N., Tiemann-Boege, I., Jabs, E., et al. (2006). Advancing age has differential effects on DNA damage, chromatin integrity, gene mutations, and aneuploidies. *Proceedings of the National Academies of Sciences, 103,* 9601–9606.

Wu, C., & Shaffer, D. R. (1987). Susceptibility to persuasive appeals as a function of source credibility and prior experience with the attitude object. *Journal of Personality and Social Psychology, 52,* 677–688.

Yackinous, C., & Guinard, J. (2002). Relation between PROP (6-n-propylthiouracil) taster status, taste anatomy and dietary intake measures for young men and women. *Appetite, 38,* 201–209.

Yale-New Haven Hospital. (2003). *Making the right choice: Speak up about complementary and alternative therapies.* Retrieved August 6, 2003, from http://www.ynhh.org/choice/cam.html

Yanagita, T. (1973). An experimental framework for evaluation of dependence liability in various types of drugs in monkeys. *Bulletin of Narcotics, 25,* 57–64.

Yang, C., & Spielman, A. (2001). The effect of a delayed weekend sleep pattern on sleep and morning functioning. *Psychology & Health, 16,* 715–725.

Yapko, M. D. (1994). Suggestibility and repressed memories of abuse: A survey of psychotherapists' beliefs. *American Journal of Clinical Hypnosis, 36,* 163–171.

Yasui-Furukori, N., Saito, M., Nakagami, T., Kaneda, A., Tateishi, T., & Kaneko, S. (2006). Association between multidrug resistance 1 (MDR1) gene polymorphisms and therapeutic response to bromperidol in schizophrenic patients: A preliminary study. *Progress in Neuro-Psychopharmacology & Biological Psychiatry, 30,* 286–291.

Yeh, S., & Lo, S. (2004). Living alone, social support, and feeling lonely among the elderly. *Social Behavior & Personality, 32,* 129–138.

Zajonc, R. B. (1980). Feeling and thinking: Preferences need no inferences. *American Psychologist, 35,* 151–175.

Zajonc, R. B. (1984). On the primacy of affect. *American Psychologist, 39,* 117–123.

Zajonc, R. B., & Sales, S. M. (1966). Social facilitation of dominant and subordinate responses. *Journal of Experimental Social Psychology, 2,* 160–168.

Zaragoza, M. S., & Mitchell, K. J. (1996). Repeated exposure to suggestion and the creation of false memories. *Psychological Science, 7,* 294–300.

Zatorre, R., Belin, P., & Penhune, V. (2002). Structure and function of the auditory cortex: Music and speech. *Trends in Cognitive Sciences, 6,* 37–46.

Zhang, D., Li, Z., Chen, X., Wang, Z., Zhang, X., Meng, X., et al. (2003). Functional comparison of primacy, middle and recency retrieval in human auditory short-term memory: An event-related fMRI study. *Cognitive Brain Research, 16,* 91–98.

Zhang, L. (2002). Thinking styles and the Big Five personality traits. *Educational Psychology, 22,* 17–31.

Zhang, X., Cohen, H., Porjesz, B., & Begleiter, H. (2001). Mismatch negativity in subjects at high risk for alcoholism. *Alcoholism: Clinical & Experimental Research, 25,* 330–337.

Zimbardo, P. G. (1972). Pathology of imprisonment. *Society, 9,* 4–8.

Zimmerman, M., Posternak, K., & Chelminski, I. (2002). Symptom severity and exclusion from antidepressant efficacy trials. *Journal of Clinical Psychopharmacology, 22,* 610–614.

Zinkernagel, C., Naef, M., Bucher, H., Ladewig, D., Gyr, N., & Battegay, M. (2001). Onset and pattern of substance use in intravenous drug users of an opiate maintenance program. *Drug & Alcohol Dependence, 64,* 105–109.

Zisapel, N. (2001). Circadian rhythm sleep disorders: Pathophysiology and potential approaches to management. *CNS Drugs, 15,* 311–328.

Zucker, A., Ostrove, J., & Stewart A. (2002). College-educated women's personality development in adulthood: Perceptions and age differences. *Psychology & Aging, 17,* 236–244.

Bell, A. P., 440
Bell, M., 82
Belloch, A., 586
Bellugi, U., 353
Belluzi, J., 176
Belsky, J., 348
Bem, D., 139
Bem, S. L., 416, 417, 418
Bendabis, S., 160
Benegal, V., 176, 178
Benes, F. M., 562
Benishay, 439
Benjafield, J. G., 8
Benjamin, L., 10
Benjamin, L. T., 43
Benjet, C., 582
Bennett, S. K., 522
Bennett, W. I., 114
Ben-Porath, Y. S., 525
Bentin, S., 74, 157
Beran, M., 290
Berckmoes, C., 75
Berger, S. A., 248
Berglund, P., 546
Berkowitz, L., 641
Bernal, M. E., 604
Bernardi, L., 167
Bernat, E., 138
Berndt, E. R., 552
Berndt, T. J., 358
Bernstein, D., 250, 252
Bernstein, I. L., 198
Berscheid, E., 616
Bersoff, D. M., 636
Beyer, J., 586
Bialystok, E., 291
Bierman, A., 364
Billiard, M., 159
Billings, E. J., 251
Bilmes, M., 503
Biondi, M., 546
Birch, H. G., 345
Bird, C., 482
Bird, T., 92
Birren, J. E., 367
Bishop, G. D., 626
Bishop, J., 349
Bishop, R., 233
Bisiach, E., 74
Biss, W., 364, 441
Bjork, R. A., 169, 243
Bjorklund, D. F., 244
Björkqvist, 426
Black, D. W., 178
Blanch, A., 510
Blasco, M., 370

Blascovich, J., 644
Blatt, S. J., 605
Blatt-Eisengart, I., 354
Bleich, A., 472
Bliese, P. D., 482
Blinn-Pike, L., 357
Bliss, T. V., 254
Bloom, B. S., 316
Bloomer, C. M., 136
Blyth, D. A., 356
Boerger, E., 162
Bogen, J. E., 76
Bohannon, J. N., III, 244
Bohman, M., 639
Boivin, D. B., 149
Bompas, A., 106
Bonanno, G. A., 373
Bonke, B., 255
Bonson, K., 174
Borbely, A. A., 152
Borell, L., 74
Bornstein, R. F., 633
Borzekowski, D., 484
Boscarino, J., 466
Bosse, R., 369
Bouchard, T., 92
Bouchard, T. J., Jr., 306,
    307, 519
Boul, L., 362
Bourassa, M., 178
Bowden, C., 592
Bowen-Reid, T., 467
Bower, G. H., 237, 264
Bowers, K., 169
Bowers, K. S., 170, 251
Brady, S., 225
Brain imaging and
    psychiatry-Part I., 69
Brandt, P., 215
Braun, A., 161
Braun, S., 342
Brawman-Mintzer, O., 545,
    592
Bray, G. A., 392
Brazelton, T., 348
Brecht, M., 384
Breckler, S. J., 630
Breedlove, 413, 438
Brennan, P., 640
Brennan, P. A., 640
Brent, D., 554
Breslau, N., 467
Brian, O., 370
Brickman, P., 378
Brieger, P., 566
Britt, R., 114

Broadbent, D. E., 233
Brobeck, J. R., 389
Brodie, M. S., 173
Brody, 444
Brody, A., 510
Brody, L. R., 428
Brooks-Gunn, J., 308, 357
Brotherton, D., 605
Brotman, A. W., 394
Broughton, R. J., 159
Broughton, W. A., 159
Brown, A., 138, 265, 549
Brown, A. L., 629
Brown, G., 579
Brown, G. W., 551
Brown, J. D., 614
Brown, P. K., 106
Brown, R., 244, 265, 352,
    353
Brown, W. A., 121
Bruch, M., 546
Brummett, B., 512
Brundage, S., 90
Brunetti, A., 284
Brunila, T., 74
Brydon, L., 477
Buchert, R., 180
Buck, L. B., 117, 118
Buckingham, H. W., Jr., 80
Buhusi, C., 174
Buijtels, H., 633
Buller, D. B., 633
Burchinal, M., 308
Burge, S., 504
Burgess, N., 253
Burke, A., 250
Burt, D. B., 244
Burton, D., 643
Busch, C. M., 362
Bush, D., 401
Bushman, B., 225, 504
Bushman, B. J., 640, 643
Busnel, M. C., 343
Buss, D., 15
Buss, D. M., 15, 419, 420,
    442, 616, 617
Bussey, K., 416
Butcher, J., 586
Butcher, J. N., 525, 527, 528
Butler, R., 372
Buunk, 406
Byne, W., 438
Byrd, 483

Cabýoglu, M., 121
Cacioppo, J. T., 482

Cahill, L., 61, 255
Calker, L., 246
Camargo, C. A., Jr., 395
Camerer, C., 279
Camp, D. S., 211
Campbell, D., 378
Campbell, F., 308
Campbell, P., 392
Canary, D. J., 428
Cannon, T. D., 561
Cannon, W. B., 63, 400
Cantalupo, C., 72
Capel, B., 89, 413
Cardoso, S. H., 2, 53
Carey, G., 519, 639
Carey, K., 173
Carlat, D. J., 395
Carli, L., 622
Carlo, 336
Carlsmith, J. M., 631
Carlson, N. R., 172
Carlsson, I., 315
Carnagey, N., 225, 643
Carpenter, S., 97
Carpenter, W. T., Jr., 579
Carrier, J., 437
Carroll, K. M., 588
Carskadon, M. A., 153,
    154, 157
Carson, R., 586, 593
Carson, R. C., 514
Carstensen, L., 248, 370
Carter, W. P., 591
Carton, J., 516
Cartwright, R., 162
Carver, C. S., 479
Case, A., 482
Case, R., 331
Casey, D. E., 590
Cash, T. F., 616
Caspi, A., 347, 356, 519
Cassell, 452
Cassels, A., 573
Castellani, A., 578
Castro, C. A., 482
Castro, F. G., 604
Cates, 446
Cathebras, P., 172
Cattapan-Ludewig, K.,
    593
Cattell, R. B., 510
Cauffman, E., 354
Cavanaugh, S., 356
Cazden, C., 353
CBS News, 547
Ceci, S. J., 250

Centers for Disease Control and Prevention (CDC), 356, 446, 447, 448, 449, 451, 452, 483, 488, 489, 554
Chabris, C., 126
Chachere, J. G., 643
Chambless, D. L., 585
Chamorro-Premuzic, T., 512
Chandler, 426
Chang, E., 82
Chao, R., 355
Chaplin, W. F., 613
Charles, S., 370
Charness, N., 369
Charney, D., 177
Chase, M. H., 153
Chassin, L., 173, 484
Chavanon, M., 510
Chelminski, I., 590
Chen-Sea, M.-J., 74
Chernyshenko, O., 522
Cherry, E. C., 126
Chesney, T., 633
Chess, S., 345
Chi, S., 510
Chilosi, A., 82
Cho, K., 151
Choi, H., 265
Choi, I., 614
Chollar, S., 290
Chomsky, N., 353
Chowdhury, R., 550
Christakis, D., 41
Christens, P., 126
Christensen, A., 578, 621
Christenson, 441, 442
Christianson, S-Å., 250
Chung, R., 355
Church, A., 522
Church, M., 388
Church, R. M., 211
Cialdini, R., 633
Cialdini, R. B., 623, 624
Clannon, 596
Clark, D. M., 244
Clark, L., 538
Clark, M. L., 358
Classen, J., 78
Clay, R., 367
Clayton, V., 40
Clément, K., 390
Clifford, E., 82
Cloitre, M., 585
Cloninger, C. R., 639

CNN.com, 636
Cobb, Y., 311
Codd, J., 291
Cohen, A., 604
Cohen, S., 468, 480, 481, 482
Cohn, E. G., 641
Cohon, M. S., 592
Colantonio, A., 468
Colby, A., 333
Cole, M., 328
Cole, R., 152
Collaer, M. L., 438
College Board, 422, 423
Colwell, J., 643
Compton, R., 127
Conca, A., 595
Condon, W. S., 348
Coney, J., 314
Conley, R. R., 69
Conrad, P., 573
Conroy, D., 387
Consumer Reports, 599
Conway, M., 248
Cooke, M., 224
Coons, P. M., 565
Cooper, H. M., 640
Cooper, R., 154
Coplan, J. D., 591
Corballis, M. C., 71
Coren, S., 151
Corenblum, B., 246
Corkill, A. J., 266
Corkin, S., 232
Cornelius, M. D., 485
Cortina, L., 460
Cosmides, L., 15
Costa, P. T., 362
Costa, P. T., Jr., 511, 514
Costa E. Silva, J. A., 159, 160
Courage, M. L., 344
Covey, S., 2
Cowan, N., 235
Cowan, P., 355
Cowley, E., 614
Cox, V. C., 642
Coyle, 543
Coyle, J., 56
Coyne, S., 224, 643
Craig, I., 307
Craik, F. I. M., 236
Craik, K. H., 13
Crambert, R. F., 367
Crano, W. D., 631
Craske, M., 588

Criglington, A., 151
Crits-Christoph, P., 575
Crockenberg, S., 347
Crogan, M., 647
Crombag, H., 175
Crone, E., 358
Cross, 522
Crouse, E., 10
Crowder, R. G., 233
Crowe, L. C., 177
Crowley, B., 468
Crowther, J., 395
Csikszentmihalyi, M., 314, 315, 378, 406
Cui, X-J., 551
Culbertson, F. M., 552
Cullen, M., 298, 312
Cunningham, M. R., 615
Cupach, W. R., 428
Cupples, A., 258
Curci, A., 245
Curran, P. J., 173
Cutting, A., 355
Cyranowski, J. M., 436, 552
Cytowic, R., 97

Dabbs, J. M., Jr., 640
Dadds, M., 521
Dahloef, P., 159, 160
Dale, N., 253
Dallard, I., 172
Damasio, A., 148
Damasio, A. R., 401
Dandy, J., 312–313
Daniels, 417
Dantzker, M., 432
Darley, J. M., 637, 638
Darroch, J., 356
Darwin, C., 403
Dasen, P. R., 328
Dauringnac, E., 486
Davalos, D., 559
Davidson, J. R. T., 68, 592
Davies, I., 344
Davies, L., 363
Davis, J., 390
Davis, L., 250
Davis, S., 254
Davis-Kean, 425
Dawkins, 449
Dawood, 446
Day, S., 602
D'Azevedo, W. A., 246
Deaux, K., 646

DeBlassie, R. R., 357
DeCasper, A. J., 341
Dedert, E., 481
DeFries, J. C., 92
Degelder, 130
Deinzer, R., 480
de Jong, P., 353
de Lacoste, M., 82
Delgado, J. M. R., 389
DeLongis, A., 461, 463
Delunas, L., 461
DelVecchio, W. F., 514
De Martino, B., 279
Demen, K., 579
Dement, 149
Dement, W., 153
Dement, W. C., 153
Denollet, J., 478
Dent, C. W., 173
Denton, K., 336
Deouell, L., 157
Deovell, L. Y., 74
DePrince, A., 252
De Raad, B., 509
Derrick, B. E., 254
DeSpelder, L., 372
Detterman, D., 311
Devanand, D. P., 595
Devine, P. G., 631, 646
De Vos, S., 370
de Waal, F., 146
Dewald, 414
Dewsbury, D. A., 10
DeYoung, C., 622
Dhand, R., 392
Di Chiara, G., 172
Dickens, W., 308
Dickey, M., 187, 188
Diefendorff, J., 404
Diehl, S. R., 561
Diekstra, R. F. W., 587
Diener, E., 378, 428
Dijksterhuis, A., 645
Dijkstra, M., 633
DiLalla, L. F., 639, 643
Dill, K. E., 225, 226, 643
Dillard, J., 633
DiMaria, C., 179, 616
Din-Dzietham, R., 468
Dion, K., 616
Dipboye, R. L., 616
Dixon, R. A., 369
Dobson, 433
Dodge, K. A., 643
Dodson, C. S., 252
Dohanich, G., 255

Frick, P., 521
Friedland, N., 464
Friedman, J. M., 390
Friedman, M., 477
Friedman, M. I., 389
Friend, R., 482
Friesen, W. V., 404
Frieswijk, 406
Fromkin, H. L., 616
Fujita, F., 428
Fulker, D. W., 92
Fulmer, I., 512
Fung, H., 552
Furnham, A., 512, 516
Furstenberg, F. F., 357

Gable, S., 388
Gadea, M., 58
Gaertner, L., 523
Gajdos, E., 586
Galambos, N., 358
Gallagher, M., 367
Gallagher, T., 576
Gallo, L., 477
Gallup, G., 146, 147
Gallup, G., Jr., 646
Galton, F., 306
Ganellen, R. J., 528
Ganey, H., 385
Gao, J-H., 60
Garavan, H., 303
Garcia, J., 198
Gardner, B. T., 288
Gardner, H., 295
Gardner, R. A., 288
Garfield, C., 276
Garma, L., 159
Garmon, L. C., 335
Garnefski, N., 587
Garrett, J., 605
Garrett, M., 605
Garry, M., 177, 251
Gartner, J., 640
Gary, M., 647
Garza-Mercer, 441, 442
Gatsua, 411
Gatz, M., 588
Gavin, J., 432
Gawin, F. H., 177
Gawronski, B., 613
Gazzaniga, M., 76, 315
Gazzola, N., 599
Ge, X., 356
Geary, N., 389, 390
Gee, C., 312
Geen, R. G., 387

Gefke, M., 364
Gehart, D., 606
Gehring, D., 579
Geiselman, R. E., 250
Geller, E., 216
Gentili, A., 160
George, M., 69
George, M. S., 550
George, T., 593, 594
George, W. H., 177
German, T., 283
Gerrits, M., 172
Gevins, A., 68
Gibbons, A., 289
Gibson, E., 344
Gibson, J., 134, 135
Giedd, J. N., 549
Gigerenzer, G., 279, 280
Gilbert, 405
Gilbert, D., 552, 553
Gilbert, D. T., 613
Gilbert-Rahola, J., 36
Giles, J., 312
Gilibert, D., 614
Gill, K., 177
Gilligan, C., 335
Ginty, D. D., 61, 149
Ginzburg, K., 472
Giraud, A., 82
Girolamo, G., 551
Glantz, L. A., 562
Glaser, 413
Glaser, R., 480
Glass, D. C., 464
Glazer, W. M., 590
Gleaves, D. J., 566
Glenberg, A., 243
Glick, 422
Global Fund to Fight
    AIDS, Tuberculosis, and
    Malaria, 451
Glover, J. A., 266
Gluck, M. A., 62, 253
Godden, D. R., 243
Goeders, N., 173
Gogtay, N., 358
Gökcebay, N., 152
Gold, M., 483
Gold, M. S., 178, 179
Goldberg, L., 511
Goldstein, A. J., 585
Goldstein, D., 280
Goleman, D., 314
Gollan, T., 265, 291
Gonsalves, B., 252
Gonzalez, R., 249

Good, C., 312
Goodglass, H., 78
Goodie, J., 477
Goodman, E., 468
Goodwin, G. M., 591
Goodwin, R., 395, 513
Goossens, L., 369
Gordon, H., 173
Gorman, C., 83
Gosling, 25
Gosling, S. D., 13
Gotlib, I., 513
Gottesman, I. I., 561, 639,
    643
Gottesmann, C., 161
Gough, H., 527
Gould, E. R., 83
Gow, A., 522
Grace, M. C., 467
Graham, D. I., 61
Graham, J. R., 527
Granic, I., 16–17, 427
Granier-Deferre, C., 343
Grant, D., 503
Grant, H., 613
Grant, P., 549
Greden, J. F., 55
Greeff, 437
Green, B. L., 467
Green, D. M., 114
Green, J. P., 175
Green, L. R., 640
Greenberg, L. S., 577
Greenwald, A., 138, 139
Greenwell, L., 384
Greer, M., 606
Gregg, 336
Gregory, R. J., 315, 527
Greist, J. H., 546, 585
Griffiths, 426
Griffiths, M., 279
Grigorenko, E., 296, 297,
    310
Gron, G., 83
Gross, J., 400
Grossenbacher, P., 97
Grossman, E. S., 99
Grossman, H. J., 303
Grossman, J., 585
Grossman, M., 428
Grosz, 417
Gruber, R., 157
Grünbaum, A., 504
Grunberg, N. E., 461
Grusec, J. E., 210
Guadagno, R., 633

Guenole, N., 522
Guilford, J. P., 314
Guilleminault, C., 159
Guinard, J., 119
Gur, R. C., 82
Gurin, J., 390
Gurman, A. S., 579
Gustavsson, A., 74
Guthrie, R., 10

Haag, L., 291
Haas, A. P., 467
Habel, U., 566
Haber, R. N., 245
Haberlandt, D., 14, 314,
    316
Hackel, L. S., 364
Hada, M., 487
Häkkänen, H., 151
Hakuta, K., 292
Halaas, J. L., 390
Halama, P., 295
Halasz, J., 8, 88
Halford, G. S., 331
Hall, 163, 439
Hall, G. S., 355
Hall, L. K., 248
Hallberg, I., 369
Haller, J., 8, 88
Halligan, P. W., 74
Hallon, S., 588, 593
Hallschmid, M., 391
Halmi, K. A., 395
Halperin, 452
Halperin, J. M., 640
Halverson, 418
Ham, P., 591
Hamer, 438, 439
Hamilton, C. S., 549
Hammersmith, S. K., 440
Hampson, S., 512
Hancock, P., 385
Hanley, 413
Hanley, S., 509
Hannover, B., 524
Hanoch, Y., 385
Happell, B., 554
Harackiewicz, A., 388
Harari, E., 503
Hardison, C., 298, 312
Hare, R., 521
Hargadon, R., 170
Harichandan, S., 522
Harkins, S., 625
Harkins, S. G., 625
Harlow, H. F., 347

Karau, S. J., 625
Karnes, F., 311
Karni, A., 153
Karniol, 417
Kass, S., 127
Kastenbaum, R., 372
Katerndahl, D., 504
Katzell, R. A., 388
Kaufman, P., 314
Kawanishi, Y., 590
Kay, 445
Kaye, 445
Kazdin, A., 582
Kean, Y. M., 546
Keating, C. R., 404
Keenan, J., 146
Keesey, 390
Keiding, N., 356
Keitner, G. I., 549
Keks, N., 554
Keller, M. B., 591
Kellett, S., 586
Kellogg, N., 504
Kelly, C., 593, 594
Kelly, K., 213
Kelner, K. L., 52
Kendler, K. S., 395, 545, 551, 561
Kennedy, J. H., 349
Kennedy, Q., 248
Kenney-Benson, G., 422, 425
Kensinger, E., 232
Kenwright, M., 602
Kermer, 553
Kerr, 626
Kertesz, A., 80
Kesner, R., 253
Kessler, R., 539
Kessler, R. C., 546, 551
Ketter, T. A., 550
Kiecolt-Glaser, J., 428, 480
Kiecolt-Glaser, J. K., 480, 482
Kihlstrom, J. F., 169, 170
Kilbride, J. E., 345
Kilbride, P. L., 345
Kilpatrick, D., 466
Kim, H., 355
Kim, J. J., 562
Kim, K. H. S., 293
Kim, Y., 523
Kinder, B. N., 177
King, B., 389
Kinnunen, T., 169
Kinnunen, U., 512

Kinomura, S., 58
Kinsey, A. C., 431, 437
Kirby, S., 313
Kirchner, T., 177
Kirkcaldy, B., 516
Kirkpatrick, L., 420
Kirsch, I., 168, 169, 170
Kisilevsky, B., 341
Kisley, M., 559
Kitayama, S., 403, 522
Kite, M. E., 646
Kittler, J., 393
Kiyatkin, E., 175
Klaczynski, P., 337
Klar, A., 72
Klatzky, R. L., 233
Klein, D., 567
Kleinman, A., 604
Kleitman, N., 153
Klerman, G. L., 575
Kliegl, R., 368
Kliegman, R., 341
Klimkowski, M., 75
Kline, D. W., 367
Kline, G., 364
Klohnen, E., 616
Kluft, R. P., 565
Knickmeyer, 427
Knowlton, B., 251
Knutson, B., 552
Kobasa, S. C., 481
Kochanska, G., 521, 636
Kochavi, D., 390
Kocsis, J. H., 593
Koehler, T., 500
Koelling, A., 198
Koerner, B., 573
Koestner, 417
Kohlberg, L., 332, 333, 334, 336, 416
Köhler, W., 219
Kokkonen, M., 509
Koltz, C., 641
Kon, M. A., 233
Konishi, M., 114
Konkel, A., 264
Kopinska, A., 114
Kopp, C. P., 342
Kopp, M., 127
Korobov, N., 360
Kosslyn, S. M., 275
Koutsky, 449
Koutstaal, W., 252
Kovacs, D., 394
Kowatch, R., 592
Kozak, M. J., 548

Kozel, F., 69
Krantz, D. S., 461
Kranzler, H. R., 545
Kraus, S. J., 631
Krcmar, M., 224
Krebs, D., 336
Krebs, D. L., 335
Kripke, D., 149, 156
Krishman, K. R. R., 68
Kroll, N. E. A., 250
Krosnick, J. A., 631
Krueger, J. M., 153
Krueger, R., 519
Krueger, W. C. F., 266
Kruk, M., 8, 88
Kübler-Ross, E., 371
Kubzansky, L., 478
Kucharska-Pietura, K., 75
Kuehnen, U., 524
Kuhn, D., 328, 626, 630
Kulik, J., 244
Kumar, R., 621
Kumpfer, K., 605
Kunda, Z., 645
Kunz, D., 149, 152
Kuo, C., 516
Kupfer, D. J., 591
Kuroda, K., 284
Kurup, P., 16
Kurup, R., 16

Laboovie, 174
Ladouceur, R., 585
Laenen, A., 292
La France, 426
Lago, T., 640
Lal, S., 11
Lam, L., 313
Lambe, E. K., 394
Lamberg, L., 159
Lambert, B. J., 152
Lambert, M., 566
Lambert, M. J., 579
Lamborn, S. D., 354, 358
Lambright, L., 16
Landry, D. W., 176
Lane, R. C., 349
Lang, A., 30, 31, 244
Lange, C. G., 399
Langer, 432, 437
Langer, E. J., 464
Langer, P., 127
Langevin, B., 159
Langlois, J. H., 615
Lao, J., 626, 630
Larkin, K., 477

Larsen, R., 420
Larson, M., 224
Larsson, H., 521
Latané, B., 625, 637, 638
Latham, G., 388
Latner, J., 394
Lau, M. L., 177
Laudenslager, M., 480
Laumann, 445
Laumann, E. O., 437
Laurent, J., 300
Lauriello, J., 590
Lave, C., 328
Lavie, P., 159
Lawrence, 415
Lawton, B., 113
Layton, L., 354
Lazar, 413
Lazarus, R. S., 400, 461, 463, 470, 472
Lebow, J. L., 579
Lecanuet, J. P., 343
Lecomte, C., 588
Lecomte, T., 588
LeDoux, J., 401
LeDoux, J. E., 61, 75, 401
Lee, C., 481
Lee, I., 253
Lee, J., 213
Lee, K-M., 293
Lee, Y., 127
Leerkes, E., 347
Lefebvre, P., 41
Lehman, D., 16
Leiblum, 446
Leichtman, M. D., 250
Leitenberg, H., 437
Leiter, V., 573
Lenhart, A., 431
Lenneberg, E., 353
Leon, M., 344
Leonardo, E., 55
Lepore, S. J., 642
Lerman, D. C., 582
Lesch, K., 551
Lester, B., 348
Leuchter, A., 590
LeVay, S., 438, 439
Levenson, R. W., 402
Levine, M., 282
Levitsky, D. A., 303
Levitt, I., 354
Levy, J., 76
Levy-Shiff, R., 341
Lewald, J., 83
Lewin, 426

Middlebrooks, J. C., 114
Miele, M., 646
Miles, D. R., 519, 639
Miles, J., 510
Miles, R., 56
Milgram, S., 611, 612, 623
Milkie, M., 364
Miller, B., 357
Miller, G., 482
Miller, G. A., 235
Miller, J., 480, 512
Miller, J. G., 636
Miller, L., 214
Miller, M. B., 315
Miller, N. E., 214, 641
Miller, N. S., 178, 179
Miller, T. Q., 478
Miller, W., 481
Millman, R., 156
Milner, B., 232
Milos, G., 393, 394, 395
Milton, J., 139
Mineka, S., 197, 586
Mirabile, R., 630
Mischel, W., 415, 513, 514
Mishra, R., 246, 330
Mistry, 246
Mistry, J., 246
Mitchell, 438
Mitchell, K. J., 251
Mitler, M. M., 159
Mitsis, E. M., 640
Moeller-Liemkueler, 418
Mogg, K., 591
Mohan, J., 477
Mohanty, A., 291
Mohr, D., 461
Moise, J., 643
Molnar, M., 551
Mombereau, C., 56
Mondloch, C., 97
Monk, T. H., 149
Monteith, M., 646
Montgomery, G., 106, 169
Montgomery, G. H., 169
Montmayeur, J-P., 118
Moradi, 349
Morales, F. R., 153
Moran, M. G., 157
Moreno, R., 188
Morgan, C. D., 529
Morgan, C. L., 244
Morgan, R., 579
Morgan, R. E., 303
Morgenstern, H., 590
Morofushi, M., 149

Morris, J. S., 61
Morris, R., 640
Morris, S., 252
Mos'cicki, E. K., 554
Moseley, B., 349
Moser, G., 461
Most, S., 125
Mount, M., 512
Mounts, N. S., 354
Mourtazaev, M. S., 157
Moynihan, J., 480, 482
Moynihan, R., 573
Mufson, L., 576
Mühlberger, A., 583
Mukerjee, M., 36
Mukherjee, R., 342
Muller, L., 606
Müller, M., 562
Mumtaz, S., 353
Munroe, R. H., 416
Munzar, P., 172
Murphy, 554, 633
Murray, B., 167
Murray, H., 386, 529
Murray, H. A., 529
Murray, J., 225
Musen, G., 251
Myers, C. E., 62, 253
Myers, D. G., 626
Myers, H., 468

Nader, K., 153
Nadon, R., 168
Nalepa, I., 591, 595
NAMI (National Alliance
    for Mental Illness), 544
Namie, G., 459
Namie, R., 459
Narita, M., 121
Narvaez, D., 334
Nash, M., 168, 169
Nash, M. R., 169, 170
National Alliance for Men-
    tal Illness (NAMI), 544
National Center for Chronic
    Disease Prevention and
    Health Promotion, 486
National Center for
    Education Statistics
    (NCES), 42
National Center for Health
    Statistics (NCHS), 356,
    391, 477, 478, 483, 484,
    488, 539, 543, 554
National Institute of Health
    (NIH), 446

National Institute of Mental
    Health (NIMH), 550,
    552
National Institute of Neu-
    rological Disorders and
    Stroke rt-PA Stroke
    Study Group, 83
National Institute on Aging,
    257
National Institute on Drug
    Abuse (NIDA), 180
National Science Founda-
    tion (NSF), 11, 489
Nawrot, M., 177
NCES (National Center
    for Education Statistics),
    42
NCHS (National Center
    for Health Statistics),
    356, 391, 477, 478, 483,
    484, 488, 539, 543, 554
Neale, M. C., 551
Needleman, H. L., 640
Neimark, E. D., 328
Neisser, U., 245, 295
Neitz, J., 92, 107
Neitz, M., 92, 107
Nelson, J. C., 591
Nelson, K., 247
Nelson, T., 148
Nestadt, G., 549
Nestor, P., 69, 253
Nettelbeck, T., 312–313
Neubauer, 423
Newberg, A., 167
Newcomb, 628
Newcombe, N., 226, 426
Newcorn, J. H., 640
Newell, B., 280
Newell, P., 162
Nezworski, M. T., 529
Nguyen, P. V., 254
Nickerson, R. S., 263
NIDA (National Institute
    on Drug Abuse), 180
Niederehe, G., 244
Nieters, J. E., 250
NIH (National Institute of
    Health), 446
NIMH (National Institute
    of Mental Health), 550,
    552
Nisbett, R. E., 613, 616
Nogrady, H., 169
Noise Pollution Council,
    113

Nordentoft, M., 342
Noriko, S., 366
Norman, S., 486
Norman, W., 511
Norris, J. E., 365
Norton, G. R., 565
Norton, M., 631
Nowell, A., 422
Noyes, R., Jr., 592
NSF (National Science
    Foundation), 11, 489
Nunn, J., 97
Nurnberg, 445
Nusbaum, H., 153
Nutt, D., 590, 591
Nyberg, L., 60

O'Brien, C. P., 25, 174
Odbert, J. S., 510
Oden, M. H., 302, 314
O'Donovan, M., 561
Ogawa, A., 394
Ogawa, K. H., 250
Ohman, A., 197
O'Kane, G., 232
Okura, Y., 258
Olatunji, B., 548
O'Leary, K. D., 616
Oleson, K. C., 645
Oliver, J. E., 643
Olivier, C., 613
Olson, M., 477, 478
O'Malley, P. M., 25
O'Neill, S., 582
Ono, H., 420
Oquendo, M., 551
O'Rahilly, S., 390
O'Regan, J., 106
O'Reilly, R. C., 253
Orman, M., 547
Ortega-Alvaro, A., 36
Osborn, D., 370
Ossorio, 484
Öst, L-G., 588
Ostensen, E., 395
Ostrove, J., 337
Otto, M. W., 548, 592
Otto, T., 254
Over, 440
Overby, K., 391
Overmeier, J. B., 214
Owen, M., 561

Padgett, T., 69
Paik, 445
Paivio, S. C., 577

Robin, M., 461
Robins, C. J., 588
Robins, R. W., 13, 14
Robinson, D., 172
Robinson, F., 3
Robinson, J., 349
Robinson, M., 513
Robinson, T., 175
Robles, 480
Robles, T., 480
Rock, I., 125, 219
Rodgers, M., 402
Rodin, J., 389, 464
Rodríguez, C., 522
Roediger, H. L., III, 237
Roehrich, L., 177
Roesch, S. C., 614
Rogers, C. R., 576
Rogers, R. J., 614
Rogge, R., 513
Rogoff, 246
Rogoff, B., 246
Roisman, G., 358
Rolke, B., 125
Romach, M., 592
Rönnqvist, L., 72
Roorda, A., 106
Rosch, E. H., 276, 291
Rose, J., 127, 486
Rose, R. J., 520
Rose, S., 81
Rose-Junius, 411
Rosekind, M. R., 158
Rosen, 445, 446
Rosenbaum, M., 244
Rosenbloom, T., 384
Rosenbluth, R., 99
Rosengren, A., 477
Rosenhan, D. L., 129
Rosenman, R. H., 477
Rosenquist, P., 594
Rosenvinge, J. H., 395
Rosenzweig, M. R., 114
Ross, 427
Ross, C. A., 565, 566
Ross, D., 224
Ross, J., 591
Ross, R., 559
Ross, S. A., 224
Rossow, I., 486
Roth, T., 159, 160
Rothblum, E., 364
Rotter, J. B., 515
Rotton, J., 641
Rouse, S. V., 528
Rowe, D., 640

Rowe, D. C., 513
Rowe, J., 370
Rowe, W., 139
Rowland, 446
Rozell, E., 313
Ruan, 448
Rubinstein, G., 606
Ruble, D., 418
Ruble, D. N., 364
Ruby, N., 149
Rudman, L., 647
Ruggero, M. A., 115
Ruiz, J., 477
Ruiz, P., 585
Rumbaugh, D., 288, 290
Ruscio, J., 472
Rushton, J., 311
Rushton, J. P., 519
Russell, T., 139
Ryan, R., 523
Ryburn, M., 300

Sachs, G., 592
Sackeim, H. A., 549, 595
Sackett, P., 298, 312
Sacks, O., 564
Saczynski, J., 368
Sadeh, A., 157
Sahoo, F., 522
Sahoo, K., 522
Salary.com, 411
Salat, D., 232
Salisch, M., 404
Salmon, J., 488
Salomon, K., 468
Salovey, P., 313, 405, 464, 646
Salthouse, T. A., 368
Sample, J., 527
Sanbonmatsu, D. M., 630
Sander, L. W., 348
Sandler, I., 463
Sandvik, E., 428
Sanes, J. N., 78
Santiago-Rivera, A., 605
Saper, C., 61
Sarrio, M., 365
Sastry, R., 176
Sateia, M. J., 159
Sattler, J., 309
Saudino, K., 347
Sauron, C., 172
Savage, M., 357
Savage-Rumbaugh, E. S., 288, 289, 290
Sawchuk, C., 548

Saxon, S., 647
Sayette, M., 177
Scammell, T., 61
Scarr, S., 307
Schachter, S., 400
Schacter, D. L., 252
Schaie, K., 363, 368, 369
Schaie, K. W., 368
Schakel, L., 313
Schauer, P., 392
Schechtman, K. B., 159
Schellenberg, E., 308
Schenck, C. H., 158
Scherer, K. R., 403, 404
Scheurink, A. J., 389
Schieber, M. H., 78
Schiff, M., 308
Schizophrenia.com, 594
Schlosberg, S., 431
Schmidt, P., 366
Schmitt, T., 15
Schneider, E., 225
Schneider, P., 602
Schneider, R., 167
Schnyder, U., 393
Schoeller, D., 488
Schofield, J. W., 355
Scholz, U., 515
Schou, M., 591
Schuckit, M., 173
Schulter, G., 402
Schultz, W., 55
Schwartz, G. E., 476
Schwartz, S., 161
Schwebke, 448
Scollon, C., 378
Scott, A., 432
Scott, S. K., 61
Scully, J., 461
Seagal, J., 472
Sears, R. R., 641
Sedikides, C., 523
Seegert, C., 215
Seeman, M., 167
Seeman, T., 167, 482
Seenoo, K., 637
Segal, Z., 167, 585
Segall, M. H., 138
Seger, C. A., 74
Self, M., 104
Seligman, M., 378, 406, 422, 425, 553
Seligman, M. E. P., 197, 214, 480, 599
Sell, 438
Selye, H., 469

Semeniuk, T., 599
Semple, M. N., 114
Sensky, T., 588
Sentenac, J., 274
Sepkowitz, 449
Serido, J., 367
Serpell R., 354
Severink, 406
Severson, S., 215
Shackelford, T., 15, 420
Shaffer, D., 554
Shaffer, D. R., 630
Shahabi, L., 481
Shanks, D., 280
Sharma, S., 158
Sharp, D., 328
Shaunessy, E., 311
Shaw, J. I., 613
Shaw, J. S., III, 250
Shaw, V. N., 177
Shears, J., 349
Sheehan, D. V., 591
Sheffield, F. D., 633
Shelton, 452
Shelton, J., 646
Shenfield, T., 291
Shephard, R., 516
Shepperd, J., 638
Sher, A. E., 159
Sher, L., 478, 550
Sherif, C. W., 644, 647
Sherif, M., 644, 645, 647
Shevrin, H., 138
Shiba, Y., 118
Shiffrin, R. M., 233
Shikani, A., 176
Shikina, I., 175
Shillito, D., 146
Shimamura, A. P., 369
Shinar, D., 127
Shiner, R., 512
Shlaer, S., 102
Shneidman, E. S., 303, 555
Shumaker, S., 255
Siegel, R., 147
Siegler, I. C., 369
Siegler, R. S., 331
Siegrist, J., 477
Sigvardsson, S., 639
Silbersweig, D., 574
Silva, C. E., 168
Silverberg, N., 291
Simon, G., 489
Simon, H., 278
Simon, H. B., 488
Simons, D., 125, 126

Tractinsky, N., 127
Trautner, 416, 419
Traverso, A., 395
Triandis, H. C., 404
Trijsburg, R., 599
Triplett, N., 624
Trivedi, M. J., 596
Troglauer, T., 126
Troxel, W., 467
Trull, T., 566
Tsai, J., 552
Tsai, S., 554
Tsaur, C., 516
Tsoh, J. Y., 395
Tulving, 239
Tulving, E., 236, 239, 243, 253, 264
Turan, K., 535
Turk, J., 342
Turner, 446
Turner, J. C., 644
Turner, P., 358
Tversky, A., 278, 280
Tweed, R., 16
Twenge, 432

Uchino, B. N., 482
Ullian, D. Z., 416
Ullrich, N., 119
Ulupinar, P., 127
Umberson, D., 364
UMTRI (University of Michigan Transportation Research Institute), 226
Underwood, B. J., 264
U.S. Census Bureau, 363, 365, 367, 369, 483
U.S. Department of Energy, 89
U.S. Department of Health and Human Services, 180, 484, 485
U.S. Food and Drug Administration (FDA), 179, 590, 591
University of Michigan Transportation Research Institute (UMTRI), 226
Urry, H., 71
Usher, 426
Ushikubo, M., 371
Utsey, S., 467, 468

Vaccarino, V., 482
Vaillant, G. E., 551

Valkonen, R., 369
Van Assema, P., 633
Van Boven, L., 613
Van Cauter, E., 157
Van der Elst, W., 369
vander Leij, A., 353
Van der Zee, K., 313
Van Domburg, R., 478
van Elst, L. T., 640
Van Groen, T., 61
Van Knippenberg, A., 645
Van Lancker, D., 74
Van Lommel, S., 292
van Raaij, W., 633
van Schie, E. G., 643
van Vianen, A., 365
Van Vugt, M., 636
Vargha-Khadem, F., 62, 253
Varley, A., 370
Varnado, P. J., 395
Vasterling, J., 467
Vaugeois, P., 178
Verdejo-García, A., 178, 180
Verhaeghen, P., 369
Vessicchio, J., 593, 594
Vetulani, J., 591, 595
Viding, E., 521
Viemerö, V., 643
Vieta, E., 592
Villegas, A., 249
Vincent, M., 565
Vingerhoets, G., 75
Visser, P., 630
Visser, P. S., 631
Vitello, P., 113
Vitouch, O., 385
Vitousek, K., 394
Voelbel, 174
Vogel, M., 60, 590
Vogel, P. J., 76
Volis, C., 646
Volkow, N. D., 180
Volling, B., 348
von Knorring, A. L., 639
Votruba, S., 488
Voyer, D., 402
Vrooman, 130
Vygotsky, L. S., 332

Wacker, J., 510
Wade, T., 179, 616
Wagner, A., 71
Wagner, A. R., 196
Wagner, D., 162

Waite, 437
Wald, G., 106
Waldron, S., 599
Wales, 414
Walitzer, K., 579
Walk, R. D., 344
Walker, 602
Walker, E., 560, 562
Walker, I., 647
Walker, L., 336
Walker, M., 153
Wall, P. D., 120
Wallace, N., 636
Wallbott, H. G., 403, 404
Walsh, B., 590
Walsh, D., 225
Walster, E., 616
Walster, G. W., 616
Walters, C. C., 210
Walton, K., 167
Wang, X., 225
Warburton, J., 337
Ward, C., 149
Wark, G. R., 335
Warner, T., 355
Warshaw, M. G., 591
Washington University School of Medicine, 76
Waterman, A., 337
Watson, D., 500, 538
Watson, J. B., 11, 194, 195
Webb, W., 149, 153
Webb, W. B., 163
Weber, R., 225
Wechsler, D., 301
Weekes, J. R., 169
Weeks, D. L., 221
Wegener, D. T., 629
Weigman, O., 643
Weinberg, M. S., 440
Weinberg, R., 307
Weiner, I. B., 528, 529
Weingarten, H. P., 389
Weissman, M. M., 552
Weisz, J., 578
Weitzman, 483
Wells, 432
Wells, D. L., 116
Wells, G. L., 249, 250
Wenk, G., 255
Wertheimer, M., 135
Wertz, 413
Wesensten, N., 152, 175
Westerhof, G., 372
Westling, B. E., 588
Weström, 447

Wetherell, J., 588
Wethington, E., 367
Wheeler, 239
Wheeler, J., 138
Wheeler, M., 253
Whisenhunt, B. L., 394
Whisman, M., 578
Whitaker-Azimitia, P. M., 640
Whitam, F. L., 439
White, D. P., 159
White, S. D., 357
Whitehead, B., 364
Whitehead, B. D., 363, 364
Whitehurst, G. J., 353
Whitman-Elia, 414
WHO (World Health Organization), 434, 446
Whorf, B. L., 290
Wickelgren, I., 367
Wicker, A. W., 631
Widom, C. S., 210, 252, 643
Wiesel, T. N., 103
Wigboldus, D., 645
Wilback, K., 616
Wilhelm, I., 636
Wilhelm, K., 466
Wilhelmsen, L., 477
Wilken, J. A., 398, 399
Wilkinson, R., 357
Williams, C. J., 631
Williams, D. R., 106
Williams, J., 258
Williams, K., 625
Williams, K. D., 625
Williams, L. M., 252
Williams, M., 167
Williamson, G. M., 480
Willis, S., 368
Wilson, F. R., 72
Wilson, G., 438, 439
Wilson, G. T., 583
Wilson, M. A., 62
Wilson, T., 394
Wilson, T. D., 616
Wilson, W., 178
Wilson, W. H., 175
Winerman, L., 11
Winograd, E., 265
Winokur, G., 549
Winter, D., 511
Wise, R., 175
Wiseman, R., 139
Witt, L., 512

Antidepressants, 590–591
disadvantages of, 593
premature ejaculation and, 446
sexual arousal and, 445
Antigens, 479
Antipsychotics, 589–590
disadvantages of, 593
smoking and, 593–594
Antiretroviral drugs, 451
Anvil (ossicle), 111–112
Anxiety, separation, 348
Anxiety disorders, 543–549
agoraphobia, 545
definition of, 543–544
generalized, 545
obsessive-compulsive disorder, 547–549
panic attacks, 544–545
panic disorder, 545–546
social phobia, 543, 546
specific phobia, 546
treatment of, 590–591
APA (American Psychological Association), 42
Aphasia, 78, 80
Applied research, 7
Approach-approach conflict, 463–464
Approach-avoidance conflict, 464
Aptitude tests, 298
Archetypes, 504
Armed Services Vocational Aptitude Battery (ASVAB), 298
Armstrong, Rebekka, 450, 451
Arousal, 382–385
aggression and, 640
Arousal theory, 382
Arthritis in late adulthood, 367–368
Artificial intelligence, 14, 283–284
Artificial neural networks (ANNs), 284
Asian Americans
health among, 483
in- and out-groups and, 645
in psychology, 11
smoking among, 484
Assimilation in Piaget's theory, 326
"Assisted suicide," 372
Association(s), loosening of, 558–559
Association areas, 71
Astin, John, 535
Astin, Mackenzie, 535
Astin, Sean, 535–536
ASVAB (Armed Services Vocational Aptitude Battery), 298
Atmospheric perspective, 134, 135

Attachment, 347–349
avoidant, 348
disorganized/disoriented, 349
resistant, 348
secure, 348
Attacking Anxiety, 579
Attention
observational learning and, 222
perception and, 125–128
Attitudes, 629–631
cognitive dissonance and, 631–632
persuasion and, 632–633
sexual. See Sexual attitudes and behavior
social, toward gays and lesbians, 441
Attraction, 614–619
factors influencing, 615–616
romantic, 616–619
Attribution, 613–614
situational, 613
Audience, imaginary, 328
Audience effects, 624
Audition, 111
Auditory canal, 111, 112
Australian Aboriginals
children of, 328, 330
women of, 246–247
Authoritarian parents, 354
Authoritative parents, 354
Autokinetic illusion, 134–135
Automatic thoughts, 588
Autonomic nervous system, 63, 64
aggression and, 640
Autonomy versus shame and doubt stage, 337
Autosomes, 89
Availability heuristic, 278, 279
Aversion therapy, 585
Avoidance-avoidance conflict, 464
Avoidance learning, 212–213
Avoidant attachment, 348
Awareness-raising campaigns, 573–574
Axons, 50, 51
AZT, 451

Babbling, 351
Backward search, 281
Balancing
brain and, 74
kinesthetic and vestibular senses and, 121–122
Bandura, Albert, 224
Barbiturates, 177
Bargaining stage of dying, 372

Bartlett, Sir Frederick, 247
Basic emotions, 402–404
Basic research, 7
Basic trust versus mistrust stage, 337
BBC Prison Experiment, 628–629
B cells, 479
Beckham, Albert Stanley, 10
Behavior
abnormal, 536–537
grossly disorganized, 559
prosocial, 636–638
sexual. See Sexual attitudes and behavior
Behavioral assessment, 523
Behavioral genetics, 92
intelligence and, 306–307
Behaviorism, 11–12, 194
Behavior modification, 214–216, 581–583
Behavior therapies, 581–586
aversion therapy, 585
based on classical conditioning, 583–586
based on observational learning, 586
based on operant conditioning, 582–583
exposure and response prevention, 585
flooding, 583, 585
Bell, Alexander Graham, 110–111
Bell curve, 301–302
Bem Sex Role Inventory (BSRI), 417
Benshoof, Tony, 2
Benzodiazepines, 177, 592
Berger, Hans, 67
Bias
confirmation, 283
in experimental research, 32–34
experimenter, 33–34
observer, 23
positive, memory and, 248
selection, 33
self-serving, 614
Biased samples, 25
Bilateral ECT, 594–595
Bilingualism, 291
Binet, Alfred, 299, 300
Binet-Simon Intelligence Scale, 299
Binocular depth cues, 132–133
Binocular disparity, 133
Biofeedback, 214
Biological clock, 149
Biological perspective on psychological disorders, 540, 541
Biological predispositions, 197–198

Biological psychology, 15–16
Biological sex, 412, 413–414
  development of, 413–414
Biomedical model of illness, 475–476
Biomedical therapies, 574, 588–596
    See also Drug therapy
  electroconvulsive therapy, 594–595
  surgical, 595–596
Biopsychosocial model of health and
    illness, 476
Biopsychosocial perspective on psy-
    chological disorders, 540, 541
Bipolar disorder, 535–536, 550
Birds, language in, 290
Blindness
  color, 92, 106
  inattentional, 125–126
Blind spot, 101, 103, 104
Blood cholesterol, 488, 489
Blood glucose, 389
Blood pressure in late adulthood, 367
Body mass index (BMI), 389–390
Body temperature, daily fluctuations
    in, 149
Body weight
  health and, 488
  obesity and weight loss and, 391–392
  variations in, 389–391
Bone conduction, 114
Bono, 451
Boring, E. G., 136
Bottom-up processing, 128
Bounded rationality, 278
Boyle, Robert, 110
Brain, 58–63, 67–85
  aggression and, 640
  aging of, 83
  AIDS and, 438
  alcohol abuse and, 486–487
  body weight and, 390–391
  cerebrum of, 69, 70–76
  circadian rhythms and, 149–150
  developing, 81–82
  drug effects on, 172–173
  EEG and, 67–68
  emotion and, 401–402
  forebrain, 58, 59, 61–63
  frontal lobes of, 76–78
  gender differences in, 82–83
  genetic influences on, 89–92
  hindbrain, 58, 59, 60
  hormonal influences on, 86–89
  hunger and, 389
  imaging of, 68–69
  learning languages and, 293
  memory and, 253–254

midbrain, 58, 59, 60
  mood disorders and, 550–551
  occipital lobes of, 79–80
  parietal lobes of, 79
  plasticity of, 63, 78, 82
  schizophrenia and, 562, 563, 593
  sexual orientation and, 438–439
  sleep cycles and, 154–155
  split, 75–76, 77
  temporal lobes of, 80–81
  vision and, 102–104
Brainstem, 58
Brain surgery, 595–596
Brightness, 105
Brightness constancy, 132
Broca, Paul, 78
Broca's area, 78, 293
BSRI (Bem Sex Role Inventory), 417
Bulimia nervosa, 395
The Bully at Work (Namie and
    Namie), 459–460
Bullying, 459–460
Burnout, 466
Bystander effect, 637–638

Caffeine, 175
California Personality Inventory
    (CPI), 527
California Test of Mental Maturity,
    301
Calkins, Mary Whiton, 10
Callous-unemotional (CU) traits, 521
Cancer, 478–479
Cannon-Bard theory of emotion, 400
Cardinal traits, 510
Careers, 365–366
Case, Robbie, 331
Case study (case history), 23–24
Catastrophes, prosocial behavior and,
    636, 638
Catastrophic events, 466–467
Catatonic schizophrenia, 560
Catharsis, 504
Cattell, Raymond, 510
CCK (cholecystokinin), 389
Cell body of neurons, 50, 51
Cell phones, using while driving,
    126–127
Central nervous system (CNS),
    57–63. *See also* See also Brain;
    Spinal cord
Central traits, 510
Cerebellum, 59, 60
Cerebral cortex, 59, 70
  of left hemisphere, 73
Cerebral hemispheres, 70, 71–76

handedness and, 72–73
  left, 71, 73
  right, 74–75
  specialization of, 71, 82
  split brain studies of, 75–76, 77
Cerebrum, 69
  contents of, 70–71
  hemispheres of, 70, 71–76
Challenge, hardiness and, 481
Chancre (in syphilis), 448
Chicken pox during pregnancy, 341
Childhood
  early, 338
  experiences in, sexual orientation
    and, 440–441
  language development in, 351–354
  middle, 338
  socialization in, 354–355
Chimpanzees, language in, 288–290
Chlamydia, 446, 447
Choices, making, as stressor, 463–464
Cholecystokinin (CCK), 389
Chromosomes, 89
  sex, 89, 92, 413
Cigarette smoking. *See* Smoking
Cingulotomy, 596
Cingulum, 596
Circadian rhythms, 149–152
  disruptions in, 151–152
  influence of, 149
Circadian theory of sleep, 152
Circumcision
  AIDS transmission and, 452
  female, 434
Clairvoyance, 139
Clark, Kenneth, 10, 11
Clark, Mamie Phipps, 10–11
Classical conditioning, 189–201
  behavior therapies based on,
    583–586
  biological predispositions and,
    197–198
  cigarette smoking and, 223
  cognitive perspective on, 196–197
  definition of, 189
  discrimination and, 193
  emotional, 194–196
  in everyday life, 198–199
  extinction and, 192, 193
  generalization and, 192, 193
  higher-order, 192
  Pavlov's contributions to, 189–192
  process of, 189–192
  spontaneous recovery and, 192
  stimulus and, 189
Claustrophobia, 546

Client-centered therapy, 13, 509, 576–577
Clinical psychologists, 42, 604
Clinical social workers (MSWs), 604
Clomipramine, 591
Closure, perceptual organization and, 130, 131
Clozapine, 590
Clusters of personality disorders, 566, 567
CNS. See Brain; Central nervous system (CNS); Spinal cord
Coaction effects, 624
Cocaine, 176–177
  during pregnancy, 342
Cochlea, 122
Cocktail party phenomenon, 126
Cognition, 275–285. See also Memory; Perception; Sensation
  artificial intelligence and, 283–284
  concepts and, 276–277
  decision making and, 277–281
  imagery and, 275–276
  problem solving and, 281–283
  social, 645
Cognitive abilities
  gender differences in, 421–426
  measurement of, 298, 301. See also Intelligence tests
Cognitive Abilities Test, 301
Cognitive appraisal, 400
Cognitive-behavioral approaches, 586–588
Cognitive development
  information processing approach to, 331
  Piaget's theory of, 326–330
  Vygotsky's sociocultural approach to, 331–332
Cognitive-developmental theory of gender role development, 416
Cognitive dissonance, 631–632
Cognitive function
  in adulthood, 363
  alcohol abuse and, 486–487
  in late adulthood, 368–369
Cognitive learning, 219–227
  cognitive maps and, 220
  by insight, 219
  latent, 220, 221
  observational (social-cognitive), 220–222, 223
  from television and electronic games, 222, 224–226
Cognitive maps, 220
Cognitive-neoassociationist model of aggression, 641–642

Cognitive perspective
  on classical conditioning, 196–197
  on psychological disorders, 541
Cognitive processes, 219
Cognitive psychology, 13–14
Cognitive theory
  of dreaming, 163
  of stress, 470–471
Cognitive therapies, 586–588
  of Beck, 588
  rational emotive therapy, 586–587
Cohort effect, 323
Coitus, 435
Collective unconscious, 504
Color blindness, 106
  red-green, 92
"Colored hearing," 99
Color vision, 104–107
  theories of, 105–107
Commitment, hardiness and, 481
Companionate love, 618, 619
Compazine, 590
Compliance, 623–624
Componential intelligence, 296, 297
Comprehensive System, 529
Compulsions, 548
Compulsive gambling, 206
Computerized axial tomography (CT scans), 68
Concept(s), 276–277
Concept-driven processing, 128
Concrete operations stage, 327–328
Conditioned response (CR), 191
Conditioned stimulus (CS), 191
Conditioning. See Classical conditioning; Operant conditioning
Conditions of worth, 509
Cones (of retina), 102
Confederates, 612
Confirmation bias, 283
Conflict
  approach-approach, 463–464
  approach-avoidance, 464
  avoidance-avoidance, 464
Conformity, 621–622
Confounding variables, 32–33
Congruence in client-centered therapy, 577
Conscience, 499
  failure to develop, 521
Conscientiousness in five-factor model, 512
Conscious in Freud's theory, 498
Consciousness, 145–182
  altered states of. See Altered states of consciousness; Psychoactive drugs; Sleep

changing views of, 147–148
circadian rhythms and, 149–152
definition of, 147
dreaming and, 161–163
psychoactive drugs and. See Psychoactive drugs
sleep and. See Sleep
Consequences Test, 315–316
Conservation in concrete operations stage, 327–328, 329
Consolidation failure, 254
Constant critic, 459
Constitutional vulnerability, schizophrenia and, 561
Consummate love, 618, 619
Contact comfort, 347
Context, memory and, 243–244
Contextual intelligence, 296, 297
Continuity, perceptual organization and, 130, 131
Continuous reinforcement, 204
Control
  dissociated, theory of, 170
  hardiness and, 481
  locus of, 515–516
Control groups, 32
Controlled substances, 172
Conventional level, 333
Convergence, 132–133
Convergent thinking, 314–315
Conversion disorder, 564
Convolutions, 71
Cooing, 351
Cooperation. See Prosocial behavior
Coping, 471–472
Cornea, 100, 101
Coronary heart disease, 476–478
Corpus callosum, 59, 70
Correlation(s), 26–29
  positive and negative, 26
Correlational method, 26–29
Corticoids, 88
Cortisol
  emotion and, 428
  memory and, 255
Counseling psychologists, 42, 604
Couple therapy, 578–579
The Courage to Heal (Bass and Davis), 250–251
Covey, Stephen, 2
Cowell, Simon, 558
CPI (California Personality Inventory), 527
CR (conditioned response), 191
Crack, 177
  during pregnancy, 342
Cramming, 238

Creativity, 314–316
Credit scores, 29
Crick, Francis, 89
Criterion-referenced achievement
    tests, 298
Critical periods, 342
Critical thinking, 40
Cross-modal perception, 129–130
Cross-sectional studies, 323, 324
Crowding, 642
Crystallized intelligence, 368
CS (conditioned stimulus), 191
CT scans (computerized axial
    tomography), 68
Culturally sensitive therapy, 604–605
Culture
    altered states of consciousness and,
        148–149
    altruism and, 636–637
    attraction and, 615–616
    cognitive development and, 328,
        330
    death and dying and, 372
    gender roles and, 416
    illusions and, 137–138
    infant development and, 345
    memory and, 246–247
    mood disorders and, 551–552, 553
    personality and, 521–523
    phonological awareness and, 354
    punishment and, 212
    sexual attitudes and behavior and,
        433–434
    social loafing and, 625
Culture-fair intelligence tests, 311
Cumulative recorders, 208
CU (callous-unemotional) traits, 521

DA (dopamine), 55
Dahmer, Jeffrey, 537
Dani people, language and, 291
Darby, Joe, 627
Dark adaptation, 102
Darwin, Charles, 9, 15
Data-driven processing, 128
Day, Sean, 99
dB (decibels), 110–111
Dean, John, 627
Death, 371–373
Decay theory, 263
Decibels (dB), 110–111
Decision making, 277–281
    elimination by aspects approach to,
        278
    framing and, 280
    heuristics in, 278–280
    intuition and, 280–281

Decision making in groups, 626–628
Declarative memory, 236, 239
"Deep Blue," 284
"Deep Junior," 284
Deep sleep, 154, 155
Defense mechanisms, 500, 501
Degeneres, Ellen, 439
Deindividuation, 628
Delta waves, 154, 155
Delusions, 558
Dement, William, 159
Dementia, 257–258
Dendrites, 50, 51
Denial, 501
Denial stage of dying, 372
Depakote (Divalproex), 550, 592
Dependent variable, 31–32
Depressants, 173, 177–178
Depression
    major, 550
    psychotic, 549
    treatment of, 590–591
Depression stage of dying, 372
Depth perception, 132–134
    in infancy, 344–345
Derailment, 558–559
Descriptive research methods, 22–29
    case study (case history), 23–24
    correlational method, 24–26
    laboratory observation, 23
    naturalistic observation, 22–23
    survey, 24–26
Designer drugs, 179–180
Development
    of biological sex, 413–414
    cognitive, 326–331
    of gender roles, 415–420
    of language, 351–354
    moral, 332–336
    prenatal, 338, 341–343
    psychosexual stages of, 500–503
    psychosocial, 336–338
    social, in adulthood, 363–367
    stages in, 323, 333–338
Developmental psychologists, 43
Developmental psychology
    approaches to studying, 323–324
    definition of, 322
    issues in, 322–323
*Diagnostic and Statistical Manual of
    Mental Disorders (DSM-IV-TR)*,
    537–539
DID (dissociative identity disorder),
    565–566
Diet, health and, 488
Dieting, 392
Difference threshold, 98–99

Diffusion of responsibility, 637–638
Diffusion tensor imaging (DTI), 69
Directive therapy, 577
Discrimination
    in classical conditioning, 193
    definition of, 643
    in operant conditioning, 209
    roots of, 644–646
Discriminative stimulus, 209
Disinhibitory effect, 222
Disorganized/disoriented attachment,
    349
Disorganized schizophrenia, 560
Displaced aggression, 641
Displacement, 501
Display rules, 404
Dissociated control, theory of, 170
Dissociative amnesia, 565
Dissociative disorders, 564–566
Dissociative fugue, 564, 565
Dissociative identity disorder (DID),
    565–566
Divalproex (depakote), 550, 592
Divergent thinking, 314–315
Diversity education, 647
Divorce, 364
Dolphins, language in, 290
Dominant-recessive pattern, 91
Door-in-the-face technique, 623
Dopamine (DA), 55
Double-blind technique, 34
"Downers," 173, 177–178
Dream(s), 153, 161–163
    cognitive theory of, 163
    content of, 161–162
    evolutionary theory of, 163
    interpretation of, 162–163
Dream analysis, 574–575
Drive(s), primary, 388
Drive-reduction theory, 380–382
Drug dependence
    physical, 174
    psychological, 174–175
Drug therapy, 573–574
    awareness-raising campaigns and,
        573–574
    disadvantages of, 593
    for mood disorders, 550
    for psychological disorders,
        589–593
Drug use during pregnancy, 342
*DSM-IV-TR (Diagnostic and Statistical
    Manual of Mental Disorders)*,
    537–539
DTI (diffusion tensor imaging), 69
Duke, Patty, 535–536, 550
Dying, 371–373

Dynamic assessment, 311
Dyspareunia, 446
Dyssomnias, 159

Ear, 111–114
Eardrum, 111, 112
Early adulthood, 338. *See also*
    Adulthood
Early childhood, 338. *See also*
    Childhood
Early intervention, intelligence and,
    307–310
"Easy" children, 345–346
Eating disorders, 392–395
Ebbinghaus, Hermann, 261
Eclectic position, 19
Ecstasy, 179–180
Ectopic pregnancy, 447
Educational psychologists, 44
EEG. *See* Electroencephalogram
    (EEG)
Ego
    in Freud's theory, 499
    in Jung's theory, 504
Egocentrism
    adolescent, 328
    in preoperational stage, 327
Ego ideal, 499
Ego integrity versus despair stage, 337
Eidetic memory, 245
Einstein, Albert, 315, 385, 510
Ejaculation, premature, 446
Electroconvulsive therapy, 594–595
Electroencephalogram (EEG), 68
    during sleep, 154–155
Electromagnetic waves, 100
Electronic games, learning from, 222,
    224–226
Elektra complex, 501, 502
Elimination by aspects, 278
Embryo, period of, 341, 342
Emerging adulthood, 358–360
Emotion(s), 379, 398–406
    basic, 402–404
    brain and, 401–402
    conditioning of, 194–196
    definition of, 398
    expression of, 402–405
    gender differences in, 428
    theories of, 398–401
Emotional intelligence, 313–314
Emotion-focused coping, 471–472
Empathy, 313–314, 636
Empty love, 618
Empty nest syndrome, 366
Encoding failure, 263

Endocrine system, 86–89
Endorphins, 56, 121
Enrichment, intelligence and,
    307–310
Enron, 627
Epinephrine, 55
    memory and, 255
    REM sleep and, 153
Episodic memory, 239
Erectile dysfunction, 444–445
Erikson, Erik, 336
Erogenous zones, 500
Escape learning, 212
Eskimo people, language and,
    290–291
ESP (extrasensory perception), 139
Estrogen
    memory and, 255
    sexual response cycle and, 436
Estrogens, 88–89
E-therapy, 602–603
Ethics in research, 34–36, 195
Ethnocentrism, 646
Euthanasia, passive and active, 372
Evolutionary psychology, 14–15
Evolutionary theory
    of dreaming, 163
    of gender role development,
        419–420
    of sleep, 152
Excitement phase of sexual response
    cycle, 435
Exemplars, 277
Exercise, health and, 488–489
Exhaustion stage of general adapta-
    tion syndrome, 470
Existential intelligence, 295
Experiential intelligence, 296, 297
Experiment(s), 28
Experimental groups, 32
Experimental method, 30–34
    bias in, 32–34
    experimental and control groups
        in, 32
    limitations of, 34
Experimental psychologists, 43
Experimenter bias, 33–34
Expert systems, 284
Explicit memory, 236, 239
Exposure and response prevention,
    585
External locus of control, 515–516
Extinction
    in classical conditioning, 192, 193
    in operant conditioning, 208
Extrasensory perception (ESP), 139

Extraversion, 510
    in five-factor model, 512
Extrinsic motivation, 380, 381
Eye, 100–102
Eyewitness testimony, 249–250
Eysenck, Hans, 510

Facial-feedback hypothesis, 405
Facilitation effect, 222
Family therapy, 578, 579
Fantasy, sexual arousal and, 437
Farsightedness, 102
Fatuous love, 619
Fears. *See also* Phobias
    hierarchy of, 583, 584
    of public speaking, overcoming,
        547
Feature detectors, 104
Fechner, Gustav, 8
Feeding center, 389
Female circumcision, 434
Female genital mutilation, 434
Female orgasmic disorder, 445–446
Female sexual arousal disorder, 444
Feminine gender role, 414
Fetal alcohol effects, 342
Fetal alcohol syndrome, 342
Fetus, 341
    period of, 341, 342
Fight-or-flight response, 63, 88, 460,
    472
    hormones and, 255
Figure-ground perception, 130, 131
FI (fixed-interval) schedule, 206
Five-factor model, 511–513
Fixations, 500
Fixed-interval (FI) schedule, 206
Fixed-ratio (FR) schedule, 204
Flashbacks, with LSD, 179
Flashbulb memories, 244–245
Flat affect, 559
Flooding, 583, 585
Fluoxetine (Prozac), 591
Flynn effect, 310
fMRI (functional MRI), 69
Foot-in-the-door technique, 623
Forebrain, 58, 59, 61–63
Forensic psychology, 42, 497
Forgetting, 261–268
    curve of, 261–262
    motivated, 265
    prospective, 265
    reasons for, 262–265
Formal academic knowledge, 296
Formal concepts, 276
Formal operations stage, 328

Fovea, 101, 102
Fragile-X syndrome, 92
Frames of mind, 295, 296
Framing, 280
Franklin, Benjamin, 2
Franklin, Jamon, 554
Franklin, Les, 554
Free association, 574
Frequency of sound waves, 110–111
Frequency theory, 115
Freud, Sigmund, 12, 24, 147, 164, 498, 639
   psychoanalytic theory of, 498–504
Frontal lobes, 76–78
FR (fixed-ratio) schedule, 204
Frustration-aggression hypothesis, 640, 641
Fugue, dissociative, 564, 565
Fullness center, 389
Full-scale IQ, 301
Fully functioning person, 509
Functional fixedness, 282–283
Functionalism, 9–10
Functional MRI (fMRI), 69
Fundamental attribution error, 614

GABA. *See* Gamma-aminobutyric acid (GABA)
Gage, Phineas, 49, 78, 83
Gamblers Anonymous, 579
Gambling, compulsive, 206
Gamma-aminobutyric acid (GABA), 56
   mood disorders and, 551
   schizophrenia and, 563
Ganzfeld procedure, 139
GAS (general adaptation syndrome), 469–470
Gastric bypass surgery, 274, 391–392
Gate-control theory, 120–121
Gatekeeper, 459
Gay men. *See* Homosexuality
Gender, 421–428
   aggression and, 640
   brain differences and, 82–83
   cognitive abilities and, 421–426
   definition of, 412
   emotion and, 428
   five personality factors and, 513
   health and, 482
   mood disorders and, 552
   psychological, 414–415
   social behavior and personality and, 426–427
   suicide and, 554, 555
Gender identity, 414

Gender roles, 414
   development of, 415–420
Gender schema theory, 418–419
Gender-sensitive therapy, 606
Gender stability, 416
Gender stereotypes, reasons for, 422
Gene-environment interactions, sexual orientation and, 439–440
General adaptation syndrome (GAS), 469–470
Generalizability, 41–42
Generalization
   in classical conditioning, 192, 194
   in operant conditioning, 209
Generalized anxiety disorder, 545
Generativity versus stagnation stage, 337
Genes, 89
Genetic counseling, 90–91
Genetic factors
   aggression and, 639–640
   alcoholism and, 487
   intelligence and, 306–307
   mood disorders and, 551
   sexual orientation and, 439
Genetics, 89–92
   behavioral, 92, 306–307
Genital(s), 413
Genital herpes, 449
Genital mutilation, female, 434
Genital stage, 502
Genital warts, 448–449
Genotype, 89, 91
Genovese, Kitty, 636
Genuineness in client-centered therapy, 577
Germinal stage, 341, 342
Gestalt psychology, 13–14, 130–132
Gestalt therapy, 577
Gibson, James, 134
GlaxoSmithKline (GSK), 573
Glial cells, 50, 52
Glucocorticoids, response to stress and, 470
Glucose, blood, 389
Glutamate, 56
   schizophrenia and, 563
Goal orientation theory, 387–388
Gonads, 87, 88–89, 413
Gonorrhea, 448
Gray matter, 70
   in schizophrenia, 563
Gregory, R. L., 137
Grieving process, 373
Grossly disorganized behavior, 559
Group influence, 624–629

decision making and, 626–628
groupthink and, 626–627
social facilitation and, 624
social loafing and, 624–625
social roles and, 628–629
Group therapy, 579
Groupthink, 626–627
GSK (GlaxoSmithKline), 573
Guilt, survivor, 467
Gustation, 118–119

Hair cells, 112
Hallucinations, 558
Hallucinogen(s), 178–180
Hallucinogen persisting perception disorder (HPPD), 179
Halo effect, 616
Hammer (ossicle), 111–112
Handedness, 72–73
Hangovers, caffeine and, 175
Happiness, quest for, 405–406
Hardiness, 481
Harlow, Harry, 347
Harris, Cathy, 627
Hartsfield Airport, 627
Hassles Scale, 461, 463
Hathaway, Starke, 525
Health, 475–484
   alcohol abuse and, 486–487
   alternative medicine and, 489–490
   biomedical model of, 475–476
   biopsychosocial model of, 476
   cancer and, 478–479
   coronary heart disease and, 476–478
   diet and exercise and, 488–489
   gender and, 482
   immune system and stress and, 479–480
   information about, on Internet, 485
   lifestyle changes and, 490
   race and, 483–484
   reducing impact of stress and illness and, 480–482
   smoking and, 484–486
Health psychology, 476
Hearing, 80, 110–115
   "colored," 99
   ear and, 111–114
   sound and, 110–111
   theories of, 114–115
Hearst, Lily, 321
Hedonic treadmill model, 378
Helmholtz, Hermann von, 8, 106, 114
Helping. *See* Prosocial behavior
Heredity, 89, 91–92

Hering, Ewald, 106
Heritability of intelligence, 306–307
Hermaphrodites, 414
Heroin during pregnancy, 342
Herpes, genital, 449
Herpes simplex virus, 449
Hertz (Hz), 110
Heterosexuals, 437. *See also* Sexual orientation
Heuristics
  in decision making, 278–280
  in problem solving, 281–282
Heuristic value, 39
Hierarchy of fears, 583, 584
Hierarchy of needs, 385–386
High blood pressure in late adulthood, 367
Higher-order conditioning, 193
Hindbrain, 58, 59, 60
Hippocampus, 61–63
  memory and, 252–253
Hispanic Americans
  health among, 483
  individualism/collectivism dimension and, 523
  prejudice against, 647–648
  in psychology, 11
  suicide among, 554, 555
Historical racism, 467
HIV. *See* Acquired immunodeficiency syndrome (AIDS); Human immunodeficiency virus (HIV)
Hodler, Marc, 627
Holland, John, 365
Homeostasis, 381
Homophobia, 441
Homosexuality, 437–442
  AIDS transmission and, 452
  determinants of, 438–441
  gay and lesbian relationships and, 441–442
  social attitudes toward gas and lesbians and, 441
Hormones, 86–89
  aggression and, 640
  body weight and, 390
  circadian rhythms and, 149, 150
  cognitive differences and, 423, 425
  emotion and, 428
  hunger and, 389
  memory and, 255
  response to stress and, 470
  sex, 88–89, 413
  sexual orientation and, 438
  sexual response cycle and, 436

social behavior and personality and, 427
Horney, Karen, 12, 505–506
Hospice care, 373
Hostility, type A personality and, 477–478
Host personality in dissociative identity disorder, 565
Hot flashes, 362
HPPD (hallucinogen persisting perception disorder), 179
HPV (human papillomavirus), 448–449
Hudson, Rock, 451
Hue, 105
Human Genome Project, 89
Human immunodeficiency virus (HIV), 450. *See also* Acquired immunodeficiency syndrome (AIDS)
  during pregnancy, 341
Humanistic personality theories, 508–509
Humanistic psychology, 12–13
Humanistic therapy, 576–577
Human papillomavirus (HPV), 448–449
Hunger, 388–395
  body weight variations and, 389–391
  eating disorders and, 392–395
  internal and external cues and, 389
  obesity and weight loss and, 391–392
Hurricane Katrina, 636, 638
Hurvich, Leon, 106
Hyperopia, 102
Hypertension in late adulthood, 367
Hypnosis, 168–170
  neodissociation theory of, 169–170
  sociocognitive theory of, 169
Hypoactive sexual desire disorder, 444
Hypochondriasis, 564
Hypothalamus, 59, 61, 62
  body weight and, 390–391
  circadian rhythms and, 149
  hunger and, 389
  lateral, 389
  sexual development and, 413
  ventromedial, 389
Hypotheses, 7
Hypothetico-deductive thinking, 328
Hz (hertz), 110

Iatmul people, 246
Id, 498–499
Identity crisis, 337

Identity versus role confusion stage, 337
Illness. *See also* Health
  biomedical model of, 475–476
  biopsychosocial model of, 476
  reducing impact of, 480–482
Illusions, 137–138
  autokinetic, 134–135
Imagery, 275–276
Imaginary audience, 328
Imipramine, 590–591
Immigrants
  culturally sensitive therapy and, 605
  prejudice against, 644
Implicit memory, 239
Impotence, 444–445
Impression formation, 612–613
Inappropriate affect, 559
Inattentional blindness, 125–126
Inclusion, 303
Independent thinking, 40
Independent variables, 31–32
Individual differences, 15–16
Individualism/collectivism dimension, 522–523
Individual psychology, 505
Indonesian tsunami, 638
Industrial/organizational (I/O) psychologists, 44, 388
Industry versus inferiority stage, 337
Infancy, 343–349
  attachment during, 347–349
  motor development during, 345, 346
  perceptual development during, 343–345
  temperament in, 345–347
Infant(s), preterm, 342–343
Infantile amnesia, 251–252
Infatuated love, 618
Inferiority complex, 505
Information processing
  bottom-up (data-driven), 128
  top-down (concept-driven), 128
Information-processing approach to cognitive development, 331
Information-processing theory, 14
In-groups, 644–645
Inhibitory effect, 222
Initiative versus guilt stage, 337
Inner ear, 112
Insight, 219
Insight therapies, 574–577
  Gestalt, 577
  humanistic, 576–577

Life stresses, mood disorders and, 551
Lifestyle
   changes in, benefits of, 490
   health and, 484–490
   sedentary, 477
Light, color vision and, 105
Light adaptation, 102
Liking, 618
   reciprocal, 615
Limbic system, 59, 61, 62
Lincoln, Abraham, 385
Linear perspective, 134, 135
Linguistic relativity hypothesis,
   290–291
Linton, Marigold, 11
Listening, active, in client-centered
   therapy, 577
Literacy, 353–354
Lithium, 550, 591
Little Albert, 194–196
Living arrangements in adulthood,
   363–364
LMFTs (licensed marriage and family
   therapists), 604
Loafing, social, 624–625
Locus of control, 515–516
Loftus, Elizabeth, 253
Longitudinal studies, 323, 324
Long-term memory, 236, 239
Long-term potentiation (LTP), 254
Loosening of associations, 558–559
Louganis, Greg, 450, 451
Love, triangular theory of, 617–619
Low-ball technique, 624
Low-birth-weight babies, 342–343
LPCs (licensed professional coun-
   selors), 604
LSD (lysergic acid diethylamide), 179
LTP (long-term potentiation), 254
Lucid dreams, 164
Lymphocytes, 479
Lysergic acid diethylamide (LSD), 179

Magnetic resonance imaging (MRI), 68
Magnetoencephalography (MEG), 69
Mainstreaming, 303
Major depression, 550
Major depressive disorder, 549–550
Male orgasmic disorder, 446
Malingering, 497
Manic episodes, 550
Manifest content, 162–163
The Man Who Tasted Shapes (Cytowic),
   99
MAO (monoamine oxidase) in-
   hibitors, 591
Marijuana, 178–179

Marplan, 591
Marriage, 364
   same-sex, 440
Marshall, Chan, 543, 546
Masculine gender role, 414
Maslow, Abraham, 12, 13, 385,
   508–509
Massed practice, 266
Masters, William, 434–435
Mastery, 261
Mastery approach orientation, 387
Mastery avoidance orientation, 387
Matching hypothesis, 616
Math ability, gender differences in,
   422–423
Mating, 616–617
Maturation, 345
MBTI (Myers-Briggs Type Indicator),
   527
McKinley, J. Charnley, 525
MDMA (methylenedioxymetham-
   phetamine), 180
Means-end analysis, 282
Medicalization, 573
Meditation, 167–168
Medulla, 58
MEG (magnetoencephalography),
   69
Melatonin, 149, 150
Mellaril, 590
Memory, 230–268
   brain and, 252–254
   context and, 243–244
   cramming and, 238
   culture and, 246–247
   declarative (explicit), 236, 239
   eidetic, 245
   episodic, 239
   eyewitness testimony and, 249–250
   flashbulb memories and, 244–245
   forgetting and. *See* Forgetting
   hormones and, 255
   improving, 237, 266–267
   long-term, 236, 239
   loss of, 255–258
   measuring, 241–242
   neuronal changes and, 253–254
   nondeclarative (implicit), 239
   as reconstruction, 247–248
   recovering repressed memories and,
      250–252
   semantic, 239, 253
   sensory, 233–234
   serial position effect and, 242–243
   short-term (working), 234–236
Menopause, 362
Mental age, 299–300

The Mentality of Apes (Köhler), 219
Mental retardation, 299, 303
Mental set, 283
"Mercy killing," 372
Metabolic rate, 390–391
Metalinguistic skills, 291
Methylenedioxymethamphetamine
   (MDMA), 180
Mexican culture, death and dying and,
   372
Microelectrodes, 68
Midbrain, 58, 59, 60
Middle adulthood, 338. *See also*
   Adulthood
Middle childhood, 338. *See also*
   Childhood
Middle ear, 111–112
Midlife crisis, 367
Minnesota Center for Twin and
   Adoption Research, 306–307
Minnesota Multiphasic Personality
   Inventory (MMPI), 497, 525, 526
Minorities. *See also* specific groups
   in psychology, 10–11
Minor tranquilizers, 177
Misinformation effect, 250
MMPI (Minnesota Multiphasic Per-
   sonality Inventory), 497, 525, 526
MMPI-2, 525–527
Modafinil, 152
Model(s), 221–222
Modeling, participant, 586
Modeling effect, 222
Moniz, Egas, 595
Monkeys, attachment studies using,
   347
Monoamine oxidase (MAO) in-
   hibitors, 591
Monoamines, 55
Monocular depth cues, 133–134, 135
Monosodium glutamate (MSG), 118
Mood disorders, 549–555
   bipolar disorder, 535–536, 550
   major depressive disorder, 549–550
   neurological correlates of, 550–551
   risk factors for, 550–553
   suicide and, 554–555
   treatment of, 590–591
Moon illusion, 137
Moore, Tracy, 558, 559
Moral development, 332–336
   ages, stages, and cultures and,
      333–335
   levels and stages of, 333
   measuring moral reasoning and,
      332–333
Mosuo culture, 411–412

Motherese, 352, 353
Motion
    perception of, 134–135
    stroboscopic, 135
Motion parallax, 134, 135
Motivated forgetting, 265
Motivation, 379–396
    biological approaches to, 380–385
    components of, 379–380
    definition of, 379
    extrinsic, 380, 381
    hunger and. *See* Hunger
    intrinsic, 380, 381
    Maslow's hierarchy of needs and,
        385–386
    sensation seeking and, 383–384
    social motives and, 386–388
    work, 388
Motives
    definition of, 379–380
    stimulus, 382–384
Motor cortex, 76–78
Motor development in infancy, 345
Motor nerves, 63
Movement and Mental Imagery
    (Washburn), 10
Mozart, Wolfgang, 315
MRI (magnetic resonance imaging),
    68
MS (multiple sclerosis), 53
MSG (monosodium glutamate), 118
MSWs (social workers), 604
Müller-Lyer illusion, 137, 138
Multiaxial system, 538, 539
Multifactorial inheritance, 92
Multiple intelligences, 295, 296
Multiple sclerosis (MS), 53
Myelin, breakdown of, in late adult-
    hood, 367
Myelination, 81
Myelin sheath, 51, 53
Myers-Briggs Type Indicator (MBTI),
    527
Myopia, 102

Naive idealism, 328
Naive subjects, 612
Narcolepsy, 159, 160
Narcotics, 172, 178
Nardil, 591
Native American(s)
    death and dying and, 372
    healing circles of, 605
    health among, 483
    illusions and, 138
    individualism/collectivism
        dimension and, 522–523

peyote use by, 148
prejudice against, 644
smoking among, 484
suicide among, 554, 555
Native American Church, 148
Nativist position on language
    development, 353
Natural concepts, 276
Naturalistic observation, 22–23
Nature-nurture debate, 306, 323
Navajo culture, illusions and, 138
NE (norepinephrine), 55
Nearsightedness, 102
Needs
    for achievement, 387–388
    for affiliation, 386
    hierarchy of, 385–386
Negative correlation, 26
Negative punishment, 210
Negative reinforcement, 203
    cigarette smoking and, 223
Negative symptoms of schizophrenia,
    559
Neodissociation theory of hypnosis,
    169–170
Neo-Freudians, 12, 504–505
Neonates, 343
Nerves
    motor, 63
    sensory, 63
Nervous system
    autonomic, 63, 64
    central, 57–63. *See also* Brain; Spinal
        cord
    parasympathetic, 63, 64
    peripheral, 57, 63–64
    sympathetic, 63, 64
Neuroleptics. *See* Antipsychotics
Neurons, 50–56
    communication between, 52–56
    memory and, 253–254
    olfactory, 116–117
    structure of, 50–52
Neuroscience, 16
Neuroticism, 510, 551
    in five-factor model, 512–513
Neurotransmitters, 53–56
    mood disorders and, 551
    schizophrenia and, 562–563
New York City Police, 627
New York Longitudinal Study, 345
Nicotine, 175
    schizophrenia and, 593–594
Nightmares, 158
Nim Chimpsky, 289
Nodes of Ranvier, 51, 53
Nondeclarative memory, 239

Nondirective therapy, 577
Norepinephrine (NE; noradrenaline),
    55, 255
    mood disorders and, 551
Norm(s), 300
    social responsibility, 636–637
Normal curve, 301–302
Norm-referenced achievement tests,
    298
NREM dreams, 161
NREM sleep, 153, 154–155
Nucleus accumbens, 172
Nutritional deficiencies, 488, 489

Obedience, 622–623
Obesity, 391–392, 488
Object permanence, 326
Object relations, 575
Observational learning, 220–222, 223
    behavior therapy based on, 586
    cigarette smoking and, 223
Observer bias, 23
Obsession(s), 548
Obsessive-compulsive disorder
    (OCD), 547–549
Occipital lobes, 79–80
Occupational Outlook Handbook, 42
Oedipus complex, 500–502
Olanzapine, 590
Olfaction, 116–117
Olfactory bulbs, 117
Olfactory epithelium, 116
Olfactory system, 116
Olsen, Mary Kate, 394
Openness in five-factor model,
    511–512
Operant conditioning, 202–217
    applications of, 214–216
    behavior therapy based on,
        582–583
    cigarette smoking and, 223
    definition of, 202
    discrimination and, 209
    escape and avoidance learning and,
        212–213
    extinction and, 208
    generalization and, 209
    learned helplessness and, 213–214
    punishment and, 209–212
    reinforcement and, 203–204
    schedules of reinforcement and,
        204–207
    shaping and, 207–208
    Skinner box and, 207–209
    Skinner's work on, 202, 207–209
    spontaneous recovery and, 208
    Thorndike's contributions to, 202

Opiates, 172
Opium, 178
Opponent-process theory, 106
Opsin, 102
Optic chiasm, 103
Optic nerve, 101
Oral stage, 502
Orgasm, 435, 436
Orgasmic disorders, 445–446
Ossicles, 111–112
Osteoporosis, 489
Otis-Lennon Mental Ability Test, 301
Out-groups, 644–645
Oval window, 112
Ovaries, 87, 88–89, 413
Overeaters Anonymous, 579
Overextension, 352
Overlearning, 5, 266
Overregularization, 352
Over-the-counter drugs, 172

Pain (in sexual pain disorders), 446
Pain sense, 119, 120–121
Pancreas, 87, 88
Panic attacks, 544–545
Panic disorder, 545–546
Papillae (of tongue), 118, 119
Paranoid schizophrenia, 559–560
Parasomnias, 158, 160
Parasympathetic nervous system, 63, 64
Parathyroid glands, 87, 88
Parathyroid hormone (PTH), 88
Parenthood, 364–365
Parenting styles, 354–355
Parietal lobes, 79
Parkinson's disease, 60
Parnate, 591
Partial reinforcement, 204
Partial reinforcement effect, 205–206
Participant modeling, 586
Passive euthanasia, 372
Passive smoking, 486
Pavlov, Ivan, 189–192
Pavlovian conditioning. *See* Classical conditioning
Paxil, 573
Peak experiences, 385, 509
Peer relationships, 355, 359
Pelvic inflammatory disease (PID), 447
Penfield, Walter, 76–78
PEN model, 510
Perception, 125–140
    attention and, 125–128
    cross-modal, 129–130

of depth, 132–134
extrasensory, 139
of motion, 134–135
perceptual organization and constancy and, 130–132
prior knowledge and, 128–129
puzzling perceptions and, 136–138
social, 612–614
subliminal, 138–139
Perceptual constancy, 130–132
Perceptual development in infancy, 343–345
Perceptual organization, 130–132
Perceptual reasoning index, 301
Perceptual set, 129
Performance approach orientation, 387–388
Performance avoidance orientation, 387–388
Period of the embryo, 341, 342
Period of the fetus, 341, 342
Period of the zygote, 341, 342
Peripheral nervous system (PNS), 57, 63–64
Perls, Thomas, 321
Permissive parents, 354–355
Persistence, motivation and, 379
Personal fables, 328
Personality, 496–530
    alter, in dissociative identity disorder, 565
    assessment of. *See* Personality assessment
    culture and, 521–523
    gender differences in, 426–427
    host, in dissociative identity disorder, 565
    humanistic theories of, 508–509
    nature versus nurture and, 519–523
    psychoanalytic theories of, 498–506
    social-cognitive theories of, 513–516
    structure of, 498–499
    trait theories of, 509–513
Personality assessment, 523–529
    interviews for, 523, 525
    observation for, 523
    personality inventories for, 525–527
    projective tests for, 528–529
    rating scales for, 525
Personality disorders, 566–567
Personality inventories, 525–527
Personal space, 642
Personal unconscious, 504
Person-centered therapy, 509, 576–577

Persuasion, 632–633
PET scans (positron emission tomography), 68
Peyote, 148
Peyotism, 148
Phallic stage, 500–503, 502
Phenotype, 89, 91
Phi phenomenon, 135
Phobias, 546
    acrophobia, 546
    agoraphobia, 545
    claustrophobia, 546
    social, 543, 546
    specific, 546
Phonemes, 287
Phonological awareness, 353–354
Physical drug dependence, 174
Physiological psychologists, 43
Physiological psychology, 15–16
Piaget, Jean, 326
PID (pelvic inflammatory disease), 447
Pineal gland, 87, 88
Pinna, 111, 112
Pituitary gland, 62, 87–88
Placebo(s), 33, 121
Placebo effect, 33
Place theory, 114–115
Plasticity of brain, 63, 78, 82
Plateau phase of sexual response cycle, 435
Play, pretend, 326
Pleasure principle, 498–499
PNS (peripheral nervous system), 57, 63–64
Polygenetic inheritance, 91–92
Polysomnograms, 152
Pons, 58, 59, 60
Ponzo illusion, 137
Pop quizzes, 472
Populations, 25
Positive bias, memory and, 248
Positive correlation, 26
Positive psychology, 378–379
Positive punishment, 209–210
Positive reinforcement, 203
Positive symptoms of schizophrenia, 558–559
Positron-emission-tomography (PET scans), 68
Postconventional level, 333
Posttraumatic stress disorder (PTSD), 466–467
Poverty, health and, 483–484
Power, Cat, 543, 546
Power, Ray, 563–564

Practical intelligence, 296, 297
Pragmatics, 287
Precognition, 139
Preconventional level, 333
Pregnancy
    drug and alcohol use during, 342
    ectopic, 447
    maternal illness during, 341
Prejudice
    definition of, 643
    persistence of, 646–648
    roots of, 644–646
    social-cognitive theory of, 645
    unlearning, 647
Premature ejaculation, 446
Prenatal development, 338, 341–343
Preoperational stage, 326–327
Presbyopia, 101, 362
Pressure sense, 79
Pretend play, 326
Preterm infants, 342–343
Primacy effect, 242, 613
Primary appraisal, 470
Primary auditory cortex, 80
Primary drives, 388. *See also* Hunger
Primary Mental Abilities Tests, 295
Primary reinforcers, 204
Primary sex characteristics, 413
Primary visual cortex, 79, 103
Principles of Psychology (James), 9
Prior knowledge, perception and,
    128–129
Private speech, 332
Proactive interference, 264
Problem-focused coping, 471
Problem solving
    algorithms for, 282
    gender differences in, 424
    heuristics in, 281–282
    obstacles to, 282–283
Processing speed index, 301
Procrastination, combating, 213
Progesterone, 88
    sexual response cycle and, 436
Projection, 501
Projective tests, 528–529
Prosocial behavior, 636–638
    bystander effect and, 637–638
    reasons for helping and, 636–637
Prospective forgetting, 265
Protective factors, 323
Prototypes, 276–277
Proximity
    attraction and, 615
    perceptual organization and, 130,
    131

Prozac (fluoxetine), 591
Pruning, 81
Psychedelics, 178–180
Psychiatric social workers (MSWs),
    604
Psychiatrists, 42, 603, 604
Psychoactive drugs, 172–182, 593
    brain and, 172–173
    depressants, 173, 177–178
    hallucinogens, 178–180
    stimulants, 173, 175–177
    substance abuse and addiction and,
    173–175
Psychoanalysis, 498, 574–575
Psychoanalysis theory, 12
Psychoanalysts, 604
Psychoanalytic personality theories,
    498–506
    defense mechanisms and, 500, 501
    Freudian, 498–504
    levels of consciousness and, 498
    neo-Freudian, 504–505
    personality structure and, 498–499
    psychosexual stages and, 500–503
Psychoanalytic psychology, 12
Psychoanalytic theory of gender role
    development, 415
Psychodynamic perspective on
    psychological disorders, 540, 541
Psychodynamic therapies, 503, 574–576
Psycholinguistics, 287
Psychological disorders, 534–567
    anxiety disorders, 543–549
    classification of, 537–539
    definition of, 536–537
    dissociative, 564–566
    mood disorders, 549–555
    personality, 566–567
    perspectives on, 540–541
    prevalence of, 539–540
    schizophrenia. *See* Schizophrenia
    somatoform, 564
    treatment for. *See* Drug therapy;
        Psychotherapy; Therapies; *specific
        treatments*
Psychological drug dependence,
    174–175
Psychological factors, sexual arousal
    and, 436–437
Psychological perspectives, 17–18
Psychological tests
    of cognitive abilities, 298. *See also*
        Intelligence tests
    of creativity, 315–316
    requirements of, 298–299
Psychologists, 42, 603, 604

clinical, 42
counseling, 42
developmental, 43
educational, 44
experimental, 43
industrial/organizational (I/O), 44
physiological, 43
social, 44
Psychology
    definition of, 5
    goals of, 7–8
    minorities in, 10–11
    schools of thought in, 11–18
    as science versus common sense,
        4–7
    women in, 10–11
Psychoneuroimmunology, 479–480
Psychopathy, 521
Psychosexual stages, 500–503
Psychosis, 558
Psychosocial development, Erikson's
    theory of, 336–338
Psychosocial stages, 336–338
Psychosurgery, 595–596
Psychotherapy, 574
    behavior, 581–586
    cognitive, 586–588
    culturally sensitive, 604–605
    e-therapy, 602–603
    family therapy and couple therapy,
        578–579
    gender-sensitive, 606
    group, 579
    insight, 503, 574–577
    relationship, 578–579
    therapeutic relationship and, 599,
        601, 603–606
Psychotic depression, 549
Psychoticism, 510
PTH (parathyroid hormone), 88
PTSD (posttraumatic stress disorder),
    466–467
Public speaking, overcoming fear of,
    547
Punishers, 202
Punishment, 209–212
    alternatives to, 211
    culture and, 212
    disadvantages of, 210–211
    making more effective, 211–212
    negative, 210
    positive, 209–210
Pupil (of eye), 100, 101
Puzzle box, 202

Question step in SQ3R method, 4

Secondary sex characteristics, 413
Secondhand smoke, 486
Secure attachment, 348
Sedentary lifestyle, 477
Selection bias, 33
Selective serotonin reuptake inhibitors (SSRIs), 591
Self-actualization, 385, 508–509, 576
Self-efficacy, 515
Self-help groups, 579
Self-medication hypothesis, 593–594
Self-serving bias, 614
Semantic memory, 239, 253
Semantics, 287
Semicircular canals, 112, 122
Sensation, 97–124
    balance and movement and, 121–122
    hearing and, 110–115
    process of, 97–100
    skin senses and, 119–121
    smell and, 116–117
    taste and, 118–119
    vision and, 100–107
Sensation seeking, 383–384
Sensorimotor stage, 326
Sensory adaption, 100
Sensory memory, 233–234
Sensory nerves, 63
Sensory receptors, 100
Separation anxiety, 348
Serial position effect, 242–243
Serotonin, 55
Serpico, Frank, 627
Set point, 378
    body weight and, 390–391
Set-point theory, 390–391
Sex, biological, 412, 413–414
Sex assignment, 413
Sex chromosomes, 89, 92, 413
Sex glands, 413
Sex hormones, 88–89, 413
Sex-linked inheritance, 92
Sex reassignment, 415
Sexual attitudes and behavior, 431–437
    culture and, 433–434
    gender differences in, 432–433
    sexual desire and arousal and, 434–437
Sexual aversion disorder, 444
Sexual Behavior in the Human Female (Kinsey), 431
Sexual Behavior in the Human Male (Kinsey), 431
Sexual desire and arousal, 434–437
    disorders of, 444–445
Sexual dysfunctions, 444–446
    of desire and arousal, 444–445

orgasmic, 445–446
    sexual pain disorders, 446
Sexually transmitted diseases (STDs), 446–453
    AIDS, 449–453
    bacterial, 447–448
    viral, 448–449
Sexual orientation, 437–442
    determinants of, 438–441
    gay and lesbian relationships and, 441–442
    social attitudes toward gays and lesbians and, 441
Sexual pain disorders, 446
Sexual response cycle, 435–436
Shading, depth perception and, 134, 135
Shadow, depth perception and, 134, 135
Shaka Franklin Foundation for Youth, 554
Shape constancy, 131–132
Shaping, 207–208
Shift workers, 152
Short-term memory, 234–236
Sign language, 352
    retrieval failure and, 265
Sildenafil (Viagra), 445
Similarity, perceptual organization and, 130, 131
Simon, Theodore, 299
Situational attribution, 613
Situation-trait debate, 513–514
16PF, 510, 511
Size constancy, 131
Skinner, B. F., 12, 202, 207–209, 380
Skinner box, 207–209
Skin senses, 119–121
Sleep, 152–160
    circadian (evolutionary) theory of, 152
    deprivation of, 156, 157–158
    dreaming and, 153, 161–163
    functions of, 152–153
    restorative theory of, 152
    sleep cycles and, 154–155
    sleep disorders and, 158–160
    types of, 153–154
    variations in, 156–157
Sleep apnea, 159, 160
Sleep cycles, 154–155
Sleep hygiene, 160
Sleep spindles, 154, 155
Sleep terrors, 158
Sleep/wakefulness cycle, 149
"Slow-to-warm-up" children, 346

Slow-wave sleep, 154
Smell sense, 116–117
Smoking
    health and, 484–486
    learning principles and, 223
    passive, 486
    during pregnancy, 342
    schizophrenia and, 593–594
Social adjustment in late adulthood, 369–370
Social anxiety disorder (SAD), 573
Social Anxiety Disorders Coalition (SADC), 573
Social attitudes toward gays and lesbians, 441
Social behavior, gender differences in, 426–427
Social cognition, 645
Social-cognitive learning, 220–222, 223
Social-cognitive theory, 513–516
    locus of control and, 515–516
    of prejudice, 645
    reciprocal determinism and, 514–515, 516
    situation-trait debate and, 513–514
Social desirability, 526
Social desirability response, 26
Social development in adulthood, 363–367
Social facilitation, 624
Socialization, 354–355
    parenting styles and, 354–355
    peer relationships and, 355, 359
Social learning theory of aggression, 642–643
Social loafing, 624–625
Social motives, 386–388
    achievement motivation and, 386–388
    work motivation and, 388
Social perception, 612–614
Social phobia, 543, 546
Social psychologists, 44
Social psychology, 610–649
    aggression and, 639–643
    attitudes and, 629–633
    attraction and, 614–619
    attribution and, 613–614
    compliance and, 623–624
    conformity and, 621–622
    definition of, 612
    group influence and, 624–629
    impression formation and, 612–613
    obedience and, 622–623
    prejudice and discrimination and, 643–648
    prosocial behavior and, 636–638

Social Readjustment Rating Scale (SRRS), 460–461, 462
Social responsibility norms, 636–637
Social roles, 628–629
Social support, 482
Social workers (MSWs), 604
Sociocognitive theory of hypnosis, 169
Sociocultural approach, 16–17
Sociocultural theory of cognitive development, 331–332
Socioeconomic status as stressor, 468
Soma of neurons, 50, 51
Somatic nervous system, 63
Somatoform disorders, 564
Somatosensory cortex, 79
Somnambulism, 158
Somniloquy, 158
Sound, 110–111
Source traits, 510
Spaced practice, 266
Spatial ability, gender differences in, 422–423
Spear, Tom, 321
Spearman, Charles, 295
Specific phobia, 546
Speech
    private, 332
    telegraphic, 352
Spinal cord, 57–58, 59
Spirochetes, 448
Split-brain operation, 75–76
Spontaneous recovery
    in classical conditioning, 192
    in operant conditioning, 208
Sports psychology, 42
SQ3R method, 3–4
SQUID (superconducting quantum interference device), 69
SRRS (Social Readjustment Rating Scale), 460–461, 462
Sry gene, 413
SSRIs (selective serotonin reuptake inhibitors), 591
Stage fright, 543
Stage(s) in development, 323, 326–328, 333–338
Stage 4 sleep, 154, 155
Standardization of tests, 299
Stanford-Binet Intelligence Scale, 300
Stanford Prison Experiment, 628
State-dependent memory effect, 244
STDs. *See* Sexually transmitted diseases (STDs)
Stelazine, 590
Stereotypes, 645–646

Stereotype threat, 311–312
Sternberg's triangular theory of love, 617–619
Stimulants, 173, 175–177
Stimulus(i), 189
    conditioned, 191
    discriminative, 209
    external, sexual arousal and, 437
    unconditioned, 190
Stimulus motives, 382–384
Stirrup (ossicle), 111–112
STP, 179
Stress, 460–473
    cognitive theory of, 470–471
    definition of, 460
    immune system and, 479–480
    reducing impact of, 480–482
    responding to, 469–473
    schizophrenia and, 561–562
    sources of. *See* Stressor(s)
Stressor(s), 460–469
    catastrophic events as, 466–467
    daily hassles as, 461, 463
    life changes as, 460–461, 462
    making choices as, 463–464
    mood disorders and, 551
    social sources of, 467–469
    in workplace, 464–466
Stressor overload, 367
Stroboscopic motion, 135
Stroke, 83
Structuralism, 8–9
Structured interviews for personality assessment, 523
Studying
    cramming and, 266
    memory improvement for, 266–267
    overlearning and, 266
Study methods, 3–4, 5
Study tips, 213
Stumbling on Happiness (Gilbert), 553
Subjective night, 151
Sublimation, 501
Subliminal perception, 138–139
Subliminal persuasion, 138
Substance abuse, 173–175, 486–487
Substantia nigra, 59, 60
Successful aging, 370–371
Suicide, 554–555
    assisted, 372
Suinn, Richard, 11
Sumner, Francis Cecil, 10
Superconducting quantum interference device (SQUID), 69
Superego, 499

Suppression, 265
Suprachiasmatic nucleus (SCN), 149
Surface traits, 510
Survey(s), as research method, 24–26
Survey step in SQ3R method, 4
Survivor guilt, 467
Swazi people, 246
Sympathetic nervous system, 63, 64
Sympathy. *See* Prosocial behavior
Synapses, 52
    development of, 81
Synaptic clefts, 51, 52
Synaptic transmission, 53–55
Synaptic vesicles, 53
Synaptogenesis, 81
Synesthesia, 99, 138
Syntax, 287, 352
Syphilis, 448
Systematic desensitization, 583, 584
Systems perspective, 16–17

Tacit knowledge, 296
Tactile information, 120
Tardive dyskinesia, 590
Targets of bullying, 459
Taste aversions, 197–198
Taste buds, 118, 119
Taste sense, 118–119
TAT (Thematic Apperception Test), 386–387, 529
T cells, 479
Telegraphic speech, 352
Telepathy, 139
Television, learning from, 222, 224–226
Temperament in infancy, 345–347
Temperature sense, 79
Temporal lobes, 80–81
Teratogens, 342
Terrorist attacks of 9/11/2001, 638
Testes, 87, 88–89, 413
Testosterone
    aggression and, 640
    sexual response cycle and, 436
Tetrahydrocannabinol (THC), 178
Texture gradient, 134, 135
Thalamus, 59, 61, 62
THC (tetrahydrocannabinol), 178
Thematic Apperception Test (TAT), 386–387, 529
Theories, 6. *See also* specific theories
    evaluating, 39
Theory of dissociated control, 170
Theory of multiple intelligences, 295, 296
Therapeutic alliance, 605

Photo Credits

Chapter 1: Pages 1, © Blend Images/Jupiter Images; 2 , © Alexander Hassenstein/Bongarts/Getty Images; 3, Fred Zimney/© www.tonybenshoof.com; 9, ©David Young-Wolff/ PhotoEdit; 13, ©Lon C. Deihl/PhotoEdit; 15, © Sonda Dawes/The Image Works; 17 L,© Mark Henley/ Panos; 17 R, © Leland Bobbe/Getty Images/Stone; 24, AP Images/Chris Pizzello; 25, © Howard Huang/Getty Images/The Image Bank; 28, © Steve Skjold/PhotoEdit

Chapter 2: Pages 48, © Dynamic Graphics/ Jupiter Images; 49, Reprinted with permission from Damasio H. Grabowski T. Frank R. Galaburda A.M. Damasio A.R.: The return of Phineas Gage: Clues about the brain from a famous patient. *Science*, 264:1102-1105, © 1994. American Association for the Advancement of Science. Courtesy of Dr. Hanna Damasio, The Dana and David Dornsife Cognitive Neuroscience Imaging Center and Brain and Creativity Institute, University of Southern California; 51, © BioPhoto/Photo Researchers, Inc.; 52, © BioPhoto/ Photo Researchers, Inc.; 56, © Bill Aron/PhotoEdit; 69, ©Alexander Tsiaras/Photo Researchers, Inc.; 80, © Anthony Edgeworth; 91, © LWA-Dann Tardif/CORBIS

Chapter 3: Pages 96, © Bob Sacha/CORBIS; 98, © Philip Condit II/Getty Images/Stone; 101, © Carolina Biological Supply Company/Phototake; 107L, © Robert Harbison; 107R, © Robert Harbison;115 TL, Image Courtesy of House Ear Institute © 2007; 115 TR, Image Courtesy of House Ear Institute © 2007; 115 B, © Meredith Davenport/Aurora Photo; 118, ©Hideo Haga/ HAGA/The Image Works; 119, © Omikron/Photo Researchers, Inc.;121, Purestock/Jupiter Images; 122, © Gregory Costanzo/ Getty Images/Taxi; 133, © 2007 Magic Eye, Inc.;135 TL, © Kent Meireis/The Image Works; 135 TML, © James Randklev/Getty Images/The Image Bank; 135 TMR, © Bernd Euler/plus 49/The Image Works; 135 TR, © Mike Yamashita/Woodfin Camp & Associates; 135 BL, © Craig Tuttle/CORBIS; 135 BM, © Randi Anglin/ Syracuse Newspaper/The Image Works; 135 BR, © Pete Turner/Getty Images/The Image Bank; 137, © Richard Lord Ente/The Image Works

Chapter 4: Pages 145, © ThinkStock LLC/ Photolibrary; 148, © Robert Frerck/Getty Images/Stone; 150, Brand X Pictures/ Jupiter Images; 151, © David Frazier/Getty Images/ Stone; 155, © Russell D. Curtis/Photo Researchers, Inc.; 156, © Jose Luis Pelaez, Inc./CORBIS; 157, Blend Images/Jupiter Images; 159, © Louis Psihoyos/SCIENCE FACTION Images; 163, MATRIX RELOADED, Keanu Reeves, Lung Yun Chao, 2003,© Warner Brothers/courtesy Everett Collection; 170, © Michael Newman/ Photo Edit; 174, © Dennis MacDonald/PhotoEdit; 176, © Tony Freeman/PhotoEdit; 179, AP Images/Noah Berger

Chapter 5: Pages 186, © Karen Kasmauski/CORBIS; 187, © Reuters/CORBIS; 195, Archives of the History of American Psychology; 197, © Kevin Laubacher/Getty Images/Taxi; 199, Courtesy of the National Fluid Milk Processor Promotion Board; 205, © Arthur Tilley/Getty Images/Taxi; 206, © Don Mason/ Blend Images/CORBIS; 208, © Nina Leen/Time & Life Pictures/ Getty Images; 211, © Dennis MacDonald/PhotoEdit; 216, © Will

& Demi McIntyre/Photo Researchers, Inc.; 224, Courtesy of Dr. Albert Bandura, Stanford University; 225, © Alex Segre/Alamy

Chapter 6: Pages 230, © Graeme Robertson/GettyImages/ Reportage; 231, © Columbia/courtesy Everett Collection; 235, © Kent Wood/Photo Researchers, Inc.; 245, © Greg Whitesell/ Getty Images; 247, © M & E Bernheim/Woodfin Camp & Associates; 248, © Royalty Free/CORBIS; 249, © Grantpix/Photo Researchers, Inc.; 254, adapted from Maguire et al., 2000; 257, © Martin Salter/The Independent

Chapter 7: Pages 273, ©Ellen Senisi /The Image Works; 275, AP Images/Jacques Brinon; 277, Image courtesy of Planeboats.com; 281, ©Jeff Greenberg/PhotoEdit; 283, ©Topham Picture Point/The Image Works; 284, AP Images/Adam Nadel; 289, ©FRANS LANTING/Minden Pictures; 292, ©Bob Daemmrich/The Image Works; 297 L, © Bernard Wolf; 297 M, © Rafael Macia/ Photo Researchers, Inc.; 297 R, © B&C Alexander/Photo Researchers, Inc.; 300, National Library of Medicine; 307, ©Portfield/Chickering/Photo Researchers, Inc.

Chapter 8: Pages 320, © Jeff Greenberg/The Image Works ; 321, Amy Snyder, © Exploratorium, www.exploratorium.edu; 323, © Amy Etra/PhotoEdit ; 324, © David Young-Wolff/PhotoEdit; 331, © Frank Siteman/ PhotoEdit; 343 L, © Francis Leroy/ Science Photo Library/Photo Researchers, Inc.; 343 R, Lennart Nilsson/ Bonniers; 343 M, Lennart Nilsson/Bonniers; 345, ©Mark Richards/PhotoEdit ; 347, © Martin Rogers/Woodfin Camp & Associates; 348, © Laura Dwight/PhotoEdit; 352, © Bob Daemmrich Photograph; 364, © PicturePartners/Alamy; 370, © Jim Craigmyle/CORBIS

Chapter 9: Pages 377, © First Light/CORBIS; 381, © Ethan Miller/Getty Images; 382, ©Anthony Neste; 383, © Don Mason/ CORBIS; 387, ©Jeff Greenberg/PhotoEdit ; 392, © Custom Medical Stock Photo/Alamy; 394, © Vince Bucci/Getty Images; 402, Courtesy of Dr. Hanna Damasio, The Dana and David Dornsife Cognitive Neuroscience Imaging Center and Brain and Creativity Institute, University of Southern California; 403, Reprinted by permission of the Human Interaction Laboratory/© Paul Ekman 1975; 404, ©David Young-Wolff/PhotoEdit

Chapter 10: Pages 410, Darryl Leniuk/Getty Images/ Digital Vision; 411,© Langevin Jacques/CORBIS Sygma; 416, © Peter Cade/Getty Images/Stone; 417, ©Arnold Gold/New Haven Register/The Image Works; 420 T, © Jorge Uzon/CORBIS; 420 B, © Arnd Wiegmann/Reuters/ CORBIS; 425, © Bettmann/CORBIS; 427 T, © Richard Hutchings/Photo Researchers, Inc.; 427 B, © Carl Glassman/The Image Works; 428, ©PhotoDisc/Getty Images; 436, © Don Mason/CORBIS; 439, Paul Drinkwater © NBC/Courtesy: Everett Collection; 440, © JIM BOURG/ Reuters/CORBIS; 451 (1985), ©Hulton Archive/ Getty Images; 451 (1986), © Stephen Chernin/Getty Images; 451 (1991), Copyright 1990 NBAE. Photo by Nathaniel S. Butler via Getty Images; 451 (1991), © Urbano Delvalle/Time Life Pictures/Getty Images; 451 (1994), © Frank Trapper/CORBIS; 451 (1995), © Allsport/ Getty Images; 451 (2002), AP Images; 451 (2006), © PIERRE VERDY/AFP/Getty Images

Chapter 11: Pages 458, © Gideon Mendel/CORBIS; 459, © Rachel Epstein/PhotoEdit ; 461, © Michael Greenlar/The Image Works; 465, © Spencer Grant/ PhotoEdit; 466, © Paul A. Souders/CORBIS; 467, © Ariel Skelley/CORBIS; 477, ©Jose Luis Pelaez, Inc./ CORBIS; 479, ©Chris Fitzgerald/The Image Works; 481, ©Ronnie Kaufman/CORBIS; 489, ©Sonda Dawes/ The Image Works; 490, © Brand X Pictures/Alamy

Chapter 12: Pages 496, © John Berry/Syracuse Newspapers/ The Image Works ; 499, © Hulton-Deutsch Collection/CORBIS; 503, © Michael Newman/Photo Edit; 506, © Bettmann/CORBIS; 514, © Ariel Skelley/ CORBIS; 515, © Jimmy Chin/National Geographic Image Collection ; 522, ©Chris Arend/Getty Images/ Stone; 529, ©Purestock/Getty Images

Chapter 13: Pages 534, © Creasource/CORBIS; 535, © Frazer Harrison/Getty Images; 537 L, ©Robert Harbison; 537 R, © Dean Conger/CORBIS; 543, Tim Mosenfelder/ Getty Images; 548, © Spencer Grant/PhotoEdit; 554, AP Images; 559, © Frazer Harrison/Getty Images; 562, Grunnitus Studio/Photo Researchers, Inc.; 563, Dr. Paul Thompson, Laboratory of Neuro Imaging at UCLA; 565, © Arthur Tilley/Getty Images/Taxi

Chapter 14: Pages 572, © Bob Daemmrich/The Image Works; 575, AP Images; 577, © Michael Rougier/Time Life Pictures/Getty Images; 578, © Royalty-Free/CORBIS ; 579, © Bruce Ayers/Getty Images/Stone; 582, © David Young-Wolff/ PhotoEdit; 583, © Rainer Jensen/ dpa/CORBIS; 595, © W & D McIntyre/Photo Researchers, Inc.; 602, © Dave & Les Jacobs/ Blend Images/CORBIS; 605, ©Michael Newman/PhotoEdit

Chapter 15: Pages 610, © Mark Richards/PhotoEdit; 611, From the film *Obedience* © 1965 by Stanley Milgram, © renewed 1993 by Alexandra Milgram, and distributed by Penn State Media Sales.; 614, © Jonathan Kirn/The Stock Connection; 615, AP Images/Aijaz Rahi; 616, © Zen Sekizawa/Getty Images/Taxi; 621, William Vandevert/ Scientific American; 626, ©Mark Richards/ PhotoEdit; 629, Philip G. Zimbardo, Inc.; 633, ©Reuters/Landov LLC; 637, ©David Young-Wolff/PhotoEdit; 638, © Robert Brenner/PhotoEdi; 640, © John Zich/zrImages/ CORBIS; 644, ©Gary A. Conner/PhotoEdit

Text and Art Credits

Explain It, p. 113: Copyright © 2006 by The New York Times Co. Reprinted with permission.

Figure 3.7, p. 115: Images Courtesy of House Ear Institute

Figure 3.11, p. 129: Copyright © 1995 by Highlights for Children, Inc., Columbus, Ohio.

Try It, p. 263: Reprinted from *Cognitive Psychology*, 11, R.S. Nickerson and M.J. Adams, "Long-term memory for a common object," pp. 287–307, exercise on p. 297, copyright © 1979, with permission from Elsevier.

Figure 6.6, p. 254: From E.A. Maguire, D.G. Gadian, I.S. Johnstrude, C.D. Good, J. Ashburner, R.S.J. Frackowiak, and C.D. Frick, "Navigation-related structural change in the hippocampi of taxi drivers," *Proceedings of the National Academy of Sciences*, 97, pp. 4398–4403, 2000. Copyright © 2000 National Academy of Sciences, U.S.A.

Try It, p. 282: From *Solve It!: A Perplexing Profusion of Puzzles* by James F. Fixx, copyright © 1978 by James F. Fixx. Used by permission of Doubleday, a division of Random House, Inc.

Figure 7.1, p. 288: Adapted with permission from *Science, 172*, David Premack, "Language in chimpanzee?," pp. 808–822, Figure 1, pp. 808–822. Copyright © 1971 AAAS.

Figure 7.2, p. 292: Reprinted from *Psychological Science, 14*, Kenji Hakuta, Ellen Bialystock, and Edward Wiley, "Critical evidence: A test of the critical-period hypothesis for second-language acquisition," pp. 31–38, copyright © 2003, with permission from Blackwell.

Figure 7.9, p. 315: Adapted from *Neuropsychologia, 38*, I. Carlsson, P.E. Wendt, and J. Risberg, "On the neurobiology of creativity: Differences in frontal activity between high and low creative subjects," pp. 873–885, copyright © 2000 Elsevier.

Figure 8.2, p. 329: From Helen Bee and Denise Boyd, *The Developing Child*, 11th edition © 2007. Published by Allyn and Bacon. Reprinted by permission of the publisher.

Figure 8.3, p. 335: From A. Colby, L. Kohlberg, J. Gibbs, and M. Lieberman, "A longitudinal study of moral judgment," *Monographs of the Society for Research in Child Development*, 48, (1–2, Serial No. 200), 1983. Copyright © 1983, with permission from Blackwell.

Figure 9.6, p. 402: Reprinted from *Nature Neuroscience, 3* (10), A.R. Damasio, T.J. Grabowski, A. Bechara, H. Damasio, L.L.B. Ponto, J. Parvizi, and R.D. Hichwa, "Subcortical and cortical brain activity during the feeling of self-generated emotions," pp. 1049–1056, Copyright © 2000, with permission from Nature Publishing Group.

Figure 10.2, p. 424: Illustrations by Jared Schneidman from "Sex Differences in the Brain" by Doreen Kimura, *Scientific American*, September 1992, pp. 120, 121. Reprinted by permission of the artist.

Try It, p. 447: From http://www.mayoclinic.com/health/stds/ QZ00037, Copyright © 2006 Mayo Foundation for Medical Education and Research (MFMER). Reprinted with permission.

Try It, p. 450: http://onhealth.webmd.com/home/interactives/ conditions/188_02asp

Figure 10.4, p. 451: *Source:* Sepkowitz (2006).

Table 11.1, p. 463: From Allen D. Kanner, James C. Coyne, C. Schaefer, and R.S. Lazarus, "Comparison of two modes of stress management: Daily hassles and uplifts versus major life events," *Journal of Behavioral Medicine*, 4, pp. 1–39, copyright © 1981. Reprinted with kind permission of Springer Science and Business Media.

Figure 11.4, p. 476: From *Dynamics of Health and Wellness* 1st edition by Green, J./Shellenberger, R. Reprinted with permission of Brooks/Cole, a division of Thomson Learning: www.thomsonrights.com. Fax: 800-730-2215

Figure 13.4, p. 560: Reprinted, with permission, from the *Annual Review of Psychology*, Volume 55 © 2004 by Annual Reviews www.annualreviews.org

Figure 13.6, p. 563: From Paul M. Thompson, Christine Vidal, Jay N. Giedd, Peter Gochman, Jonathan Blumenthal, Robert Nicolson, Arthur W. Toga, & Judith L. Rapoport, "Mapping adolescent brain change reveals dynamic wave of accelerated gray matter loss in very early-onset schizophrenia," *Proceedings of the National Academy of Sciences*, 98, pp. 11650–11655. Figure 5, p. 11563 (September 25, 2001). Copyright © 2001 National Academy of Sciences, U.S.A.